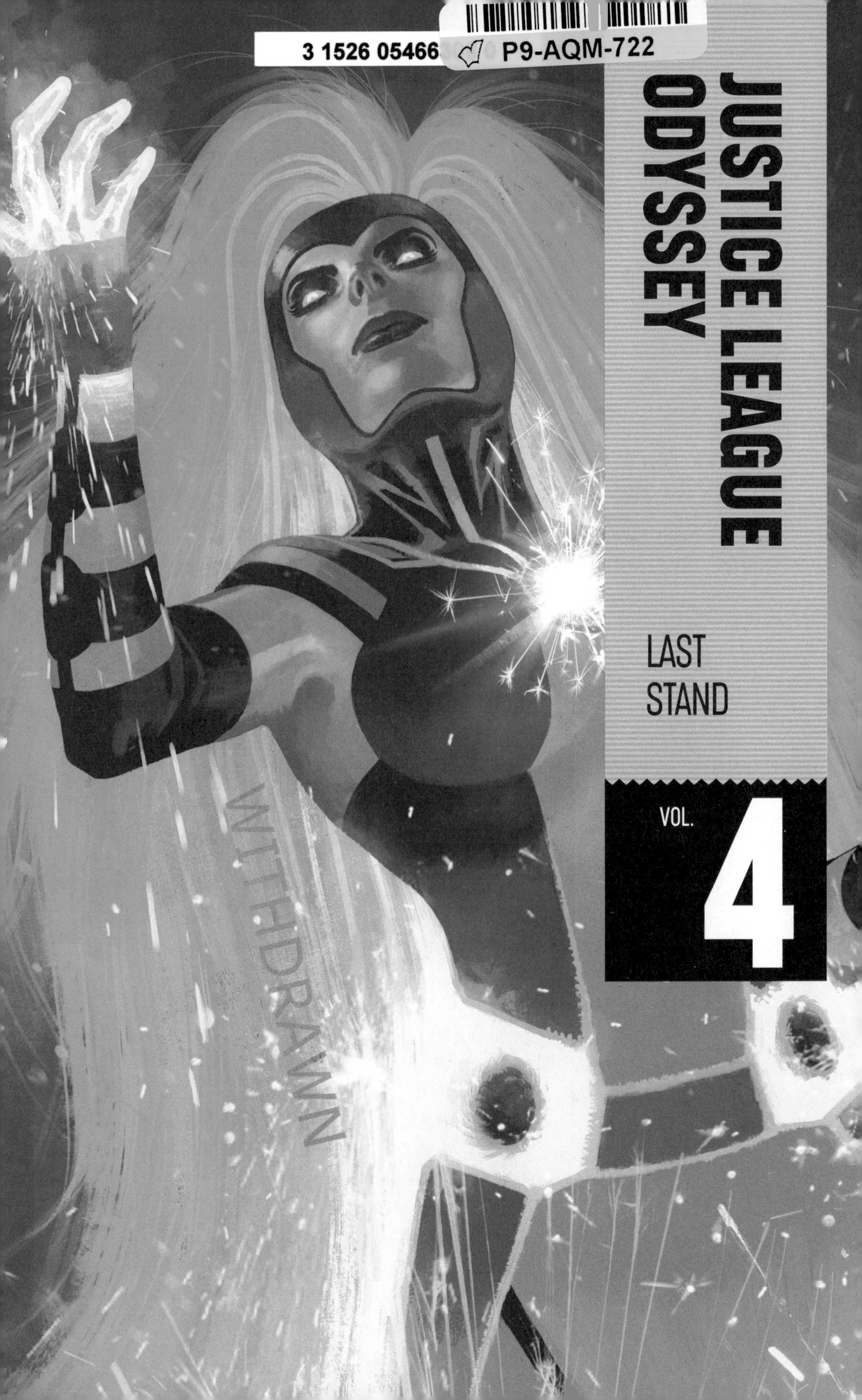

JUSTICE LEAGUE ODYSSEY
LAST STAND
VOL. 4
WITHDRAWN

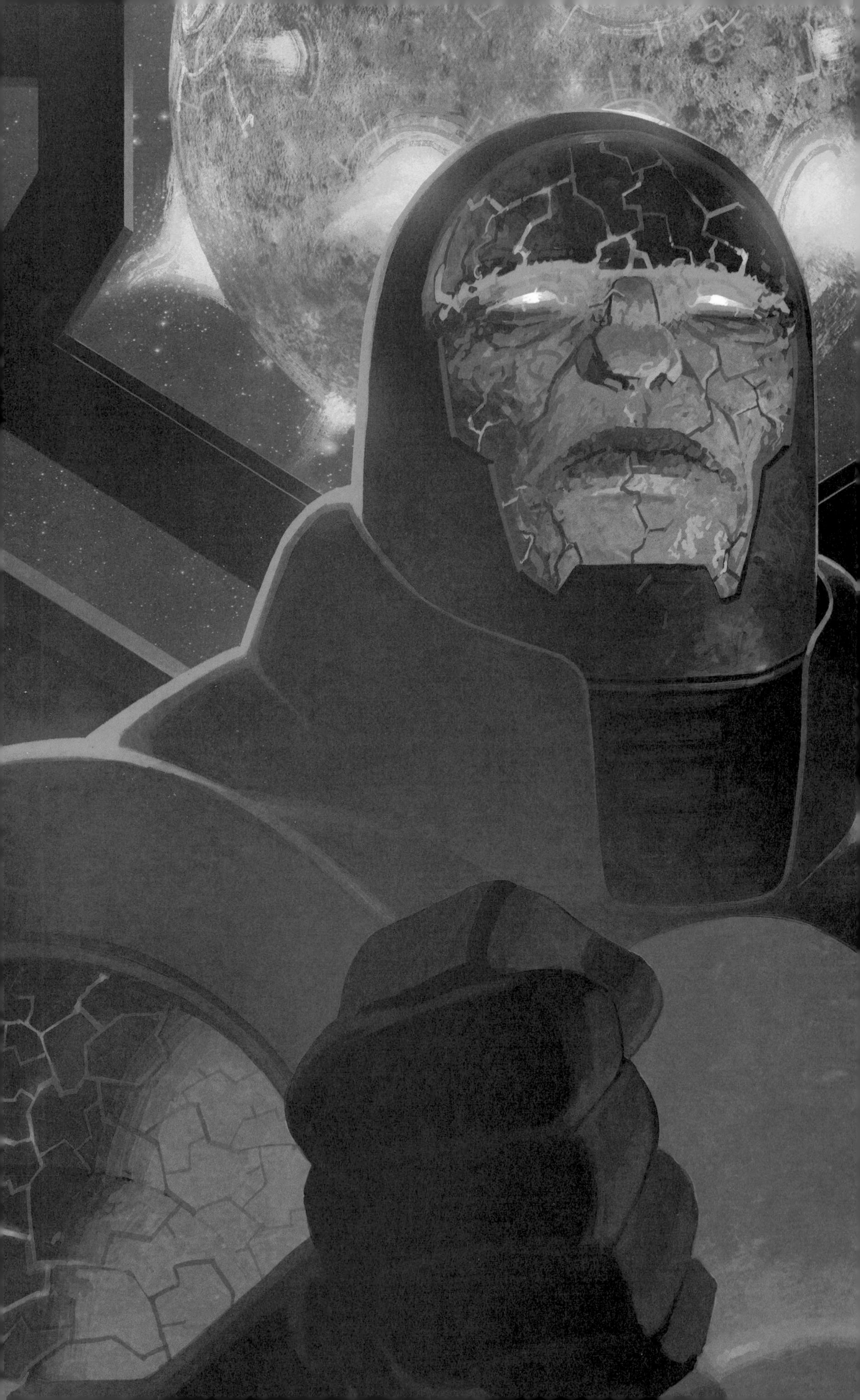

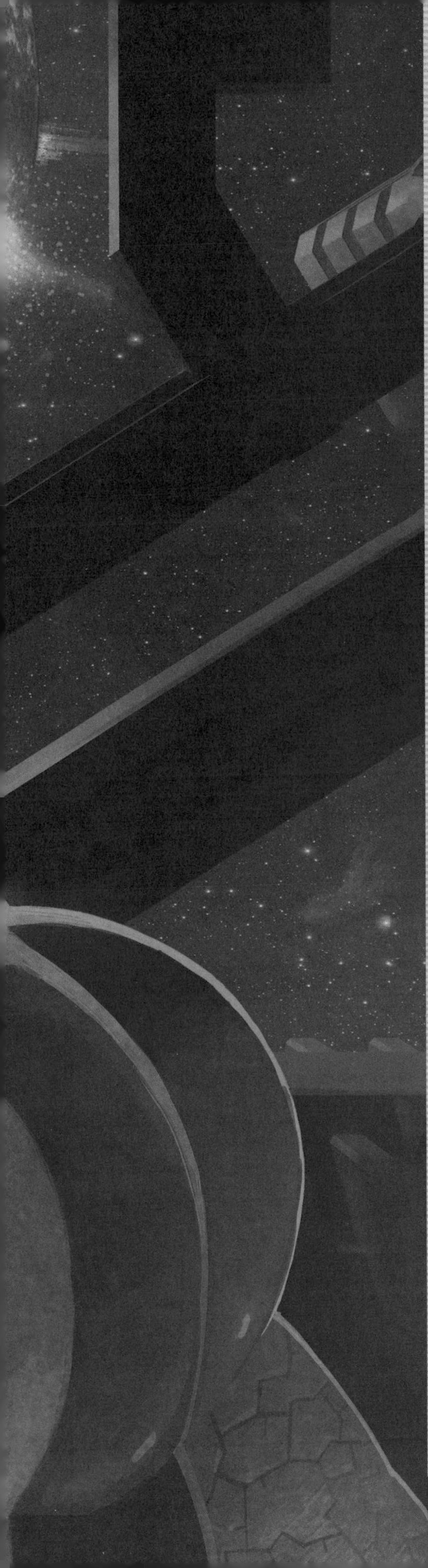

JUSTICE LEAGUE ODYSSEY

LAST STAND

writer

DAN ABNETT

artists

WILL CONRAD
CLIFF RICHARDS

colorist

RAIN BEREDO

letterer

DERON BENNETT

collection cover art

SKAN

VOL. **4**

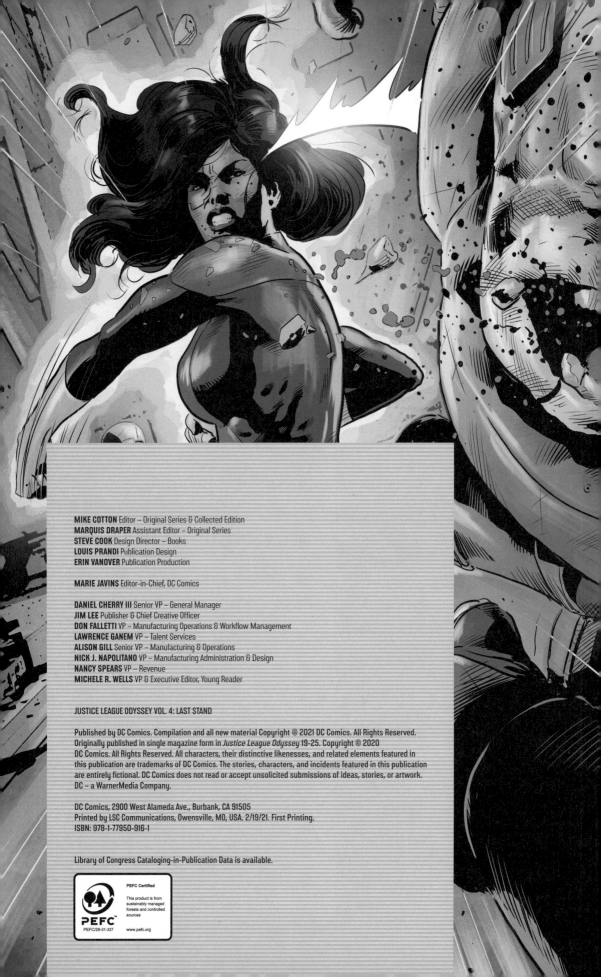

MIKE COTTON Editor – Original Series & Collected Edition
MARQUIS DRAPER Assistant Editor – Original Series
STEVE COOK Design Director – Books
LOUIS PRANDI Publication Design
ERIN VANOVER Publication Production

MARIE JAVINS Editor-in-Chief, DC Comics

DANIEL CHERRY III Senior VP – General Manager
JIM LEE Publisher & Chief Creative Officer
DON FALLETTI VP – Manufacturing Operations & Workflow Management
LAWRENCE GANEM VP – Talent Services
ALISON GILL Senior VP – Manufacturing & Operations
NICK J. NAPOLITANO VP – Manufacturing Administration & Design
NANCY SPEARS VP – Revenue
MICHELE R. WELLS VP & Executive Editor, Young Reader

JUSTICE LEAGUE ODYSSEY VOL. 4: LAST STAND

DC Comics, 2900 West Alameda Ave., Burbank, CA 91505
Printed by LSC Communications, Owensville, MO, USA. 2/19/21. First Printing.
ISBN: 978-1-77950-916-1

Library of Congress Cataloging-in-Publication Data is available.

PEFC Certified

This product is from sustainably managed forests and controlled sources

PEFC
PEFC/29-31-337

www.pefc.org

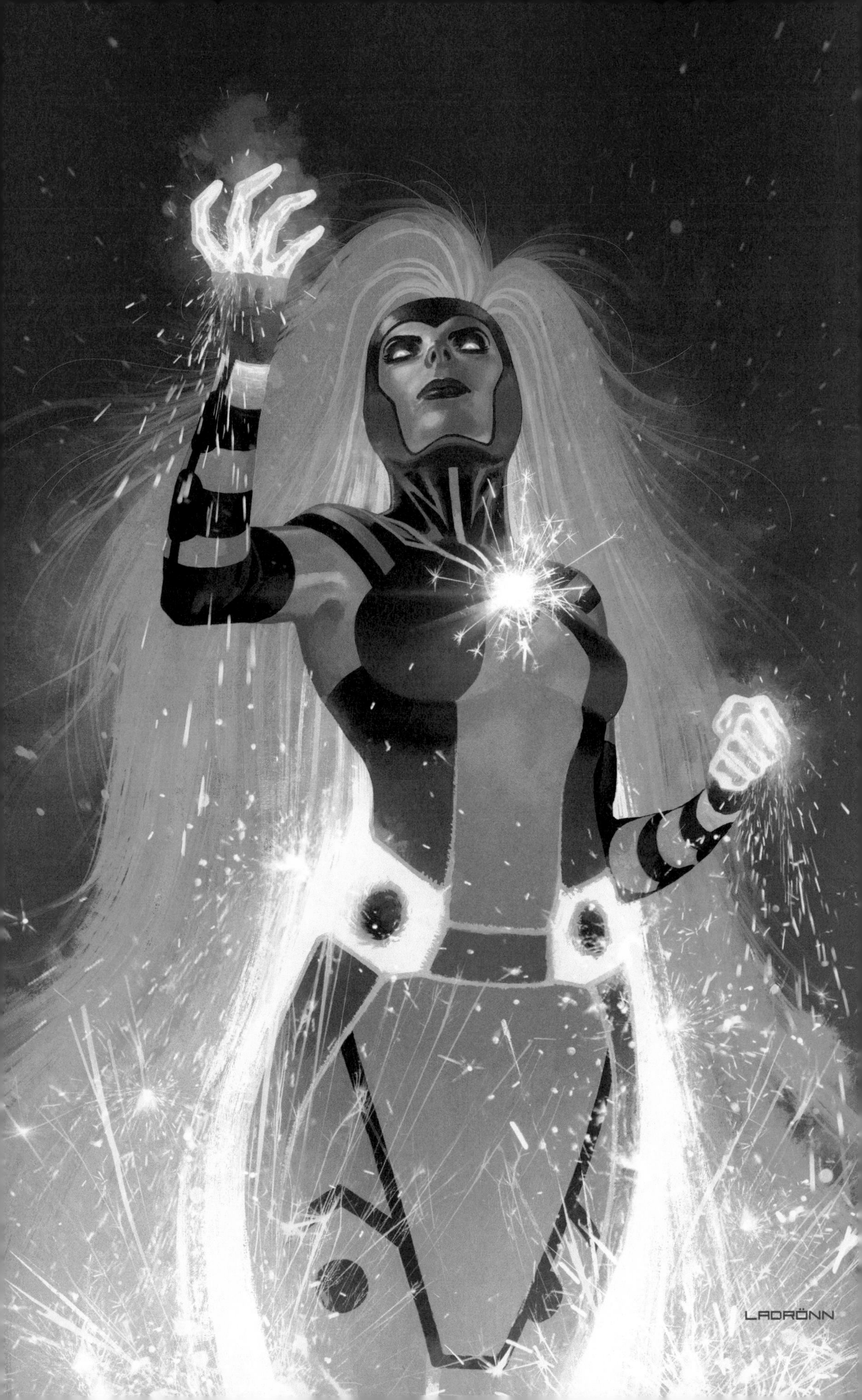
LADRÖNN

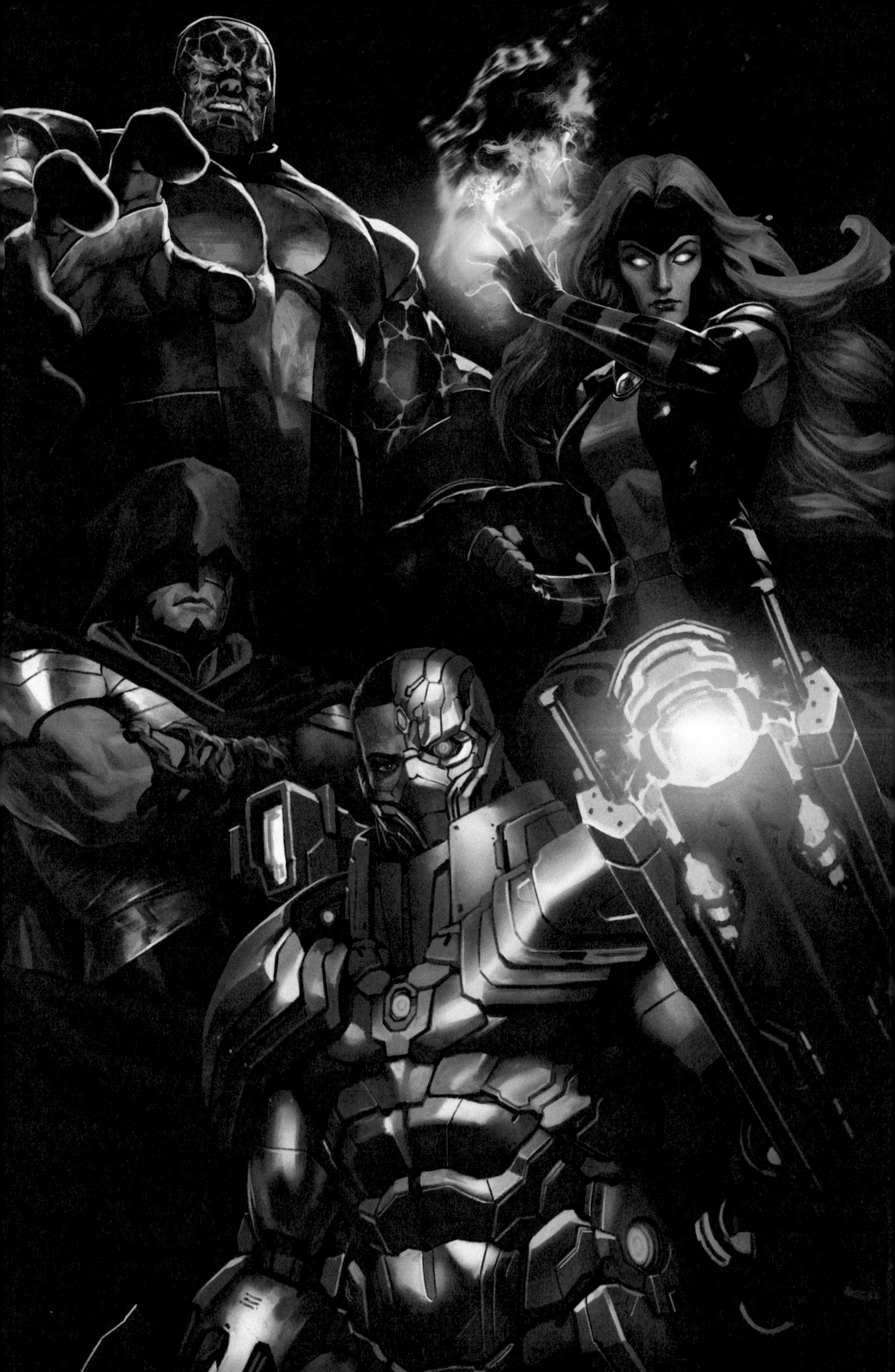

Justice League Odyssey **#19** variant cover by **SKAN**

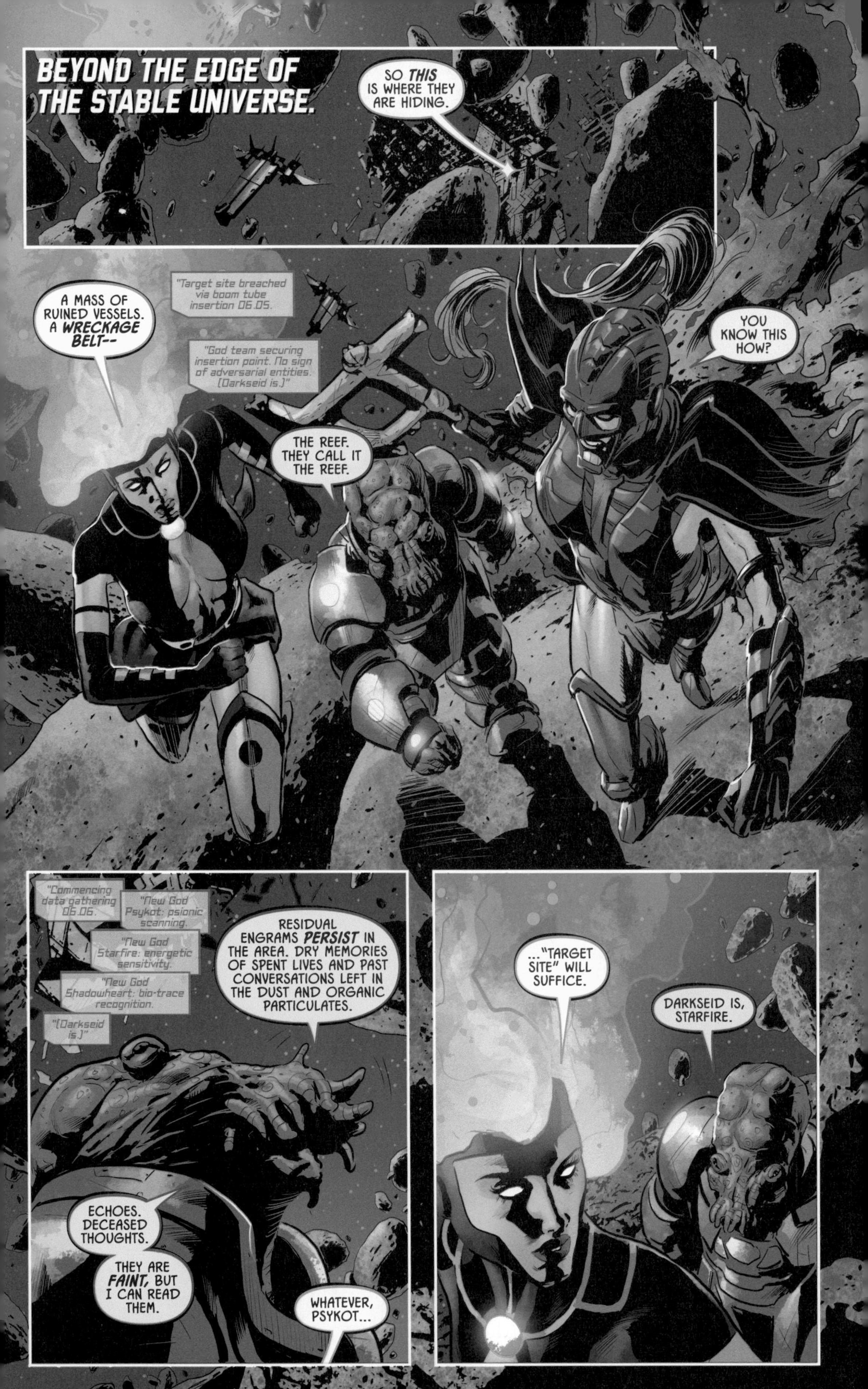
BEYOND THE EDGE OF THE STABLE UNIVERSE.
SO THIS IS WHERE THEY ARE HIDING.
A MASS OF RUINED VESSELS. A WRECKAGE BELT--
"Target site breached via boom tube insertion 06.05.
"God team securing insertion point. No sign of adversarial entities. [Darkseid is.]"
YOU KNOW THIS HOW?
THE REEF. THEY CALL IT THE REEF.
"Commencing data gathering 06.06.
"New God Psykot: psionic scanning.
"New God Starfire: energetic sensitivity.
"New God Shadowheart: bio-trace recognition.
"[Darkseid is.]"
RESIDUAL ENGRAMS PERSIST IN THE AREA. DRY MEMORIES OF SPENT LIVES AND PAST CONVERSATIONS LEFT IN THE DUST AND ORGANIC PARTICULATES.
ECHOES. DECEASED THOUGHTS.
THEY ARE FAINT, BUT I CAN READ THEM.
WHATEVER, PSYKOT...
..."TARGET SITE" WILL SUFFICE.
DARKSEID IS, STARFIRE.

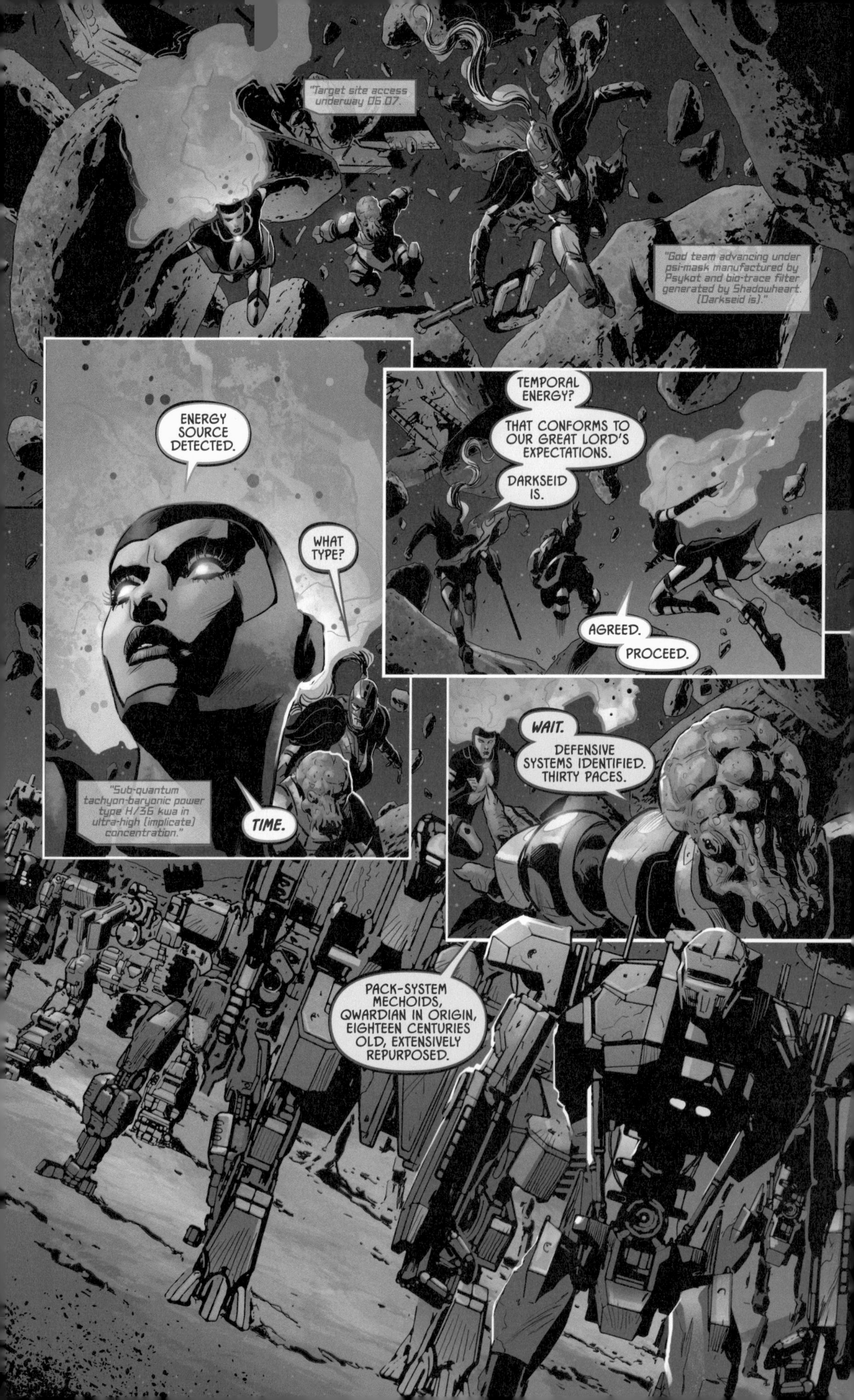
"Target site access underway 06.07."
"God team advancing under psi-mask manufactured by Psykot and bio-trace filter generated by Shadowheart. (Darkseid is)."
ENERGY SOURCE DETECTED.
WHAT TYPE?
"Sub-quantum tachyon-baryonic power type H/36 kwa in ultra-high (implicate) concentration."
TIME.
TEMPORAL ENERGY?
THAT CONFORMS TO OUR GREAT LORD'S EXPECTATIONS.
DARKSEID IS.
AGREED.
PROCEED.
WAIT.
DEFENSIVE SYSTEMS IDENTIFIED. THIRTY PACES.
PACK-SYSTEM MECHOIDS, QWARDIAN IN ORIGIN, EIGHTEEN CENTURIES OLD, EXTENSIVELY REPURPOSED.

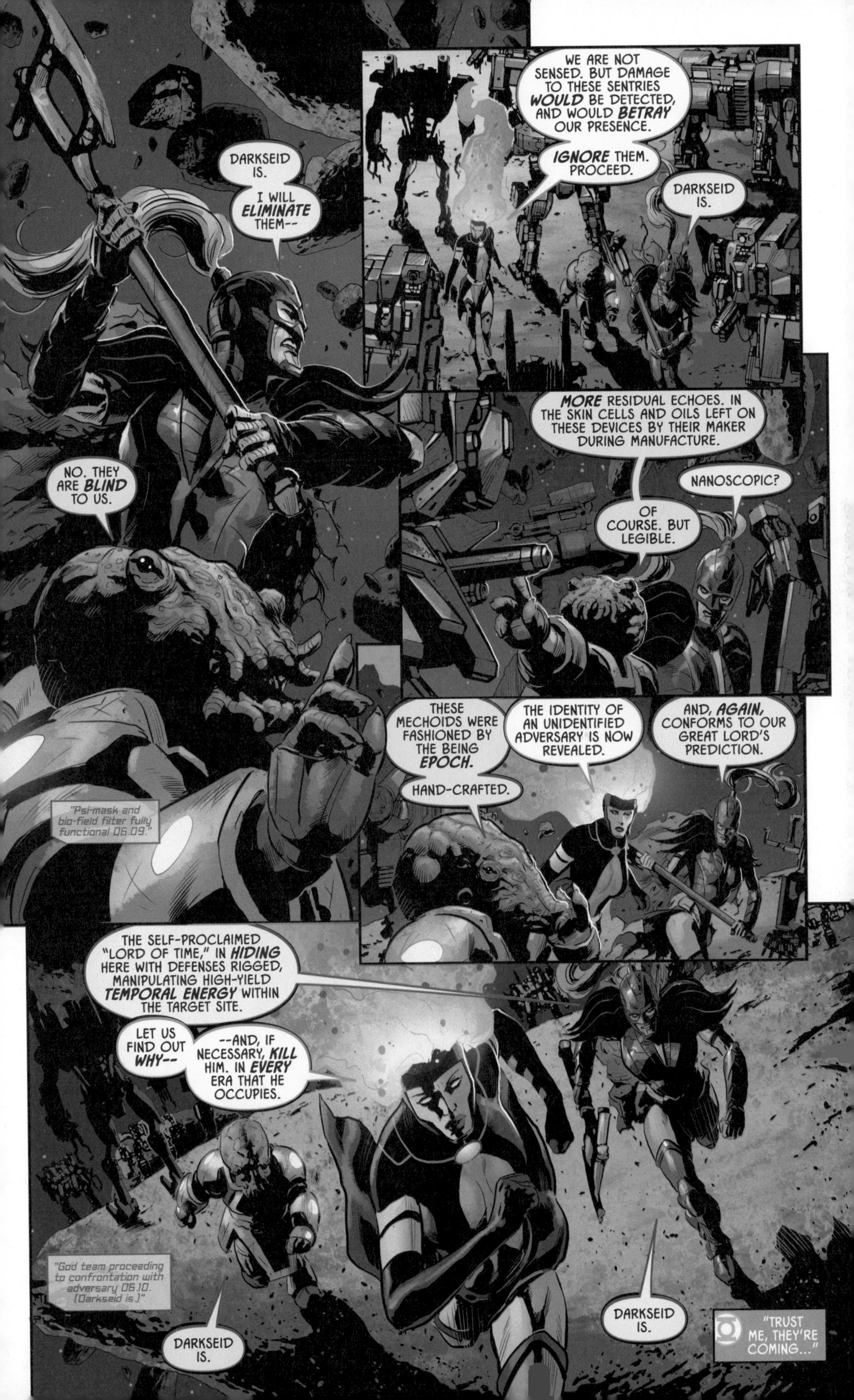
DARKSEID IS.
I WILL ELIMINATE THEM--
WE ARE NOT SENSED. BUT DAMAGE TO THESE SENTRIES WOULD BE DETECTED, AND WOULD BETRAY OUR PRESENCE.
IGNORE THEM. PROCEED.
DARKSEID IS.
NO. THEY ARE BLIND TO US.
MORE RESIDUAL ECHOES. IN THE SKIN CELLS AND OILS LEFT ON THESE DEVICES BY THEIR MAKER DURING MANUFACTURE.
NANOSCOPIC?
OF COURSE. BUT LEGIBLE.
"Psi-mask and bio-field filter fully functional 06.09."
THESE MECHOIDS WERE FASHIONED BY THE BEING EPOCH.
HAND-CRAFTED.
THE IDENTITY OF AN UNIDENTIFIED ADVERSARY IS NOW REVEALED.
AND, AGAIN, CONFORMS TO OUR GREAT LORD'S PREDICTION.
THE SELF-PROCLAIMED "LORD OF TIME," IN HIDING HERE WITH DEFENSES RIGGED, MANIPULATING HIGH-YIELD TEMPORAL ENERGY WITHIN THE TARGET SITE.
LET US FIND OUT WHY--
--AND, IF NECESSARY, KILL HIM. IN EVERY ERA THAT HE OCCUPIES.
"God team proceeding to confrontation with adversary 06.10. (Darkseid is.)"
DARKSEID IS.
DARKSEID IS.
"TRUST ME, THEY'RE COMING..."

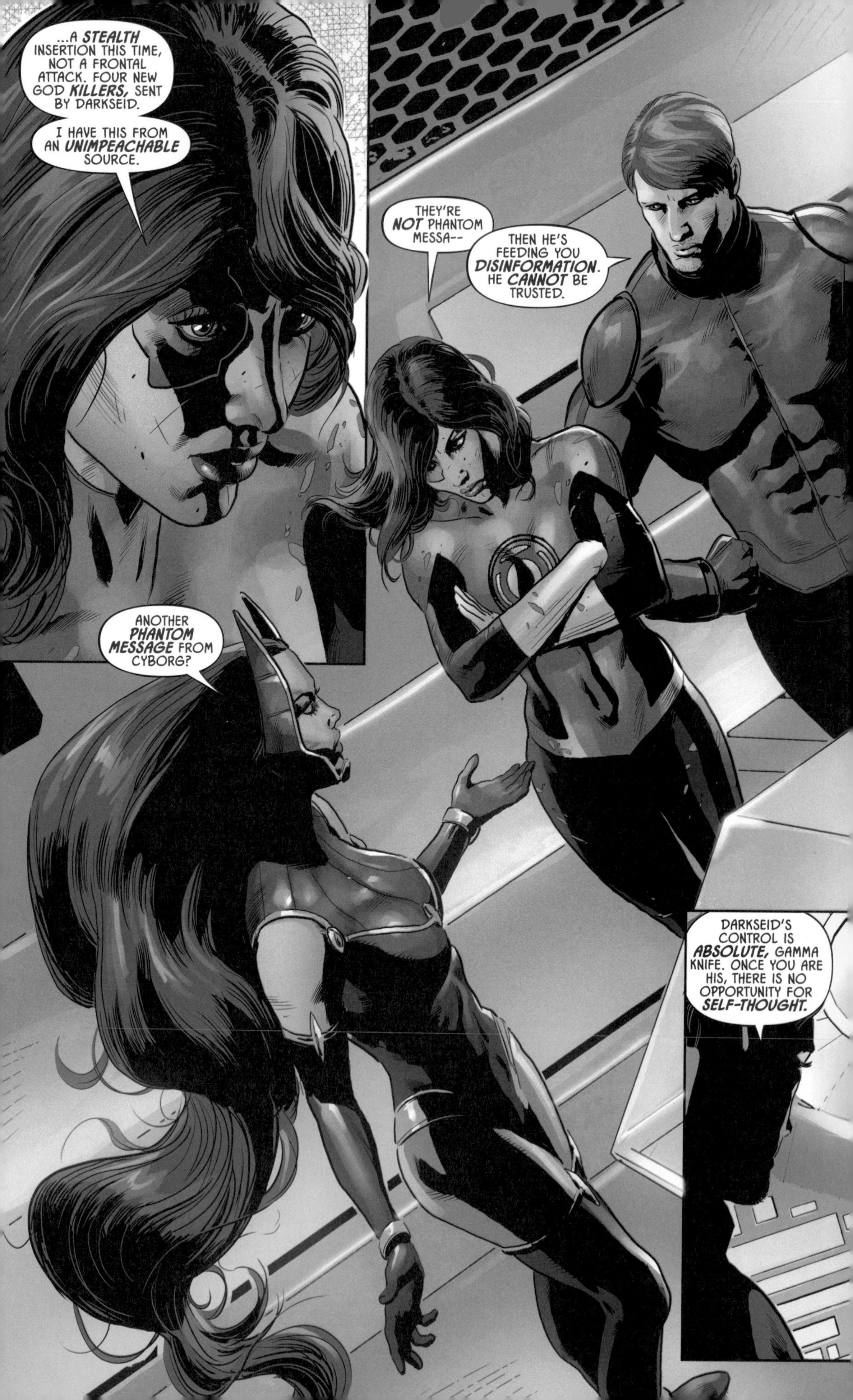
...A STEALTH INSERTION THIS TIME, NOT A FRONTAL ATTACK. FOUR NEW GOD KILLERS, SENT BY DARKSEID.
I HAVE THIS FROM AN UNIMPEACHABLE SOURCE.
THEY'RE NOT PHANTOM MESSA--
THEN HE'S FEEDING YOU DISINFORMATION. HE CANNOT BE TRUSTED.
ANOTHER PHANTOM MESSAGE FROM CYBORG?
DARKSEID'S CONTROL IS ABSOLUTE, GAMMA KNIFE. ONCE YOU ARE HIS, THERE IS NO OPPORTUNITY FOR SELF-THOUGHT.

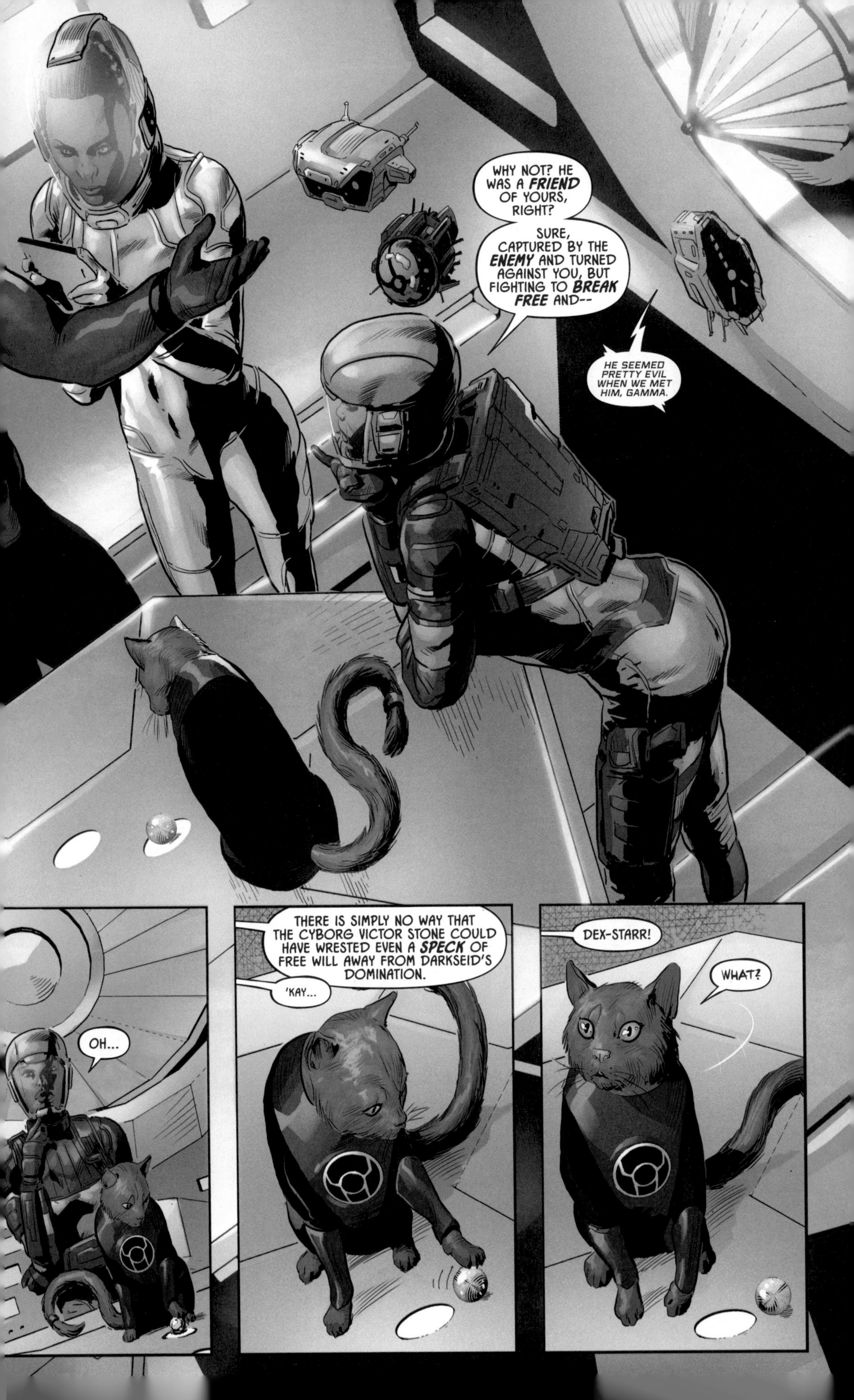
WHY NOT? HE WAS A FRIEND OF YOURS, RIGHT?
SURE, CAPTURED BY THE ENEMY AND TURNED AGAINST YOU, BUT FIGHTING TO BREAK FREE AND--
HE SEEMED PRETTY EVIL WHEN WE MET HIM, GAMMA.
OH...
THERE IS SIMPLY NO WAY THAT THE CYBORG VICTOR STONE COULD HAVE WRESTED EVEN A SPECK OF FREE WILL AWAY FROM DARKSEID'S DOMINATION.
'KAY...
DEX-STARR!
WHAT?

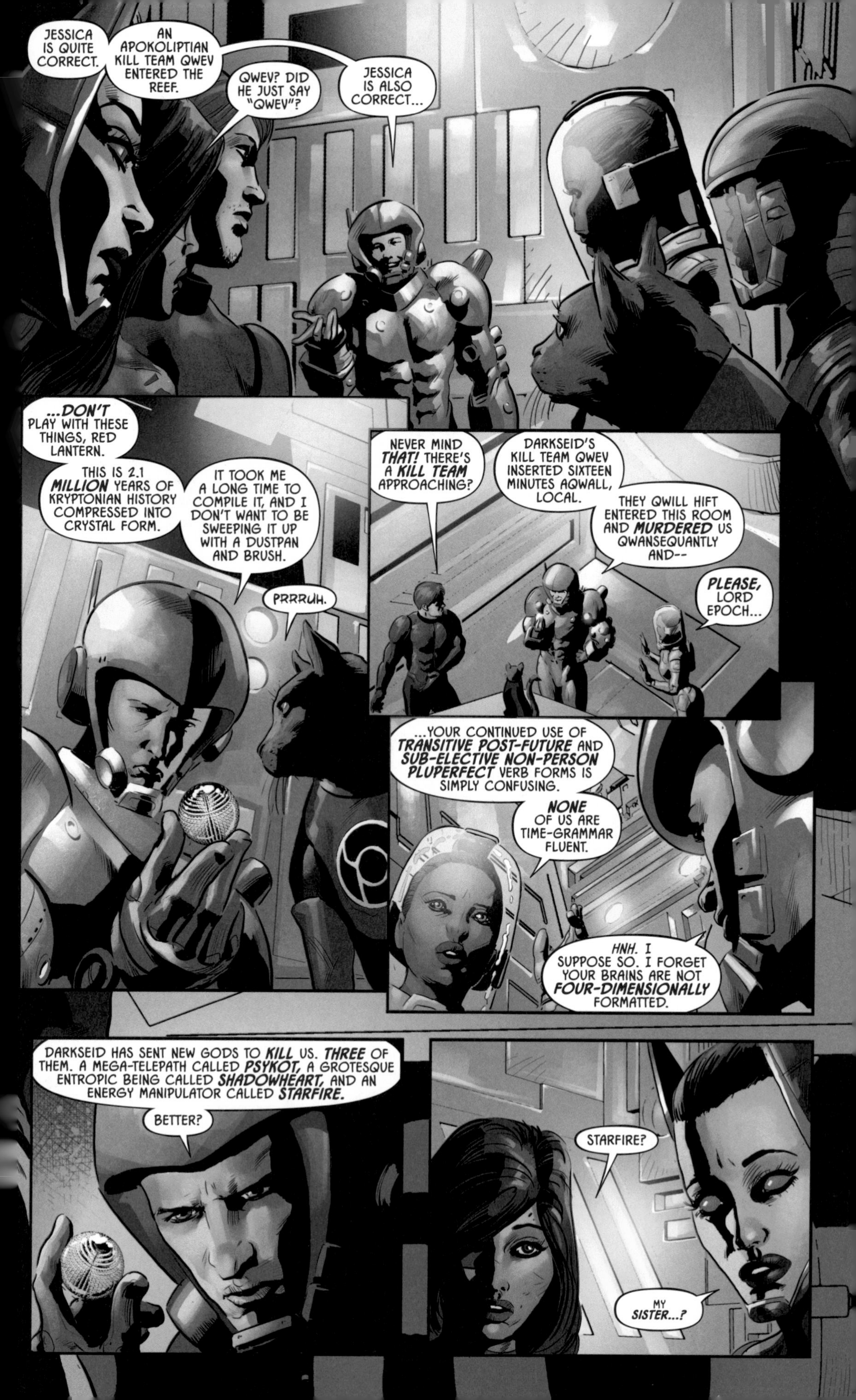
JESSICA IS QUITE CORRECT.
AN APOKOLIPTIAN KILL TEAM QWEV ENTERED THE REEF.
QWEV? DID HE JUST SAY "QWEV"?
JESSICA IS ALSO CORRECT...
...DON'T PLAY WITH THESE THINGS, RED LANTERN.
THIS IS 2.1 MILLION YEARS OF KRYPTONIAN HISTORY COMPRESSED INTO CRYSTAL FORM.
IT TOOK ME A LONG TIME TO COMPILE IT, AND I DON'T WANT TO BE SWEEPING IT UP WITH A DUSTPAN AND BRUSH.
PRRRUH.
NEVER MIND THAT! THERE'S A KILL TEAM APPROACHING?
DARKSEID'S KILL TEAM QWEV INSERTED SIXTEEN MINUTES AQWALL, LOCAL.
THEY QWILL HIFT ENTERED THIS ROOM AND MURDERED US QWANSEQUANTLY AND--
PLEASE, LORD EPOCH...
...YOUR CONTINUED USE OF TRANSITIVE POST-FUTURE AND SUB-ELECTIVE NON-PERSON PLUPERFECT VERB FORMS IS SIMPLY CONFUSING.
NONE OF US ARE TIME-GRAMMAR FLUENT.
HNH. I SUPPOSE SO. I FORGET YOUR BRAINS ARE NOT FOUR-DIMENSIONALLY FORMATTED.
DARKSEID HAS SENT NEW GODS TO KILL US. THREE OF THEM. A MEGA-TELEPATH CALLED PSYKOT, A GROTESQUE ENTROPIC BEING CALLED SHADOWHEART, AND AN ENERGY MANIPULATOR CALLED STARFIRE.
BETTER?
STARFIRE?
MY SISTER...?

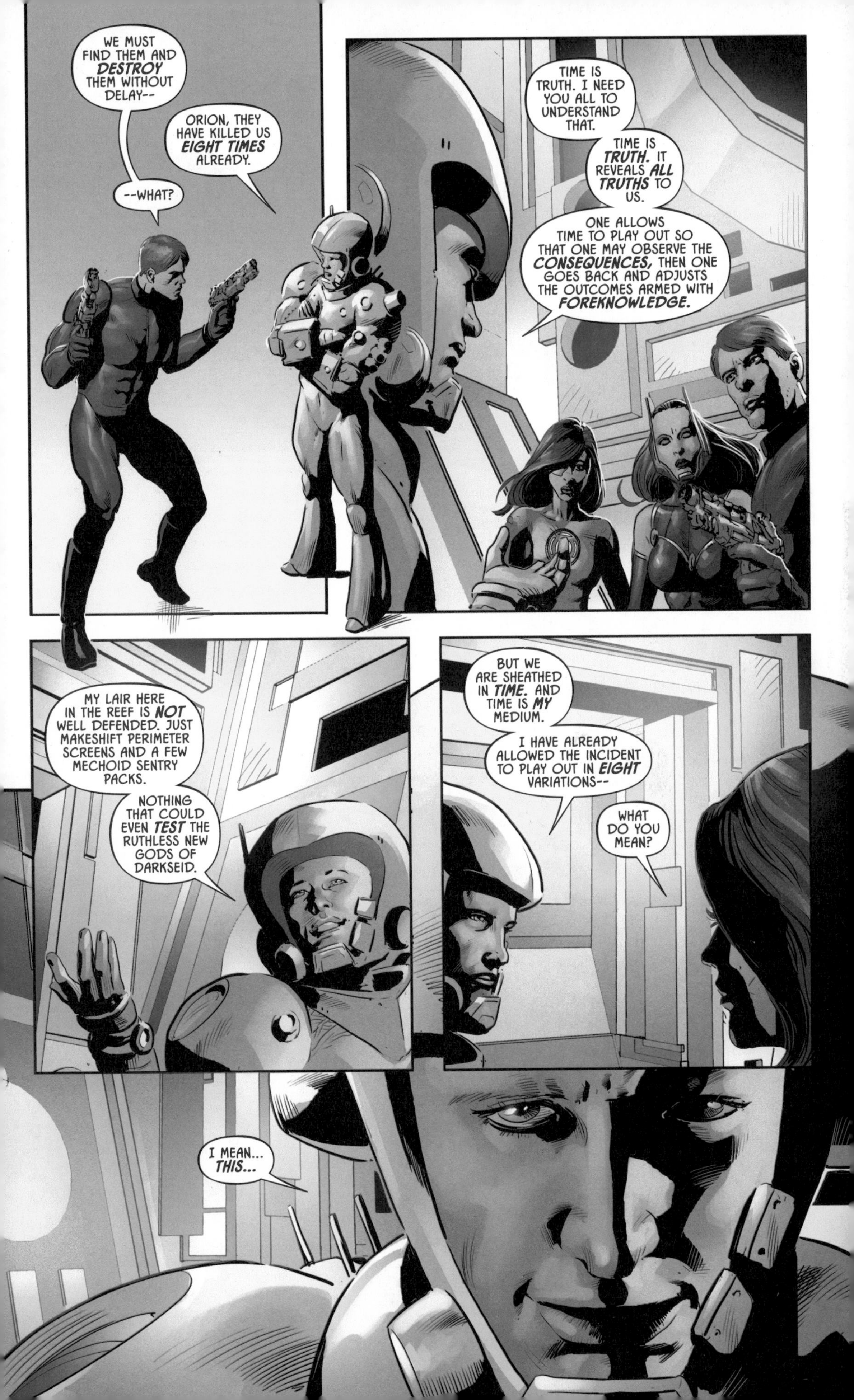

WE MUST FIND THEM AND **DESTROY** THEM WITHOUT DELAY--
ORION, THEY HAVE KILLED US **EIGHT TIMES** ALREADY.
--WHAT?
TIME IS TRUTH. I NEED YOU ALL TO UNDERSTAND THAT.
TIME IS **TRUTH.** IT REVEALS **ALL TRUTHS** TO US.
ONE ALLOWS TIME TO PLAY OUT SO THAT ONE MAY OBSERVE THE **CONSEQUENCES,** THEN ONE GOES BACK AND ADJUSTS THE OUTCOMES ARMED WITH **FOREKNOWLEDGE.**
MY LAIR HERE IN THE REEF IS **NOT** WELL DEFENDED. JUST MAKESHIFT PERIMETER SCREENS AND A FEW MECHOID SENTRY PACKS.
NOTHING THAT COULD EVEN **TEST** THE RUTHLESS NEW GODS OF DARKSEID.
BUT WE ARE SHEATHED IN **TIME.** AND TIME IS **MY** MEDIUM.
I HAVE ALREADY ALLOWED THE INCIDENT TO PLAY OUT IN **EIGHT** VARIATIONS--
WHAT DO YOU MEAN?
I MEAN... **THIS...**

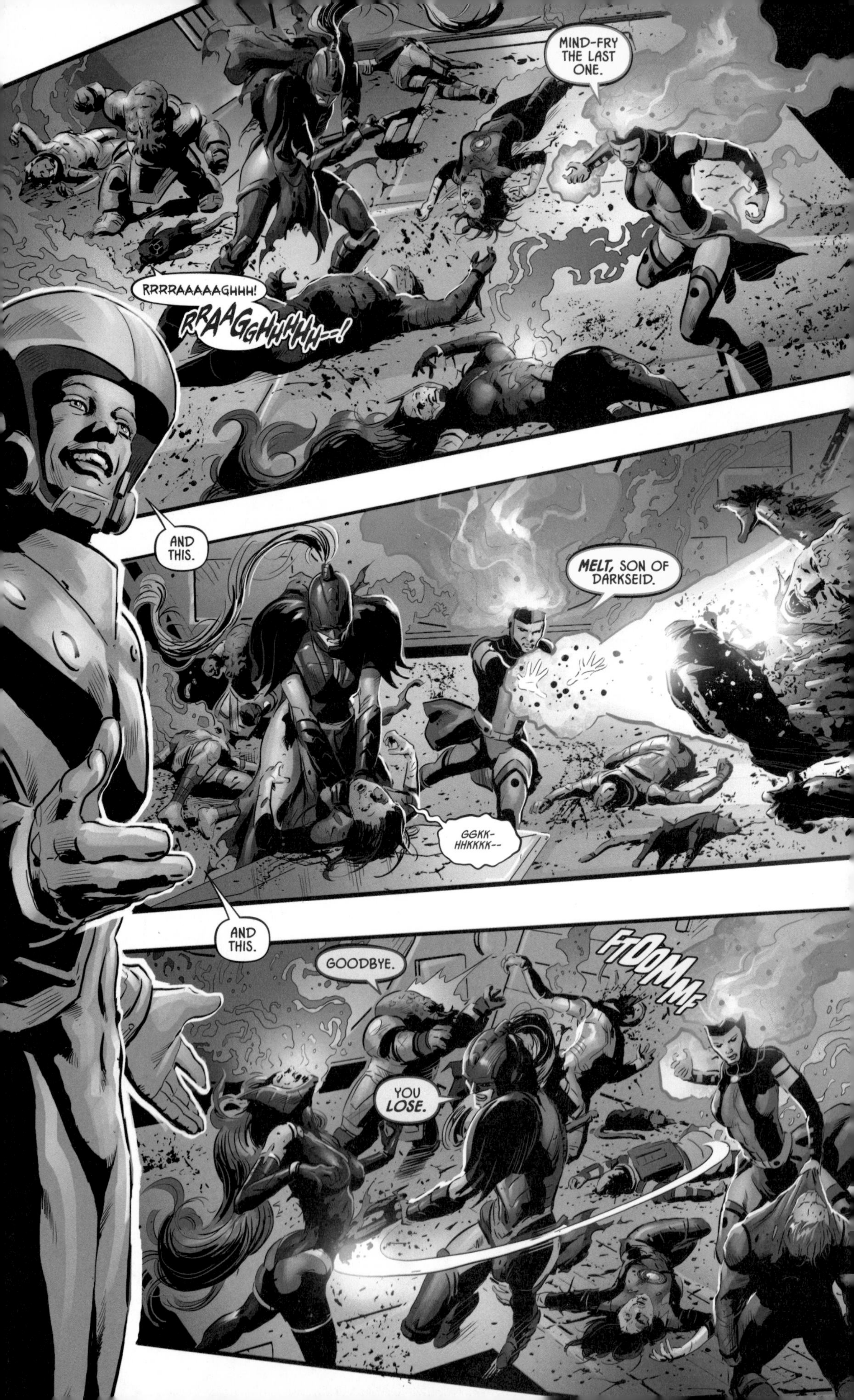
MIND-FRY THE LAST ONE.
RRRRAAAAAGHHH!
RRAAGGHHHHH--!
AND THIS.
MELT, SON OF DARKSEID.
GGKK-HHKKKK--
AND THIS.
GOODBYE.
FTOOMMF
YOU LOSE.

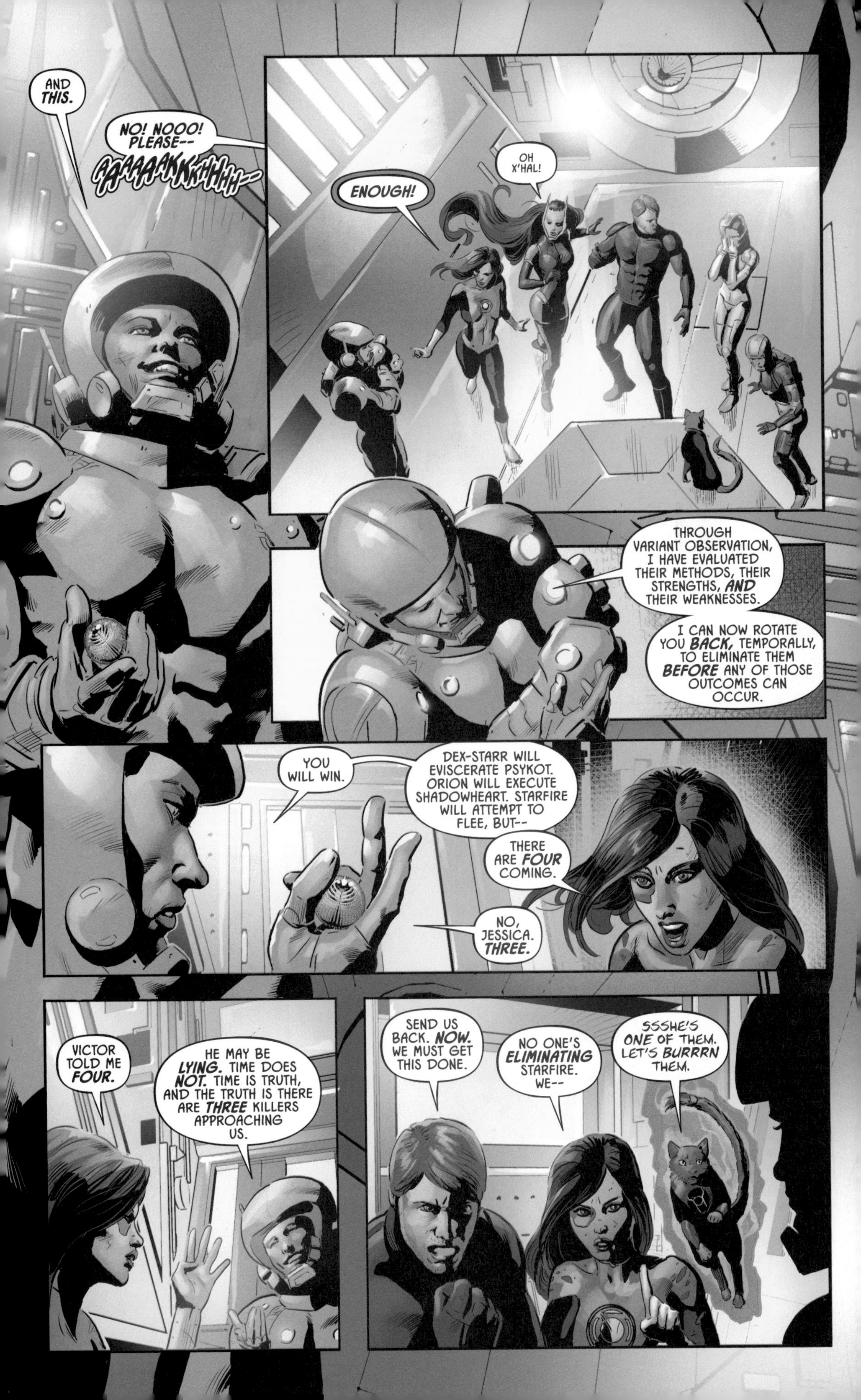
AND THIS.
NO! NOOO! PLEASE--
AAAAAKKHHHH--
OH X'HAL!
ENOUGH!
THROUGH VARIANT OBSERVATION, I HAVE EVALUATED THEIR METHODS, THEIR STRENGTHS, AND THEIR WEAKNESSES.
I CAN NOW ROTATE YOU BACK, TEMPORALLY, TO ELIMINATE THEM BEFORE ANY OF THOSE OUTCOMES CAN OCCUR.
YOU WILL WIN.
DEX-STARR WILL EVISCERATE PSYKOT. ORION WILL EXECUTE SHADOWHEART. STARFIRE WILL ATTEMPT TO FLEE, BUT--
THERE ARE FOUR COMING.
NO, JESSICA. THREE.
VICTOR TOLD ME FOUR.
HE MAY BE LYING. TIME DOES NOT. TIME IS TRUTH, AND THE TRUTH IS THERE ARE THREE KILLERS APPROACHING US.
SEND US BACK. NOW. WE MUST GET THIS DONE.
NO ONE'S ELIMINATING STARFIRE. WE--
SSSHE'S ONE OF THEM. LET'S BURRRN THEM.

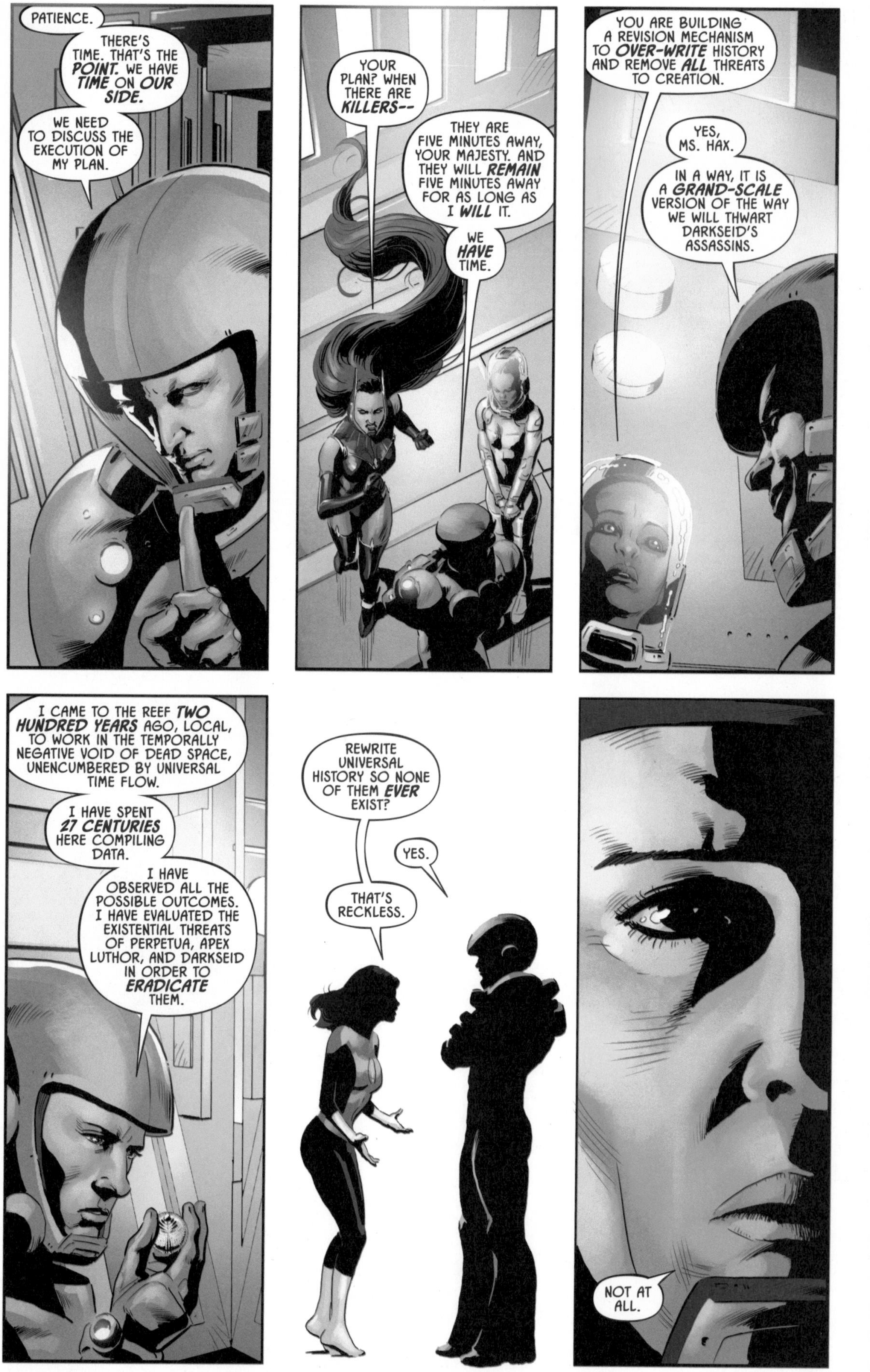
PATIENCE.
THERE'S TIME. THAT'S THE POINT. WE HAVE TIME ON OUR SIDE.
WE NEED TO DISCUSS THE EXECUTION OF MY PLAN.
YOUR PLAN? WHEN THERE ARE KILLERS--
THEY ARE FIVE MINUTES AWAY, YOUR MAJESTY. AND THEY WILL REMAIN FIVE MINUTES AWAY FOR AS LONG AS I WILL IT.
WE HAVE TIME.
YOU ARE BUILDING A REVISION MECHANISM TO OVER-WRITE HISTORY AND REMOVE ALL THREATS TO CREATION.
YES, MS. HAX.
IN A WAY, IT IS A GRAND-SCALE VERSION OF THE WAY WE WILL THWART DARKSEID'S ASSASSINS.
I CAME TO THE REEF TWO HUNDRED YEARS AGO, LOCAL, TO WORK IN THE TEMPORALLY NEGATIVE VOID OF DEAD SPACE, UNENCUMBERED BY UNIVERSAL TIME FLOW.
I HAVE SPENT 27 CENTURIES HERE COMPILING DATA.
I HAVE OBSERVED ALL THE POSSIBLE OUTCOMES. I HAVE EVALUATED THE EXISTENTIAL THREATS OF PERPETUA, APEX LUTHOR, AND DARKSEID IN ORDER TO ERADICATE THEM.
REWRITE UNIVERSAL HISTORY SO NONE OF THEM EVER EXIST?
YES.
THAT'S RECKLESS.
NOT AT ALL.

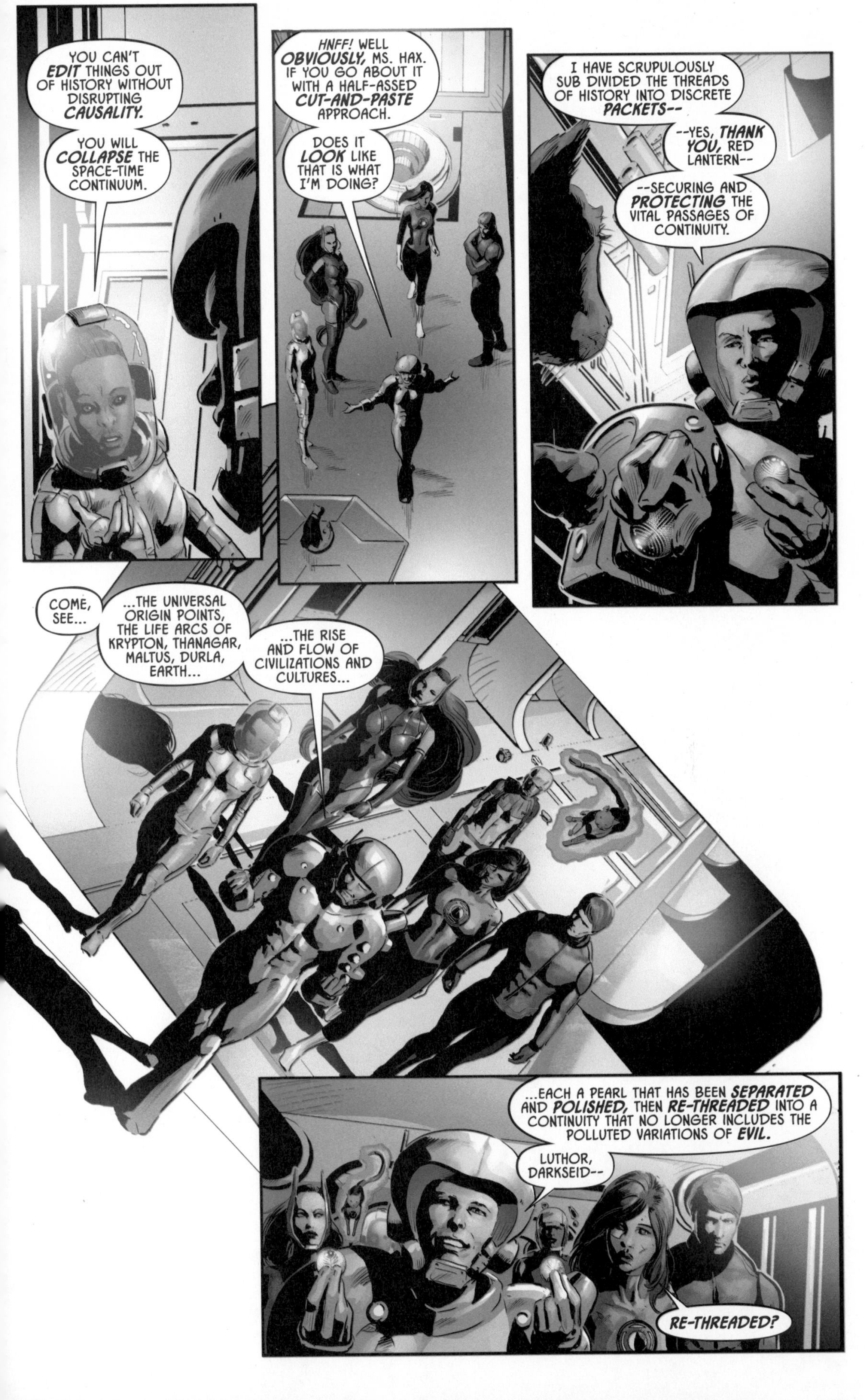
YOU CAN'T EDIT THINGS OUT OF HISTORY WITHOUT DISRUPTING CAUSALITY.
YOU WILL COLLAPSE THE SPACE-TIME CONTINUUM.
HNFF! WELL OBVIOUSLY, MS. HAX. IF YOU GO ABOUT IT WITH A HALF-ASSED CUT-AND-PASTE APPROACH.
DOES IT LOOK LIKE THAT IS WHAT I'M DOING?
I HAVE SCRUPULOUSLY SUB DIVIDED THE THREADS OF HISTORY INTO DISCRETE PACKETS--
--YES, THANK YOU, RED LANTERN--
--SECURING AND PROTECTING THE VITAL PASSAGES OF CONTINUITY.
COME, SEE...
...THE UNIVERSAL ORIGIN POINTS, THE LIFE ARCS OF KRYPTON, THANAGAR, MALTUS, DURLA, EARTH...
...THE RISE AND FLOW OF CIVILIZATIONS AND CULTURES...
...EACH A PEARL THAT HAS BEEN SEPARATED AND POLISHED, THEN RE-THREADED INTO A CONTINUITY THAT NO LONGER INCLUDES THE POLLUTED VARIATIONS OF EVIL.
LUTHOR, DARKSEID--
RE-THREADED?

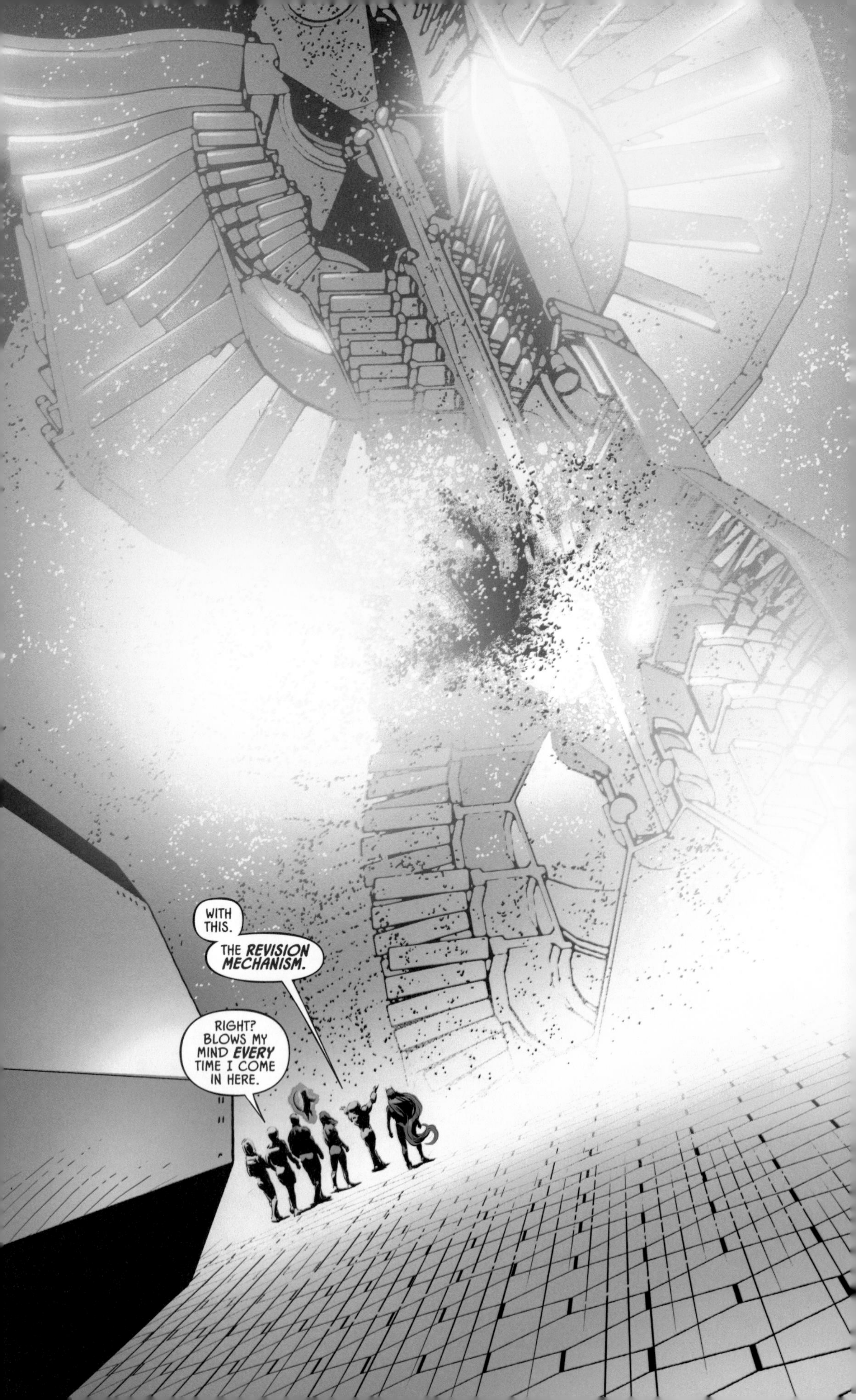
WITH THIS.
THE REVISION MECHANISM.
RIGHT? BLOWS MY MIND EVERY TIME I COME IN HERE.

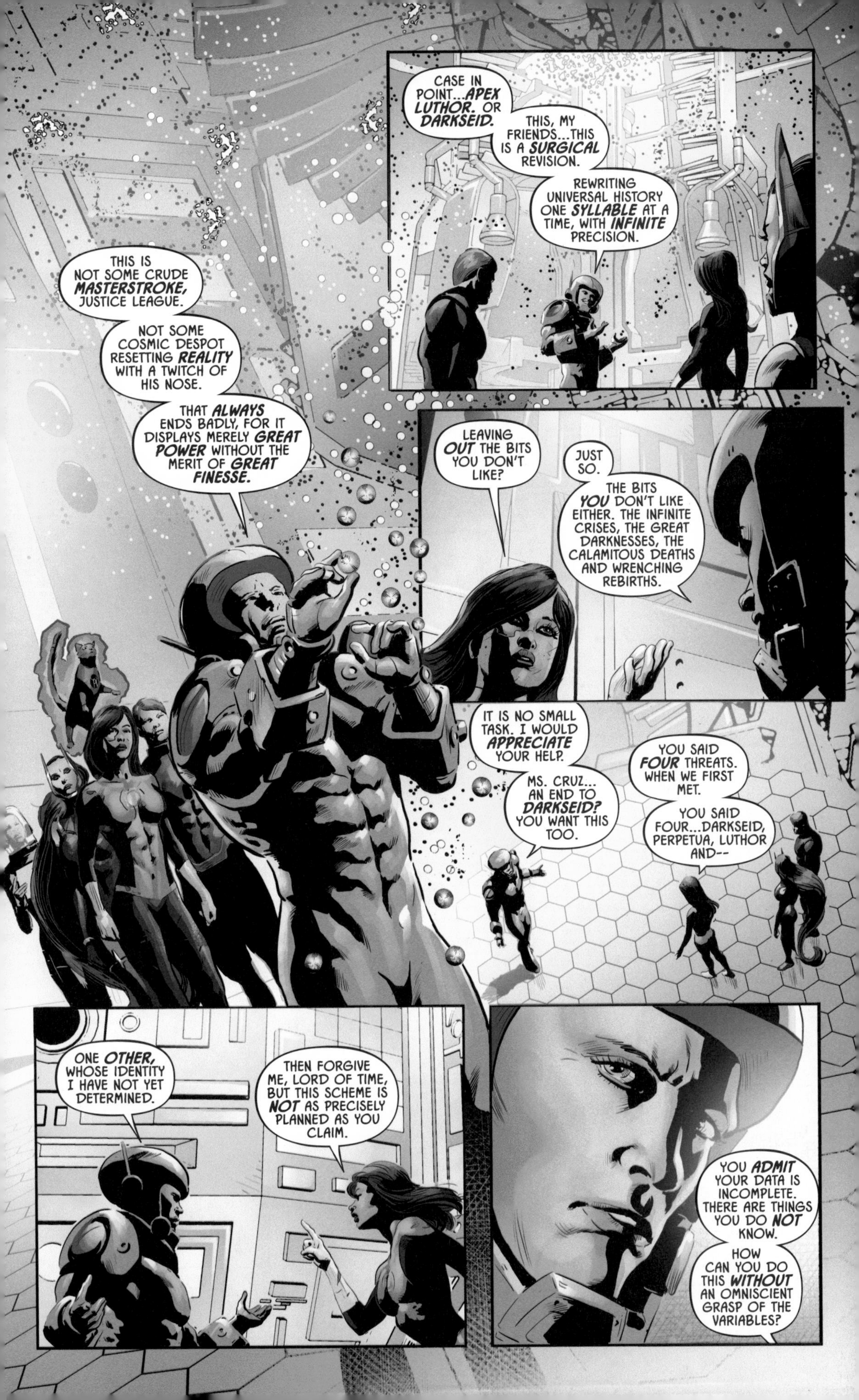
THIS IS NOT SOME CRUDE MASTERSTROKE, JUSTICE LEAGUE.
NOT SOME COSMIC DESPOT RESETTING REALITY WITH A TWITCH OF HIS NOSE.
THAT ALWAYS ENDS BADLY, FOR IT DISPLAYS MERELY GREAT POWER WITHOUT THE MERIT OF GREAT FINESSE.
CASE IN POINT...APEX LUTHOR. OR DARKSEID.
THIS, MY FRIENDS...THIS IS A SURGICAL REVISION.
REWRITING UNIVERSAL HISTORY ONE SYLLABLE AT A TIME, WITH INFINITE PRECISION.
LEAVING OUT THE BITS YOU DON'T LIKE?
JUST SO.
THE BITS YOU DON'T LIKE EITHER. THE INFINITE CRISES, THE GREAT DARKNESSES, THE CALAMITOUS DEATHS AND WRENCHING REBIRTHS.
IT IS NO SMALL TASK. I WOULD APPRECIATE YOUR HELP.
MS. CRUZ... AN END TO DARKSEID? YOU WANT THIS TOO.
YOU SAID FOUR THREATS. WHEN WE FIRST MET.
YOU SAID FOUR...DARKSEID, PERPETUA, LUTHOR AND--
ONE OTHER, WHOSE IDENTITY I HAVE NOT YET DETERMINED.
THEN FORGIVE ME, LORD OF TIME, BUT THIS SCHEME IS NOT AS PRECISELY PLANNED AS YOU CLAIM.
YOU ADMIT YOUR DATA IS INCOMPLETE. THERE ARE THINGS YOU DO NOT KNOW.
HOW CAN YOU DO THIS WITHOUT AN OMNISCIENT GRASP OF THE VARIABLES?

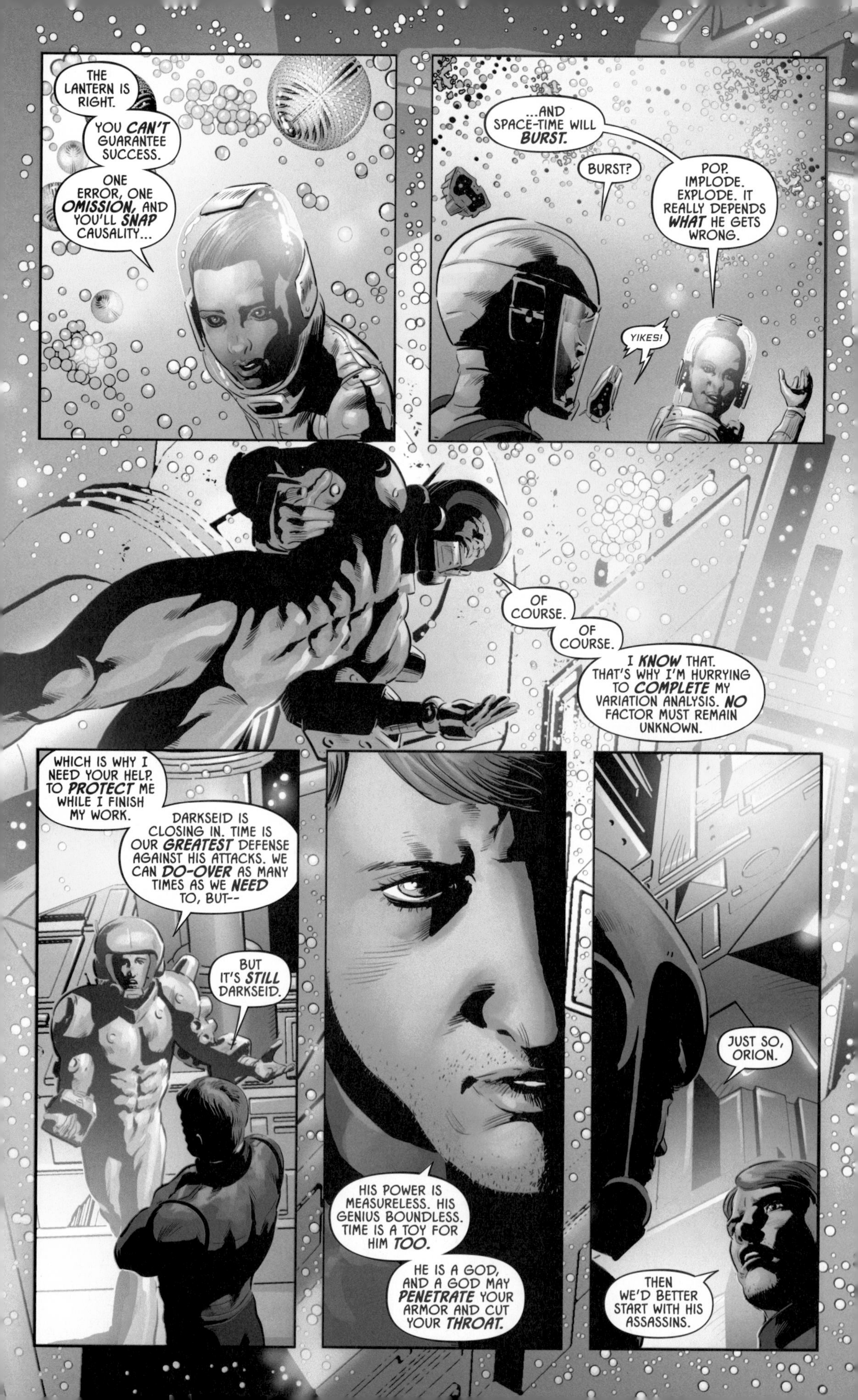
THE LANTERN IS RIGHT.
YOU CAN'T GUARANTEE SUCCESS.
ONE ERROR, ONE OMISSION, AND YOU'LL SNAP CAUSALITY...
...AND SPACE-TIME WILL BURST.
BURST?
POP. IMPLODE. EXPLODE. IT REALLY DEPENDS WHAT HE GETS WRONG.
YIKES!
OF COURSE.
OF COURSE.
I KNOW THAT. THAT'S WHY I'M HURRYING TO COMPLETE MY VARIATION ANALYSIS. NO FACTOR MUST REMAIN UNKNOWN.
WHICH IS WHY I NEED YOUR HELP. TO PROTECT ME WHILE I FINISH MY WORK.
DARKSEID IS CLOSING IN. TIME IS OUR GREATEST DEFENSE AGAINST HIS ATTACKS. WE CAN DO-OVER AS MANY TIMES AS WE NEED TO, BUT--
BUT IT'S STILL DARKSEID.
HIS POWER IS MEASURELESS. HIS GENIUS BOUNDLESS. TIME IS A TOY FOR HIM TOO.
HE IS A GOD, AND A GOD MAY PENETRATE YOUR ARMOR AND CUT YOUR THROAT.
JUST SO, ORION.
THEN WE'D BETTER START WITH HIS ASSASSINS.

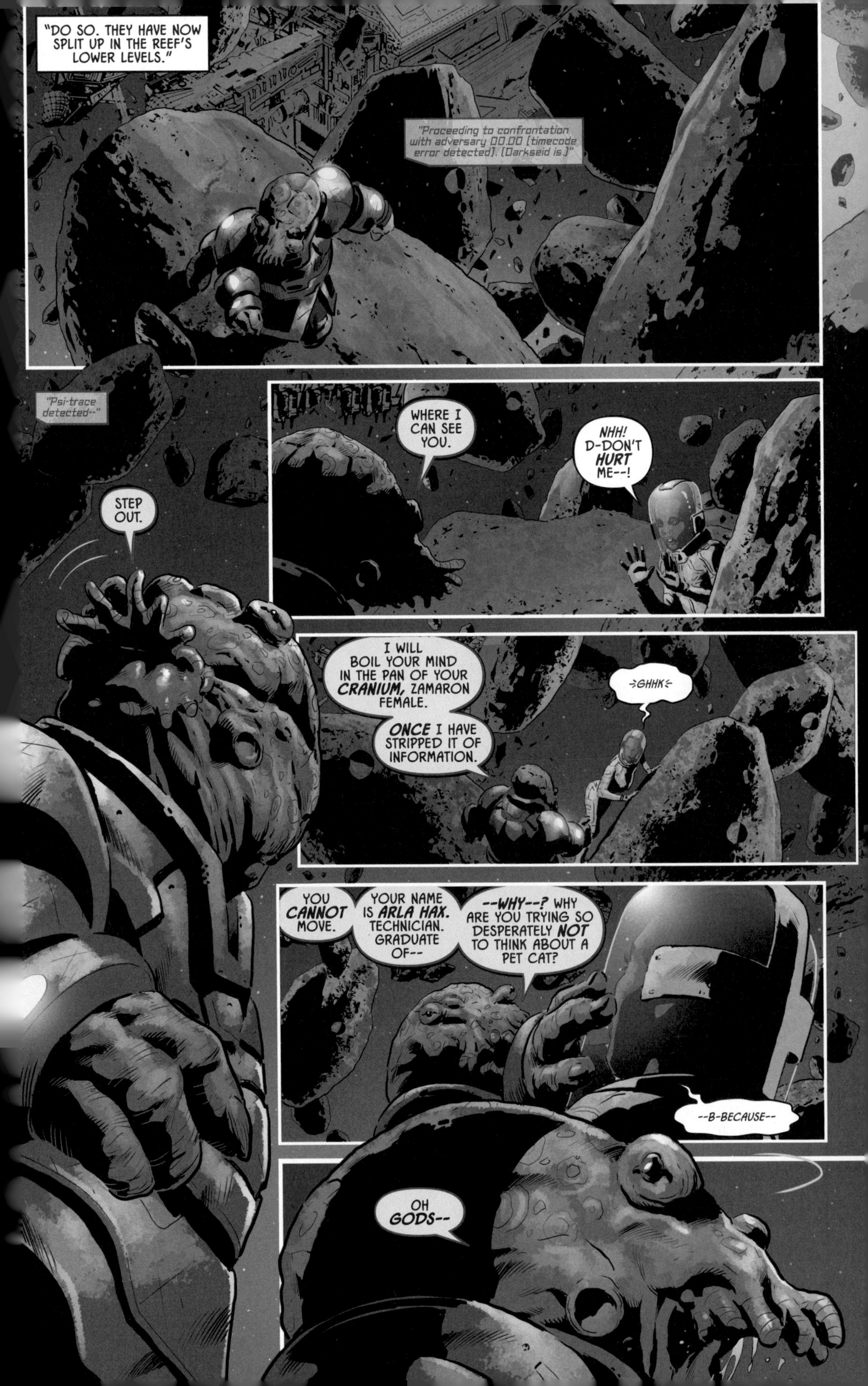
"DO SO. THEY HAVE NOW SPLIT UP IN THE REEF'S LOWER LEVELS."
"Proceeding to confrontation with adversary 00.00 [timecode error detected]. [Darkseid is.]"
"Psi-trace detected--"
STEP OUT.
WHERE I CAN SEE YOU.
NHH! D-DON'T HURT ME--!
I WILL BOIL YOUR MIND IN THE PAN OF YOUR CRANIUM, ZAMARON FEMALE.
ONCE I HAVE STRIPPED IT OF INFORMATION.
GHHK
YOU CANNOT MOVE.
YOUR NAME IS ARLA HAX. TECHNICIAN. GRADUATE OF--
--WHY--? WHY ARE YOU TRYING SO DESPERATELY NOT TO THINK ABOUT A PET CAT?
--B-BECAUSE--
OH GODS--

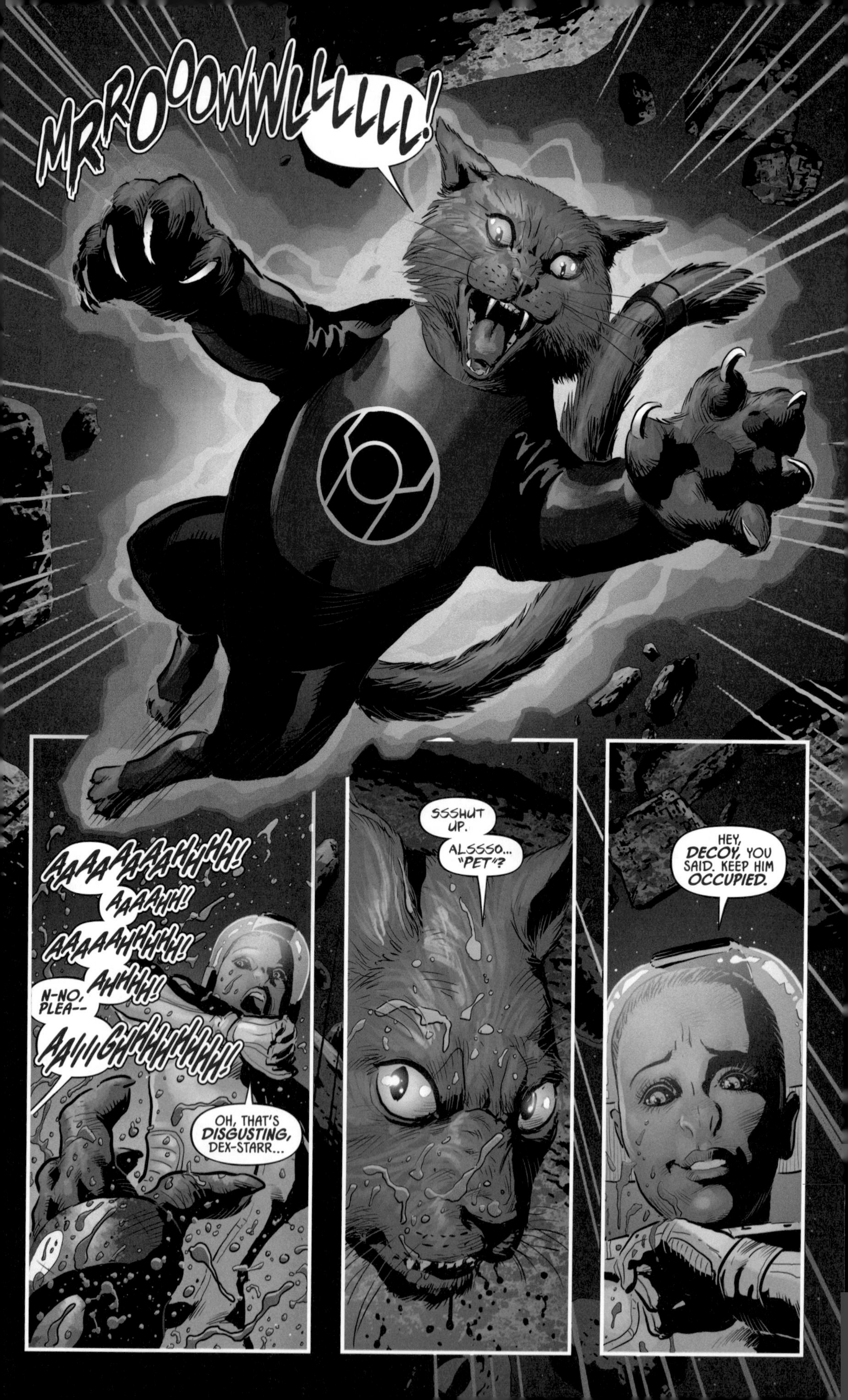
MRROOOWWLLLLLL!
AAAAAAAAAHHHH!
AAAAHH!
AAAAAHHHHH!
AHHHH!
N-NO, PLEA--
AAIIIGHHHHHHHH!
OH, THAT'S DISGUSTING, DEX-STARR...
SSSHUT UP.
ALSSSO... "PET"?
HEY, DECOY, YOU SAID. KEEP HIM OCCUPIED.

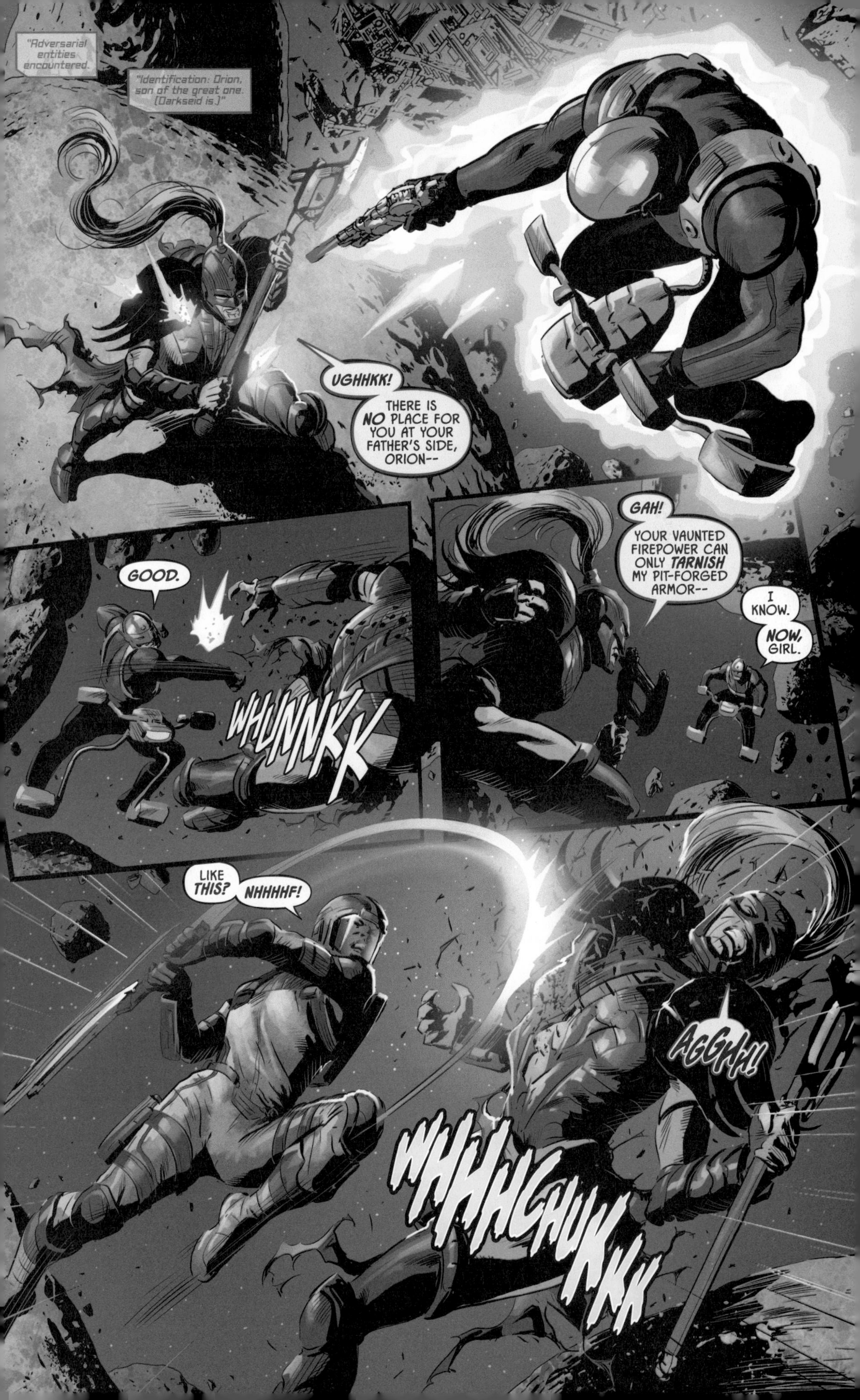
"Adversarial entities encountered.
"Identification: Orion, son of the great one. [Darkseid is.]"
UGHHKK!
THERE IS NO PLACE FOR YOU AT YOUR FATHER'S SIDE, ORION--
GOOD.
WHUNNKK
GAH!
YOUR VAUNTED FIREPOWER CAN ONLY TARNISH MY PIT-FORGED ARMOR--
I KNOW.
NOW, GIRL.
LIKE THIS?
NHHHHF!
AGGHH!
WHHHCHUKKK

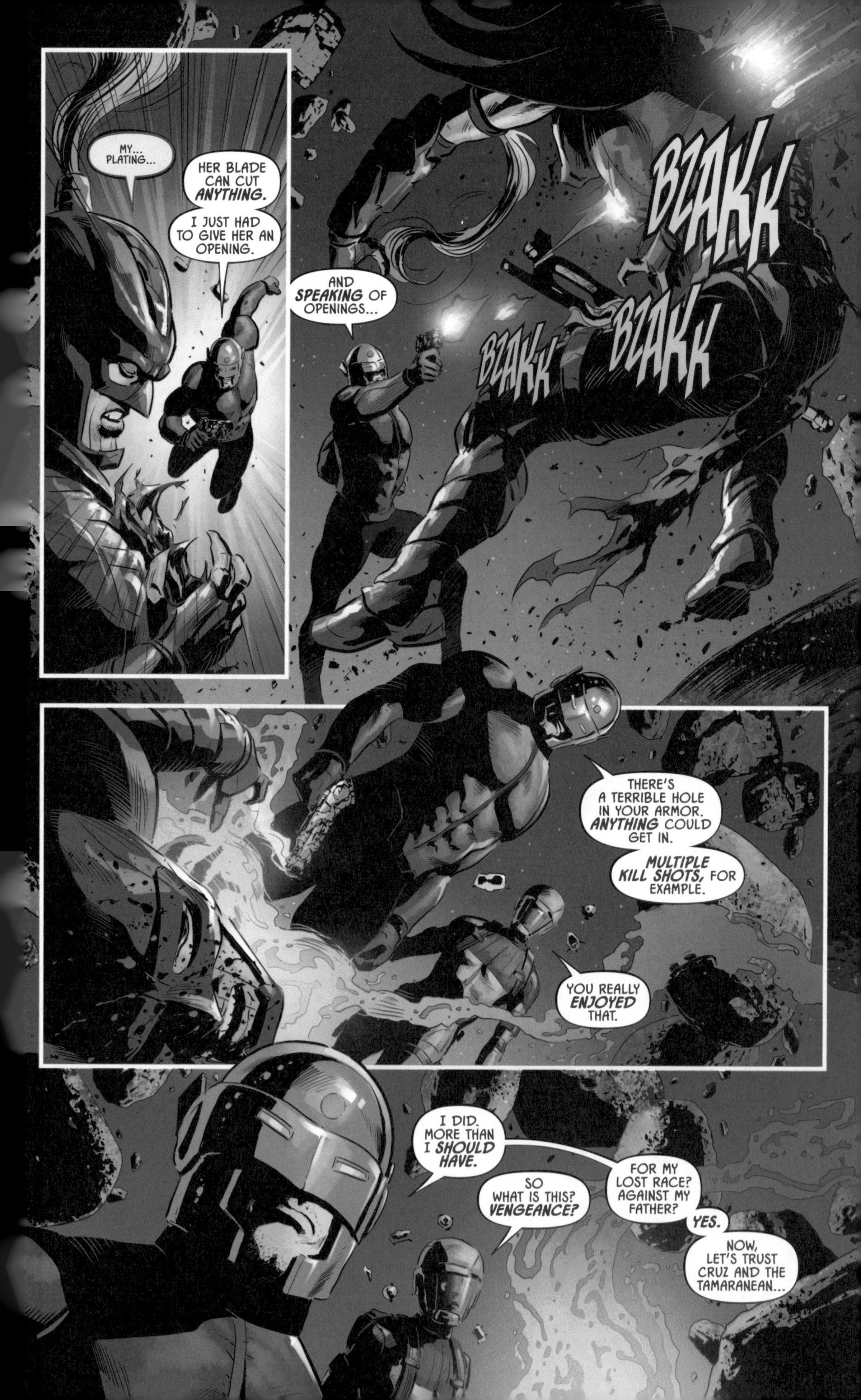
MY... PLATING...
HER BLADE CAN CUT ANYTHING.
I JUST HAD TO GIVE HER AN OPENING.
AND SPEAKING OF OPENINGS...
BZAKK
BZAKK
BZAKK
THERE'S A TERRIBLE HOLE IN YOUR ARMOR. ANYTHING COULD GET IN.
MULTIPLE KILL SHOTS, FOR EXAMPLE.
YOU REALLY ENJOYED THAT.
I DID. MORE THAN I SHOULD HAVE.
SO WHAT IS THIS? VENGEANCE?
FOR MY LOST RACE? AGAINST MY FATHER?
YES.
NOW, LET'S TRUST CRUZ AND THE TAMARANEAN...

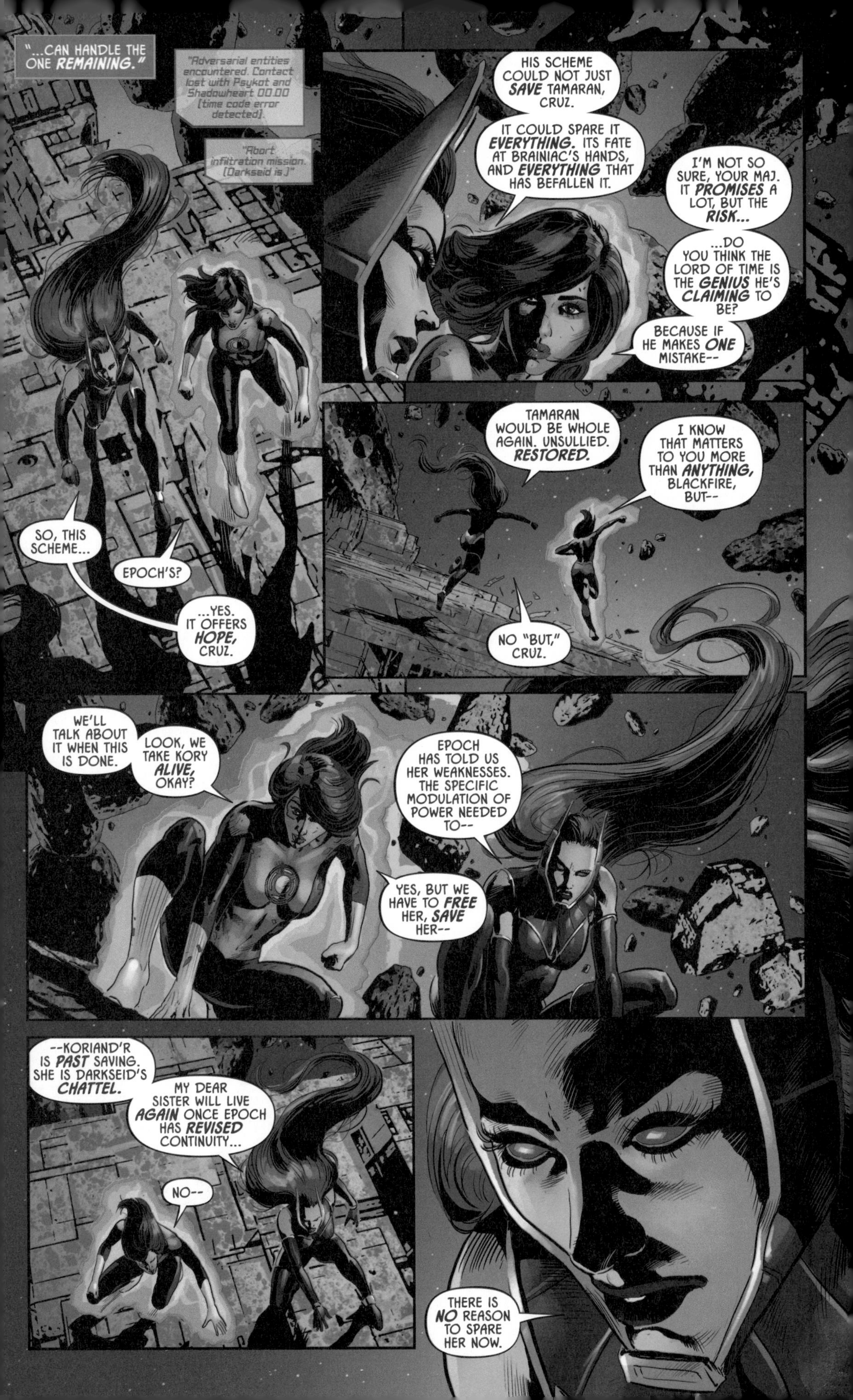

"...CAN HANDLE THE ONE REMAINING."
"Adversarial entities encountered. Contact lost with Psykot and Shadowheart 00.00 [time code error detected]
"Abort infiltration mission. [Darkseid is]"
HIS SCHEME COULD NOT JUST SAVE TAMARAN, CRUZ.
IT COULD SPARE IT EVERYTHING. ITS FATE AT BRAINIAC'S HANDS, AND EVERYTHING THAT HAS BEFALLEN IT.
I'M NOT SO SURE, YOUR MAJ. IT PROMISES A LOT, BUT THE RISK...
...DO YOU THINK THE LORD OF TIME IS THE GENIUS HE'S CLAIMING TO BE?
BECAUSE IF HE MAKES ONE MISTAKE--
SO, THIS SCHEME...
EPOCH'S?
...YES. IT OFFERS HOPE, CRUZ.
TAMARAN WOULD BE WHOLE AGAIN. UNSULLIED. RESTORED.
I KNOW THAT MATTERS TO YOU MORE THAN ANYTHING, BLACKFIRE, BUT--
NO "BUT," CRUZ.
WE'LL TALK ABOUT IT WHEN THIS IS DONE.
LOOK, WE TAKE KORY ALIVE, OKAY?
EPOCH HAS TOLD US HER WEAKNESSES. THE SPECIFIC MODULATION OF POWER NEEDED TO--
YES, BUT WE HAVE TO FREE HER, SAVE HER--
--KORIAND'R IS PAST SAVING. SHE IS DARKSEID'S CHATTEL.
MY DEAR SISTER WILL LIVE AGAIN ONCE EPOCH HAS REVISED CONTINUITY...
NO--
THERE IS NO REASON TO SPARE HER NOW.

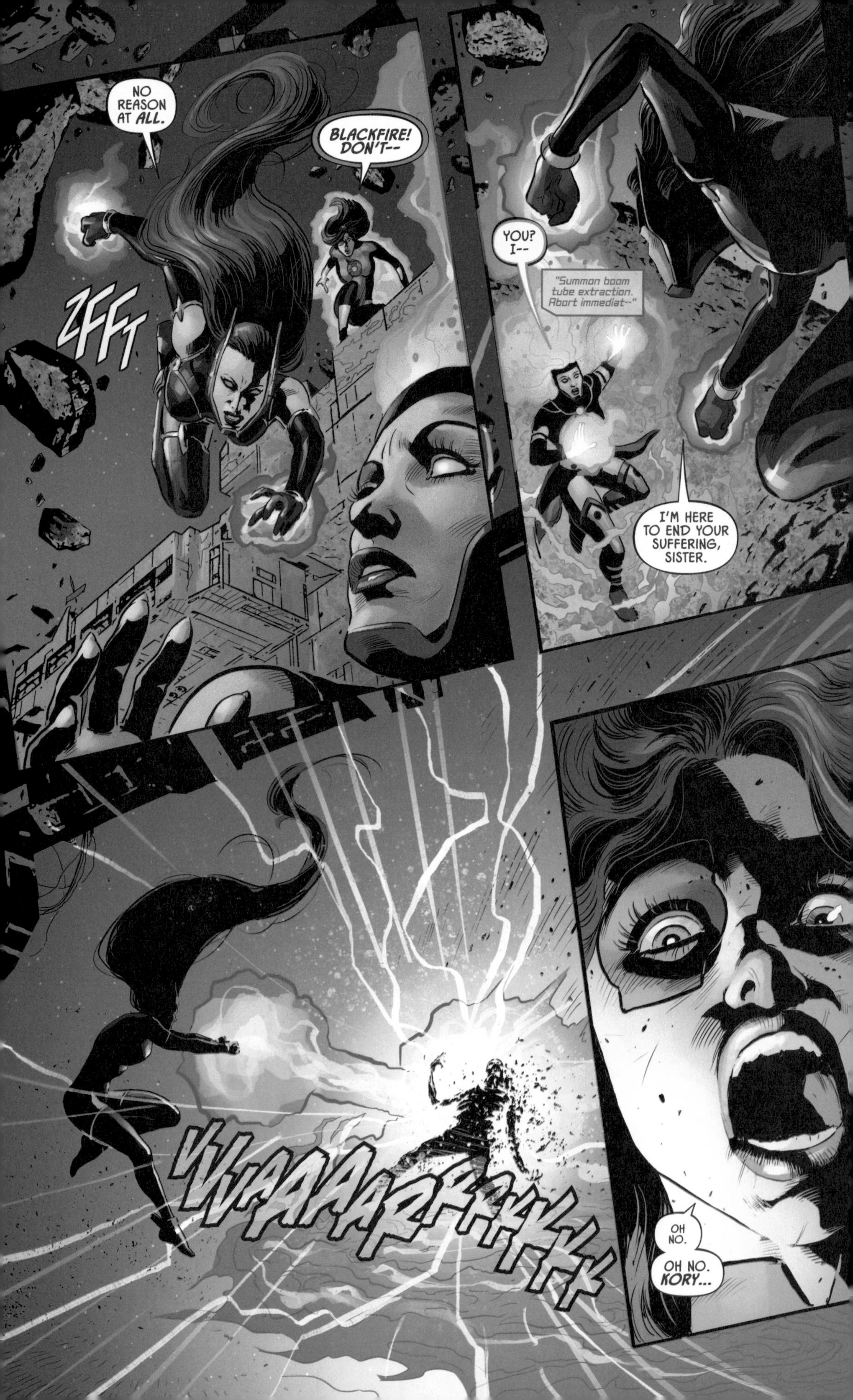
NO REASON AT ALL.
BLACKFIRE! DON'T--
ZFFT
YOU? I--
"Summon boom tube extraction. Abort immediat--"
I'M HERE TO END YOUR SUFFERING, SISTER.
VVRAAAAPKKKK
OH NO.
OH NO. KORY...

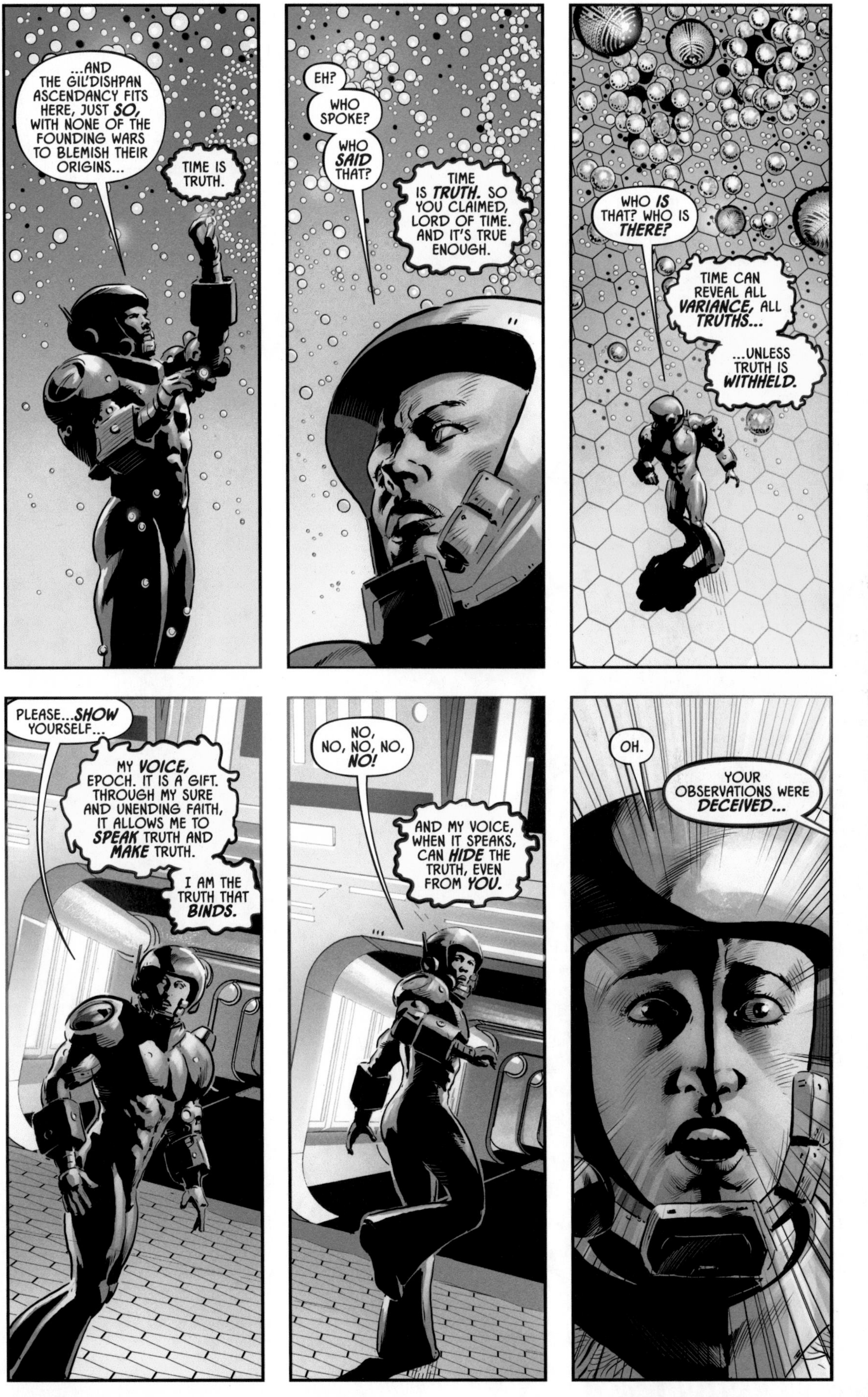
...AND THE GIL'DISHPAN ASCENDANCY FITS HERE, JUST SO, WITH NONE OF THE FOUNDING WARS TO BLEMISH THEIR ORIGINS...
TIME IS TRUTH.
EH?
WHO SPOKE?
WHO SAID THAT?
TIME IS TRUTH. SO YOU CLAIMED, LORD OF TIME. AND IT'S TRUE ENOUGH.
WHO IS THAT? WHO IS THERE?
TIME CAN REVEAL ALL VARIANCE, ALL TRUTHS...
...UNLESS TRUTH IS WITHHELD.
PLEASE...SHOW YOURSELF...
MY VOICE, EPOCH. IT IS A GIFT. THROUGH MY SURE AND UNENDING FAITH, IT ALLOWS ME TO SPEAK TRUTH AND MAKE TRUTH.
I AM THE TRUTH THAT BINDS.
NO, NO, NO, NO, NO!
AND MY VOICE, WHEN IT SPEAKS, CAN HIDE THE TRUTH, EVEN FROM YOU.
OH.
YOUR OBSERVATIONS WERE DECEIVED...

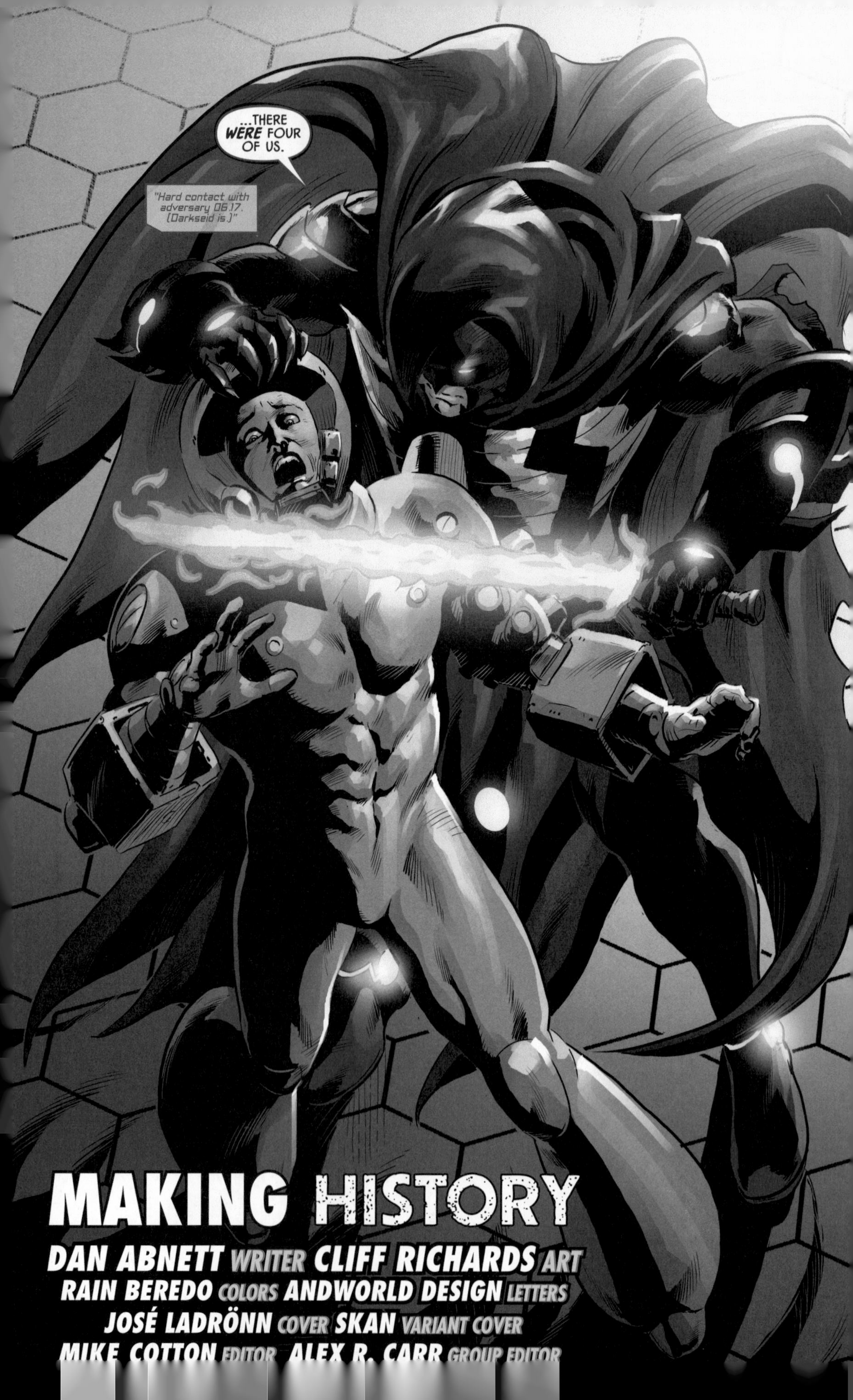
"Hard contact with adversary 06.17. (Darkseid is.)"
...THERE WERE FOUR OF US.
MAKING HISTORY
DAN ABNETT WRITER CLIFF RICHARDS ART
RAIN BEREDO COLORS ANDWORLD DESIGN LETTERS
JOSÉ LADRÖNN COVER SKAN VARIANT COVER
MIKE COTTON EDITOR ALEX R. CARR GROUP EDITOR

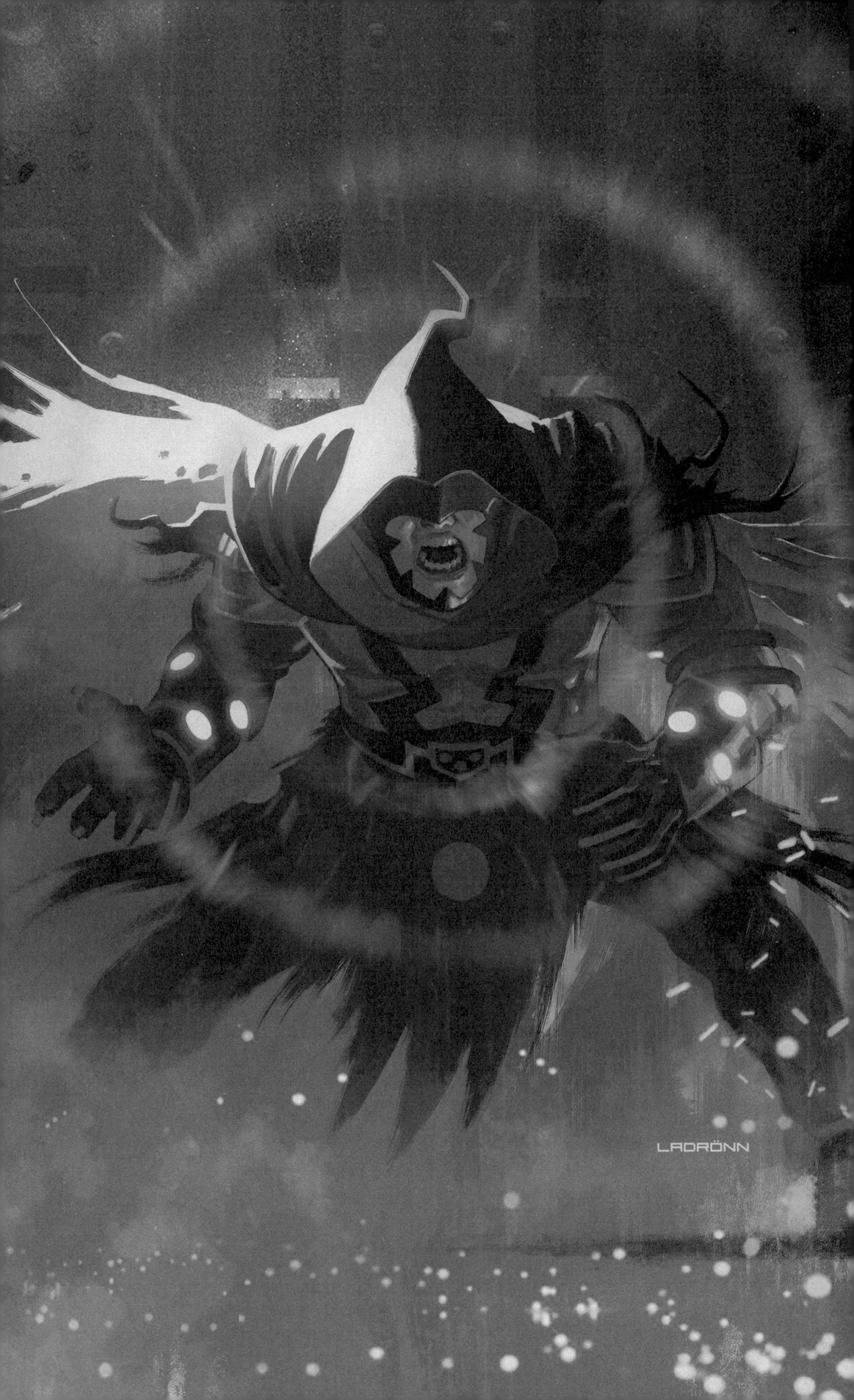
LADRÖNN

Justice League Odyssey #20 variant cover by **SKAN**

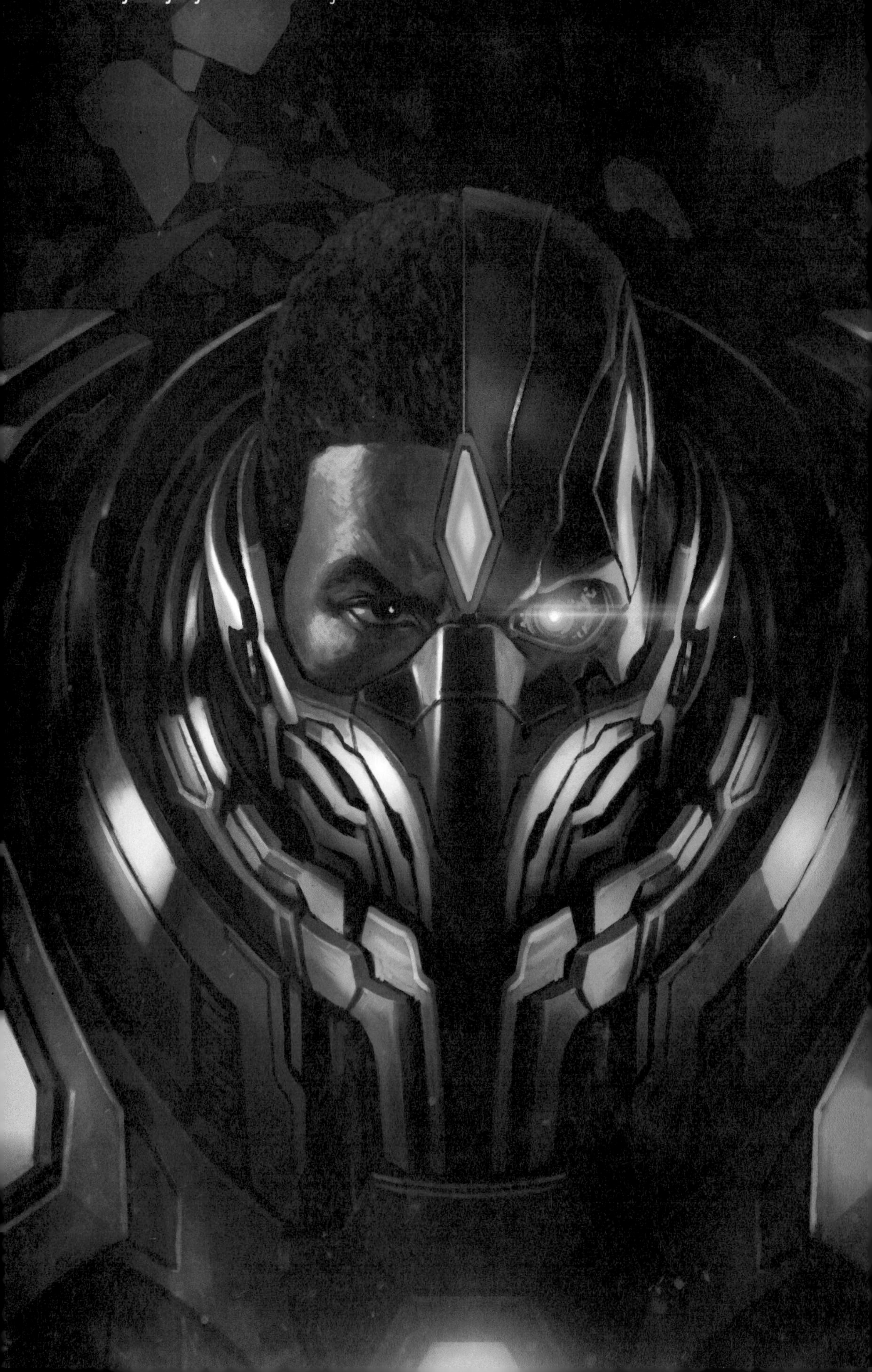

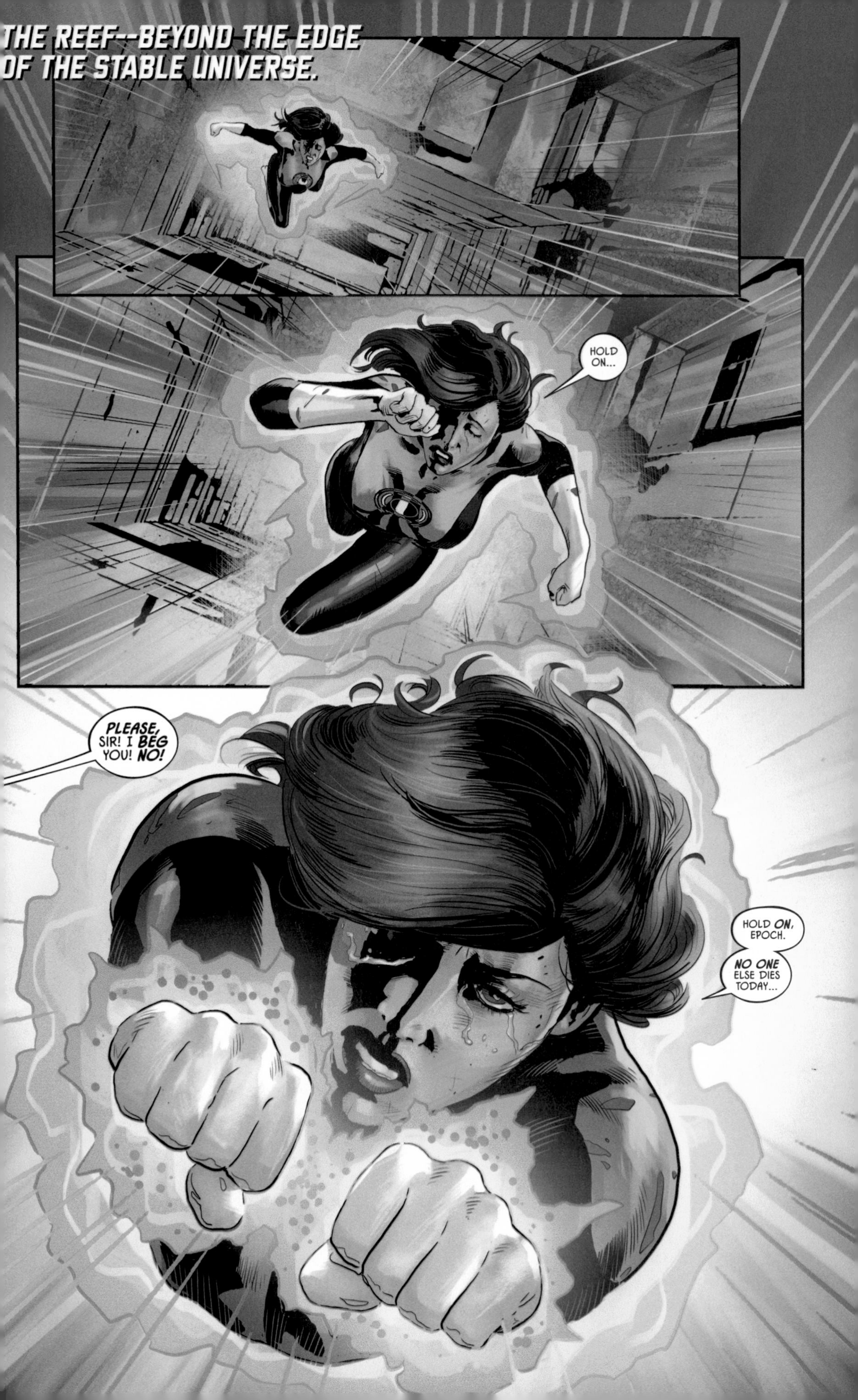
THE REEF--BEYOND THE EDGE OF THE STABLE UNIVERSE.
HOLD ON...
PLEASE, SIR! I BEG YOU! NO!
HOLD ON, EPOCH.
NO ONE ELSE DIES TODAY...

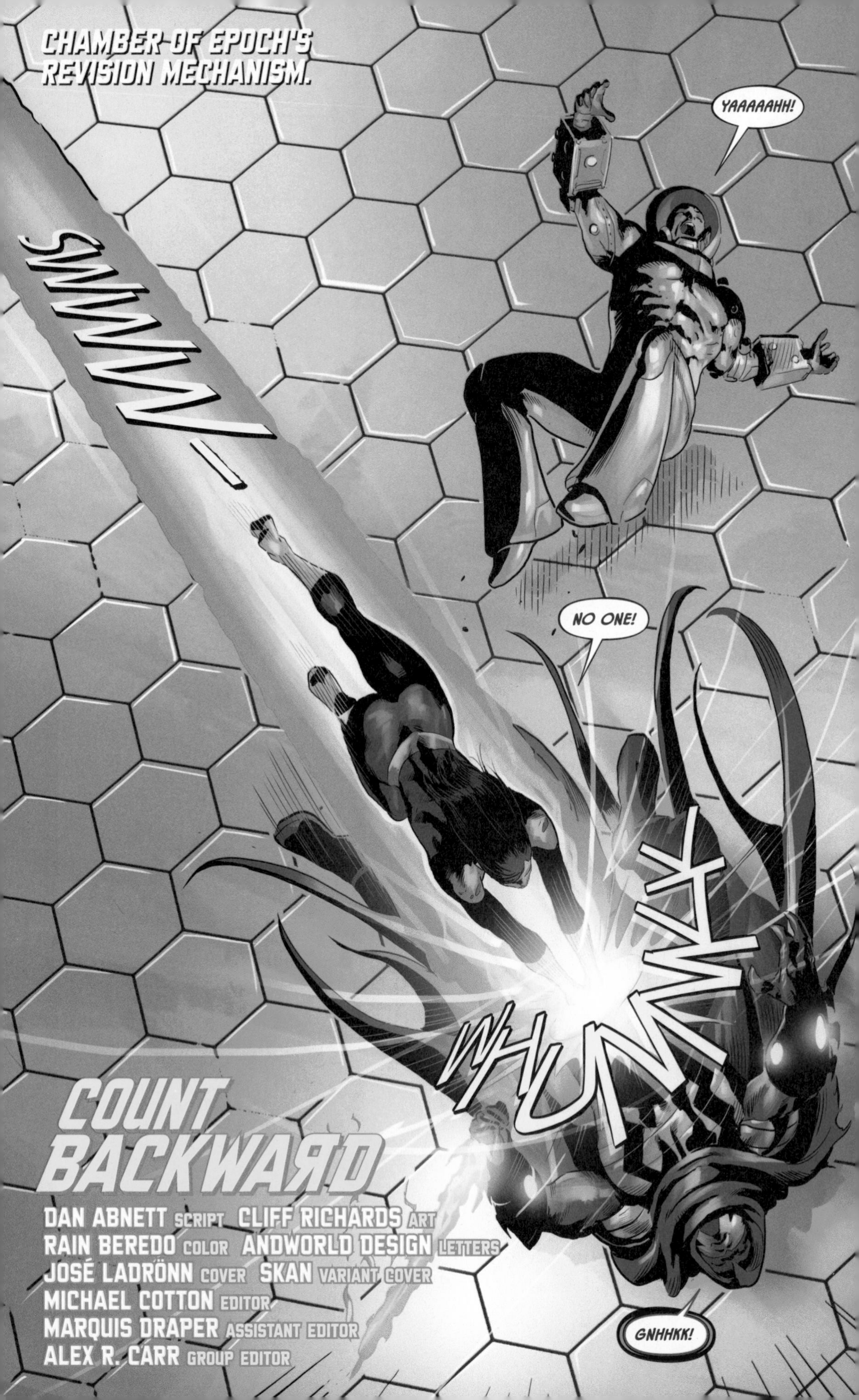
CHAMBER OF EPOCH'S REVISION MECHANISM.
YAAAAAHH!
NO ONE!
GNHHKK!
COUNT BACKWARD
DAN ABNETT SCRIPT CLIFF RICHARDS ART
RAIN BEREDO COLOR ANDWORLD DESIGN LETTERS
JOSÉ LADRÖNN COVER SKAN VARIANT COVER
MICHAEL COTTON EDITOR
MARQUIS DRAPER ASSISTANT EDITOR
ALEX R. CARR GROUP EDITOR

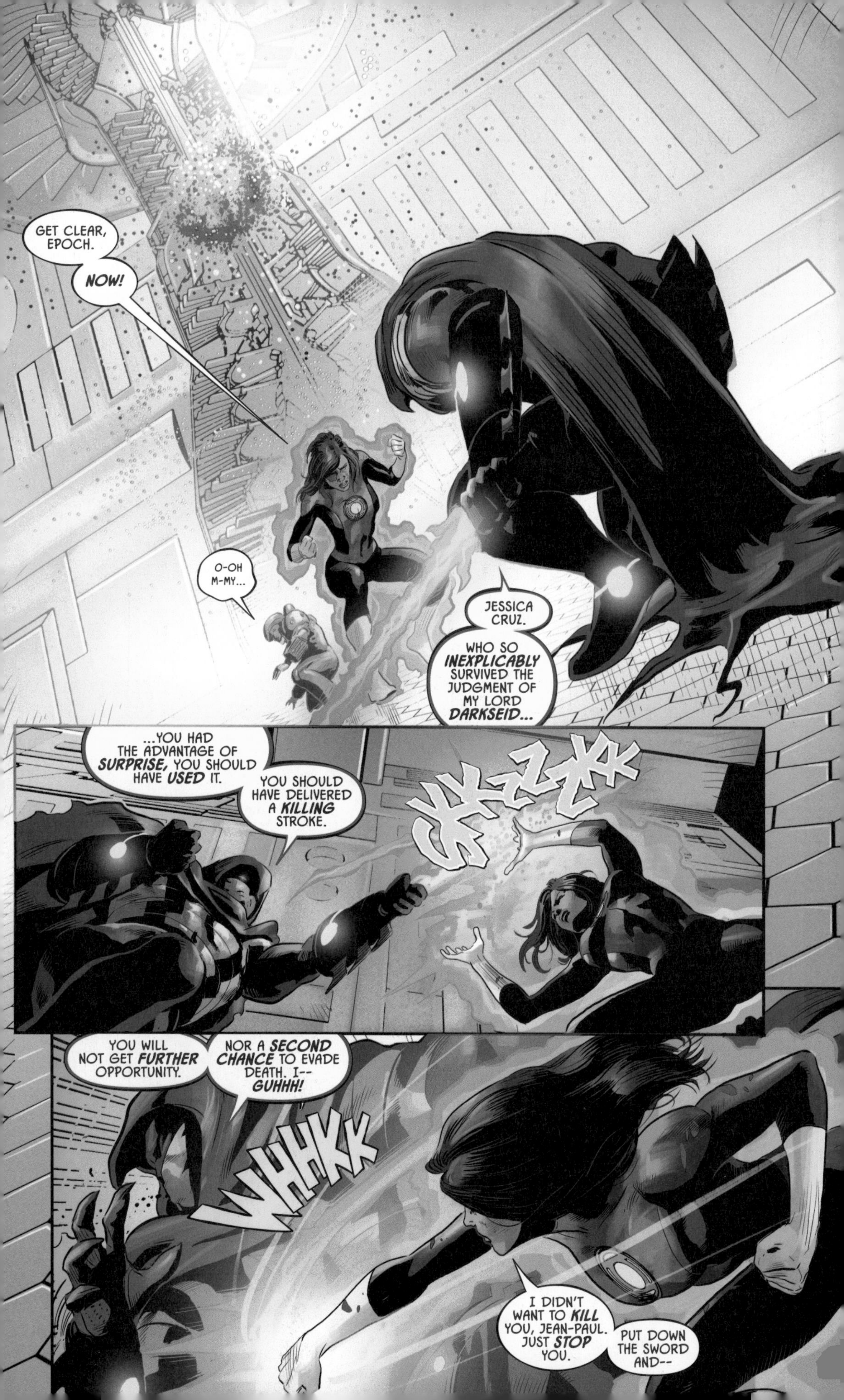
GET CLEAR, EPOCH.
NOW!
O-OH M-MY...
JESSICA CRUZ.
WHO SO INEXPLICABLY SURVIVED THE JUDGMENT OF MY LORD DARKSEID...
...YOU HAD THE ADVANTAGE OF SURPRISE, YOU SHOULD HAVE USED IT.
YOU SHOULD HAVE DELIVERED A KILLING STROKE.
SKKZZZKK
YOU WILL NOT GET FURTHER OPPORTUNITY.
NOR A SECOND CHANCE TO EVADE DEATH. I-- GUHHH!
WHHKK
I DIDN'T WANT TO KILL YOU, JEAN-PAUL. JUST STOP YOU.
PUT DOWN THE SWORD AND--

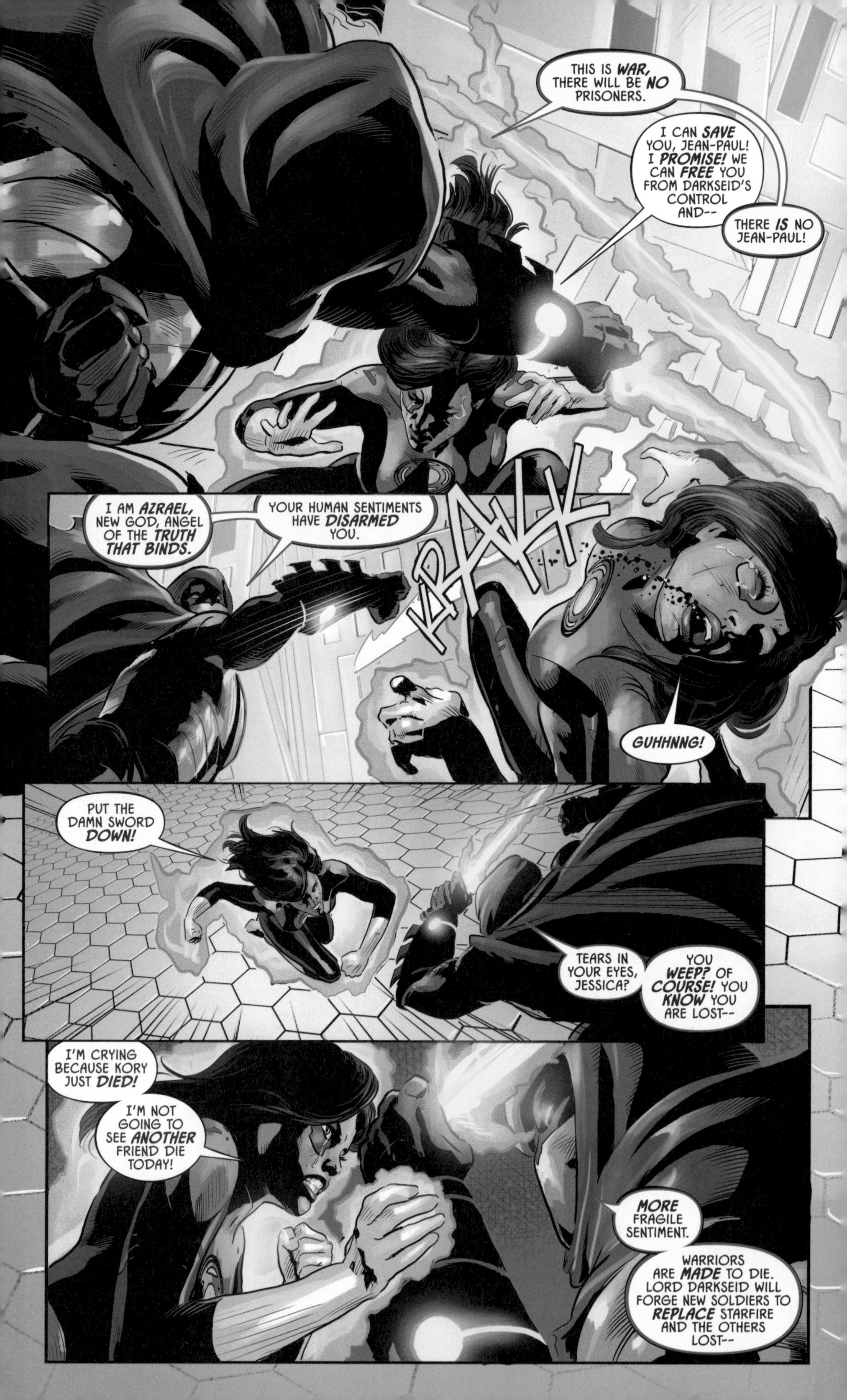
THIS IS WAR, THERE WILL BE NO PRISONERS.
I CAN SAVE YOU, JEAN-PAUL! I PROMISE! WE CAN FREE YOU FROM DARKSEID'S CONTROL AND--
THERE IS NO JEAN-PAUL!
I AM AZRAEL, NEW GOD, ANGEL OF THE TRUTH THAT BINDS.
YOUR HUMAN SENTIMENTS HAVE DISARMED YOU.
KRAKK
GUHHNNG!
PUT THE DAMN SWORD DOWN!
TEARS IN YOUR EYES, JESSICA?
YOU WEEP? OF COURSE! YOU KNOW YOU ARE LOST--
I'M CRYING BECAUSE KORY JUST DIED!
I'M NOT GOING TO SEE ANOTHER FRIEND DIE TODAY!
MORE FRAGILE SENTIMENT.
WARRIORS ARE MADE TO DIE. LORD DARKSEID WILL FORGE NEW SOLDIERS TO REPLACE STARFIRE AND THE OTHERS LOST--

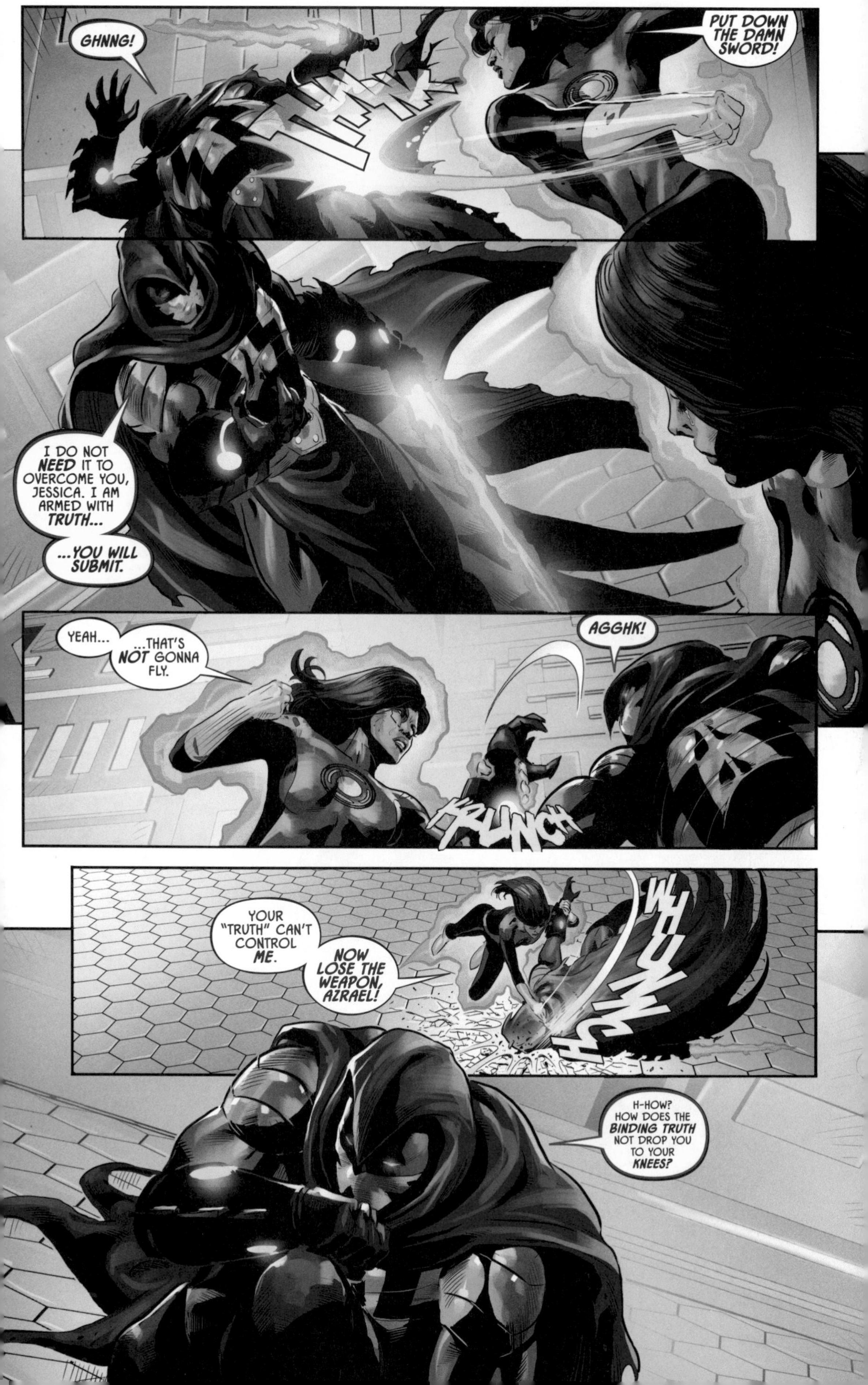
GHNNG!
PUT DOWN THE DAMN SWORD!
I DO NOT NEED IT TO OVERCOME YOU, JESSICA. I AM ARMED WITH TRUTH...
...YOU WILL SUBMIT.
YEAH...
...THAT'S NOT GONNA FLY.
AGGHK!
KRUNCH
YOUR "TRUTH" CAN'T CONTROL ME.
NOW LOSE THE WEAPON, AZRAEL!
WHOOOMSH
H-HOW? HOW DOES THE BINDING TRUTH NOT DROP YOU TO YOUR KNEES?

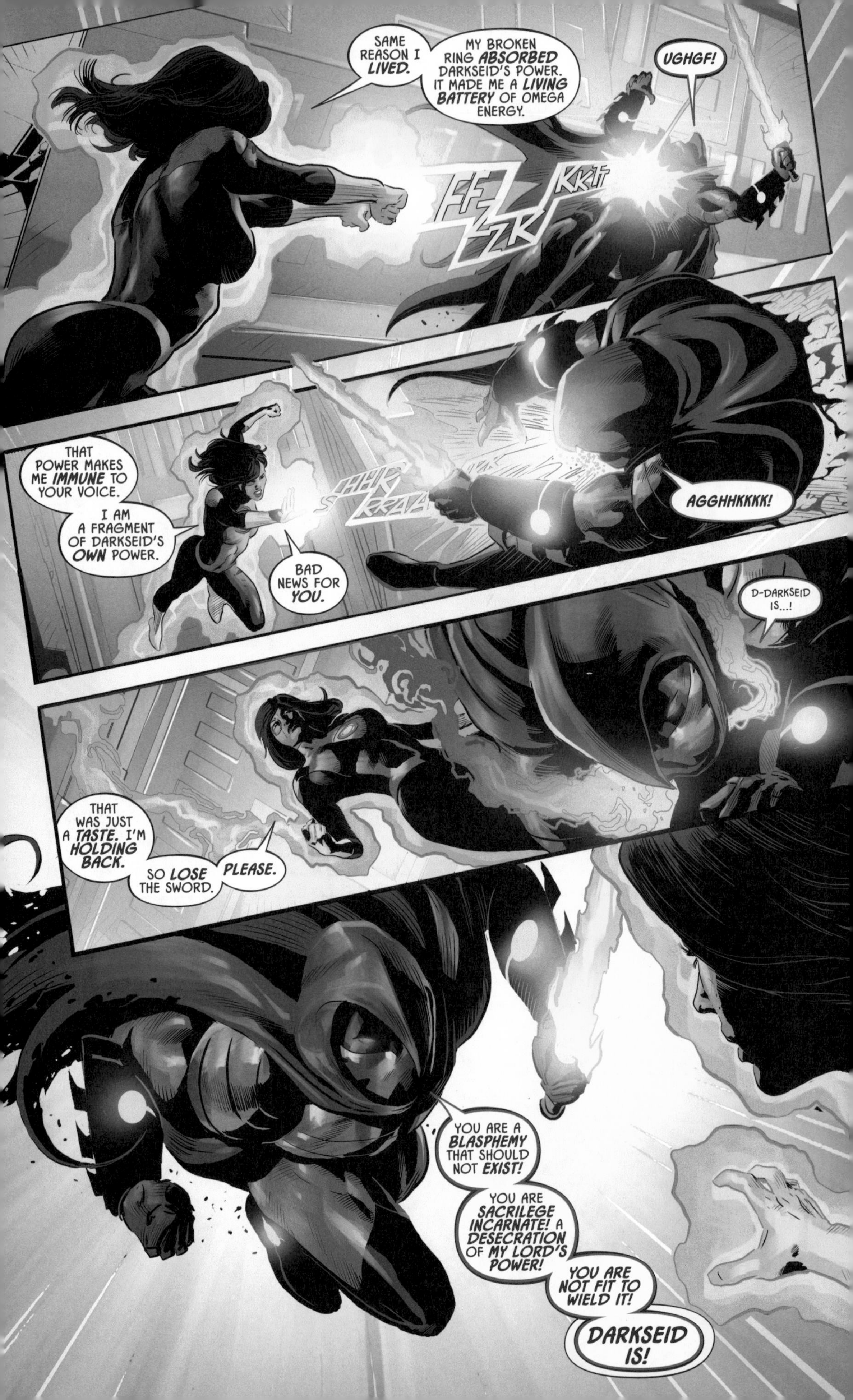
SAME REASON I *LIVED.*
MY BROKEN RING *ABSORBED* DARKSEID'S POWER. IT MADE ME A *LIVING BATTERY* OF OMEGA ENERGY.
UGHGF!
FFZZZKKT
THAT POWER MAKES ME *IMMUNE* TO YOUR VOICE.
I AM A FRAGMENT OF DARKSEID'S *OWN* POWER.
BAD NEWS FOR *YOU.*
AGGHHKKKK!
D-DARKSEID IS...!
THAT WAS JUST A *TASTE.* I'M *HOLDING BACK.*
SO *LOSE* THE SWORD.
PLEASE.
YOU ARE A *BLASPHEMY* THAT SHOULD NOT *EXIST!*
YOU ARE *SACRILEGE INCARNATE!* A *DESECRATION* OF *MY LORD'S POWER!*
YOU ARE NOT FIT TO WIELD IT!
DARKSEID IS!

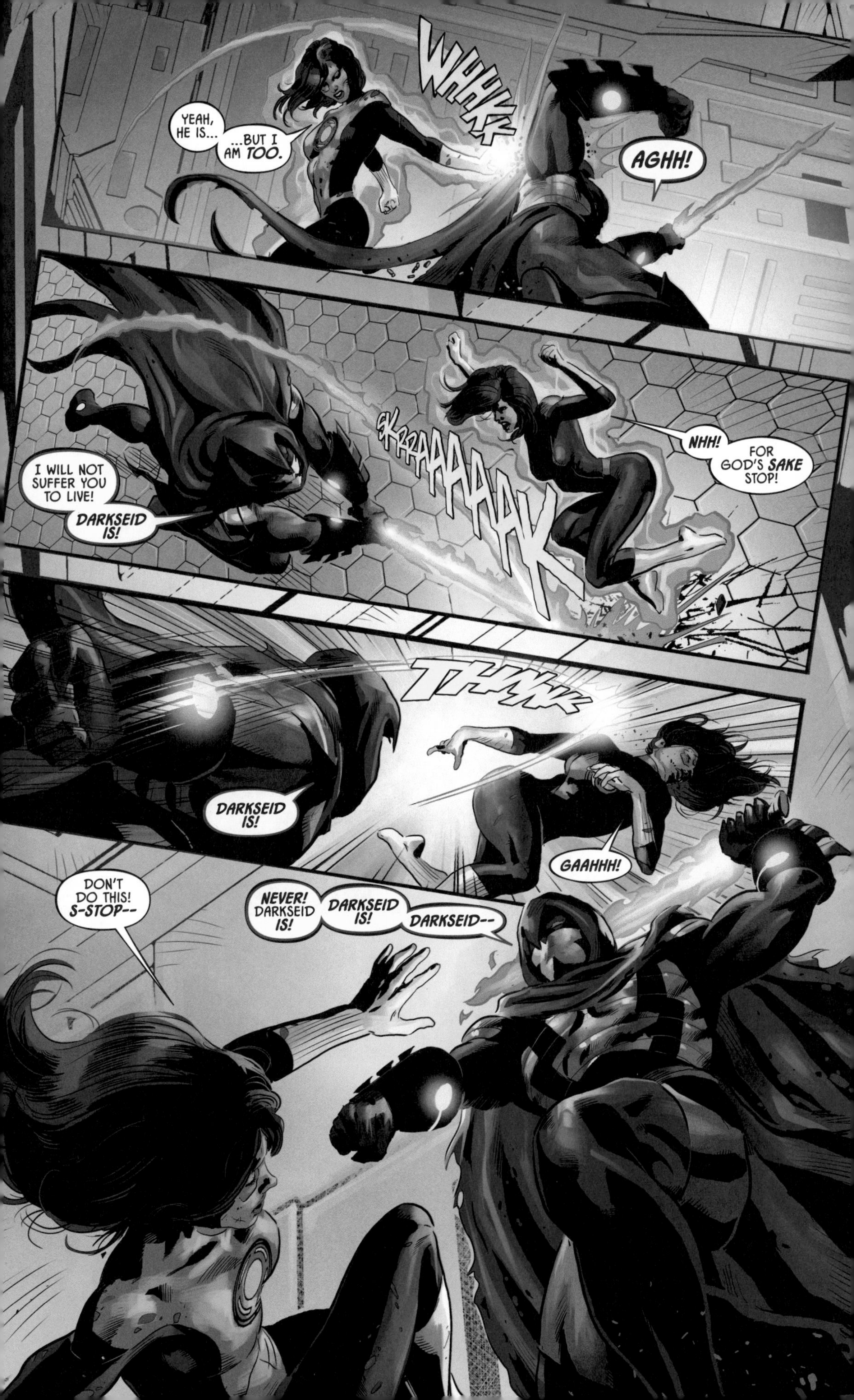
YEAH, HE IS...
...BUT I AM TOO.
WHHKK
AGHH!
I WILL NOT SUFFER YOU TO LIVE!
DARKSEID IS!
SKRRAAAAAAK
NHH!
FOR GOD'S SAKE STOP!
THUNK
DARKSEID IS!
GAAHHH!
DON'T DO THIS! S-STOP--
NEVER! DARKSEID IS!
DARKSEID IS!
DARKSEID--

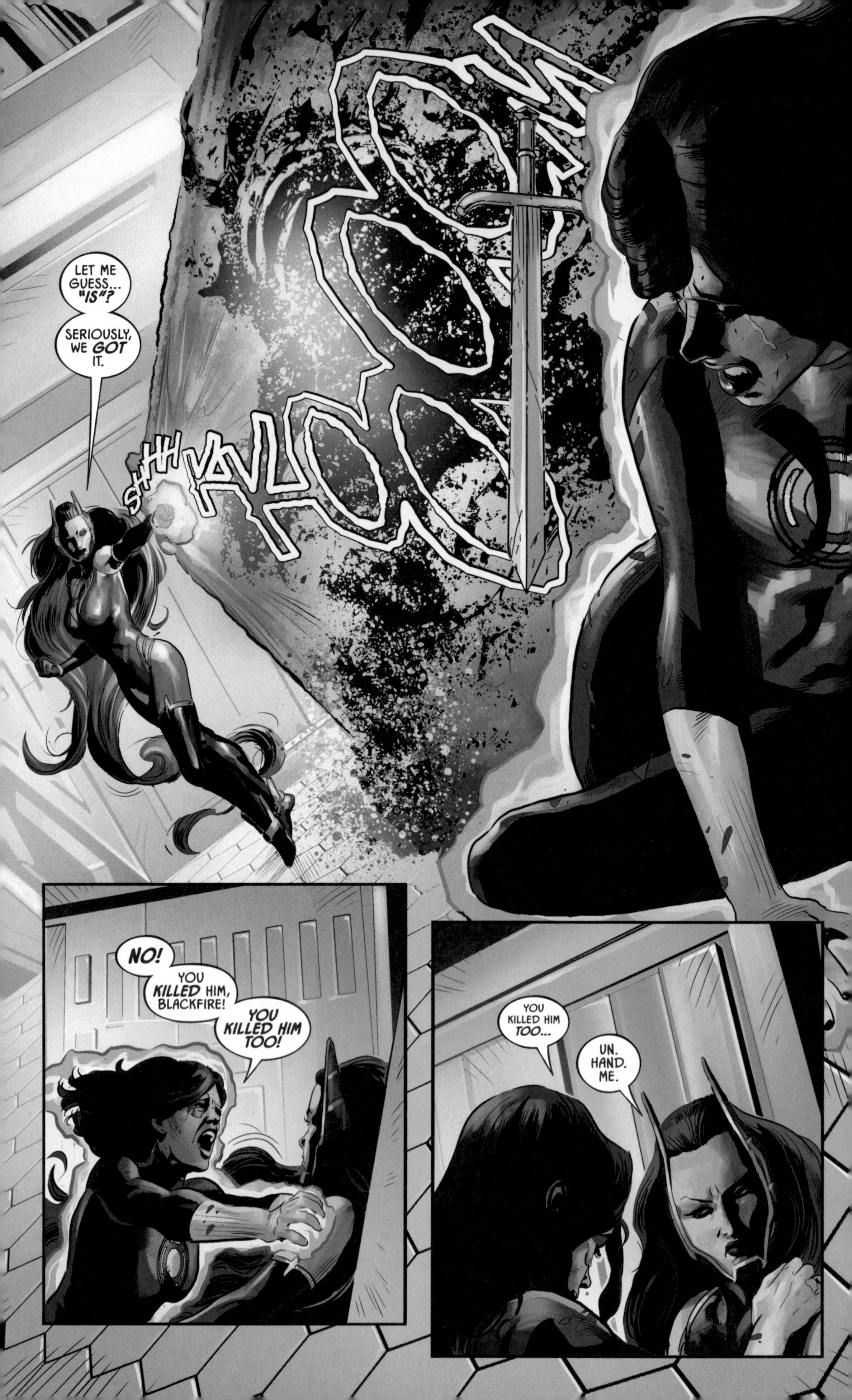
LET ME GUESS... "IS"?
SERIOUSLY, WE GOT IT.
SHHVAVLOOM
NO!
YOU KILLED HIM, BLACKFIRE!
YOU KILLED HIM TOO!
YOU KILLED HIM TOO...
UN. HAND. ME.

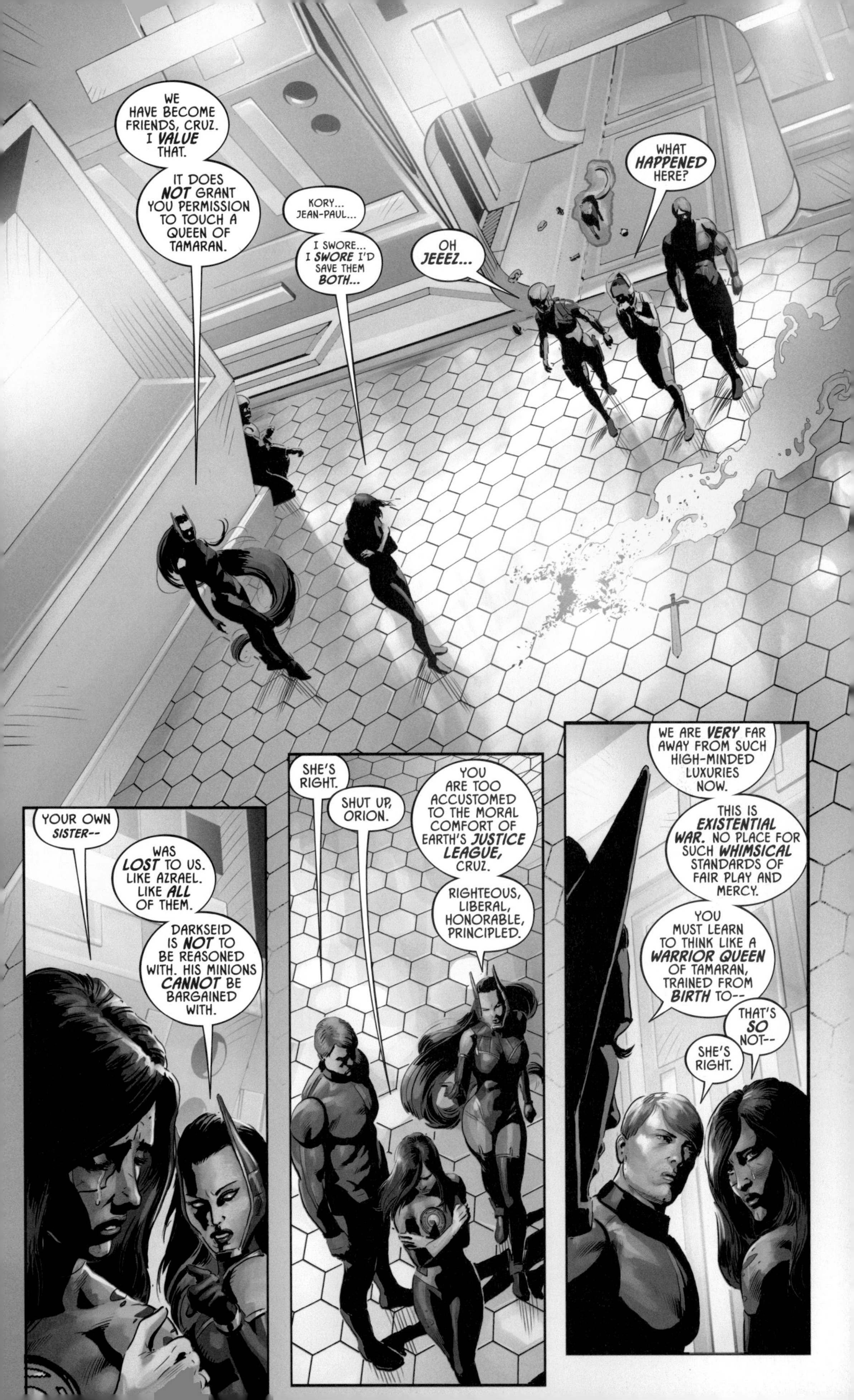
WE HAVE BECOME FRIENDS, CRUZ. I VALUE THAT.
IT DOES NOT GRANT YOU PERMISSION TO TOUCH A QUEEN OF TAMARAN.
KORY... JEAN-PAUL...
I SWORE... I SWORE I'D SAVE THEM BOTH...
OH JEEEZ...
WHAT HAPPENED HERE?
YOUR OWN SISTER--
WAS LOST TO US. LIKE AZRAEL. LIKE ALL OF THEM.
DARKSEID IS NOT TO BE REASONED WITH. HIS MINIONS CANNOT BE BARGAINED WITH.
SHE'S RIGHT.
SHUT UP, ORION.
YOU ARE TOO ACCUSTOMED TO THE MORAL COMFORT OF EARTH'S JUSTICE LEAGUE, CRUZ.
RIGHTEOUS, LIBERAL, HONORABLE, PRINCIPLED.
WE ARE VERY FAR AWAY FROM SUCH HIGH-MINDED LUXURIES NOW.
THIS IS EXISTENTIAL WAR. NO PLACE FOR SUCH WHIMSICAL STANDARDS OF FAIR PLAY AND MERCY.
YOU MUST LEARN TO THINK LIKE A WARRIOR QUEEN OF TAMARAN, TRAINED FROM BIRTH TO--
THAT'S SO NOT--
SHE'S RIGHT.

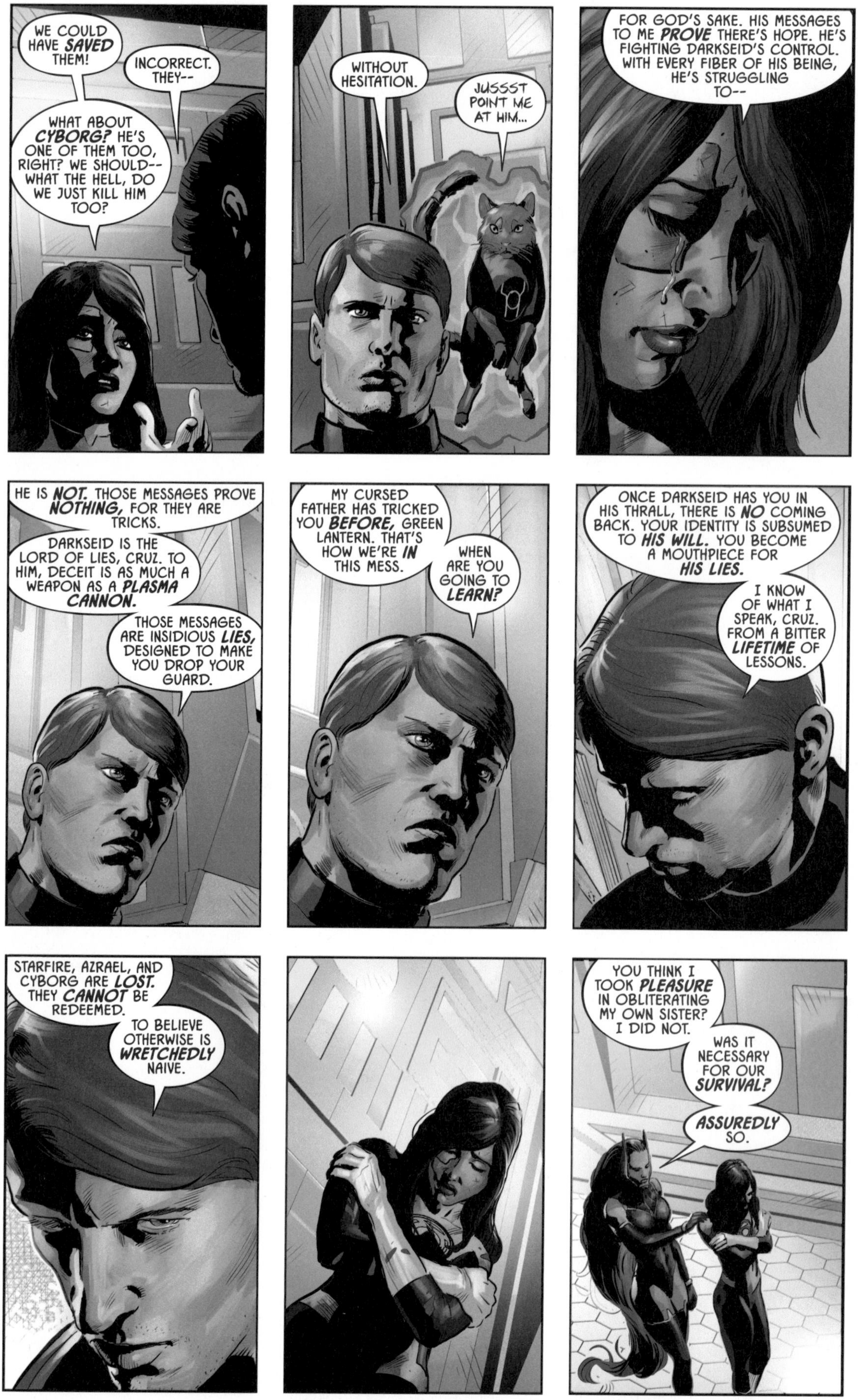
WE COULD HAVE SAVED THEM!
INCORRECT. THEY--
WHAT ABOUT CYBORG? HE'S ONE OF THEM TOO, RIGHT? WE SHOULD-- WHAT THE HELL, DO WE JUST KILL HIM TOO?
WITHOUT HESITATION.
JUSSST POINT ME AT HIM...
FOR GOD'S SAKE. HIS MESSAGES TO ME PROVE THERE'S HOPE. HE'S FIGHTING DARKSEID'S CONTROL. WITH EVERY FIBER OF HIS BEING, HE'S STRUGGLING TO--
HE IS NOT. THOSE MESSAGES PROVE NOTHING, FOR THEY ARE TRICKS.
DARKSEID IS THE LORD OF LIES, CRUZ. TO HIM, DECEIT IS AS MUCH A WEAPON AS A PLASMA CANNON.
THOSE MESSAGES ARE INSIDIOUS LIES, DESIGNED TO MAKE YOU DROP YOUR GUARD.
MY CURSED FATHER HAS TRICKED YOU BEFORE, GREEN LANTERN. THAT'S HOW WE'RE IN THIS MESS.
WHEN ARE YOU GOING TO LEARN?
ONCE DARKSEID HAS YOU IN HIS THRALL, THERE IS NO COMING BACK. YOUR IDENTITY IS SUBSUMED TO HIS WILL. YOU BECOME A MOUTHPIECE FOR HIS LIES.
I KNOW OF WHAT I SPEAK, CRUZ. FROM A BITTER LIFETIME OF LESSONS.
STARFIRE, AZRAEL, AND CYBORG ARE LOST. THEY CANNOT BE REDEEMED.
TO BELIEVE OTHERWISE IS WRETCHEDLY NAIVE.
YOU THINK I TOOK PLEASURE IN OBLITERATING MY OWN SISTER? I DID NOT.
WAS IT NECESSARY FOR OUR SURVIVAL?
ASSUREDLY SO.

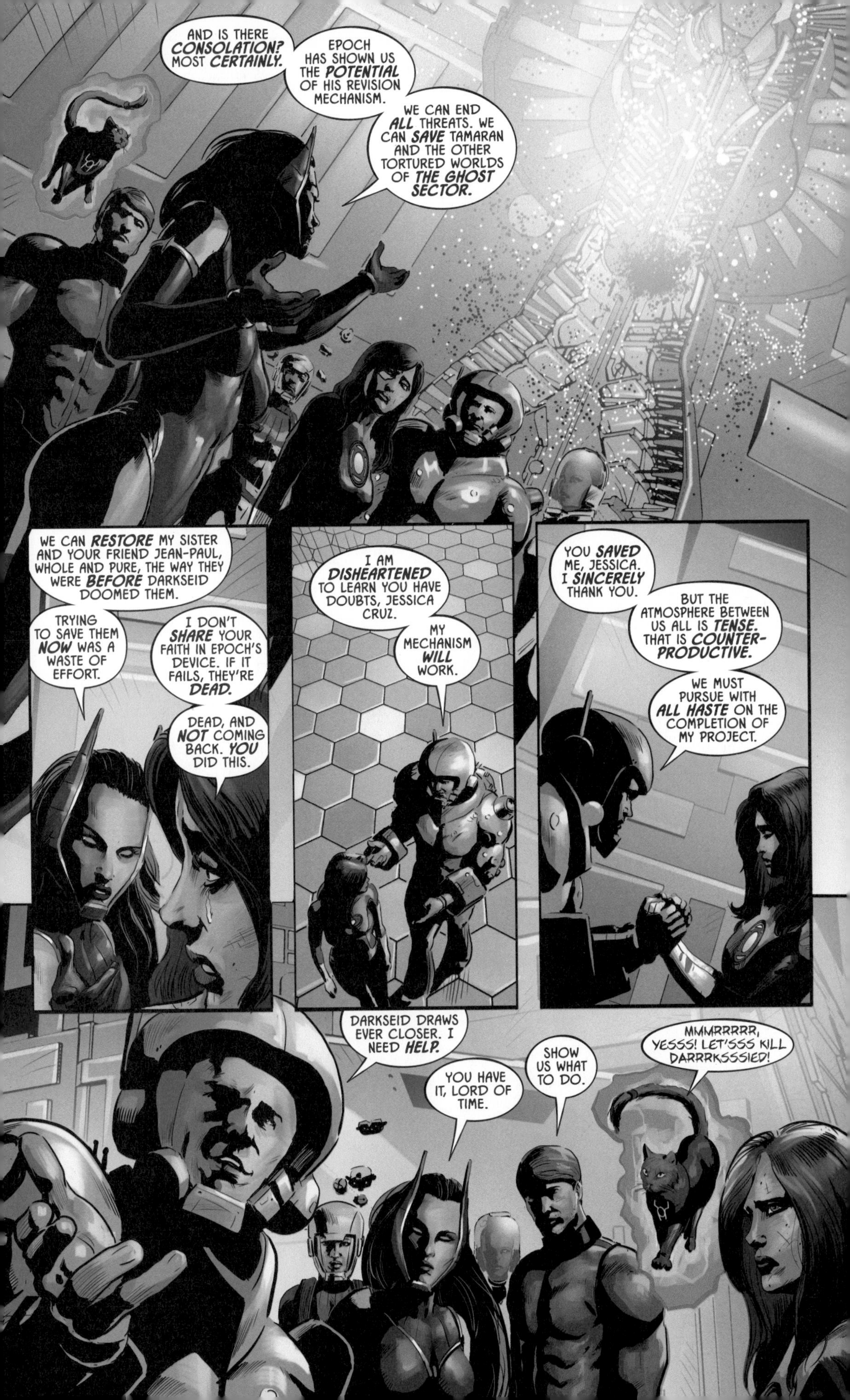
AND IS THERE CONSOLATION? MOST CERTAINLY.
EPOCH HAS SHOWN US THE POTENTIAL OF HIS REVISION MECHANISM.
WE CAN END ALL THREATS. WE CAN SAVE TAMARAN AND THE OTHER TORTURED WORLDS OF THE GHOST SECTOR.
WE CAN RESTORE MY SISTER AND YOUR FRIEND JEAN-PAUL, WHOLE AND PURE, THE WAY THEY WERE BEFORE DARKSEID DOOMED THEM.
TRYING TO SAVE THEM NOW WAS A WASTE OF EFFORT.
I DON'T SHARE YOUR FAITH IN EPOCH'S DEVICE. IF IT FAILS, THEY'RE DEAD.
DEAD, AND NOT COMING BACK. YOU DID THIS.
I AM DISHEARTENED TO LEARN YOU HAVE DOUBTS, JESSICA CRUZ.
MY MECHANISM WILL WORK.
YOU SAVED ME, JESSICA. I SINCERELY THANK YOU.
BUT THE ATMOSPHERE BETWEEN US ALL IS TENSE. THAT IS COUNTER-PRODUCTIVE.
WE MUST PURSUE WITH ALL HASTE ON THE COMPLETION OF MY PROJECT.
DARKSEID DRAWS EVER CLOSER. I NEED HELP.
YOU HAVE IT, LORD OF TIME.
SHOW US WHAT TO DO.
MMMRRRRR, YESSS! LET'SSS KILL DARRRKSSSIED!

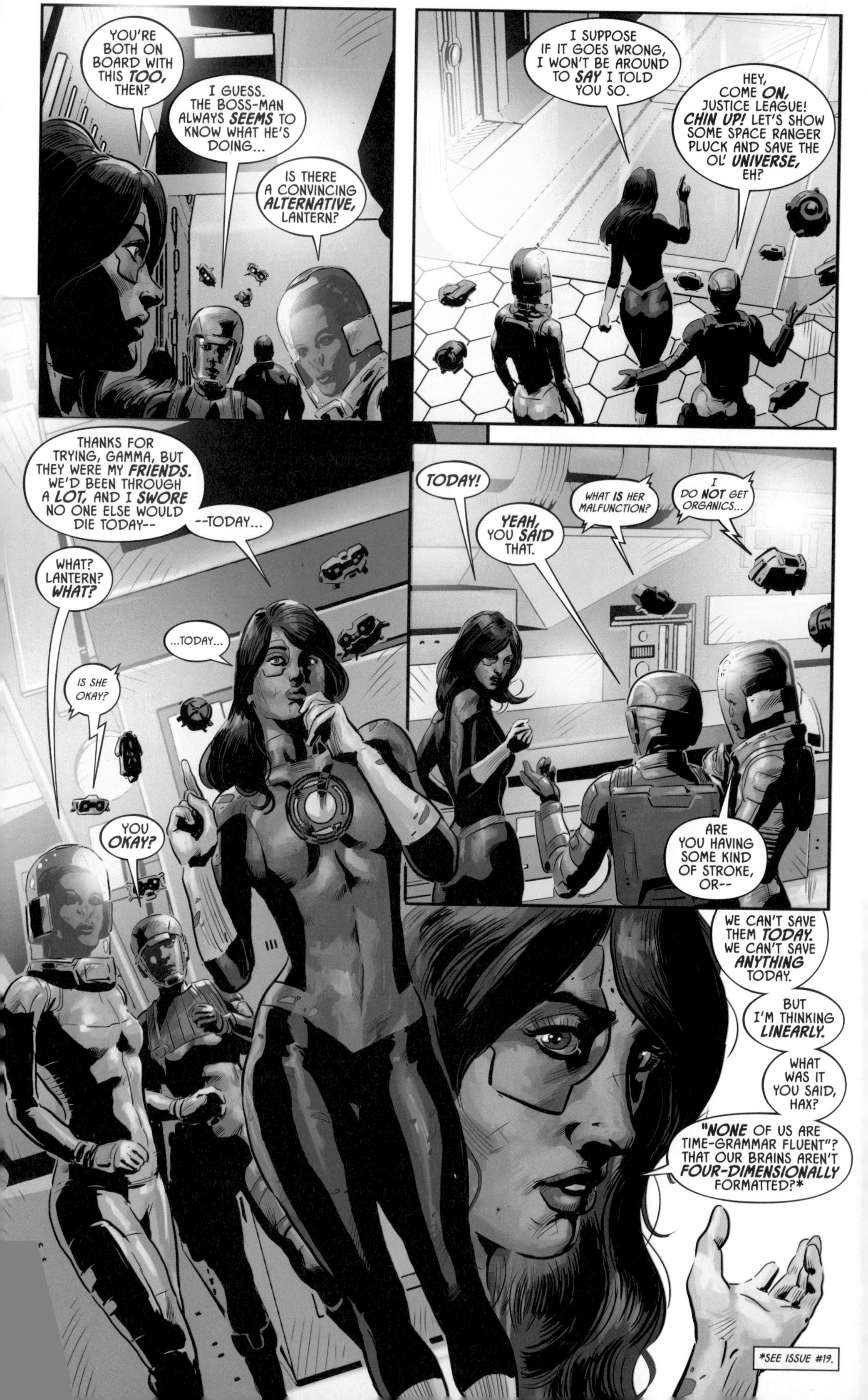
YOU'RE BOTH ON BOARD WITH THIS TOO, THEN?
I GUESS. THE BOSS-MAN ALWAYS SEEMS TO KNOW WHAT HE'S DOING...
IS THERE A CONVINCING ALTERNATIVE, LANTERN?
I SUPPOSE IF IT GOES WRONG, I WON'T BE AROUND TO SAY I TOLD YOU SO.
HEY, COME ON, JUSTICE LEAGUE! CHIN UP! LET'S SHOW SOME SPACE RANGER PLUCK AND SAVE THE OL' UNIVERSE, EH?
THANKS FOR TRYING, GAMMA, BUT THEY WERE MY FRIENDS. WE'D BEEN THROUGH A LOT, AND I SWORE NO ONE ELSE WOULD DIE TODAY--
--TODAY...
WHAT? LANTERN? WHAT?
...TODAY...
IS SHE OKAY?
YOU OKAY?
TODAY!
YEAH, YOU SAID THAT.
WHAT IS HER MALFUNCTION?
I DO NOT GET ORGANICS...
ARE YOU HAVING SOME KIND OF STROKE, OR--
WE CAN'T SAVE THEM TODAY. WE CAN'T SAVE ANYTHING TODAY.
BUT I'M THINKING LINEARLY.
WHAT WAS IT YOU SAID, HAX?
"NONE OF US ARE TIME-GRAMMAR FLUENT"? THAT OUR BRAINS AREN'T FOUR-DIMENSIONALLY FORMATTED?*
*SEE ISSUE #19.

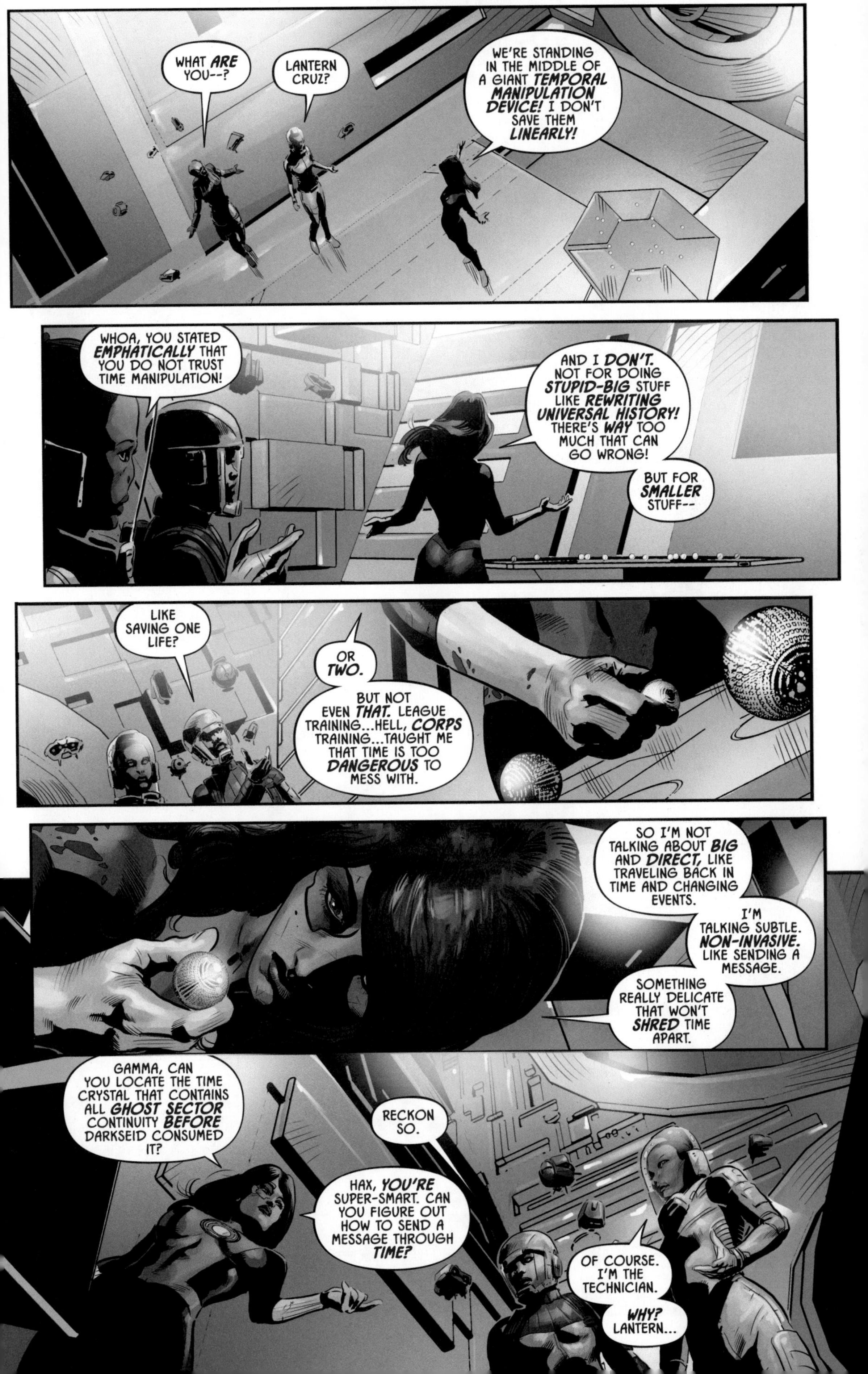
WHAT ARE YOU--?
LANTERN CRUZ?
WE'RE STANDING IN THE MIDDLE OF A GIANT TEMPORAL MANIPULATION DEVICE! I DON'T SAVE THEM LINEARLY!
WHOA, YOU STATED EMPHATICALLY THAT YOU DO NOT TRUST TIME MANIPULATION!
AND I DON'T. NOT FOR DOING STUPID-BIG STUFF LIKE REWRITING UNIVERSAL HISTORY! THERE'S WAY TOO MUCH THAT CAN GO WRONG!
BUT FOR SMALLER STUFF--
LIKE SAVING ONE LIFE?
OR TWO.
BUT NOT EVEN THAT. LEAGUE TRAINING...HELL, CORPS TRAINING...TAUGHT ME THAT TIME IS TOO DANGEROUS TO MESS WITH.
SO I'M NOT TALKING ABOUT BIG AND DIRECT, LIKE TRAVELING BACK IN TIME AND CHANGING EVENTS.
I'M TALKING SUBTLE. NON-INVASIVE. LIKE SENDING A MESSAGE.
SOMETHING REALLY DELICATE THAT WON'T SHRED TIME APART.
GAMMA, CAN YOU LOCATE THE TIME CRYSTAL THAT CONTAINS ALL GHOST SECTOR CONTINUITY BEFORE DARKSEID CONSUMED IT?
RECKON SO.
HAX, YOU'RE SUPER-SMART. CAN YOU FIGURE OUT HOW TO SEND A MESSAGE THROUGH TIME?
OF COURSE. I'M THE TECHNICIAN.
WHY? LANTERN...

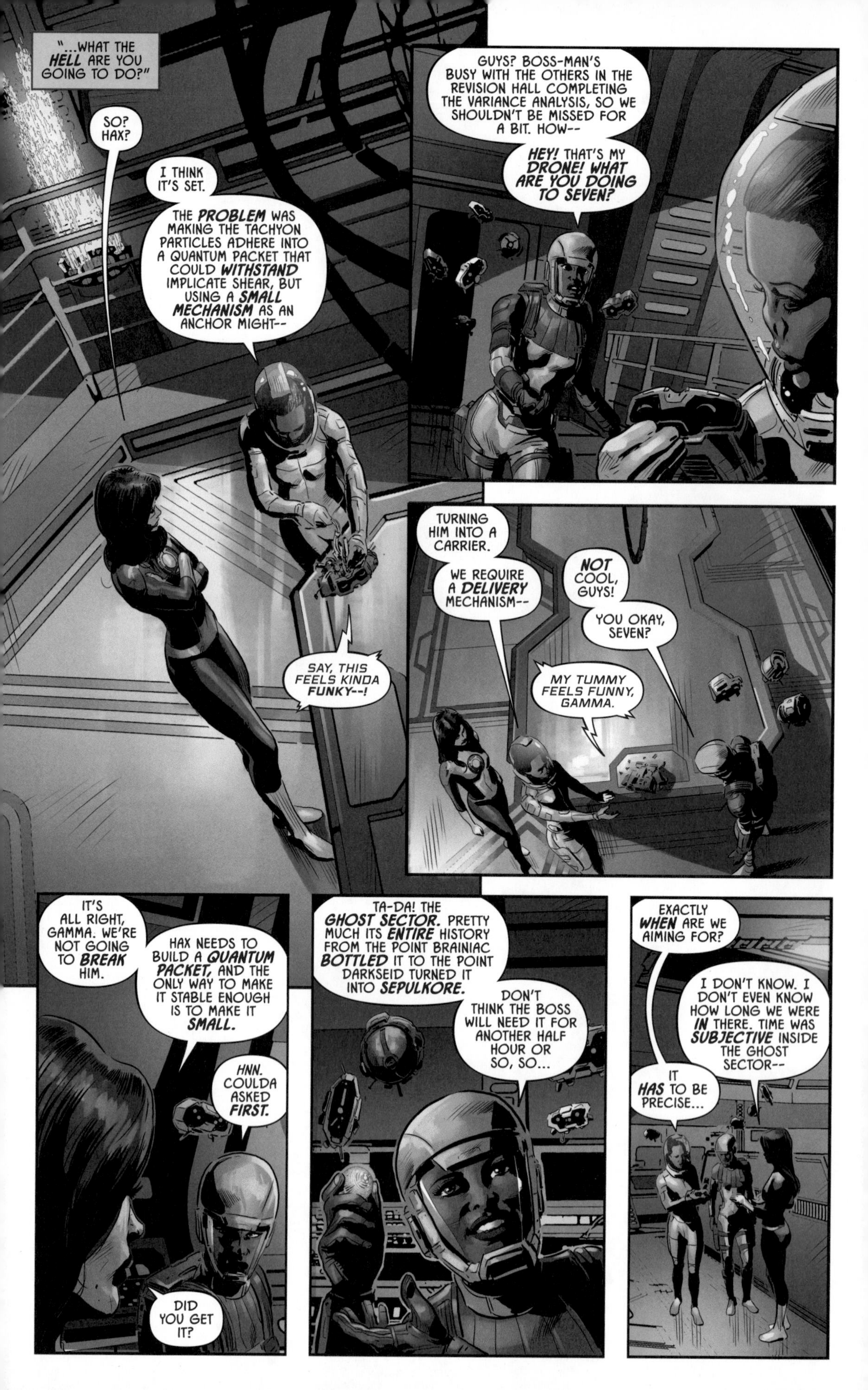
"...WHAT THE HELL ARE YOU GOING TO DO?"
SO? HAX?
I THINK IT'S SET.
THE PROBLEM WAS MAKING THE TACHYON PARTICLES ADHERE INTO A QUANTUM PACKET THAT COULD WITHSTAND IMPLICATE SHEAR, BUT USING A SMALL MECHANISM AS AN ANCHOR MIGHT--
SAY, THIS FEELS KINDA FUNKY--!
GUYS? BOSS-MAN'S BUSY WITH THE OTHERS IN THE REVISION HALL COMPLETING THE VARIANCE ANALYSIS, SO WE SHOULDN'T BE MISSED FOR A BIT. HOW--
HEY! THAT'S MY DRONE! WHAT ARE YOU DOING TO SEVEN?
TURNING HIM INTO A CARRIER.
WE REQUIRE A DELIVERY MECHANISM--
NOT COOL, GUYS!
YOU OKAY, SEVEN?
MY TUMMY FEELS FUNNY, GAMMA.
IT'S ALL RIGHT, GAMMA. WE'RE NOT GOING TO BREAK HIM.
HAX NEEDS TO BUILD A QUANTUM PACKET, AND THE ONLY WAY TO MAKE IT STABLE ENOUGH IS TO MAKE IT SMALL.
HNN. COULDA ASKED FIRST.
DID YOU GET IT?
TA-DA! THE GHOST SECTOR. PRETTY MUCH ITS ENTIRE HISTORY FROM THE POINT BRAINIAC BOTTLED IT TO THE POINT DARKSEID TURNED IT INTO SEPULKORE.
DON'T THINK THE BOSS WILL NEED IT FOR ANOTHER HALF HOUR OR SO, SO...
EXACTLY WHEN ARE WE AIMING FOR?
I DON'T KNOW. I DON'T EVEN KNOW HOW LONG WE WERE IN THERE. TIME WAS SUBJECTIVE INSIDE THE GHOST SECTOR--
IT HAS TO BE PRECISE...

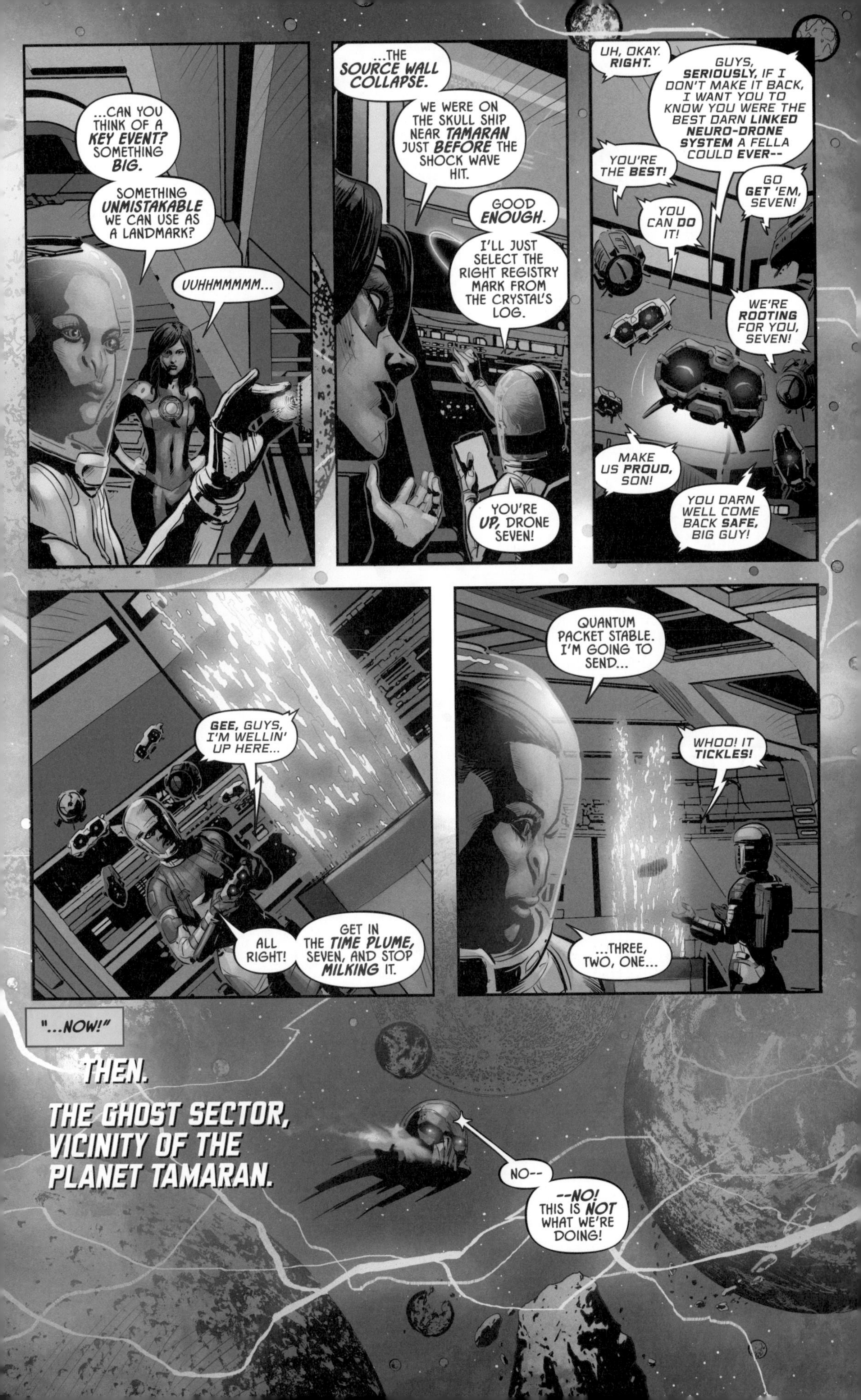
...CAN YOU THINK OF A KEY EVENT? SOMETHING BIG.
SOMETHING UNMISTAKABLE WE CAN USE AS A LANDMARK?
UUHHMMMMM...
...THE SOURCE WALL COLLAPSE.
WE WERE ON THE SKULL SHIP NEAR TAMARAN JUST BEFORE THE SHOCK WAVE HIT.
GOOD ENOUGH.
I'LL JUST SELECT THE RIGHT REGISTRY MARK FROM THE CRYSTAL'S LOG.
YOU'RE UP, DRONE SEVEN!
UH, OKAY. RIGHT.
GUYS, SERIOUSLY, IF I DON'T MAKE IT BACK, I WANT YOU TO KNOW YOU WERE THE BEST DARN LINKED NEURO-DRONE SYSTEM A FELLA COULD EVER--
YOU'RE THE BEST!
YOU CAN DO IT!
GO GET 'EM, SEVEN!
WE'RE ROOTING FOR YOU, SEVEN!
MAKE US PROUD, SON!
YOU DARN WELL COME BACK SAFE, BIG GUY!
GEE, GUYS, I'M WELLIN' UP HERE...
ALL RIGHT!
GET IN THE TIME PLUME, SEVEN, AND STOP MILKING IT.
QUANTUM PACKET STABLE. I'M GOING TO SEND...
WHOO! IT TICKLES!
...THREE, TWO, ONE...
"...NOW!"
THEN.
THE GHOST SECTOR, VICINITY OF THE PLANET TAMARAN.
NO--
--NO! THIS IS NOT WHAT WE'RE DOING!

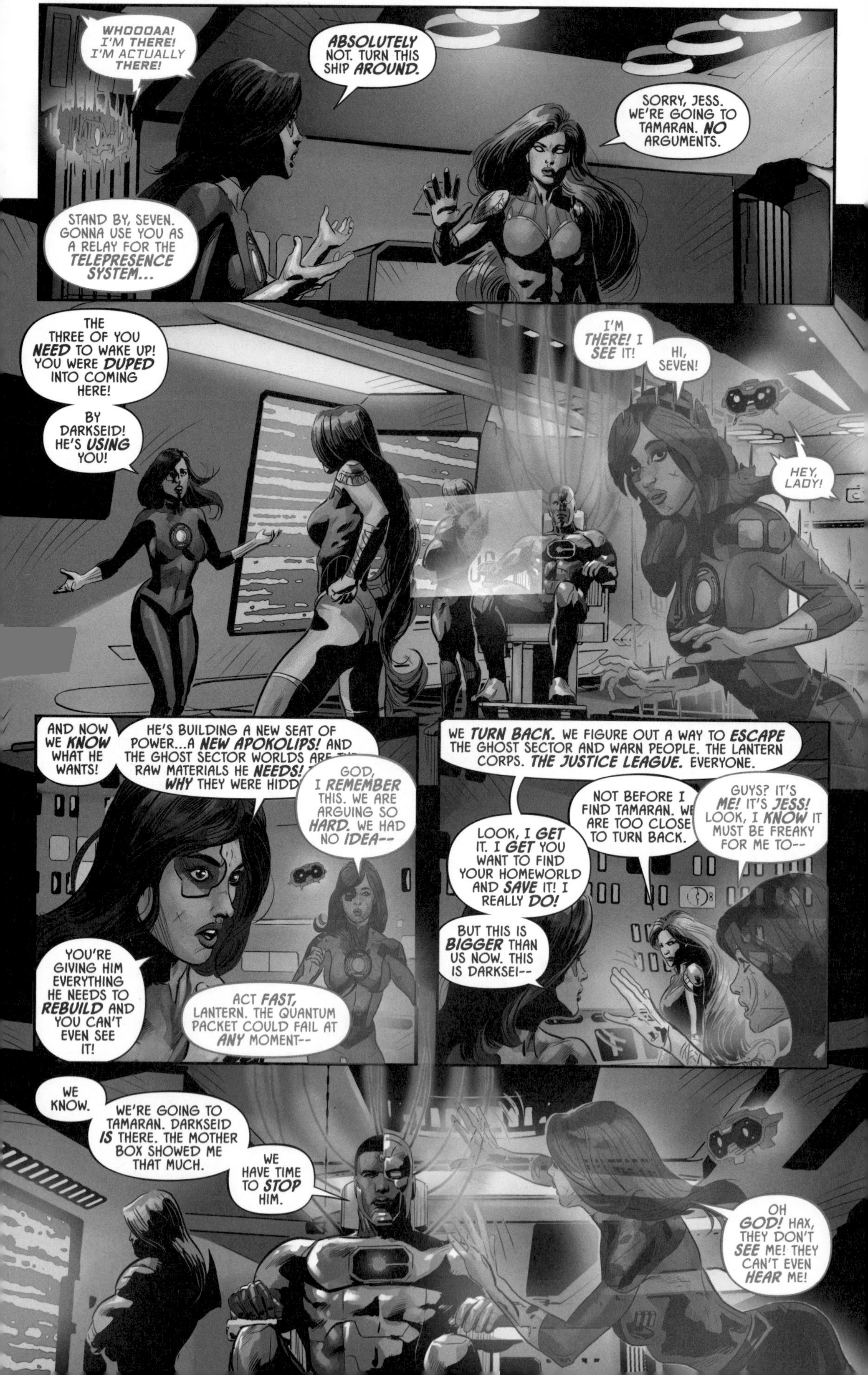
WHOOOAA! I'M THERE! I'M ACTUALLY THERE!
ABSOLUTELY NOT. TURN THIS SHIP AROUND.
SORRY, JESS. WE'RE GOING TO TAMARAN. NO ARGUMENTS.
STAND BY, SEVEN. GONNA USE YOU AS A RELAY FOR THE TELEPRESENCE SYSTEM...
THE THREE OF YOU NEED TO WAKE UP! YOU WERE DUPED INTO COMING HERE!
BY DARKSEID! HE'S USING YOU!
I'M THERE! I SEE IT!
HI, SEVEN!
HEY, LADY!
AND NOW WE KNOW WHAT HE WANTS!
HE'S BUILDING A NEW SEAT OF POWER...A NEW APOKOLIPS! AND THE GHOST SECTOR WORLDS ARE RAW MATERIALS HE NEEDS! WHY THEY WERE HIDD
GOD, I REMEMBER THIS. WE ARE ARGUING SO HARD. WE HAD NO IDEA--
YOU'RE GIVING HIM EVERYTHING HE NEEDS TO REBUILD AND YOU CAN'T EVEN SEE IT!
ACT FAST, LANTERN. THE QUANTUM PACKET COULD FAIL AT ANY MOMENT--
WE TURN BACK. WE FIGURE OUT A WAY TO ESCAPE THE GHOST SECTOR AND WARN PEOPLE. THE LANTERN CORPS. THE JUSTICE LEAGUE. EVERYONE.
LOOK, I GET IT. I GET YOU WANT TO FIND YOUR HOMEWORLD AND SAVE IT! I REALLY DO!
BUT THIS IS BIGGER THAN US NOW. THIS IS DARKSEI--
NOT BEFORE I FIND TAMARAN. WE ARE TOO CLOSE TO TURN BACK.
GUYS? IT'S ME! IT'S JESS! LOOK, I KNOW IT MUST BE FREAKY FOR ME TO--
WE KNOW.
WE'RE GOING TO TAMARAN. DARKSEID IS THERE. THE MOTHER BOX SHOWED ME THAT MUCH.
WE HAVE TIME TO STOP HIM.
OH GOD! HAX, THEY DON'T SEE ME! THEY CAN'T EVEN HEAR ME!

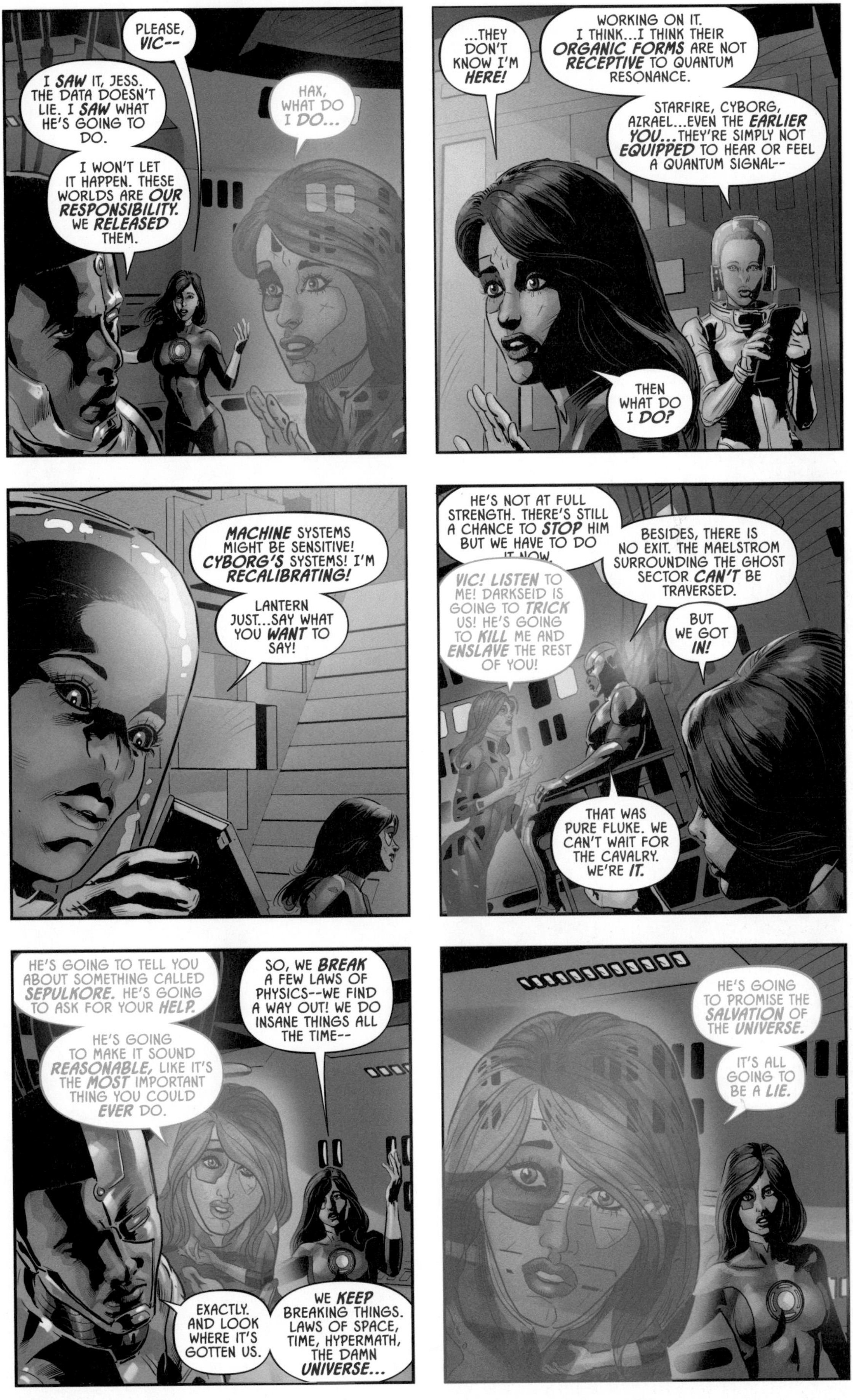
PLEASE, VIC--
I SAW IT, JESS. THE DATA DOESN'T LIE. I SAW WHAT HE'S GOING TO DO.
I WON'T LET IT HAPPEN. THESE WORLDS ARE OUR RESPONSIBILITY. WE RELEASED THEM.
HAX, WHAT DO I DO...
...THEY DON'T KNOW I'M HERE!
WORKING ON IT. I THINK...I THINK THEIR ORGANIC FORMS ARE NOT RECEPTIVE TO QUANTUM RESONANCE.
STARFIRE, CYBORG, AZRAEL...EVEN THE EARLIER YOU...THEY'RE SIMPLY NOT EQUIPPED TO HEAR OR FEEL A QUANTUM SIGNAL--
THEN WHAT DO I DO?
MACHINE SYSTEMS MIGHT BE SENSITIVE! CYBORG'S SYSTEMS! I'M RECALIBRATING!
LANTERN JUST...SAY WHAT YOU WANT TO SAY!
HE'S NOT AT FULL STRENGTH. THERE'S STILL A CHANCE TO STOP HIM BUT WE HAVE TO DO IT NOW.
VIC! LISTEN TO ME! DARKSEID IS GOING TO TRICK US! HE'S GOING TO KILL ME AND ENSLAVE THE REST OF YOU!
BESIDES, THERE IS NO EXIT. THE MAELSTROM SURROUNDING THE GHOST SECTOR CAN'T BE TRAVERSED.
BUT WE GOT IN!
THAT WAS PURE FLUKE. WE CAN'T WAIT FOR THE CAVALRY. WE'RE IT.
HE'S GOING TO TELL YOU ABOUT SOMETHING CALLED SEPULKORE. HE'S GOING TO ASK FOR YOUR HELP.
HE'S GOING TO MAKE IT SOUND REASONABLE, LIKE IT'S THE MOST IMPORTANT THING YOU COULD EVER DO.
SO, WE BREAK A FEW LAWS OF PHYSICS--WE FIND A WAY OUT! WE DO INSANE THINGS ALL THE TIME--
EXACTLY. AND LOOK WHERE IT'S GOTTEN US.
WE KEEP BREAKING THINGS. LAWS OF SPACE, TIME, HYPERMATH, THE DAMN UNIVERSE...
HE'S GOING TO PROMISE THE SALVATION OF THE UNIVERSE.
IT'S ALL GOING TO BE A LIE.

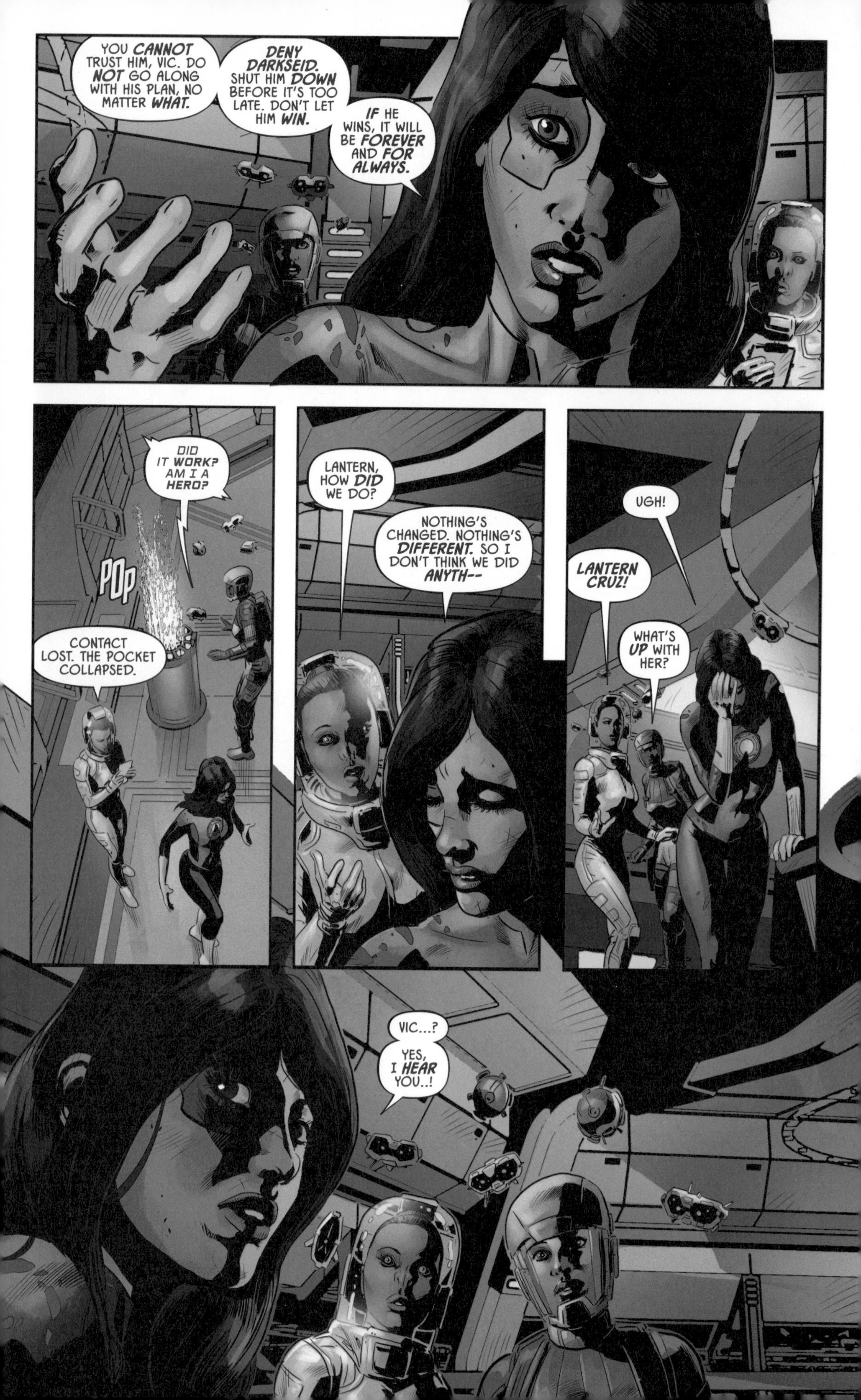
YOU CANNOT TRUST HIM, VIC. DO NOT GO ALONG WITH HIS PLAN, NO MATTER WHAT.
DENY DARKSEID. SHUT HIM DOWN BEFORE IT'S TOO LATE. DON'T LET HIM WIN.
IF HE WINS, IT WILL BE FOREVER AND FOR ALWAYS.
DID IT WORK? AM I A HERO?
POP
CONTACT LOST. THE POCKET COLLAPSED.
LANTERN, HOW DID WE DO?
NOTHING'S CHANGED. NOTHING'S DIFFERENT. SO I DON'T THINK WE DID ANYTH--
UGH!
LANTERN CRUZ!
WHAT'S UP WITH HER?
VIC...?
YES, I HEAR YOU..!

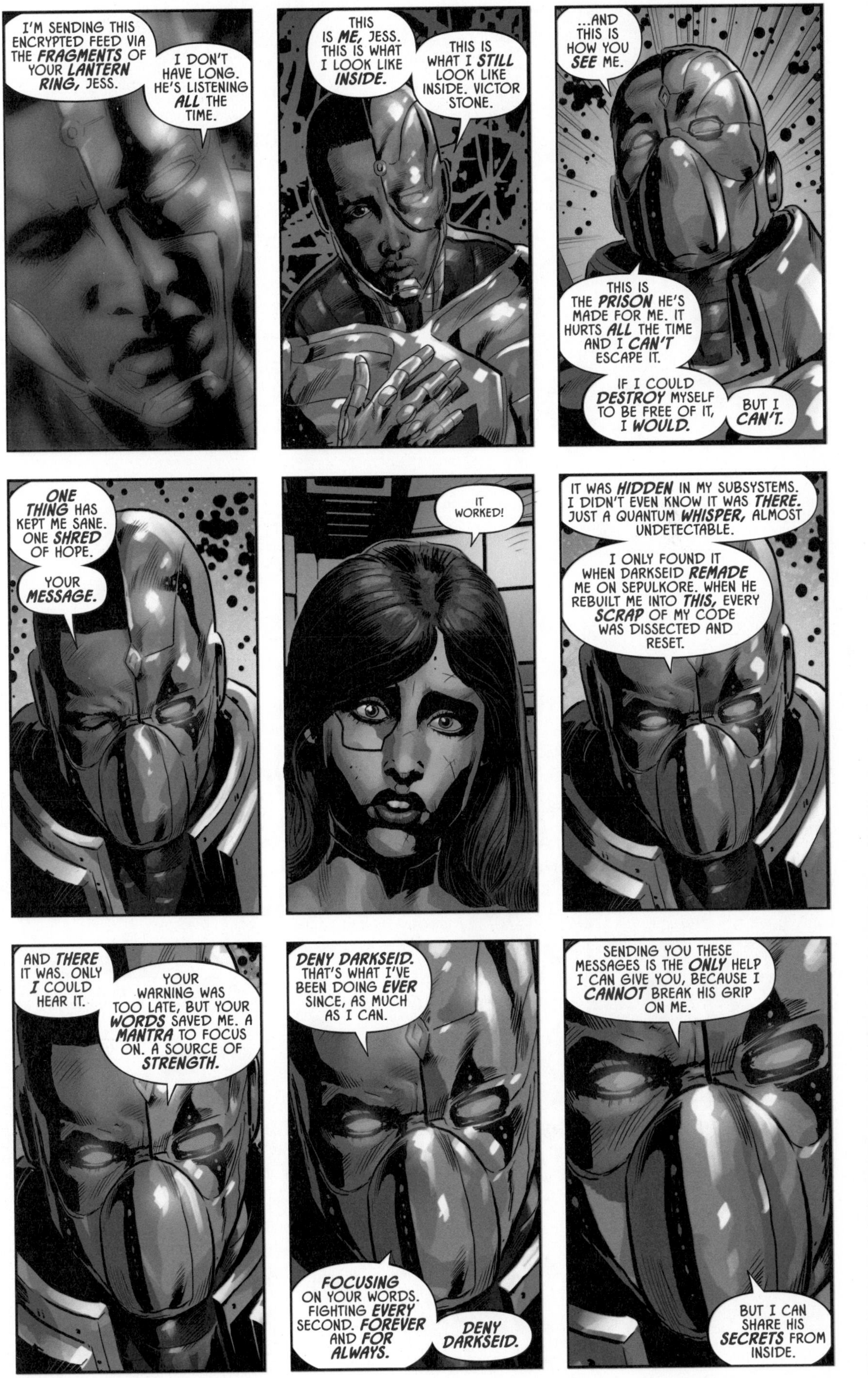
I'M SENDING THIS ENCRYPTED FEED VIA THE FRAGMENTS OF YOUR LANTERN RING, JESS.
I DON'T HAVE LONG. HE'S LISTENING ALL THE TIME.
THIS IS ME, JESS. THIS IS WHAT I LOOK LIKE INSIDE.
THIS IS WHAT I STILL LOOK LIKE INSIDE. VICTOR STONE.
...AND THIS IS HOW YOU SEE ME.
THIS IS THE PRISON HE'S MADE FOR ME. IT HURTS ALL THE TIME AND I CAN'T ESCAPE IT.
IF I COULD DESTROY MYSELF TO BE FREE OF IT, I WOULD.
BUT I CAN'T.
ONE THING HAS KEPT ME SANE. ONE SHRED OF HOPE.
YOUR MESSAGE.
IT WORKED!
IT WAS HIDDEN IN MY SUBSYSTEMS. I DIDN'T EVEN KNOW IT WAS THERE. JUST A QUANTUM WHISPER, ALMOST UNDETECTABLE.
I ONLY FOUND IT WHEN DARKSEID REMADE ME ON SEPULKORE. WHEN HE REBUILT ME INTO THIS, EVERY SCRAP OF MY CODE WAS DISSECTED AND RESET.
AND THERE IT WAS. ONLY I COULD HEAR IT.
YOUR WARNING WAS TOO LATE, BUT YOUR WORDS SAVED ME. A MANTRA TO FOCUS ON. A SOURCE OF STRENGTH.
DENY DARKSEID. THAT'S WHAT I'VE BEEN DOING EVER SINCE, AS MUCH AS I CAN.
FOCUSING ON YOUR WORDS. FIGHTING EVERY SECOND. FOREVER AND FOR ALWAYS.
DENY DARKSEID.
SENDING YOU THESE MESSAGES IS THE ONLY HELP I CAN GIVE YOU, BECAUSE I CANNOT BREAK HIS GRIP ON ME.
BUT I CAN SHARE HIS SECRETS FROM INSIDE.

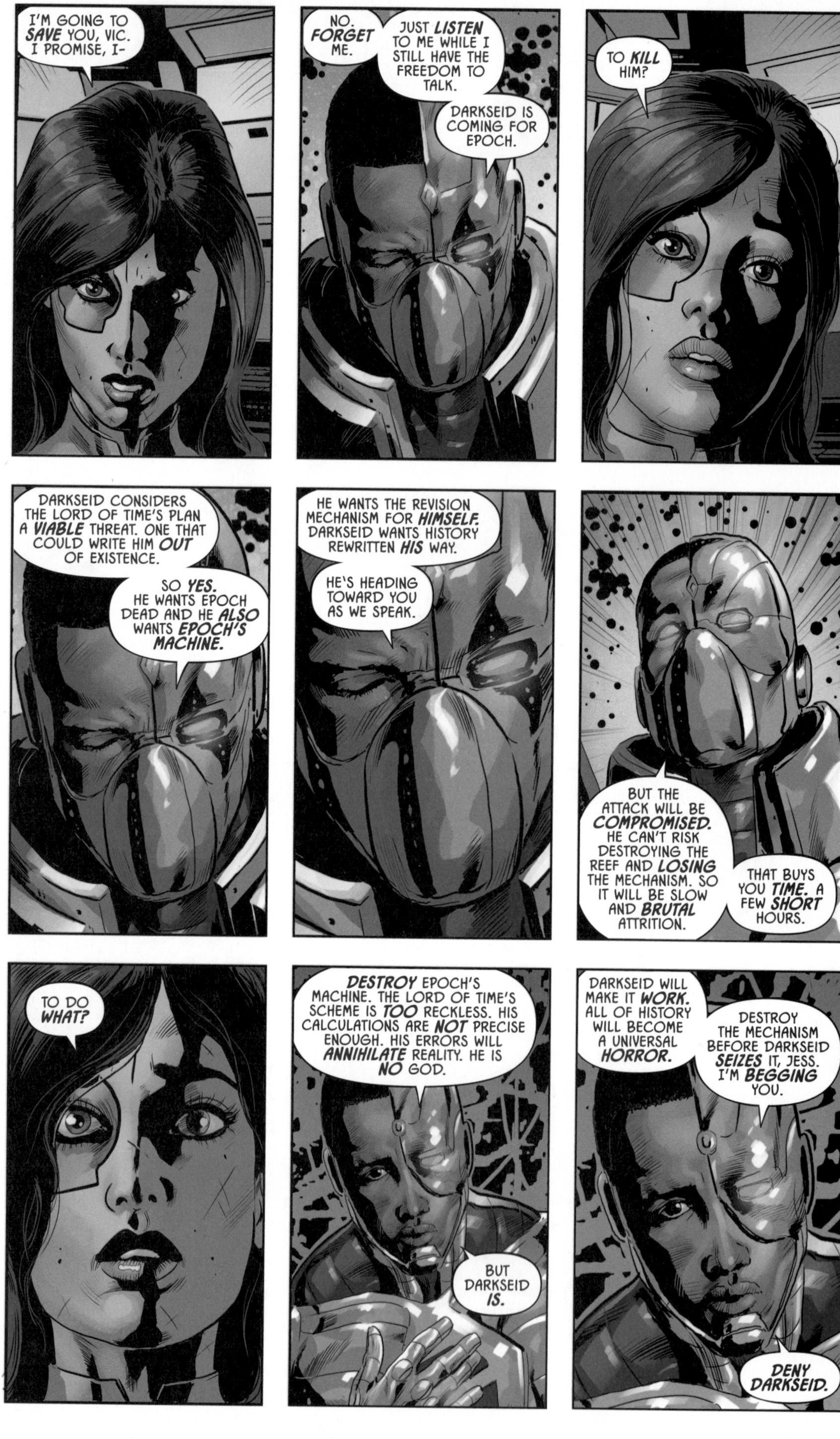
I'M GOING TO SAVE YOU, VIC. I PROMISE, I-
NO. FORGET ME.
JUST LISTEN TO ME WHILE I STILL HAVE THE FREEDOM TO TALK.
DARKSEID IS COMING FOR EPOCH.
TO KILL HIM?
DARKSEID CONSIDERS THE LORD OF TIME'S PLAN A VIABLE THREAT. ONE THAT COULD WRITE HIM OUT OF EXISTENCE.
SO YES. HE WANTS EPOCH DEAD AND HE ALSO WANTS EPOCH'S MACHINE.
HE WANTS THE REVISION MECHANISM FOR HIMSELF. DARKSEID WANTS HISTORY REWRITTEN HIS WAY.
HE'S HEADING TOWARD YOU AS WE SPEAK.
BUT THE ATTACK WILL BE COMPROMISED. HE CAN'T RISK DESTROYING THE REEF AND LOSING THE MECHANISM. SO IT WILL BE SLOW AND BRUTAL ATTRITION.
THAT BUYS YOU TIME. A FEW SHORT HOURS.
TO DO WHAT?
DESTROY EPOCH'S MACHINE. THE LORD OF TIME'S SCHEME IS TOO RECKLESS. HIS CALCULATIONS ARE NOT PRECISE ENOUGH. HIS ERRORS WILL ANNIHILATE REALITY. HE IS NO GOD.
BUT DARKSEID IS.
DARKSEID WILL MAKE IT WORK. ALL OF HISTORY WILL BECOME A UNIVERSAL HORROR.
DESTROY THE MECHANISM BEFORE DARKSEID SEIZES IT, JESS. I'M BEGGING YOU.
DENY DARKSEID.

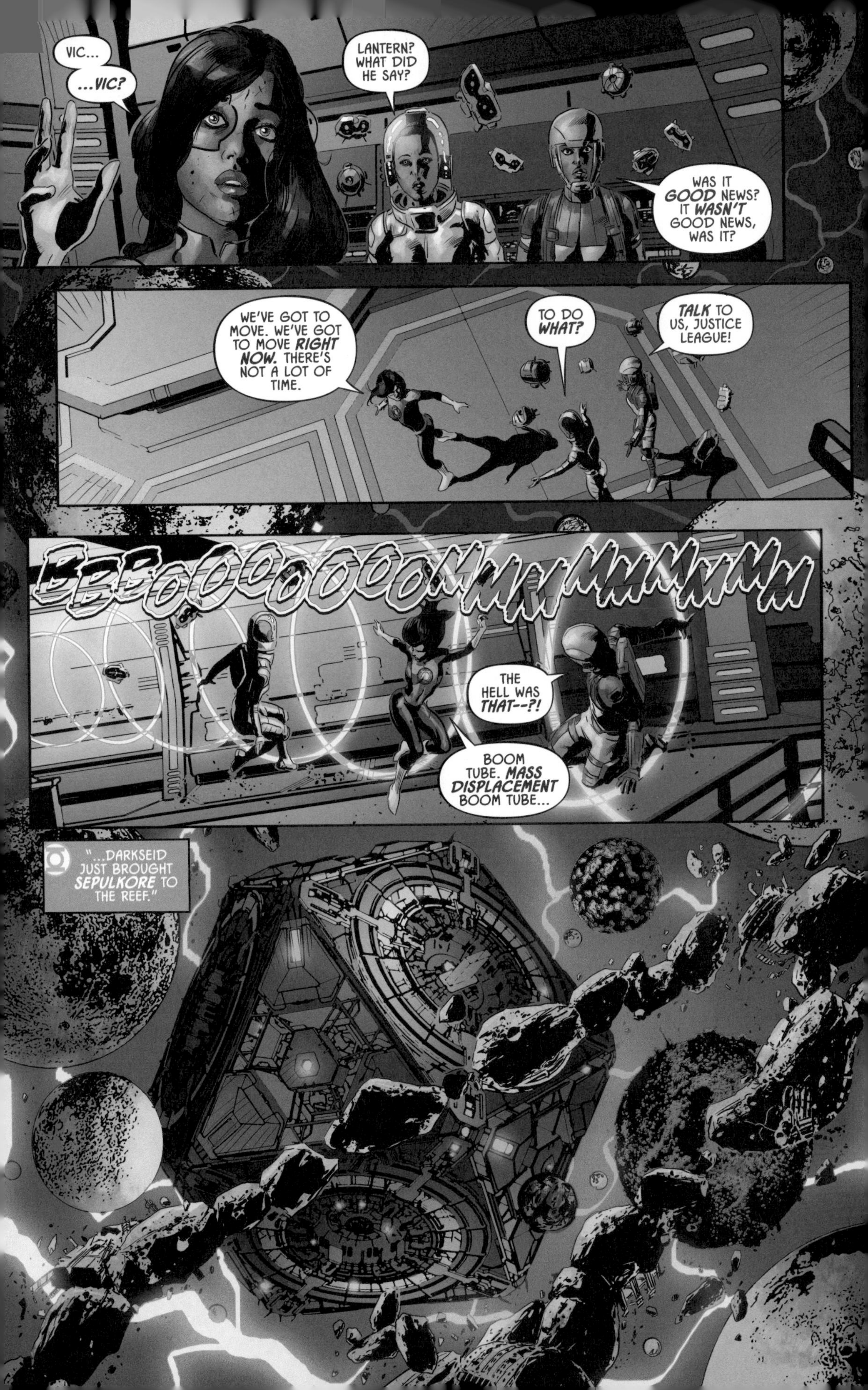
VIC...
...VIC?
LANTERN? WHAT DID HE SAY?
WAS IT GOOD NEWS? IT WASN'T GOOD NEWS, WAS IT?
WE'VE GOT TO MOVE. WE'VE GOT TO MOVE RIGHT NOW. THERE'S NOT A LOT OF TIME.
TO DO WHAT?
TALK TO US, JUSTICE LEAGUE!
BBBOOOOOOOOOMMMMMMMMMM
THE HELL WAS THAT--?!
BOOM TUBE. MASS DISPLACEMENT BOOM TUBE...
"...DARKSEID JUST BROUGHT SEPULKORE TO THE REEF."

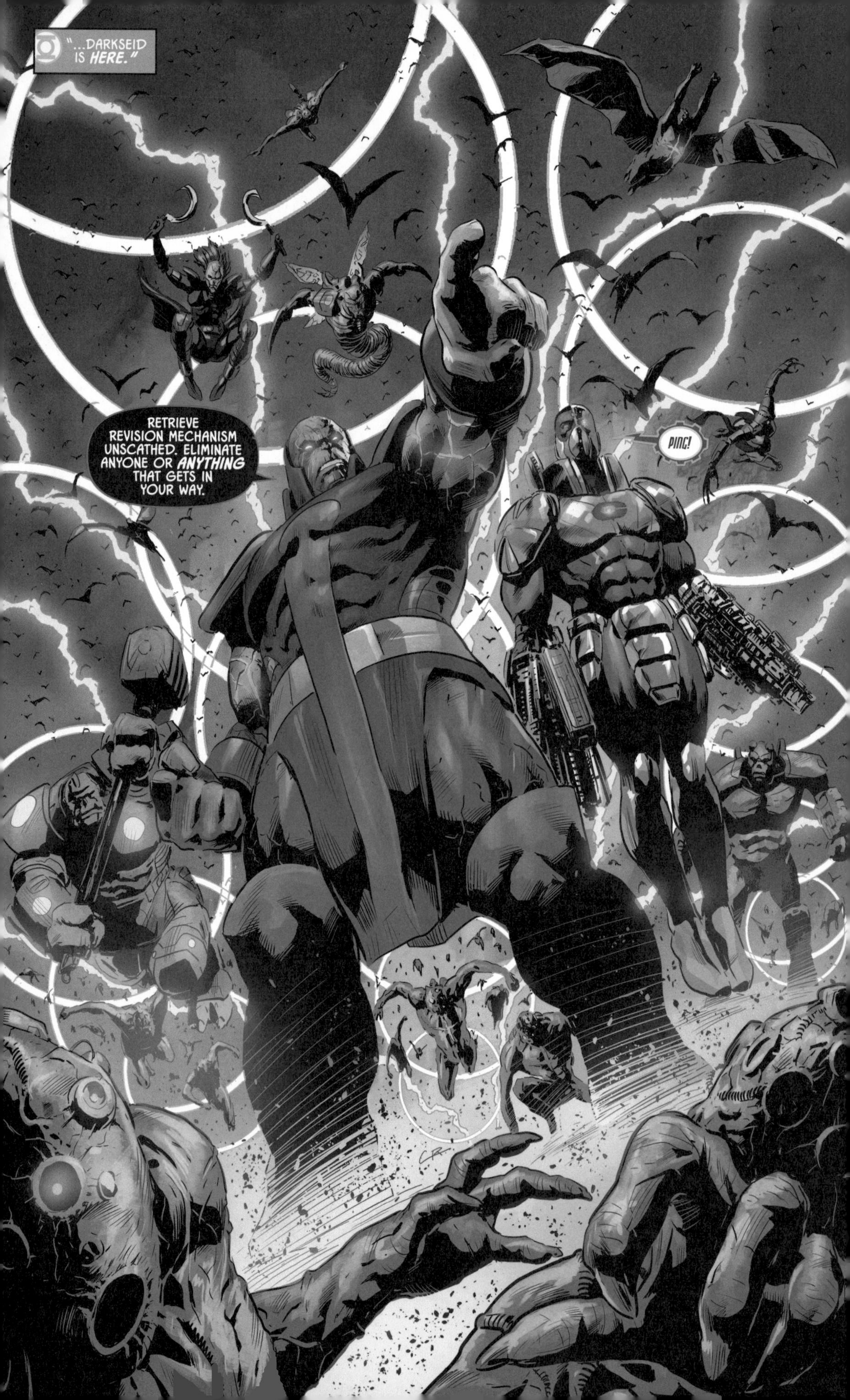
"...DARKSEID IS HERE."
RETRIEVE REVISION MECHANISM UNSCATHED. ELIMINATE ANYONE OR ANYTHING THAT GETS IN YOUR WAY.
PING!

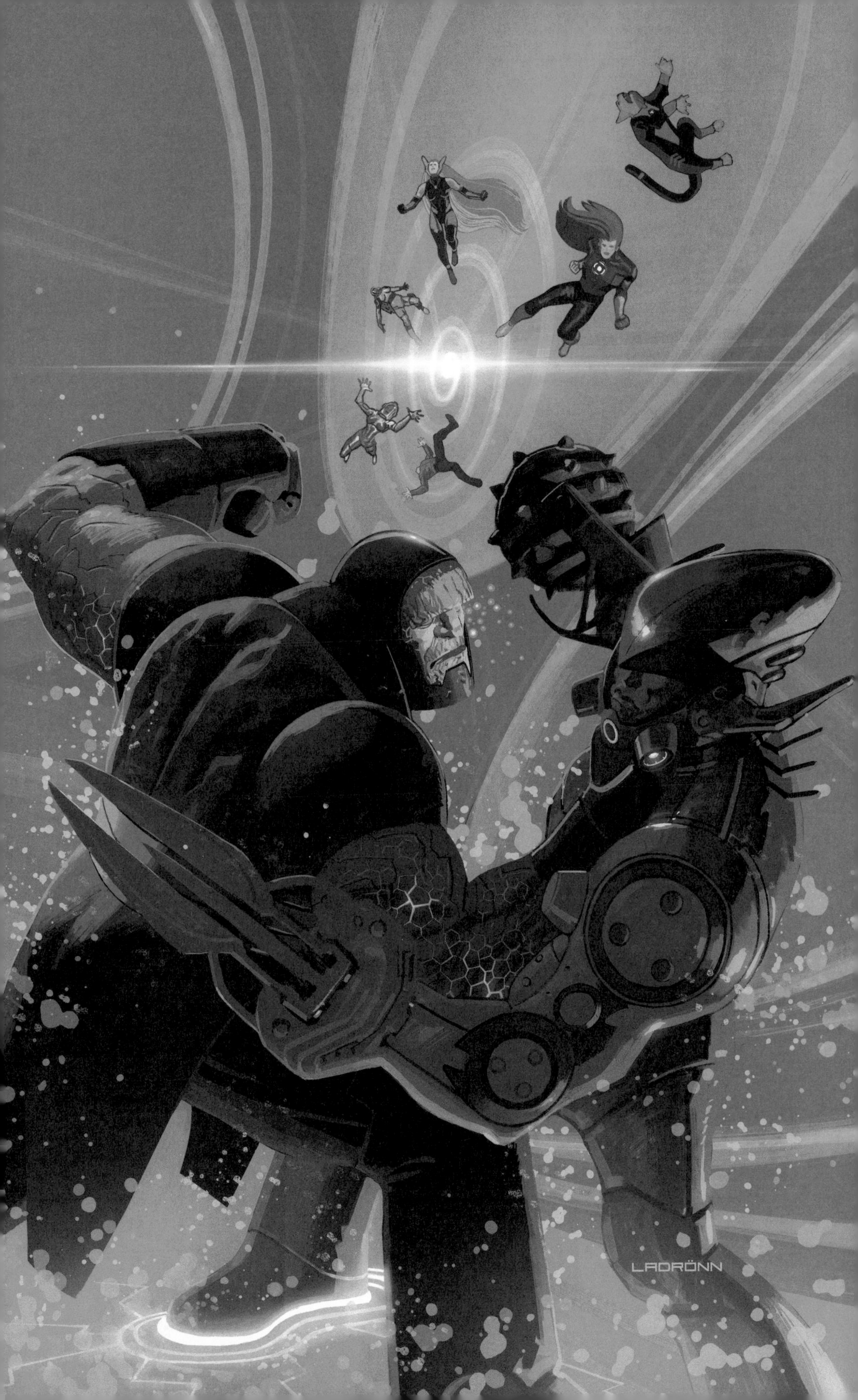
LADRÖNN

Justice League Odyssey **#21** variant cover by **SKAN**

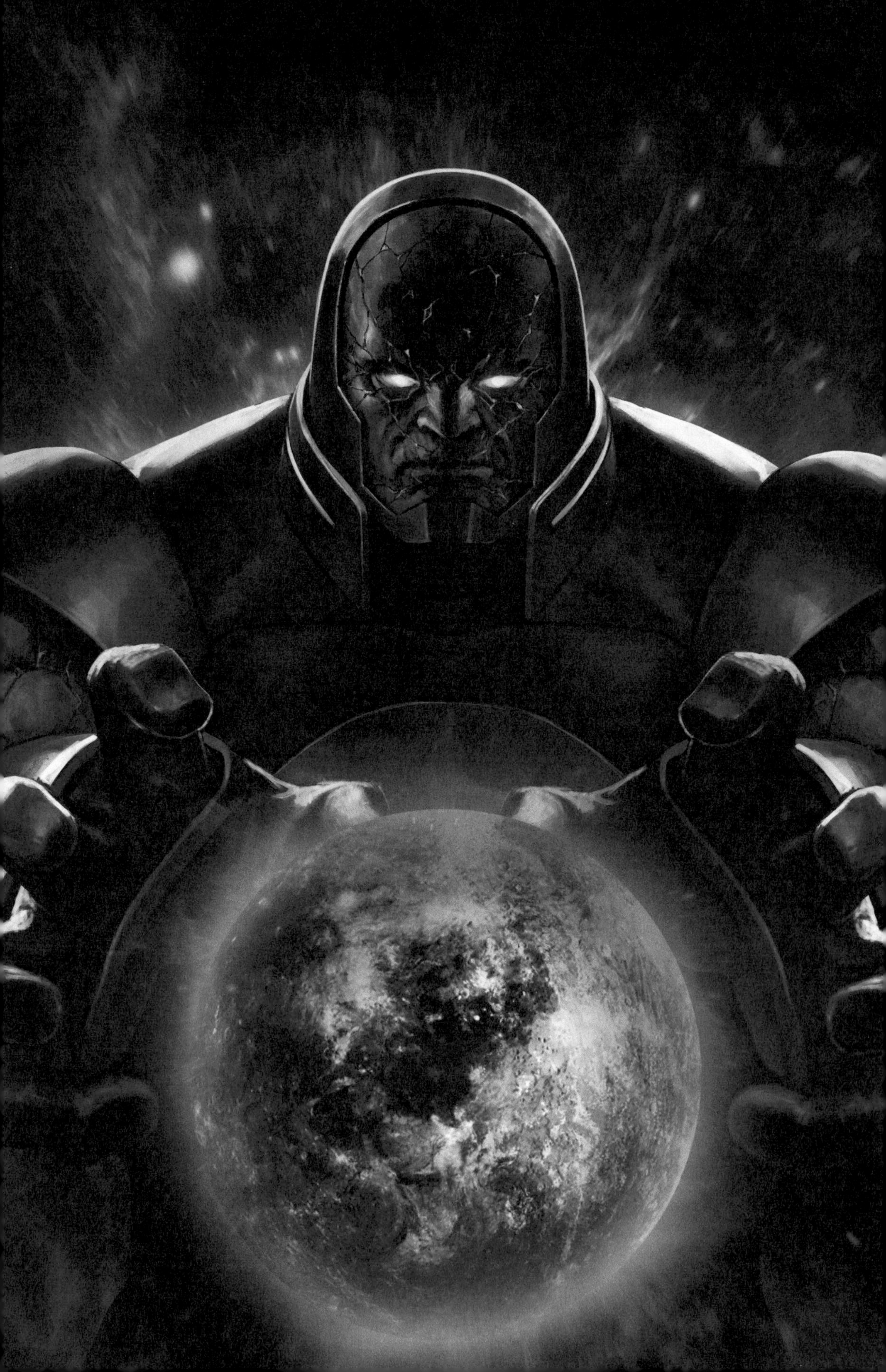

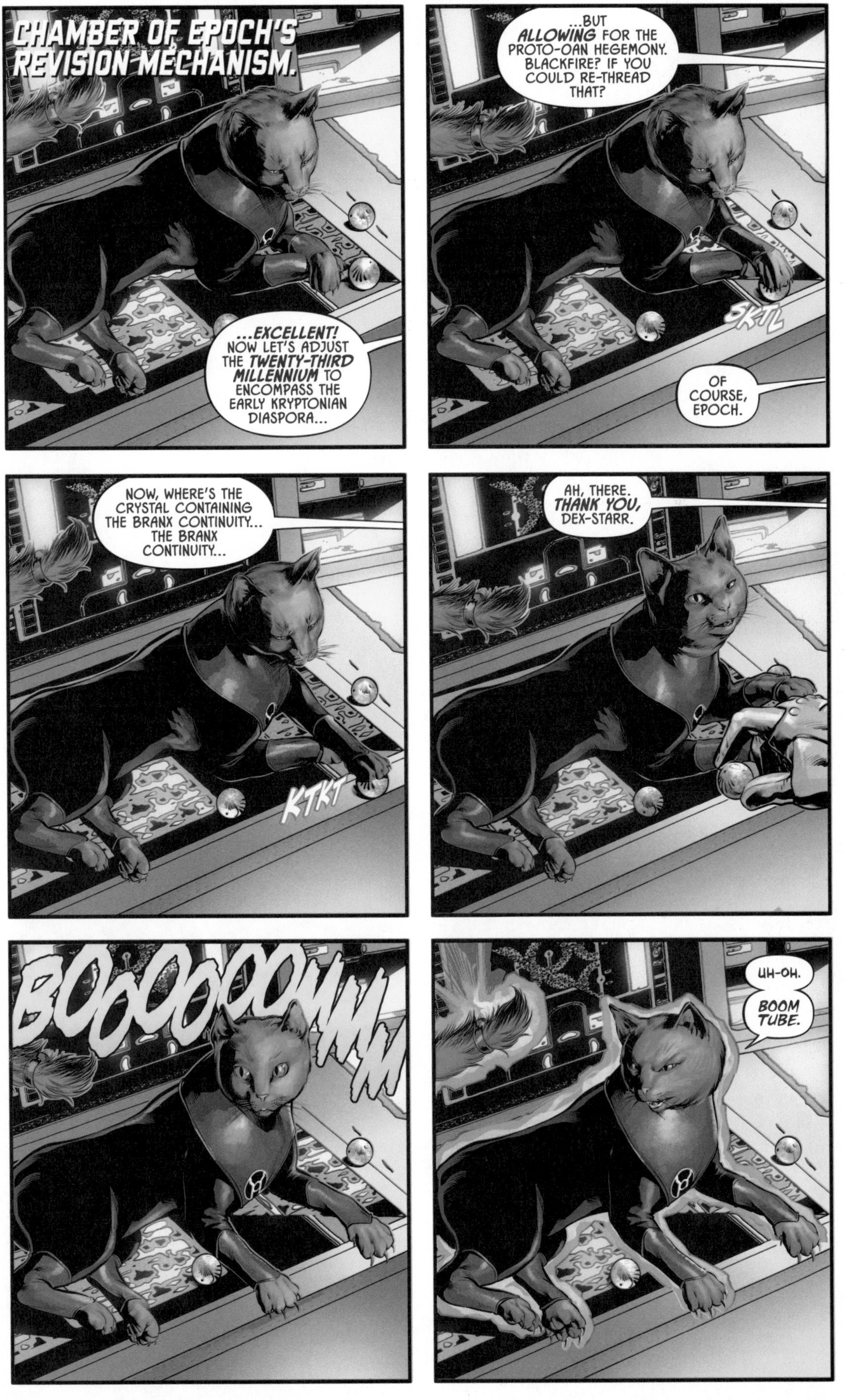
CHAMBER OF EPOCH'S REVISION MECHANISM.
...EXCELLENT! NOW LET'S ADJUST THE TWENTY-THIRD MILLENNIUM TO ENCOMPASS THE EARLY KRYPTONIAN DIASPORA...
...BUT ALLOWING FOR THE PROTO-OAN HEGEMONY. BLACKFIRE? IF YOU COULD RE-THREAD THAT?
SKTL
OF COURSE, EPOCH.
NOW, WHERE'S THE CRYSTAL CONTAINING THE BRANX CONTINUITY... THE BRANX CONTINUITY...
KTKT
AH, THERE. THANK YOU, DEX-STARR.
BOOOOOOMMM
UH-OH.
BOOM TUBE.

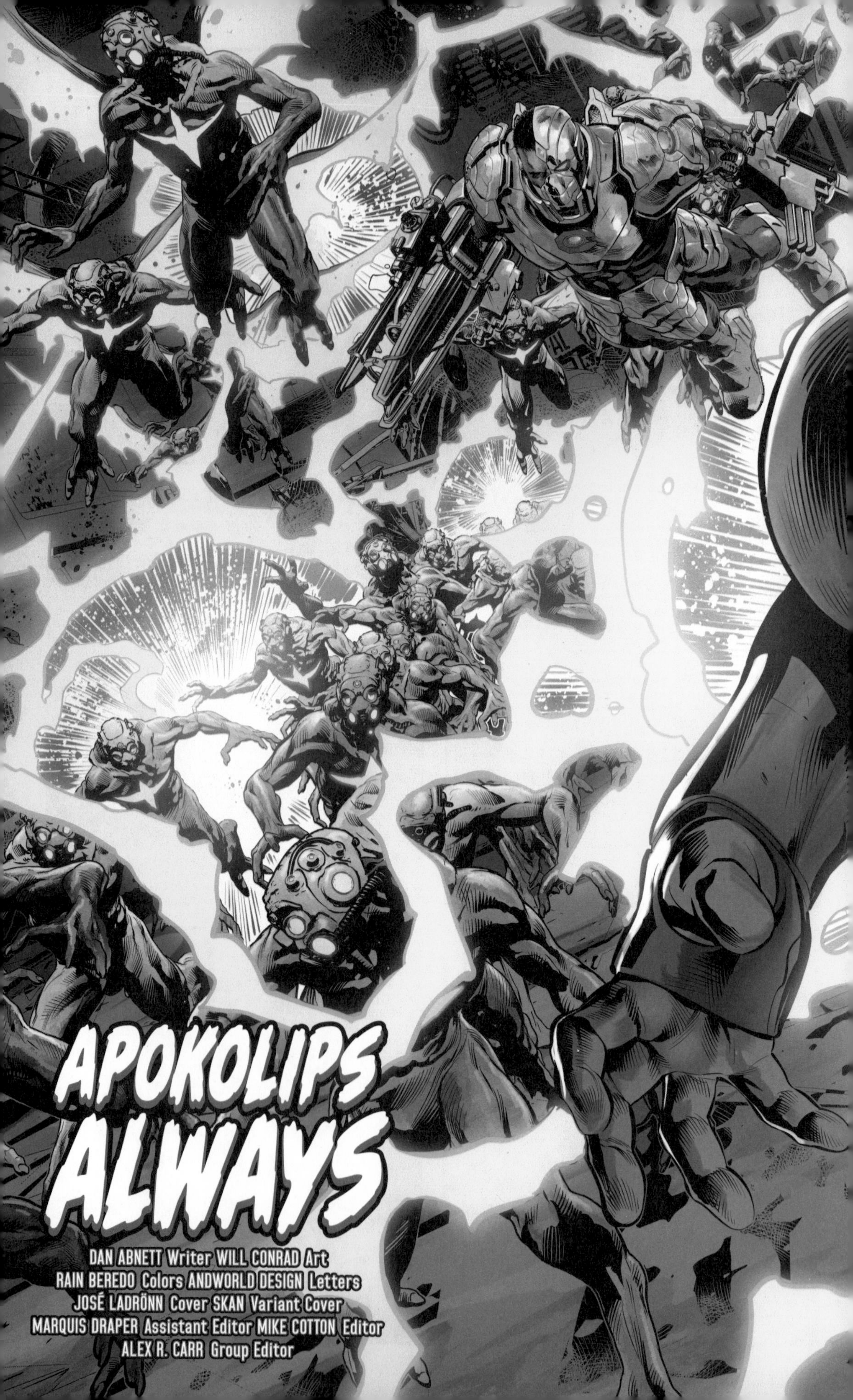
APOKOLIPS
ALWAYS
DAN ABNETT Writer WILL CONRAD Art
RAIN BEREDO Colors ANDWORLD DESIGN Letters
JOSÉ LADRÖNN Cover SKAN Variant Cover
MARQUIS DRAPER Assistant Editor MIKE COTTON Editor
ALEX R. CARR Group Editor

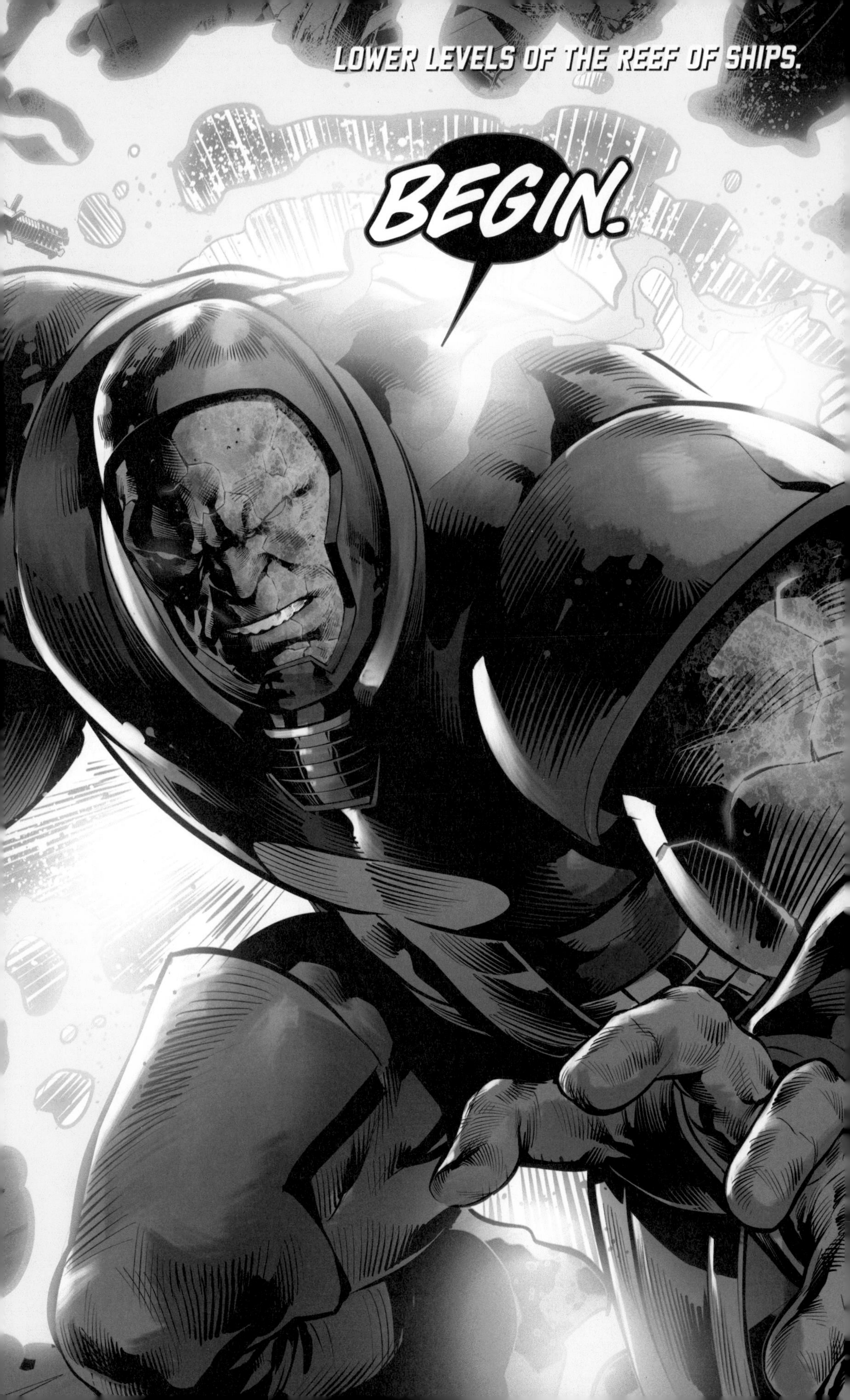
LOWER LEVELS OF THE REEF OF SHIPS.
BEGIN.

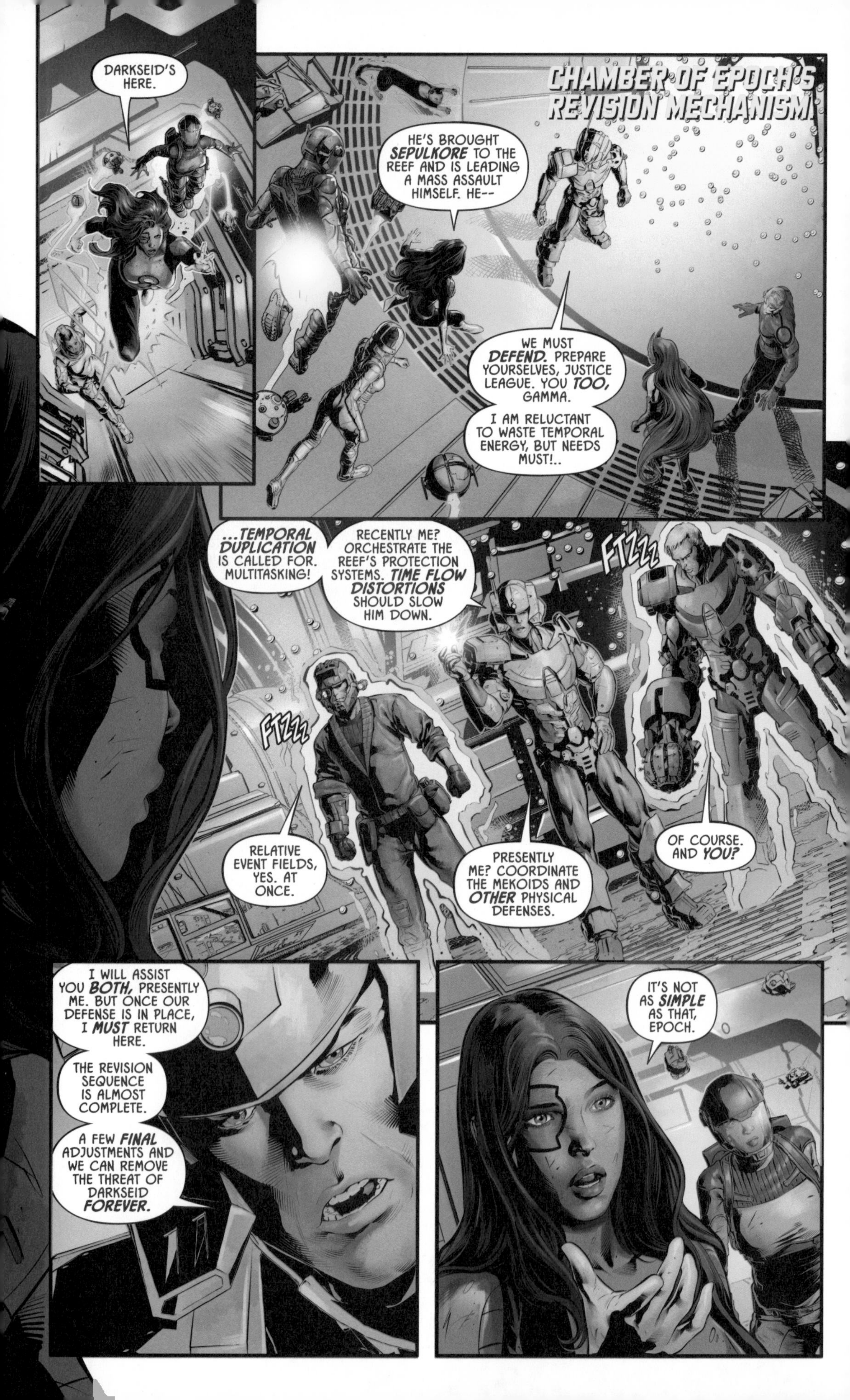
DARKSEID'S HERE.
CHAMBER OF EPOCH'S REVISION MECHANISM!
HE'S BROUGHT SEPULKORE TO THE REEF AND IS LEADING A MASS ASSAULT HIMSELF. HE--
WE MUST DEFEND. PREPARE YOURSELVES, JUSTICE LEAGUE. YOU TOO, GAMMA.
I AM RELUCTANT TO WASTE TEMPORAL ENERGY, BUT NEEDS MUST!..
...TEMPORAL DUPLICATION IS CALLED FOR. MULTITASKING!
RECENTLY ME? ORCHESTRATE THE REEF'S PROTECTION SYSTEMS. TIME FLOW DISTORTIONS SHOULD SLOW HIM DOWN.
FTZZZ
FTZZZ
RELATIVE EVENT FIELDS, YES. AT ONCE.
OF COURSE. AND YOU?
PRESENTLY ME? COORDINATE THE MEKOIDS AND OTHER PHYSICAL DEFENSES.
I WILL ASSIST YOU BOTH, PRESENTLY ME. BUT ONCE OUR DEFENSE IS IN PLACE, I MUST RETURN HERE.
THE REVISION SEQUENCE IS ALMOST COMPLETE.
A FEW FINAL ADJUSTMENTS AND WE CAN REMOVE THE THREAT OF DARKSEID FOREVER.
IT'S NOT AS SIMPLE AS THAT, EPOCH.

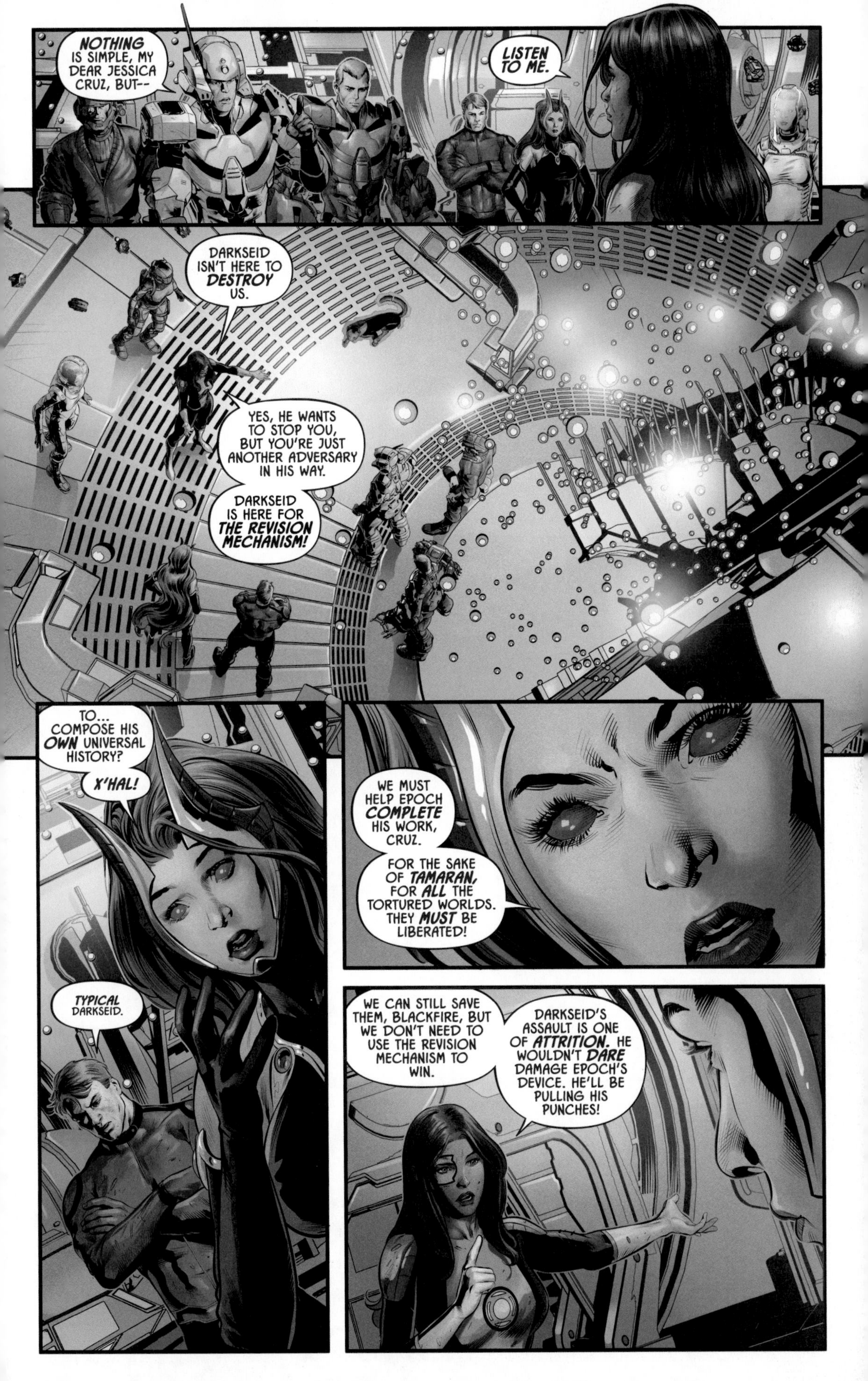

NOTHING IS SIMPLE, MY DEAR JESSICA CRUZ, BUT--
LISTEN TO ME.
DARKSEID ISN'T HERE TO DESTROY US.
YES, HE WANTS TO STOP YOU, BUT YOU'RE JUST ANOTHER ADVERSARY IN HIS WAY.
DARKSEID IS HERE FOR THE REVISION MECHANISM!
TO... COMPOSE HIS OWN UNIVERSAL HISTORY?
X'HAL!
WE MUST HELP EPOCH COMPLETE HIS WORK, CRUZ.
FOR THE SAKE OF TAMARAN, FOR ALL THE TORTURED WORLDS. THEY MUST BE LIBERATED!
TYPICAL DARKSEID.
WE CAN STILL SAVE THEM, BLACKFIRE, BUT WE DON'T NEED TO USE THE REVISION MECHANISM TO WIN.
DARKSEID'S ASSAULT IS ONE OF ATTRITION. HE WOULDN'T DARE DAMAGE EPOCH'S DEVICE. HE'LL BE PULLING HIS PUNCHES!

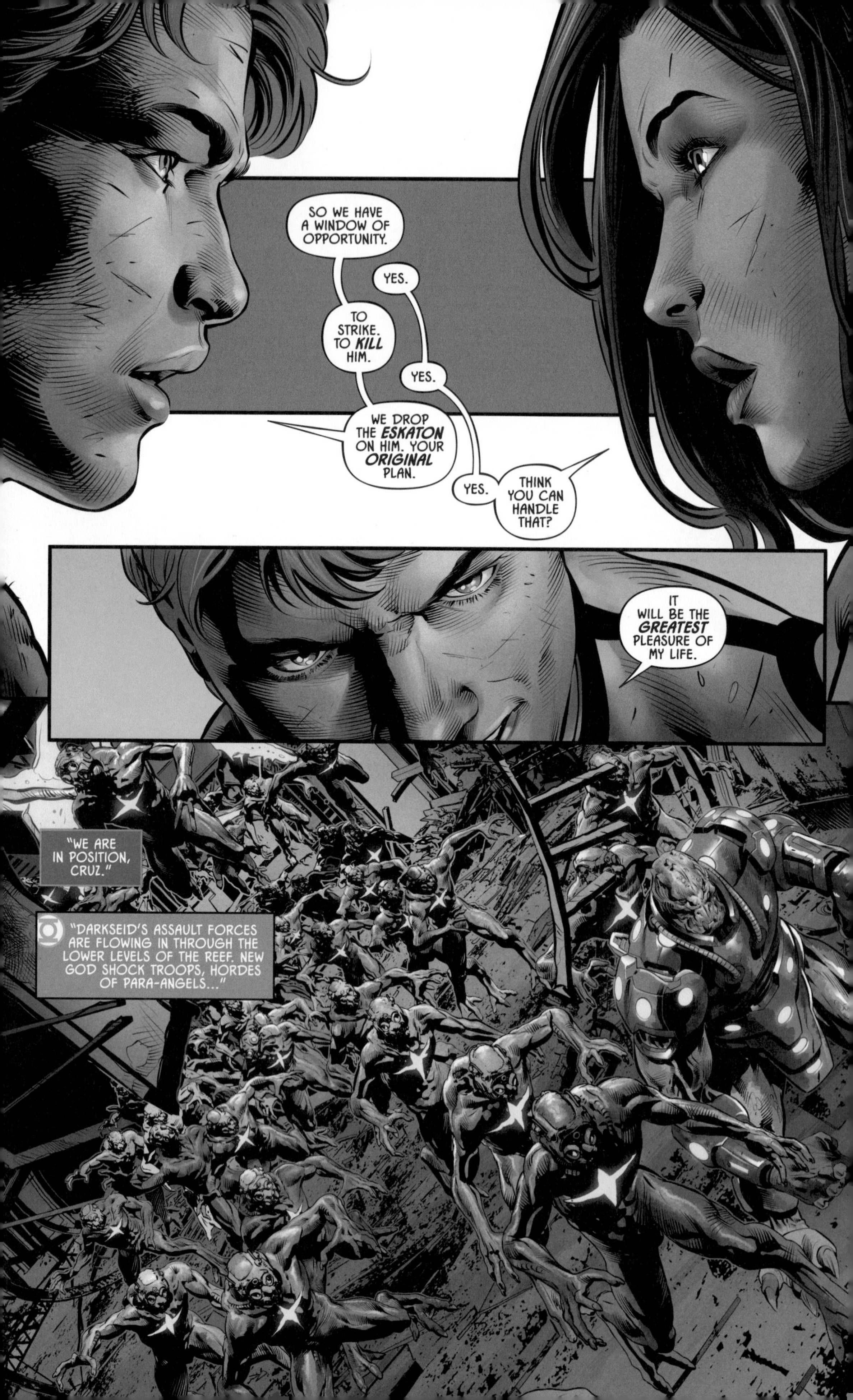
SO WE HAVE A WINDOW OF OPPORTUNITY.
YES.
TO STRIKE. TO KILL HIM.
YES.
WE DROP THE ESKATON ON HIM. YOUR ORIGINAL PLAN.
YES.
THINK YOU CAN HANDLE THAT?
IT WILL BE THE GREATEST PLEASURE OF MY LIFE.
"WE ARE IN POSITION, CRUZ."
"DARKSEID'S ASSAULT FORCES ARE FLOWING IN THROUGH THE LOWER LEVELS OF THE REEF. NEW GOD SHOCK TROOPS, HORDES OF PARA-ANGELS..."

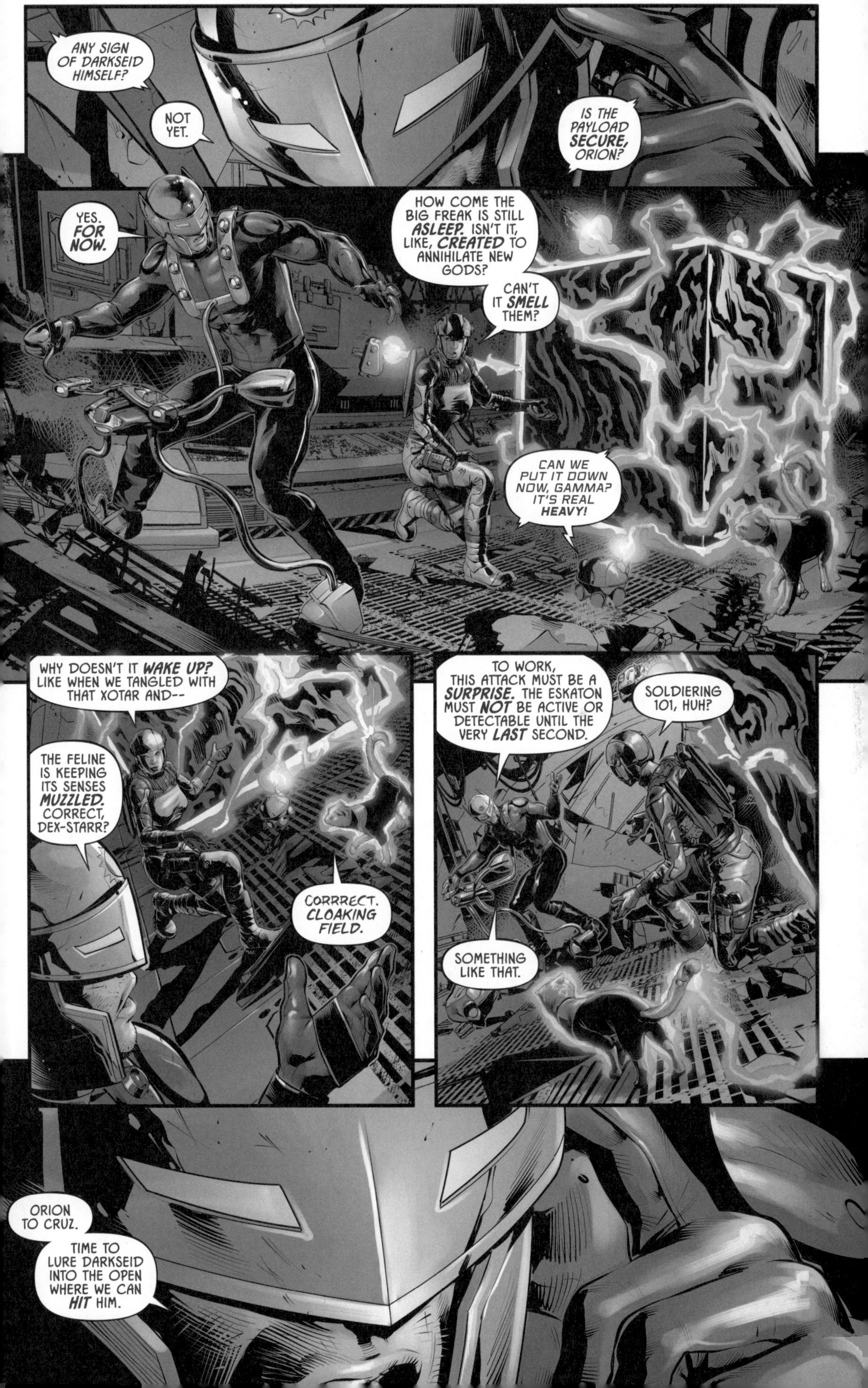

ANY SIGN OF DARKSEID HIMSELF?
NOT YET.
IS THE PAYLOAD SECURE, ORION?
YES. FOR NOW.
HOW COME THE BIG FREAK IS STILL ASLEEP. ISN'T IT, LIKE, CREATED TO ANNIHILATE NEW GODS?
CAN'T IT SMELL THEM?
CAN WE PUT IT DOWN NOW, GAMMA? IT'S REAL HEAVY!
WHY DOESN'T IT WAKE UP? LIKE WHEN WE TANGLED WITH THAT XOTAR AND--
THE FELINE IS KEEPING ITS SENSES MUZZLED. CORRECT, DEX-STARR?
CORRRECT. CLOAKING FIELD.
TO WORK, THIS ATTACK MUST BE A SURPRISE. THE ESKATON MUST NOT BE ACTIVE OR DETECTABLE UNTIL THE VERY LAST SECOND.
SOLDIERING 101, HUH?
SOMETHING LIKE THAT.
ORION TO CRUZ.
TIME TO LURE DARKSEID INTO THE OPEN WHERE WE CAN HIT HIM.

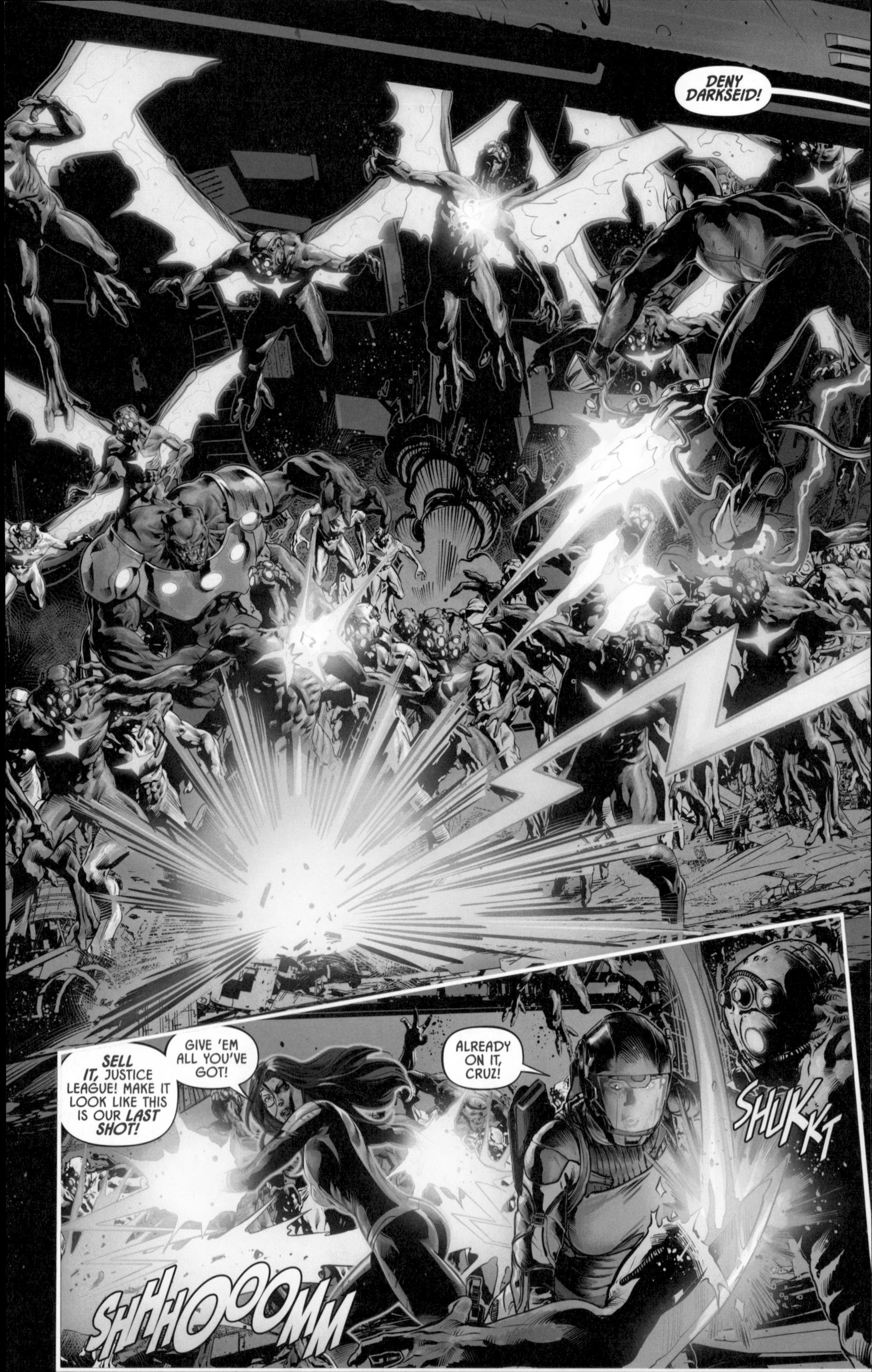
DENY DARKSEID!
SELL IT, JUSTICE LEAGUE! MAKE IT LOOK LIKE THIS IS OUR LAST SHOT!
GIVE 'EM ALL YOU'VE GOT!
ALREADY ON IT, CRUZ!
SHUKKT
SHHHOOOMM

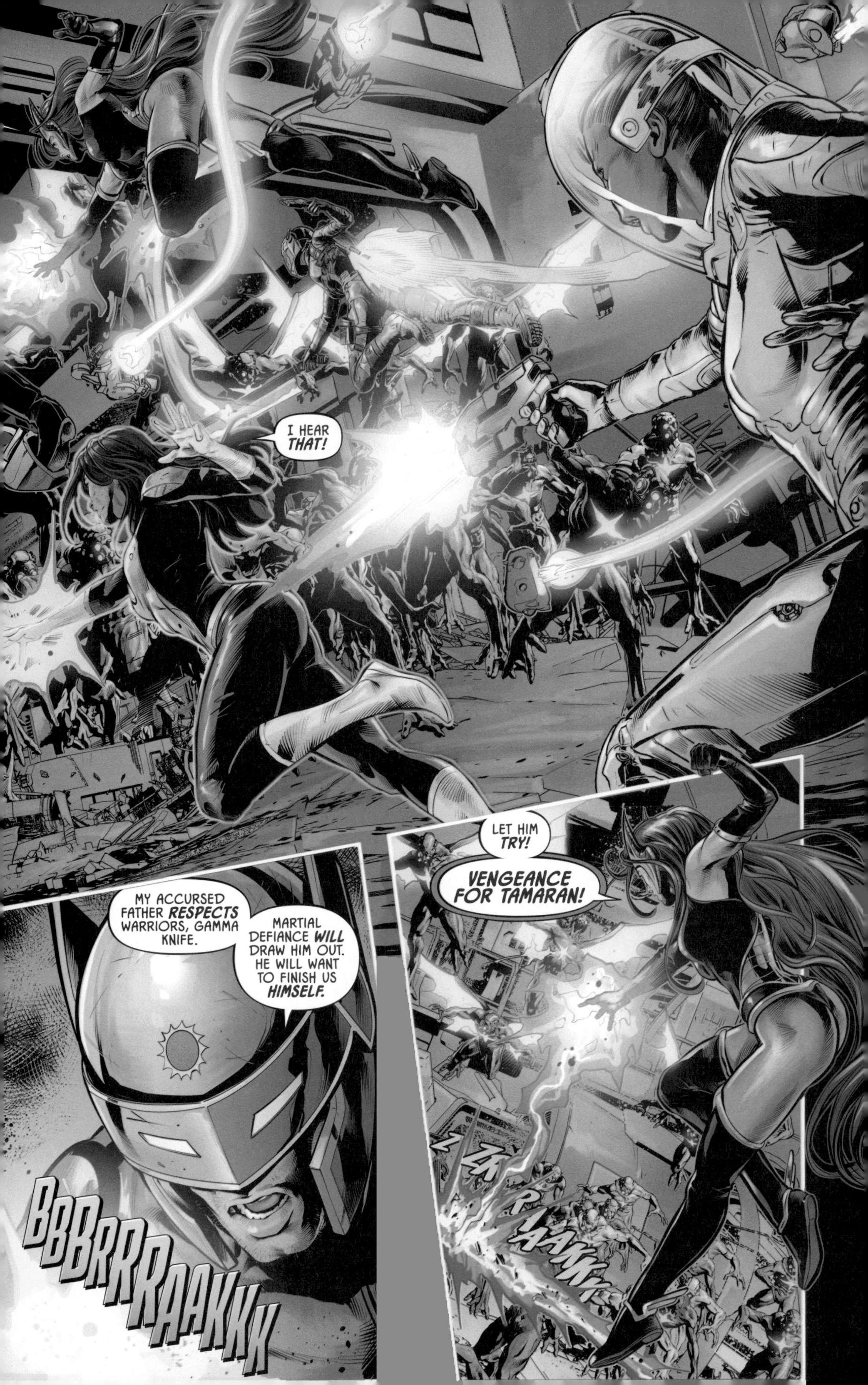
I HEAR THAT!
MY ACCURSED FATHER RESPECTS WARRIORS, GAMMA KNIFE.
MARTIAL DEFIANCE WILL DRAW HIM OUT. HE WILL WANT TO FINISH US HIMSELF.
BBBRRRAAKKKK
LET HIM TRY!
VENGEANCE FOR TAMARAN!
ZZKRRAAKKK

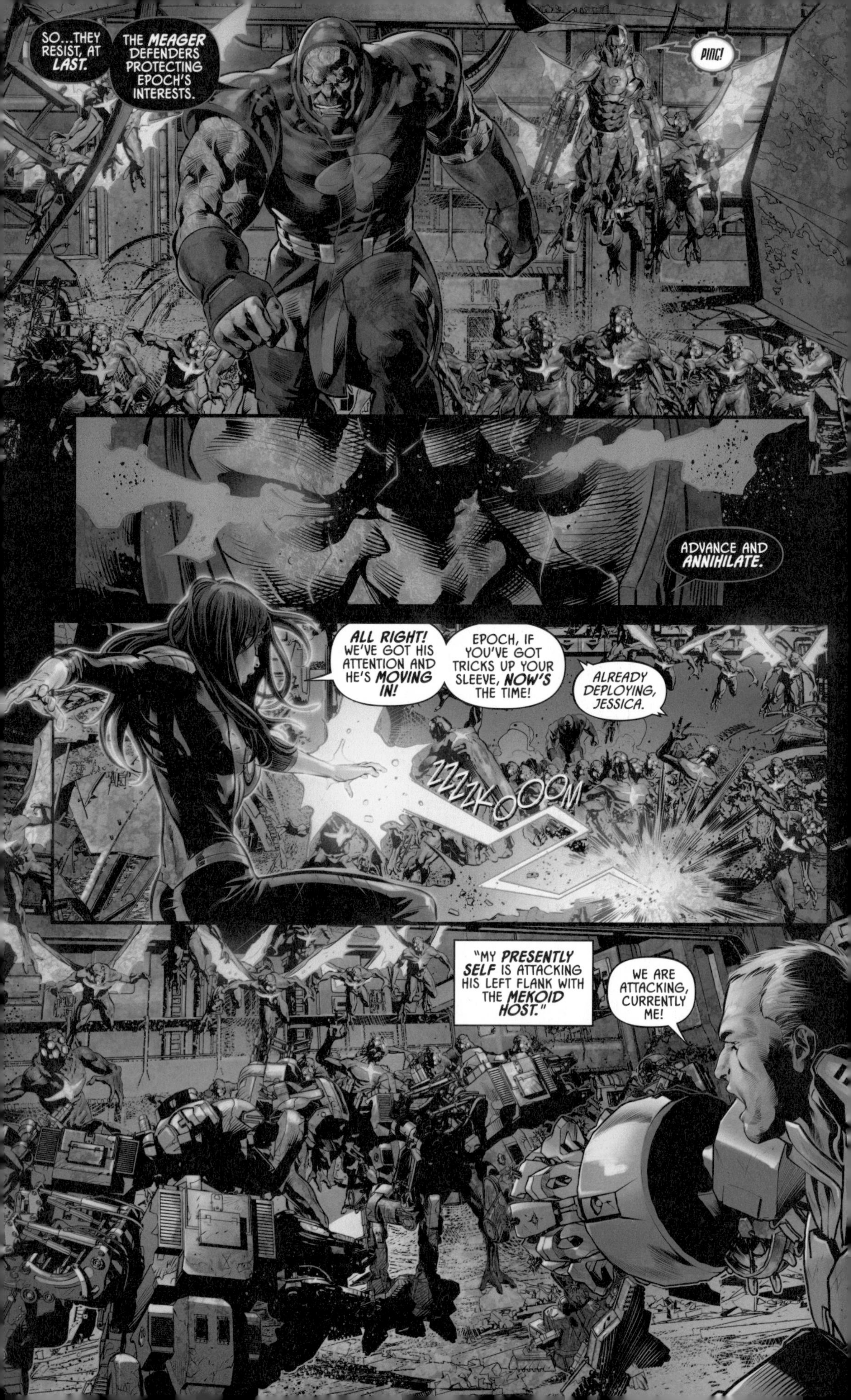
SO...THEY RESIST, AT LAST.
THE MEAGER DEFENDERS PROTECTING EPOCH'S INTERESTS.
PING!
ADVANCE AND ANNIHILATE.
ALL RIGHT! WE'VE GOT HIS ATTENTION AND HE'S MOVING IN!
EPOCH, IF YOU'VE GOT TRICKS UP YOUR SLEEVE, NOW'S THE TIME!
ALREADY DEPLOYING, JESSICA.
ZZZKOOOM
"MY PRESENTLY SELF IS ATTACKING HIS LEFT FLANK WITH THE MEKOID HOST."
WE ARE ATTACKING, CURRENTLY ME!

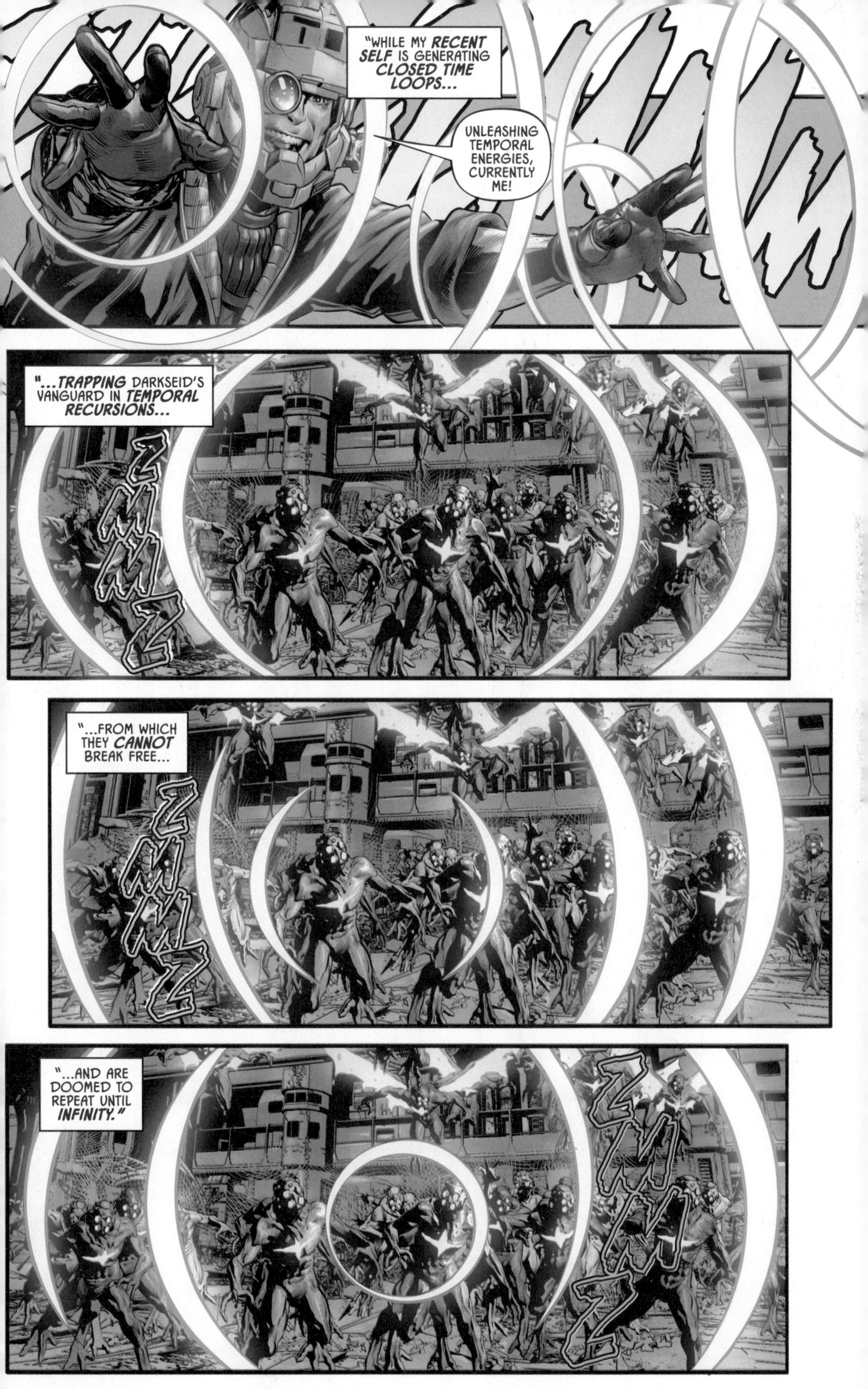
"WHILE MY RECENT SELF IS GENERATING CLOSED TIME LOOPS...
UNLEASHING TEMPORAL ENERGIES, CURRENTLY ME!
"...TRAPPING DARKSEID'S VANGUARD IN TEMPORAL RECURSIONS...
ZMMMZ
"...FROM WHICH THEY CANNOT BREAK FREE...
ZMMMZ
"...AND ARE DOOMED TO REPEAT UNTIL INFINITY."
ZMMMZ

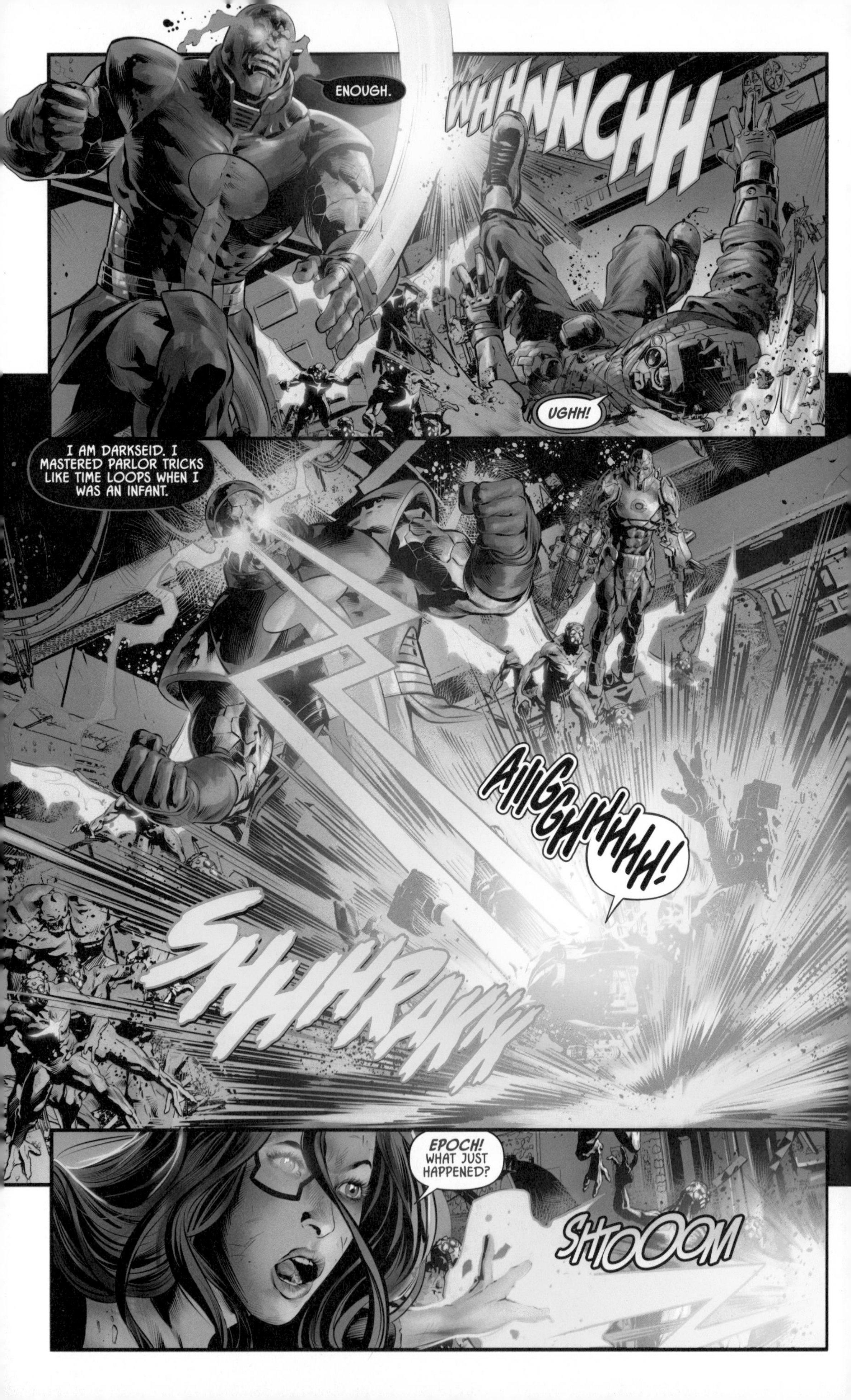
ENOUGH.
WHHNNCHH
UGHH!
I AM DARKSEID. I MASTERED PARLOR TRICKS LIKE TIME LOOPS WHEN I WAS AN INFANT.
AIIGHHHHH!
SHHHRAKK
EPOCH! WHAT JUST HAPPENED?
SHOOOM

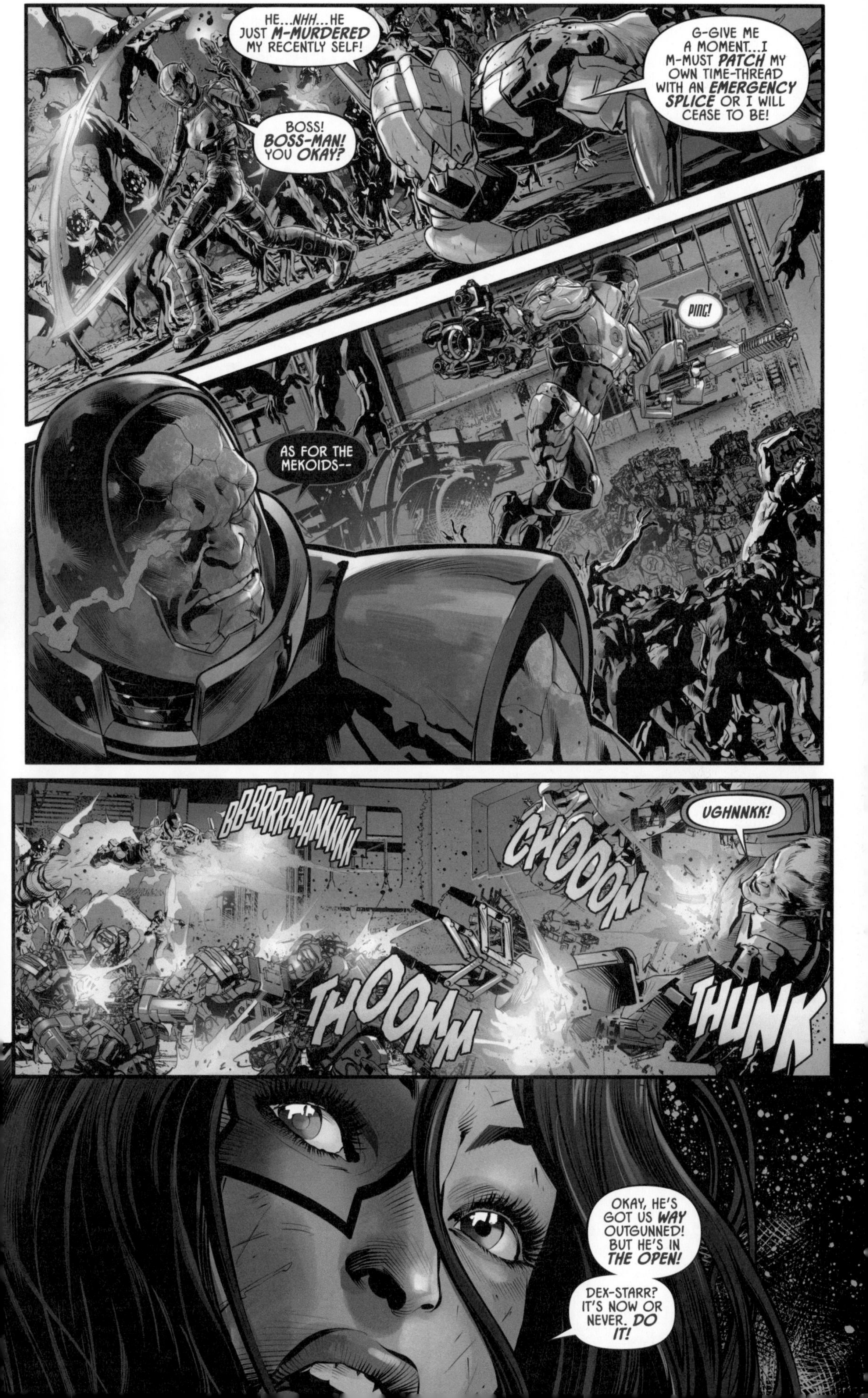

HE...NHH...HE JUST M-MURDERED MY RECENTLY SELF!
BOSS! BOSS-MAN! YOU OKAY?
G-GIVE ME A MOMENT...I M-MUST PATCH MY OWN TIME-THREAD WITH AN EMERGENCY SPLICE OR I WILL CEASE TO BE!
PING!
AS FOR THE MEKOIDS--
BBBRRRRAAAKKKKK
CHOOOM
UGHNNKK!
THOOMM
THUNK
OKAY, HE'S GOT US WAY OUTGUNNED! BUT HE'S IN THE OPEN!
DEX-STARR? IT'S NOW OR NEVER. DO IT!

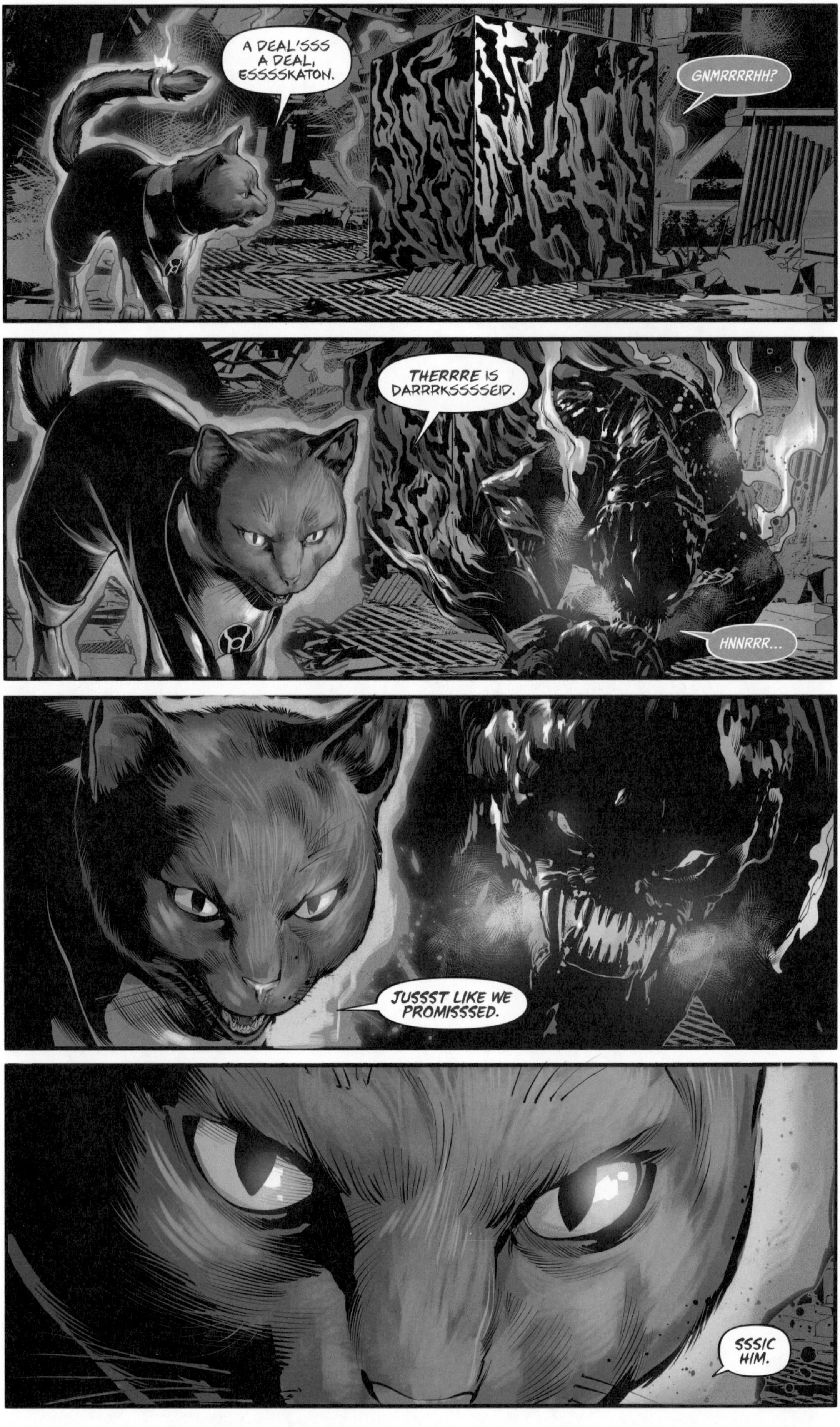
A DEAL'SSS A DEAL, ESSSSKATON.
GNMRRRRHH?
THERRRE IS DARRRKSSSSEID.
HNNRRR...
JUSSST LIKE WE PROMISSSED.
SSSIC HIM.

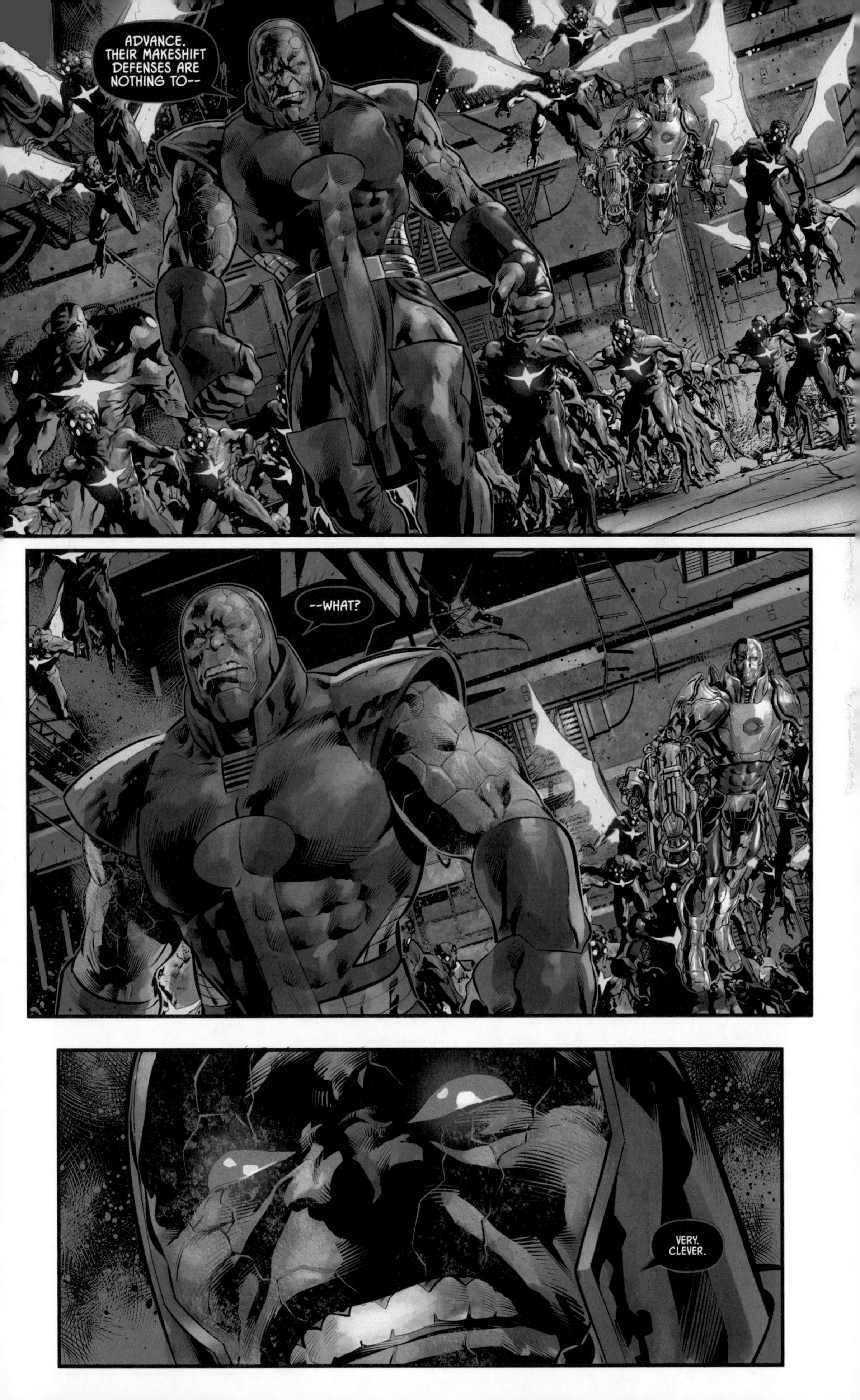
ADVANCE. THEIR MAKESHIFT DEFENSES ARE NOTHING TO--
--WHAT?
VERY. CLEVER.

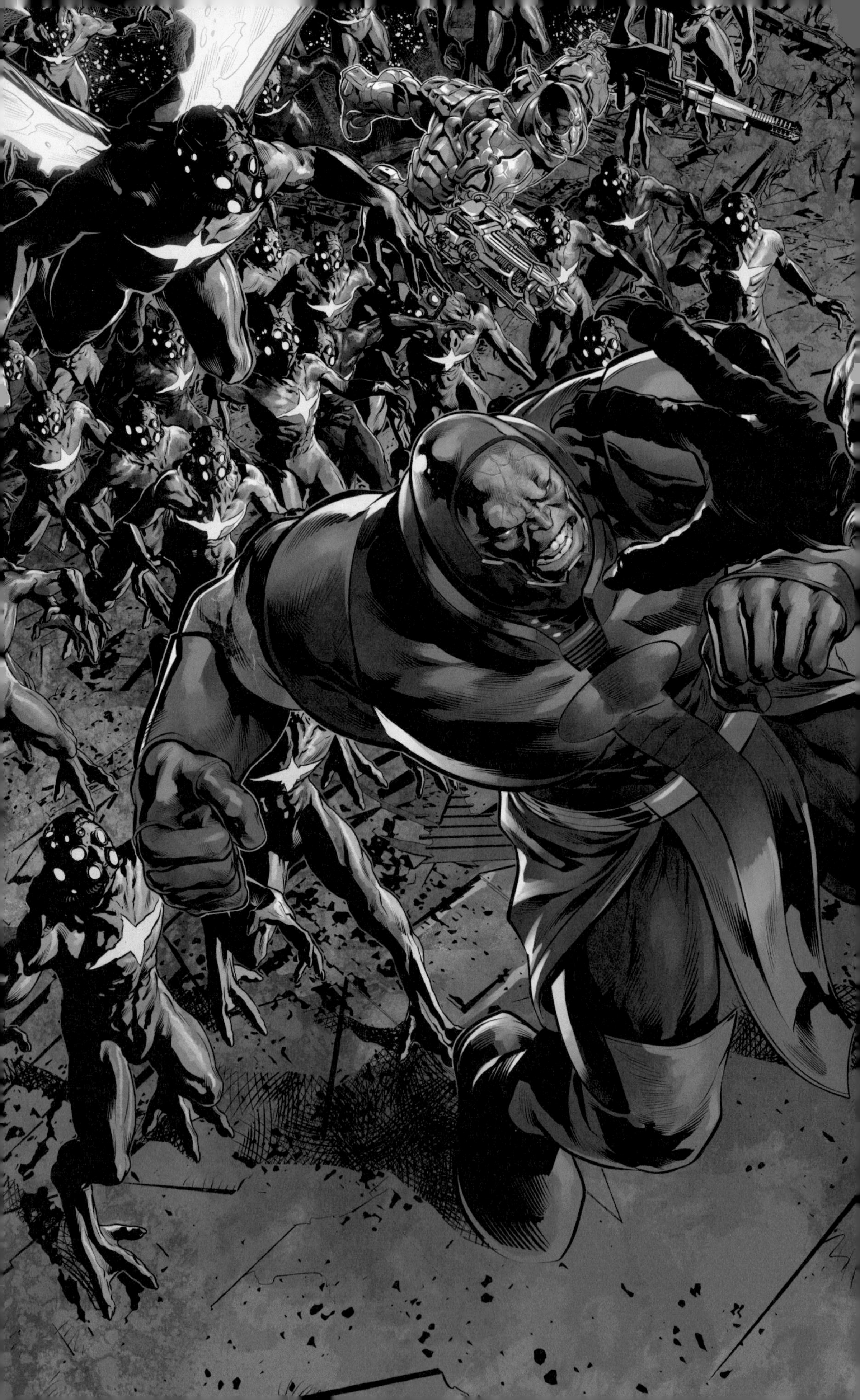

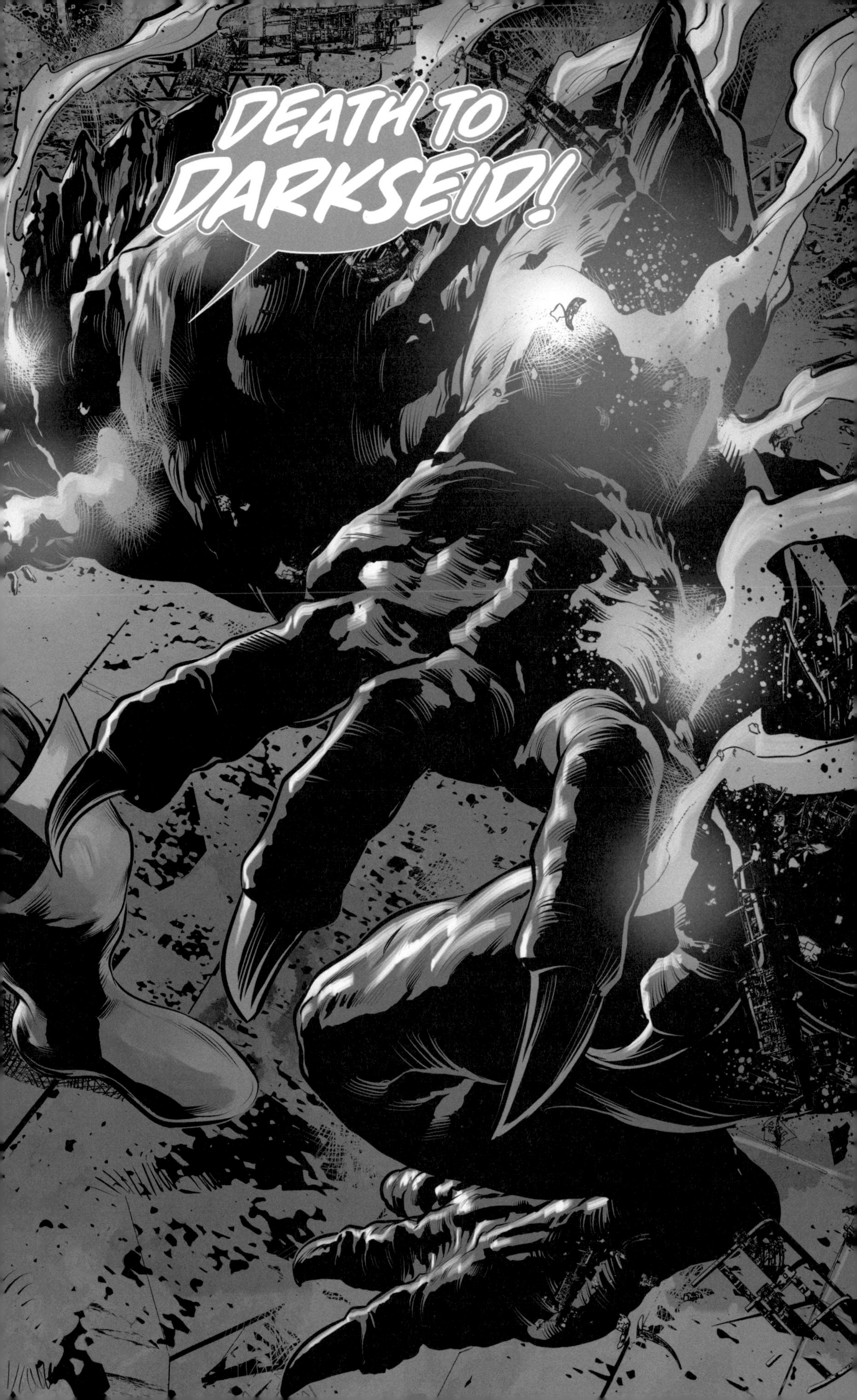
DEATH TO DARKSEID!

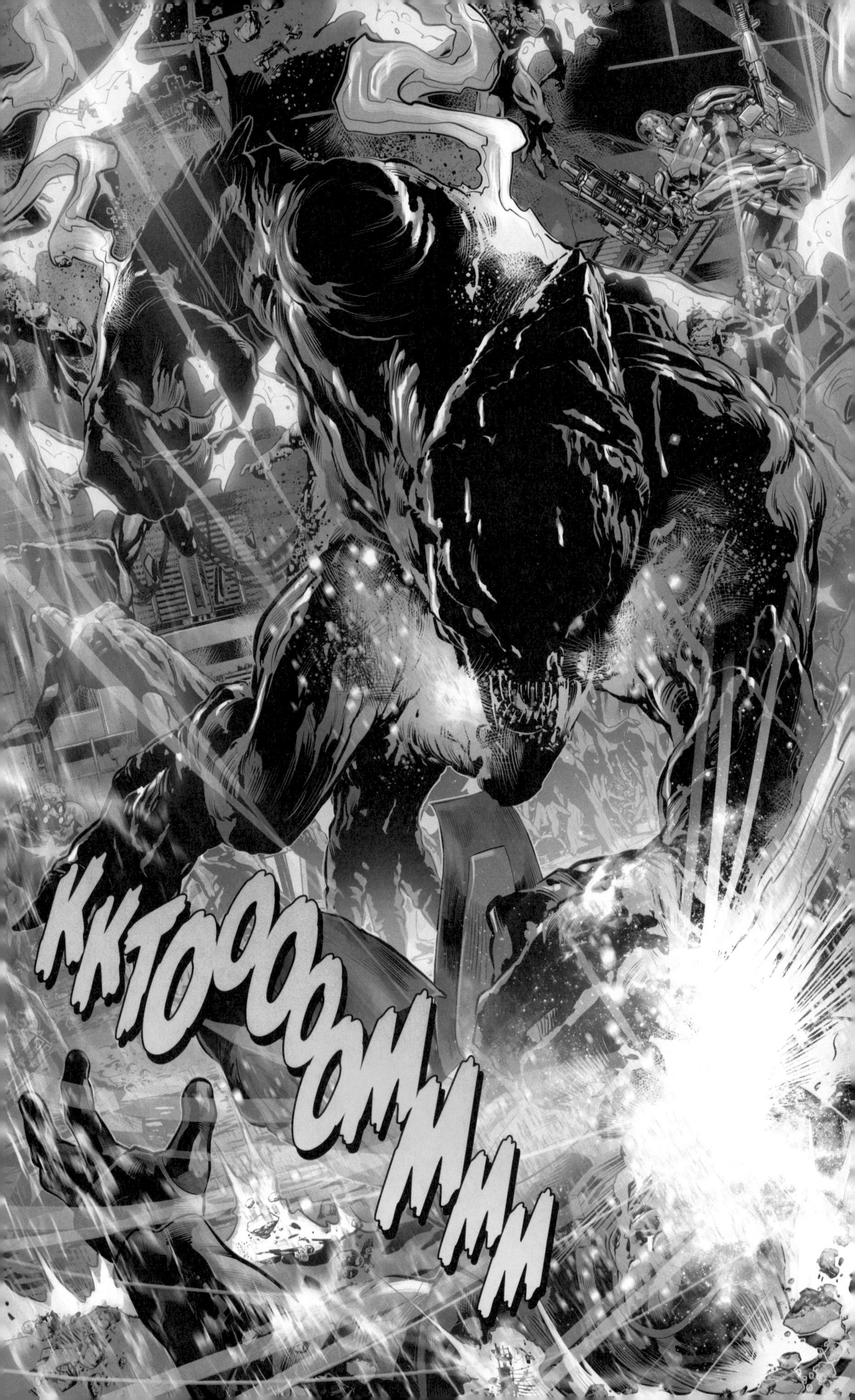
KKTOOOOOMMMM

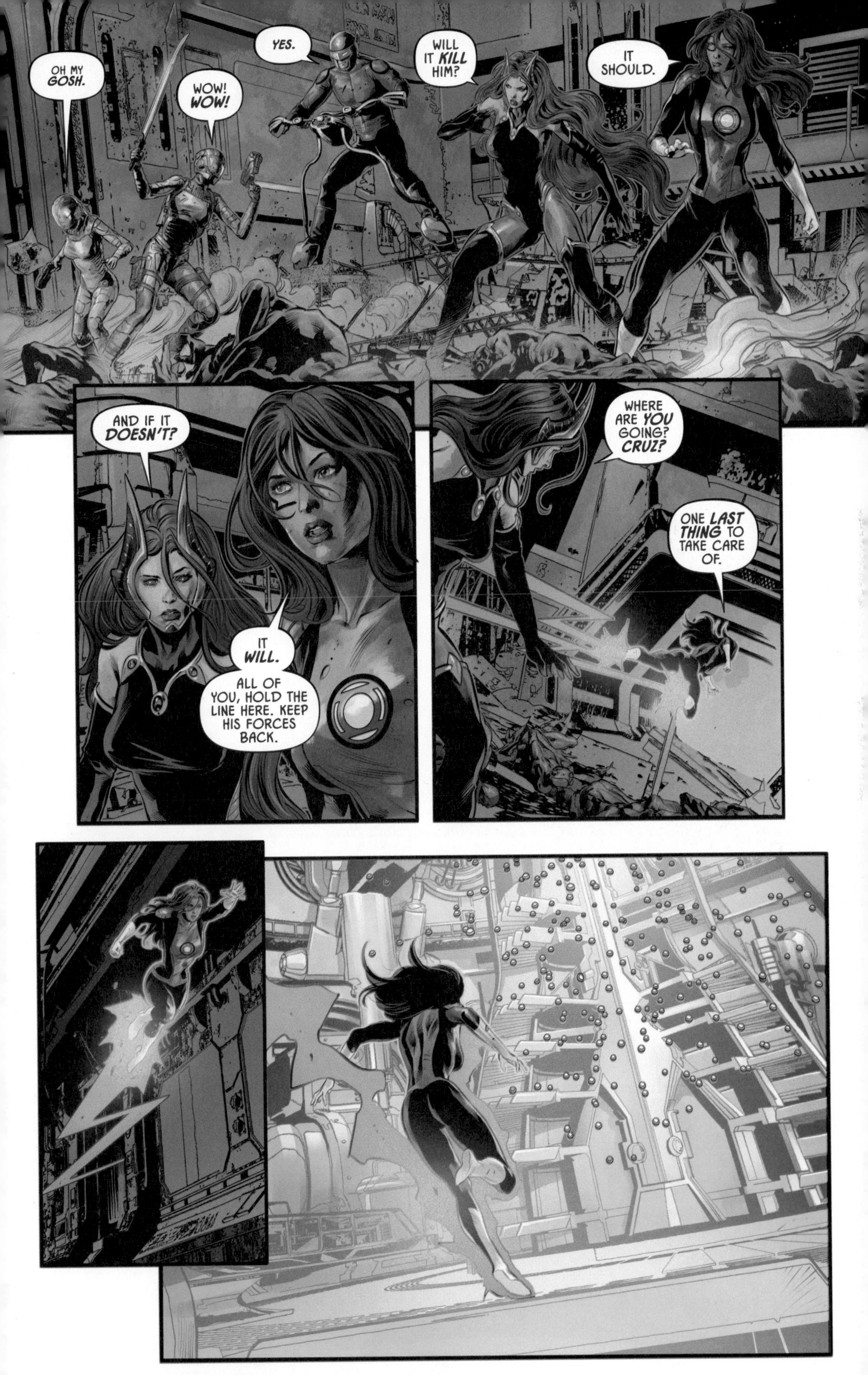
OH MY GOSH.
WOW! WOW!
YES.
WILL IT KILL HIM?
IT SHOULD.
AND IF IT DOESN'T?
IT WILL.
ALL OF YOU, HOLD THE LINE HERE. KEEP HIS FORCES BACK.
WHERE ARE YOU GOING? CRUZ?
ONE LAST THING TO TAKE CARE OF.

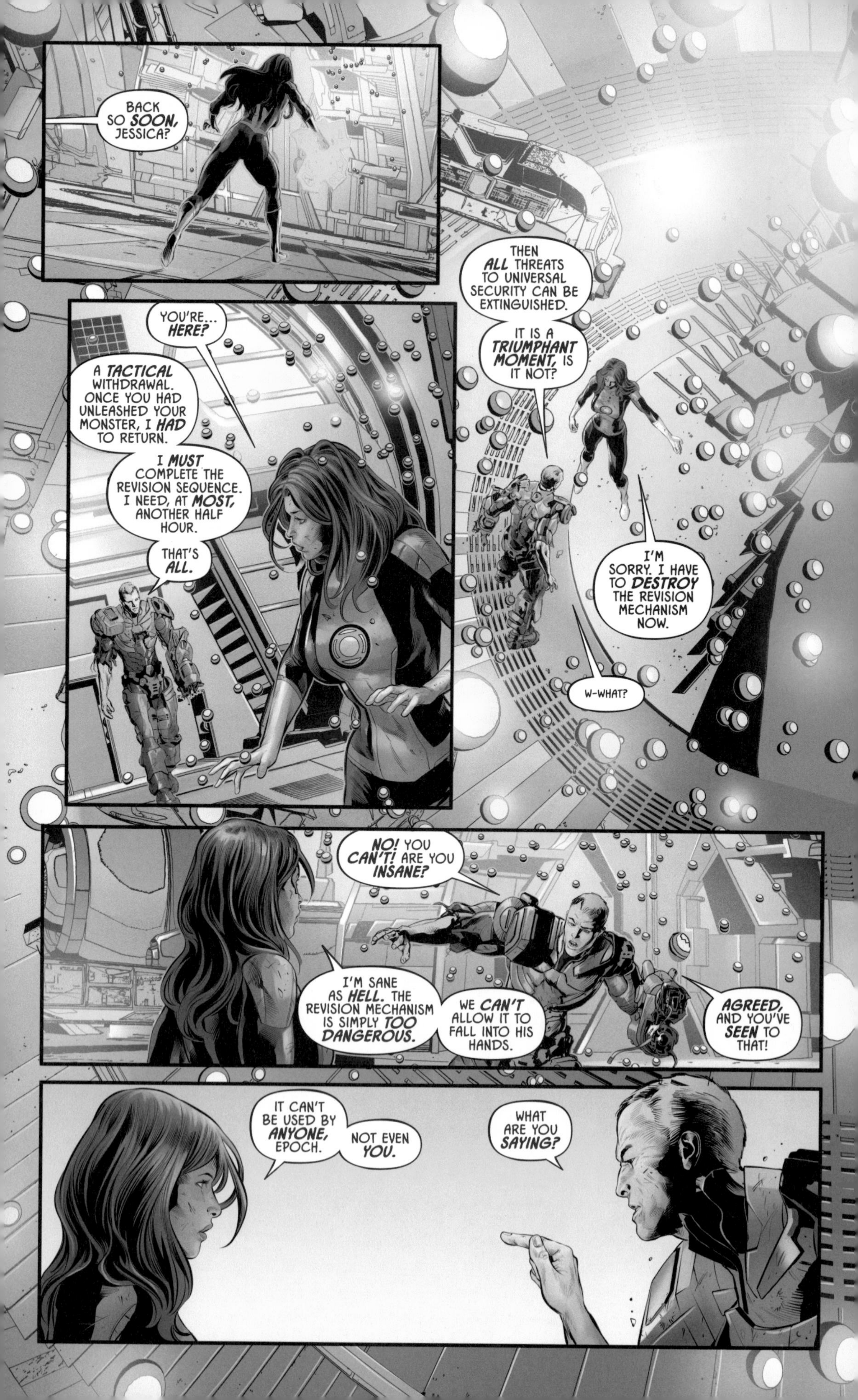
BACK SO SOON, JESSICA?
YOU'RE... HERE?
A TACTICAL WITHDRAWAL. ONCE YOU HAD UNLEASHED YOUR MONSTER, I HAD TO RETURN.
I MUST COMPLETE THE REVISION SEQUENCE. I NEED, AT MOST, ANOTHER HALF HOUR.
THAT'S ALL.
THEN ALL THREATS TO UNIVERSAL SECURITY CAN BE EXTINGUISHED.
IT IS A TRIUMPHANT MOMENT, IS IT NOT?
I'M SORRY. I HAVE TO DESTROY THE REVISION MECHANISM NOW.
W-WHAT?
NO! YOU CAN'T! ARE YOU INSANE?
I'M SANE AS HELL. THE REVISION MECHANISM IS SIMPLY TOO DANGEROUS.
WE CAN'T ALLOW IT TO FALL INTO HIS HANDS.
AGREED, AND YOU'VE SEEN TO THAT!
IT CAN'T BE USED BY ANYONE, EPOCH.
NOT EVEN YOU.
WHAT ARE YOU SAYING?

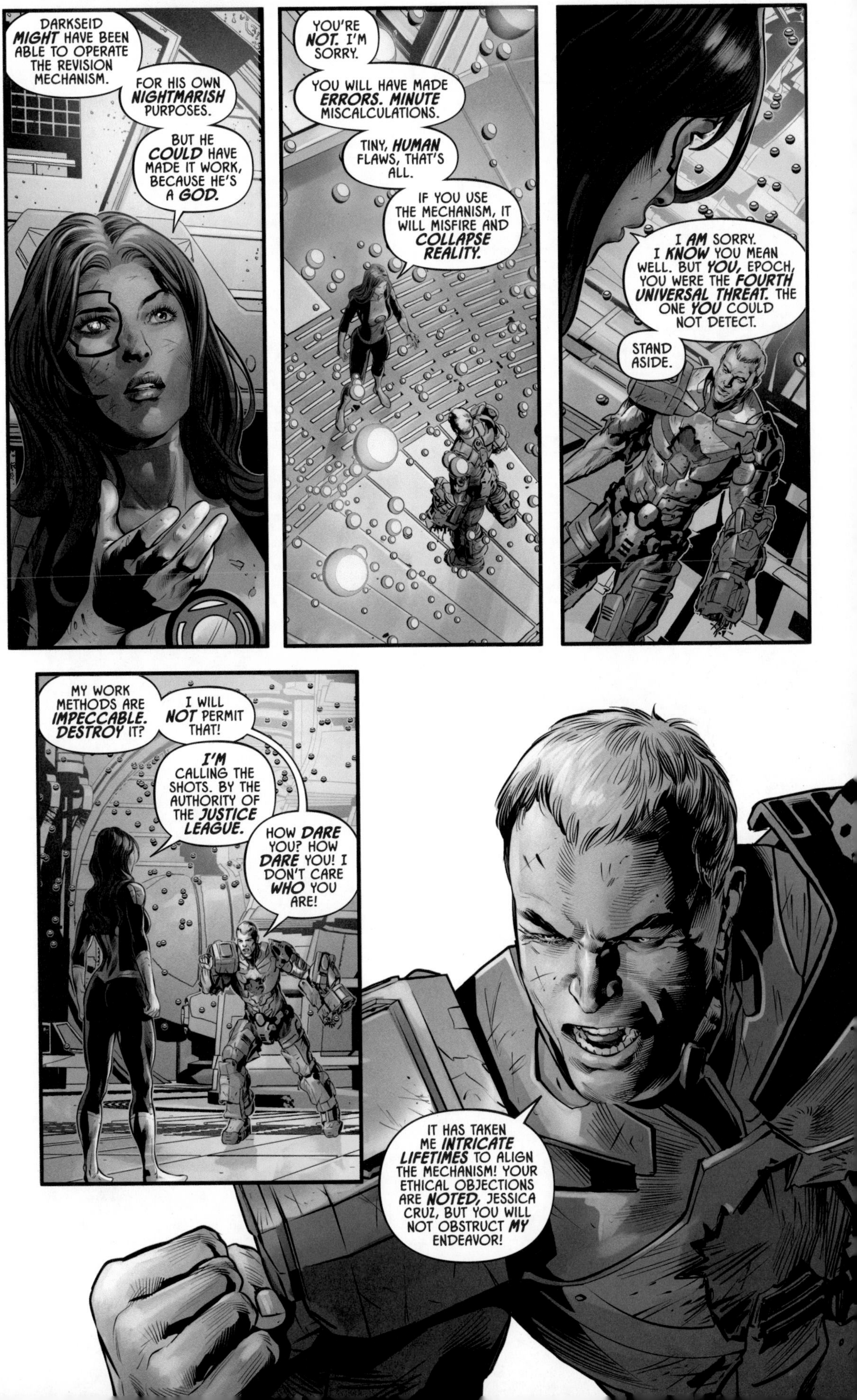
DARKSEID MIGHT HAVE BEEN ABLE TO OPERATE THE REVISION MECHANISM.
FOR HIS OWN NIGHTMARISH PURPOSES.
BUT HE COULD HAVE MADE IT WORK, BECAUSE HE'S A GOD.
YOU'RE NOT. I'M SORRY.
YOU WILL HAVE MADE ERRORS. MINUTE MISCALCULATIONS.
TINY, HUMAN FLAWS, THAT'S ALL.
IF YOU USE THE MECHANISM, IT WILL MISFIRE AND COLLAPSE REALITY.
I AM SORRY. I KNOW YOU MEAN WELL. BUT YOU, EPOCH, YOU WERE THE FOURTH UNIVERSAL THREAT. THE ONE YOU COULD NOT DETECT.
STAND ASIDE.
MY WORK METHODS ARE IMPECCABLE. DESTROY IT?
I WILL NOT PERMIT THAT!
I'M CALLING THE SHOTS. BY THE AUTHORITY OF THE JUSTICE LEAGUE.
HOW DARE YOU? HOW DARE YOU! I DON'T CARE WHO YOU ARE!
IT HAS TAKEN ME INTRICATE LIFETIMES TO ALIGN THE MECHANISM! YOUR ETHICAL OBJECTIONS ARE NOTED, JESSICA CRUZ, BUT YOU WILL NOT OBSTRUCT MY ENDEAVOR!

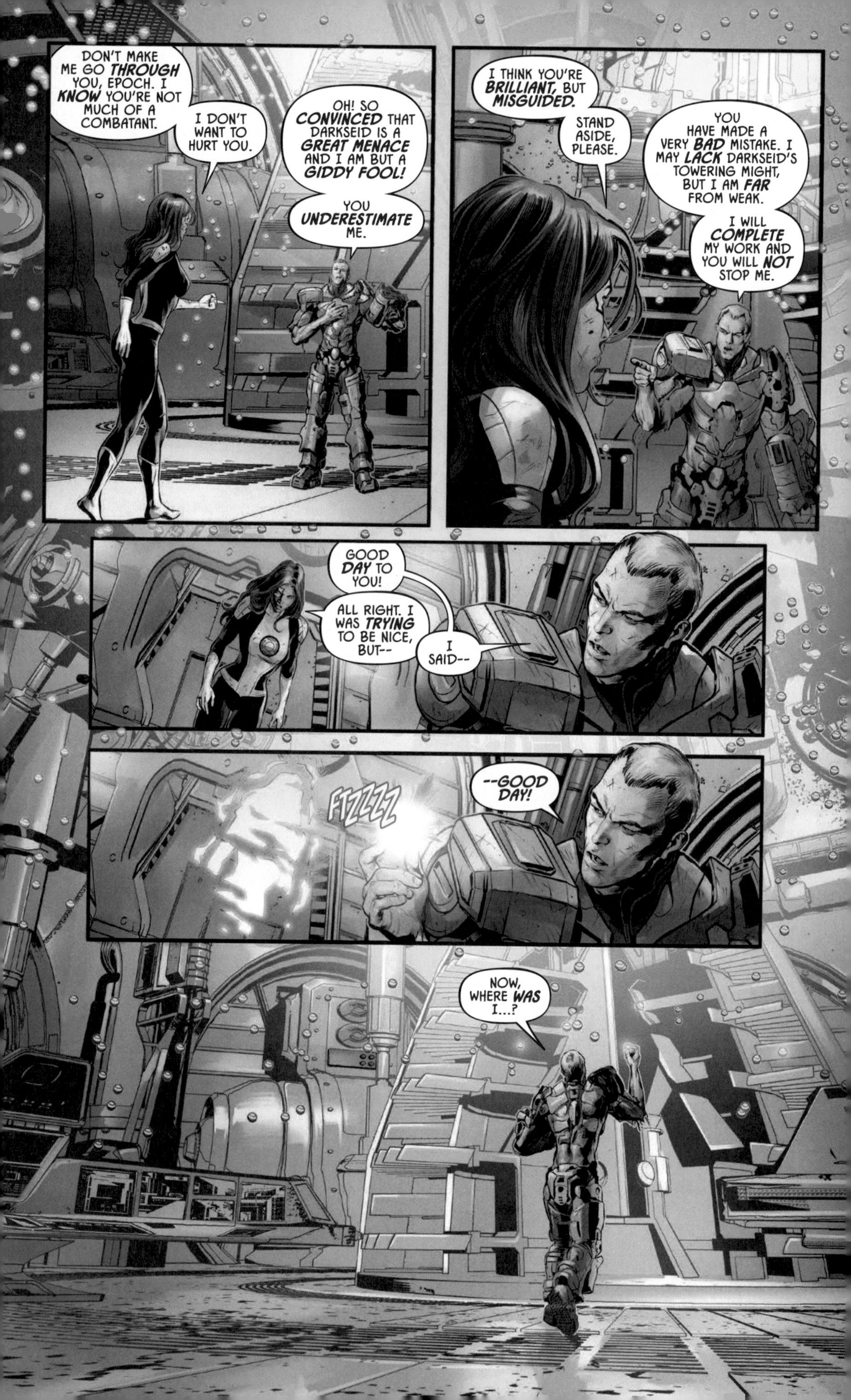
DON'T MAKE ME GO THROUGH YOU, EPOCH. I KNOW YOU'RE NOT MUCH OF A COMBATANT.
I DON'T WANT TO HURT YOU.
OH! SO CONVINCED THAT DARKSEID IS A GREAT MENACE AND I AM BUT A GIDDY FOOL!
YOU UNDERESTIMATE ME.
I THINK YOU'RE BRILLIANT, BUT MISGUIDED.
STAND ASIDE, PLEASE.
YOU HAVE MADE A VERY BAD MISTAKE. I MAY LACK DARKSEID'S TOWERING MIGHT, BUT I AM FAR FROM WEAK.
I WILL COMPLETE MY WORK AND YOU WILL NOT STOP ME.
GOOD DAY TO YOU!
ALL RIGHT. I WAS TRYING TO BE NICE, BUT--
I SAID--
FTZZZZ
--GOOD DAY!
NOW, WHERE WAS I...?

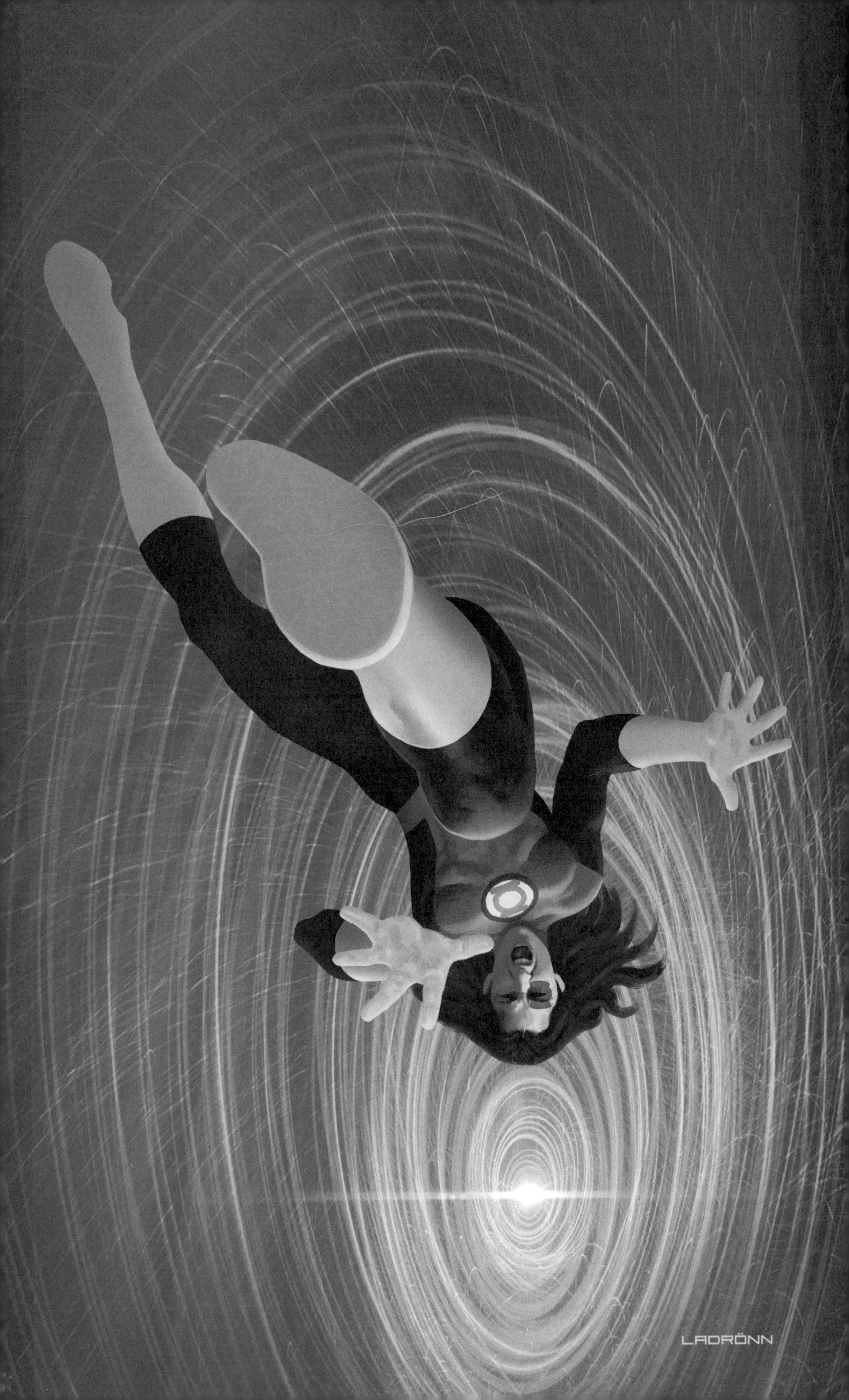
LADRÖNN

Justice League Odyssey **#22** variant cover by **SKAN**

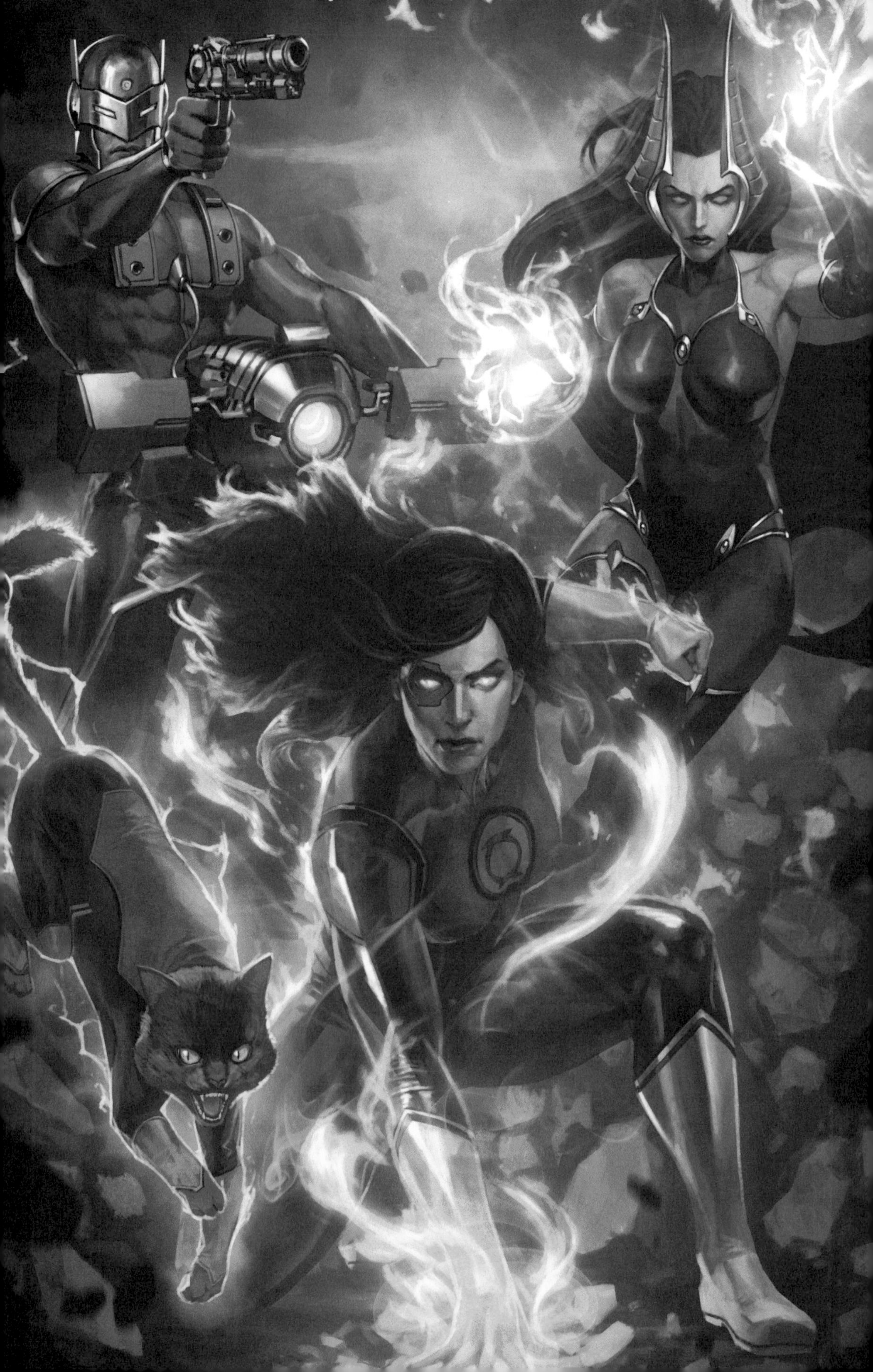

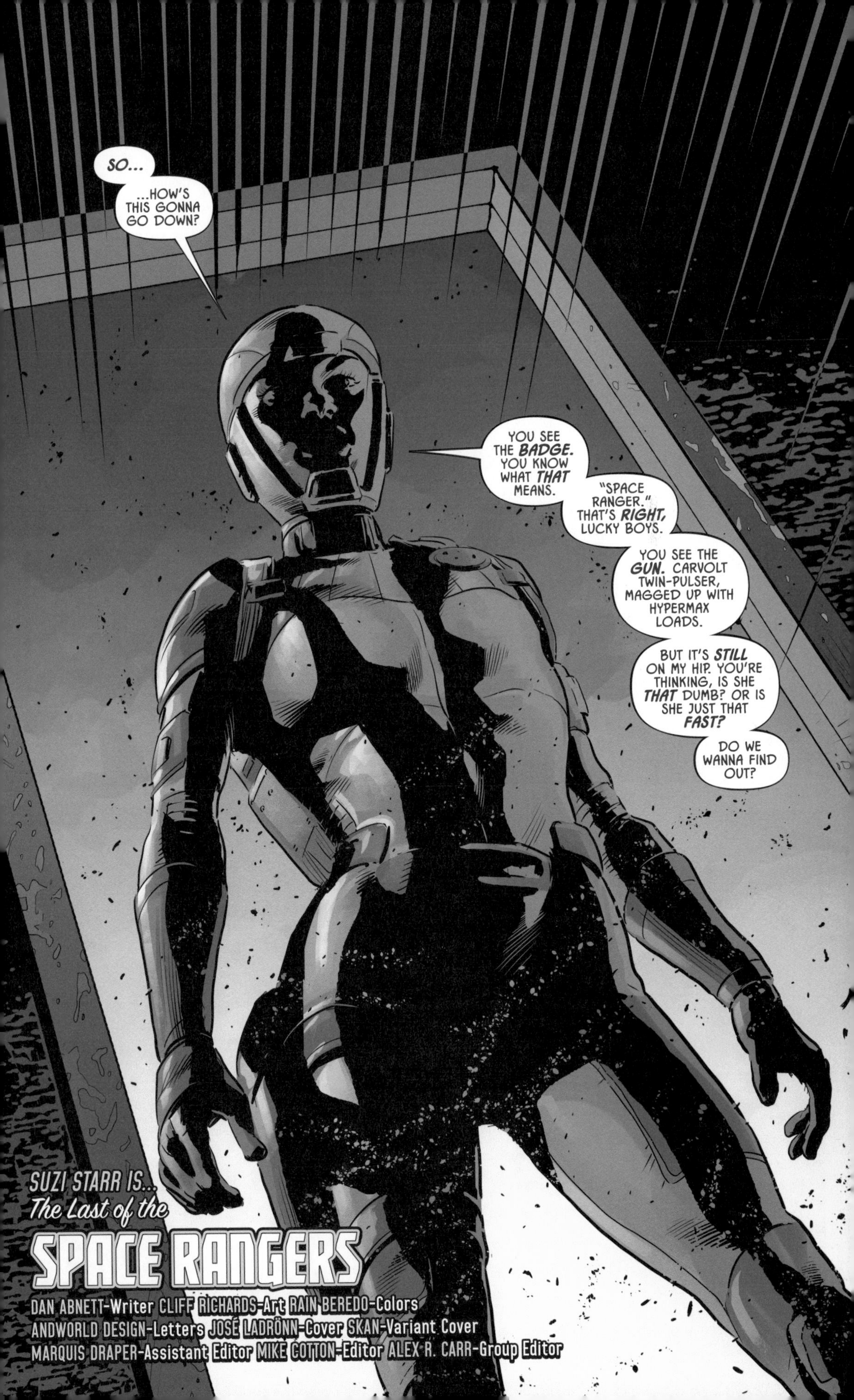
SO...
...HOW'S THIS GONNA GO DOWN?
YOU SEE THE BADGE. YOU KNOW WHAT THAT MEANS.
"SPACE RANGER." THAT'S RIGHT, LUCKY BOYS.
YOU SEE THE GUN. CARVOLT TWIN-PULSER, MAGGED UP WITH HYPERMAX LOADS.
BUT IT'S STILL ON MY HIP. YOU'RE THINKING, IS SHE THAT DUMB? OR IS SHE JUST THAT FAST?
DO WE WANNA FIND OUT?
SUZI STARR IS...
The Last of the
SPACE RANGERS
DAN ABNETT-Writer CLIFF RICHARDS-Art RAIN BEREDO-Colors
ANDWORLD DESIGN-Letters JOSÉ LADRÖNN-Cover SKAN-Variant Cover
MARQUIS DRAPER-Assistant Editor MIKE COTTON-Editor ALEX R. CARR-Group Editor

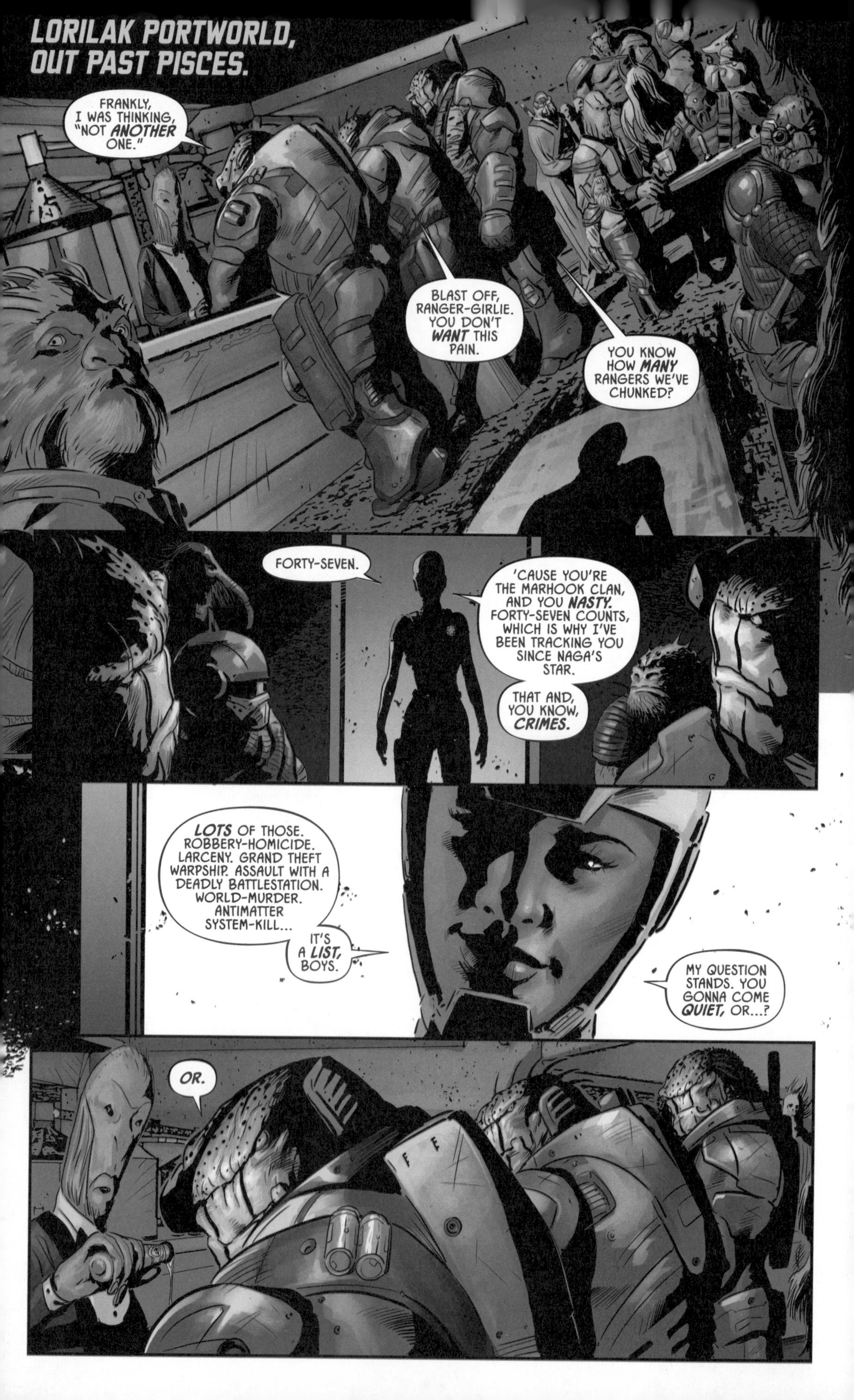
LORILAK PORTWORLD, OUT PAST PISCES.
FRANKLY, I WAS THINKING, "NOT ANOTHER ONE."
BLAST OFF, RANGER-GIRLIE. YOU DON'T WANT THIS PAIN.
YOU KNOW HOW MANY RANGERS WE'VE CHUNKED?
FORTY-SEVEN.
'CAUSE YOU'RE THE MARHOOK CLAN, AND YOU NASTY. FORTY-SEVEN COUNTS, WHICH IS WHY I'VE BEEN TRACKING YOU SINCE NAGA'S STAR.
THAT AND, YOU KNOW, CRIMES.
LOTS OF THOSE. ROBBERY-HOMICIDE. LARCENY. GRAND THEFT WARPSHIP. ASSAULT WITH A DEADLY BATTLESTATION. WORLD-MURDER. ANTIMATTER SYSTEM-KILL...
IT'S A LIST, BOYS.
MY QUESTION STANDS. YOU GONNA COME QUIET, OR...?
OR.

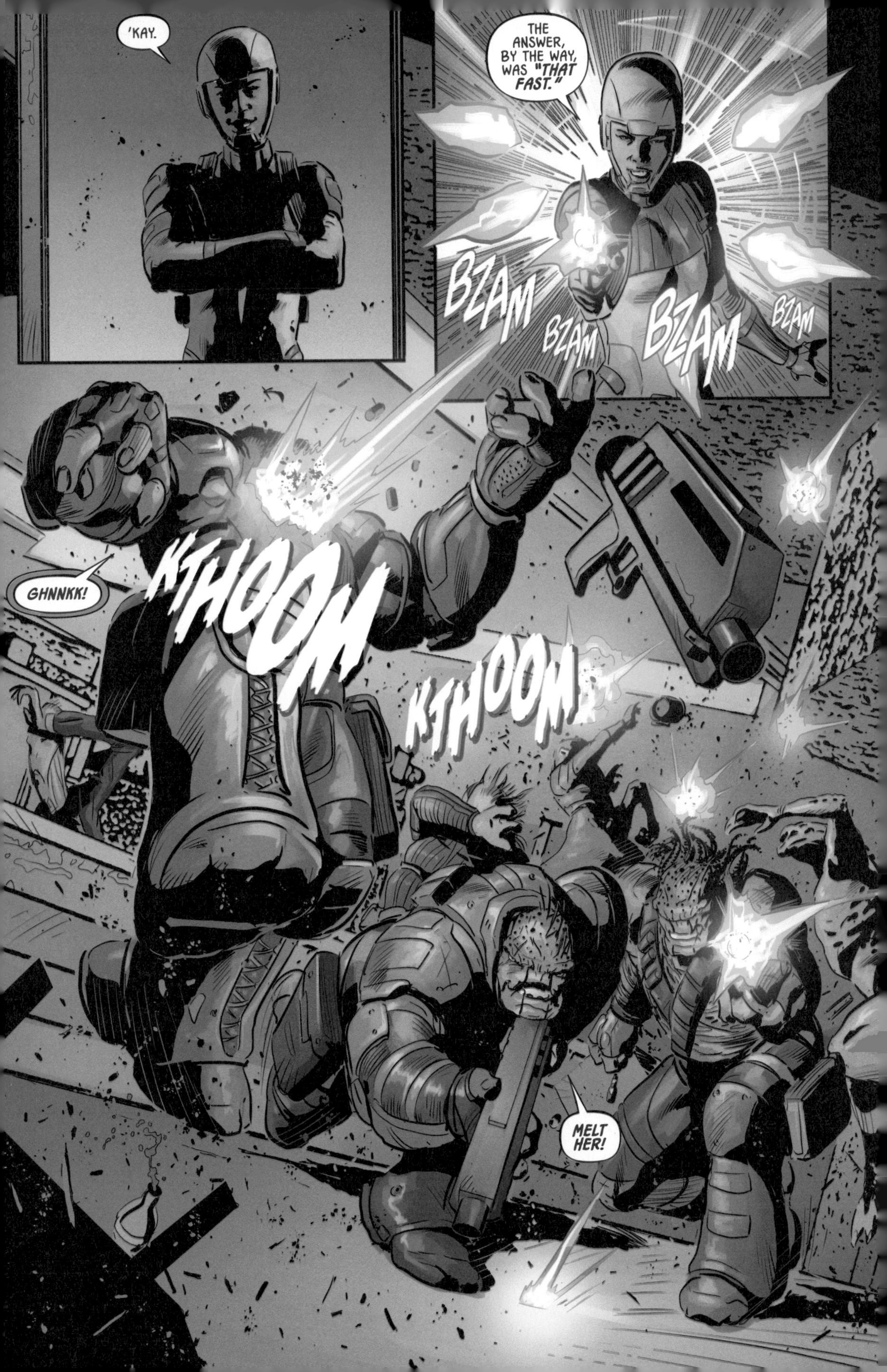
'KAY.
THE ANSWER, BY THE WAY, WAS "THAT FAST."
BZAM
BZAM
BZAM
BZAM
GHNNKK!
KTHOOM
KTHOOM
MELT HER!

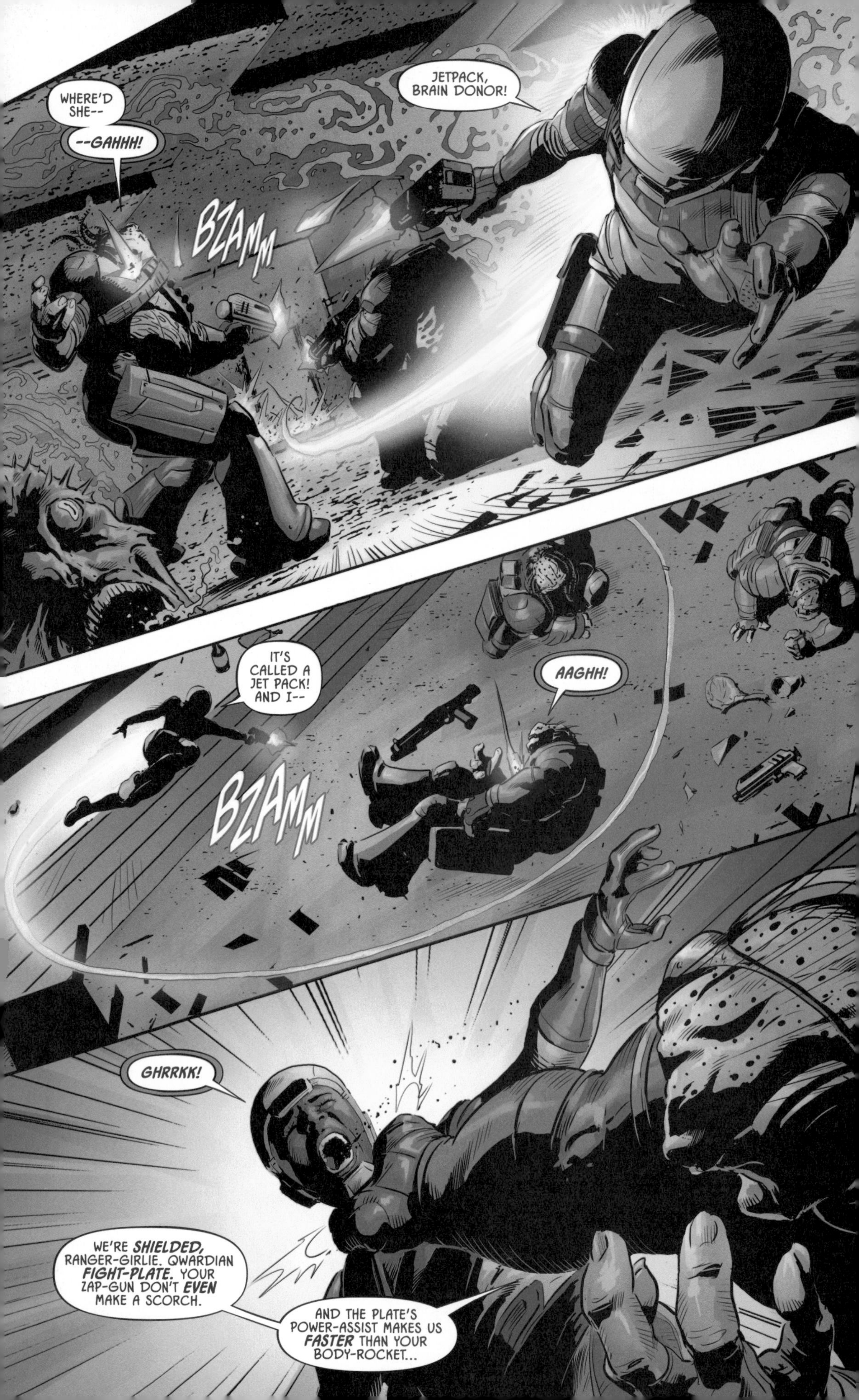

WHERE'D SHE--
--GAHHH!
JETPACK, BRAIN DONOR!
BZAMM
IT'S CALLED A JET PACK! AND I--
AAGHH!
BZAMM
GHRRKK!
WE'RE SHIELDED, RANGER-GIRLIE. QWARDIAN FIGHT-PLATE. YOUR ZAP-GUN DON'T EVEN MAKE A SCORCH.
AND THE PLATE'S POWER-ASSIST MAKES US FASTER THAN YOUR BODY-ROCKET...

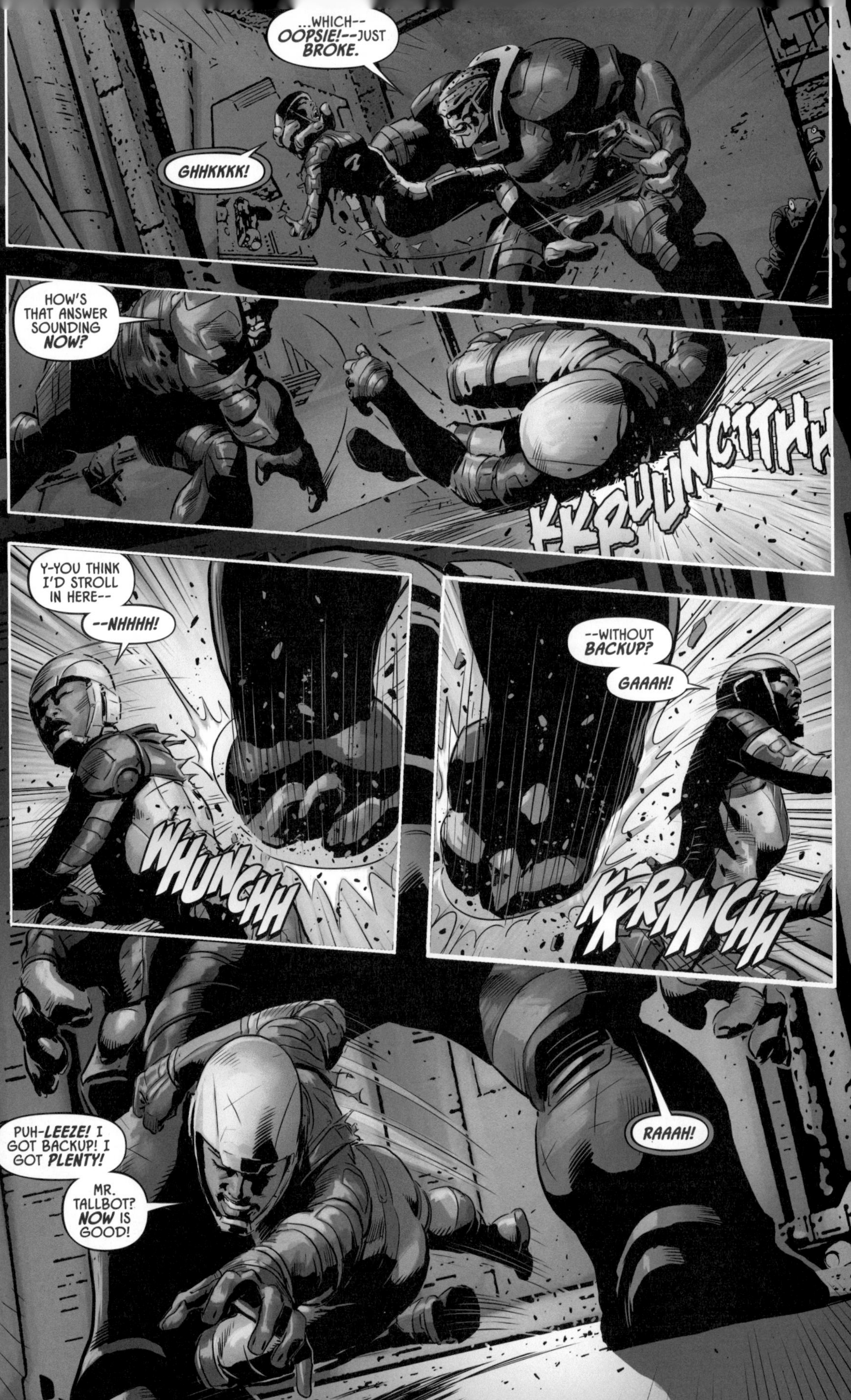

...WHICH-- OOPSIE!--JUST BROKE.
GHHKKKK!
HOW'S THAT ANSWER SOUNDING NOW?
KKRUUNCTTHH
Y-YOU THINK I'D STROLL IN HERE--
--NHHHH!
WHUNCHH
--WITHOUT BACKUP?
GAAAH!
KKRNNCHH
PUH-LEEZE! I GOT BACKUP! I GOT PLENTY!
MR. TALLBOT? NOW IS GOOD!
RAAAH!

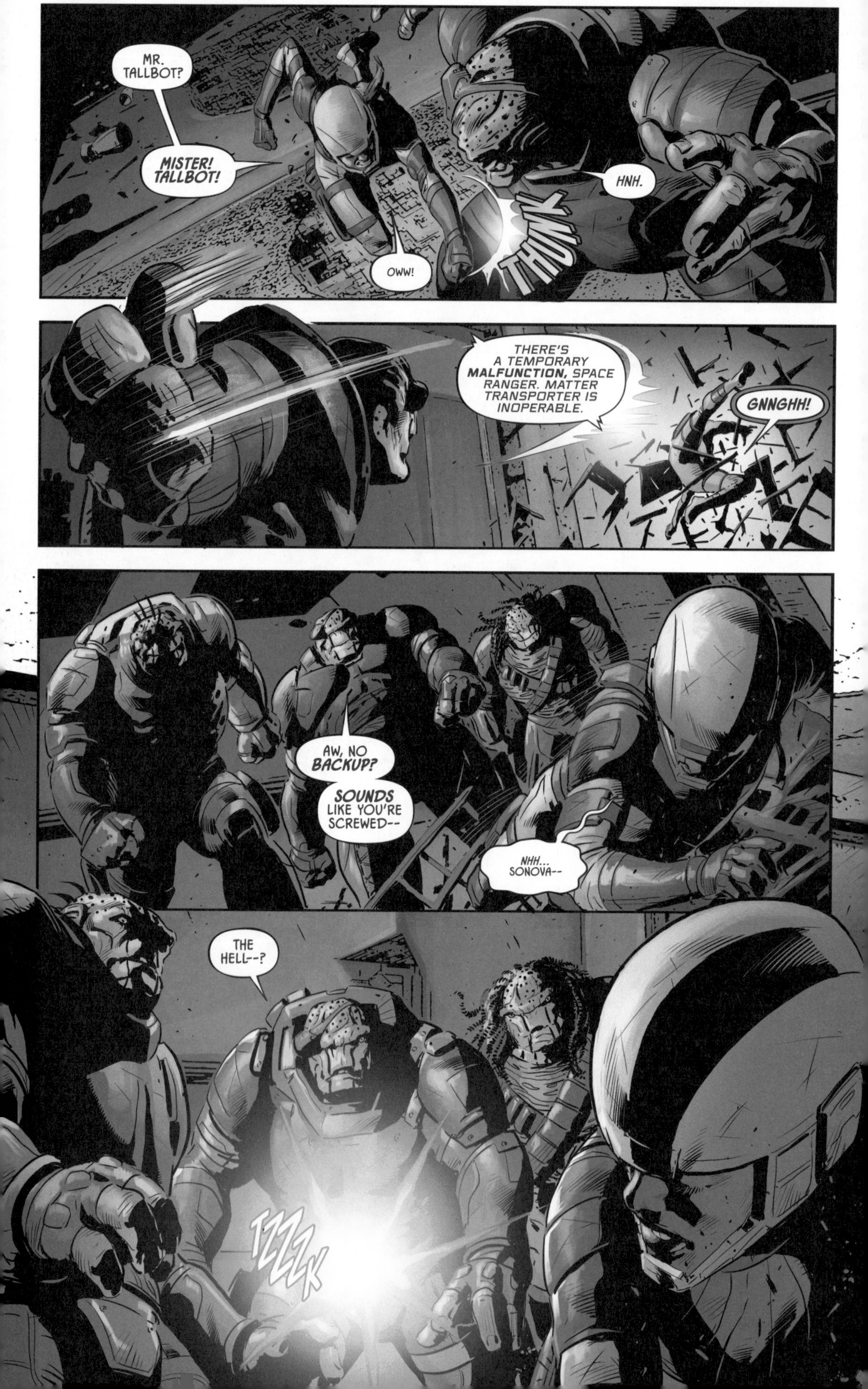

MR. TALLBOT?
MISTER! TALLBOT!
HNH.
THUNK
OWW!
THERE'S A TEMPORARY MALFUNCTION, SPACE RANGER. MATTER TRANSPORTER IS INOPERABLE.
GNNGHH!
AW, NO BACKUP?
SOUNDS LIKE YOU'RE SCREWED--
NHH... SONOVA--
THE HELL--?
TZZZK

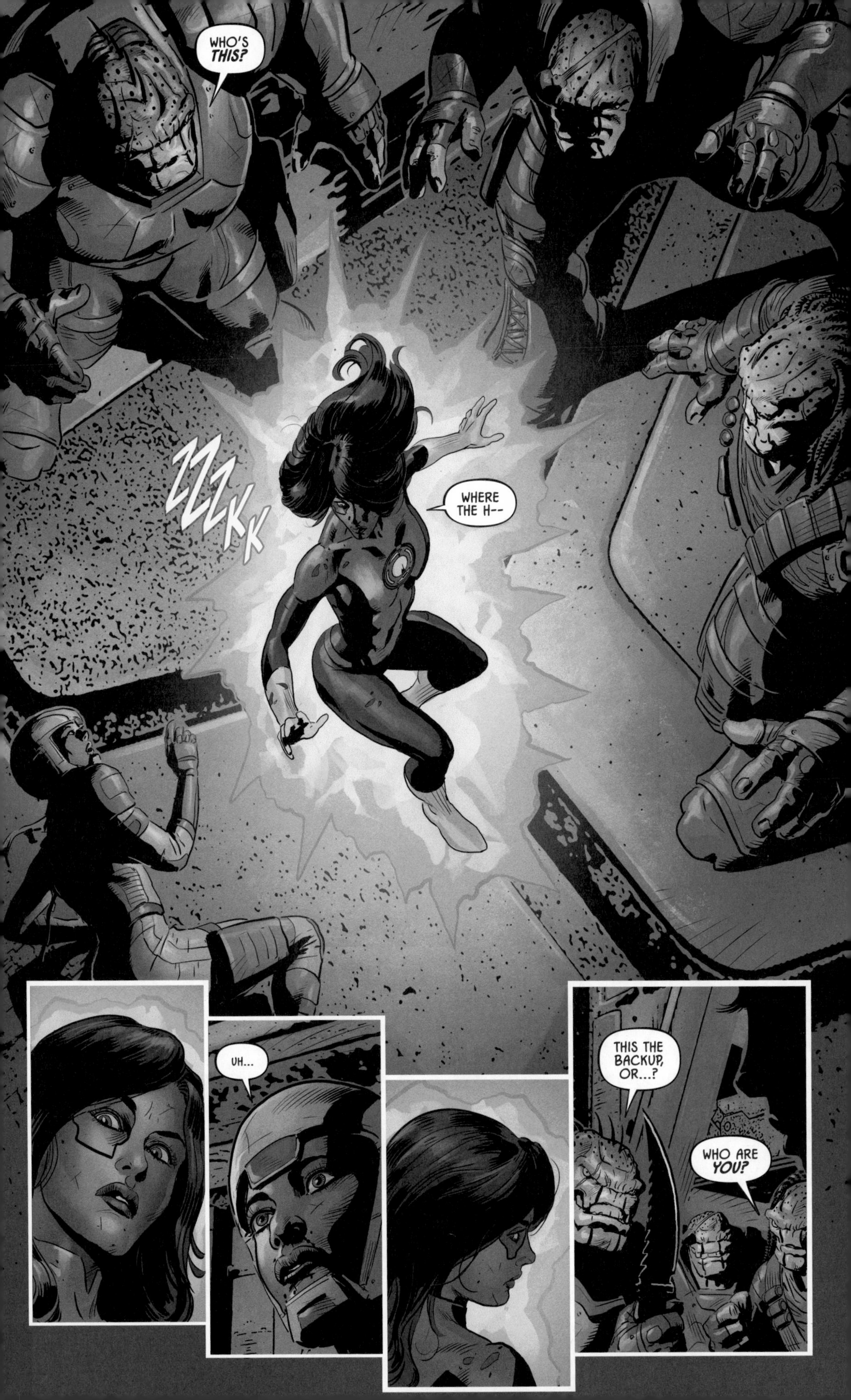
WHO'S *THIS?*
ZZZKK
WHERE THE H--
UH...
THIS THE BACKUP, OR...?
WHO ARE *YOU?*

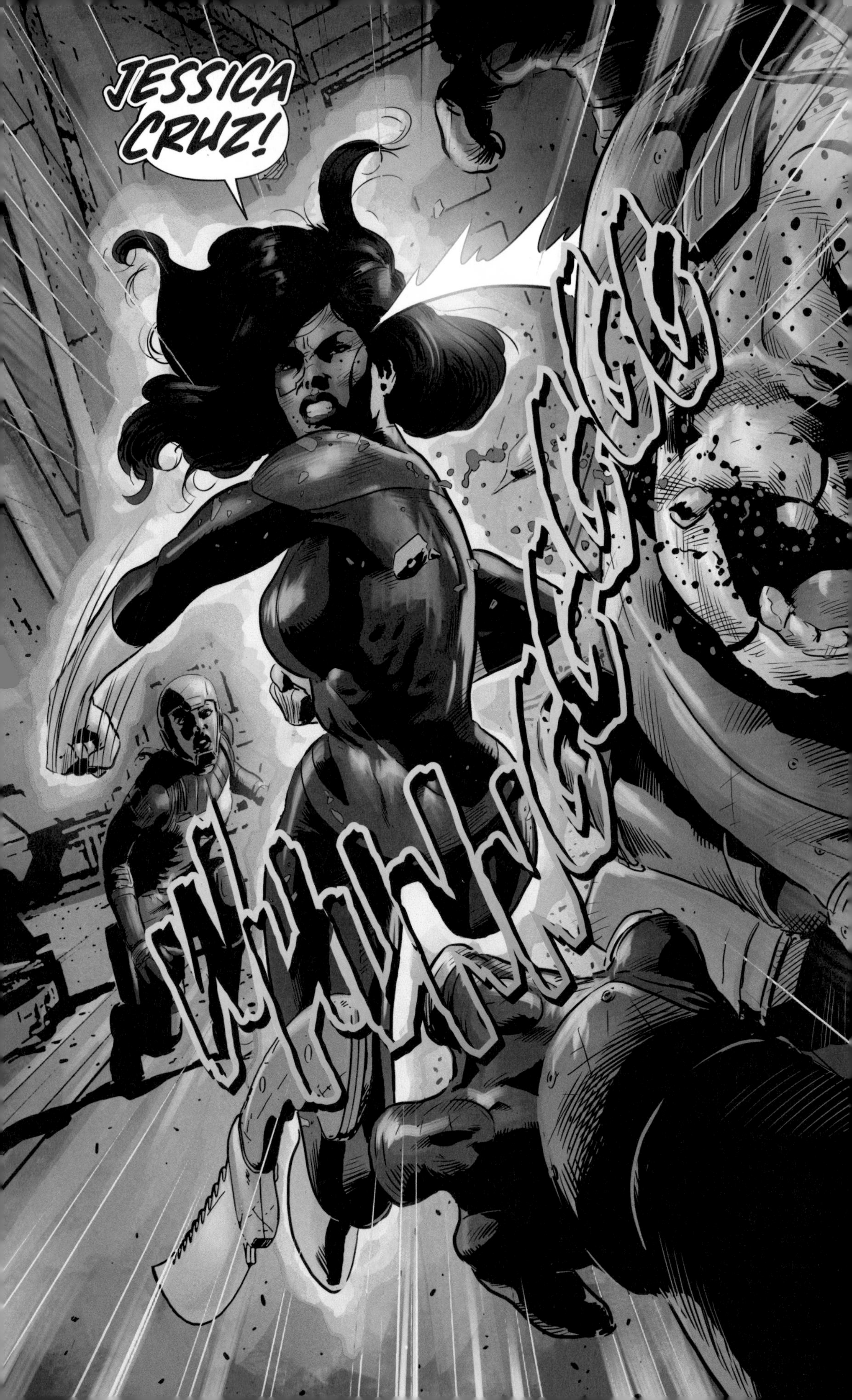
JESSICA CRUZ!

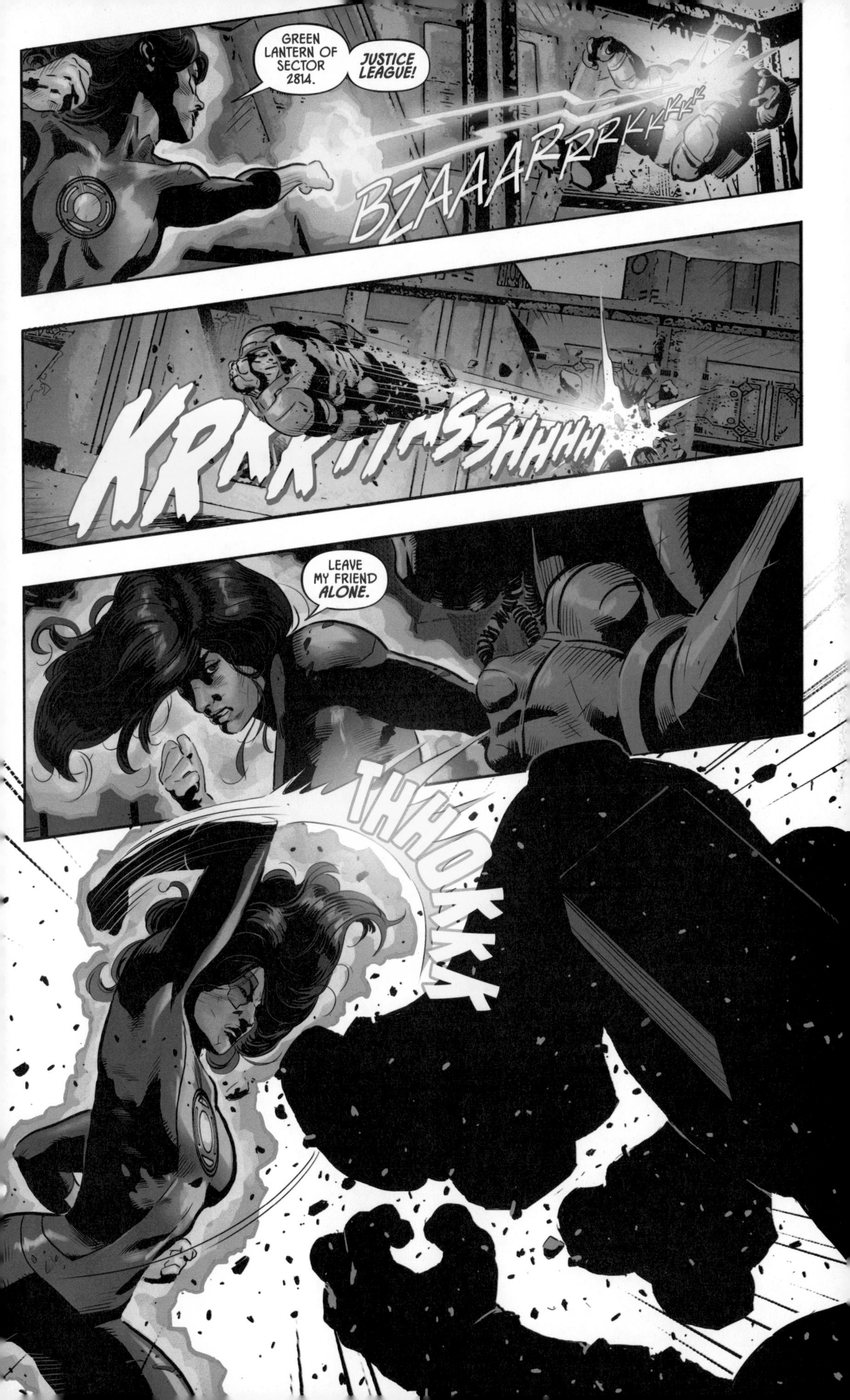
GREEN LANTERN OF SECTOR 2814.
JUSTICE LEAGUE!
BZAAARRRKKKK
KRAKKTHSSHHHH
LEAVE MY FRIEND ALONE.
THHOKKK

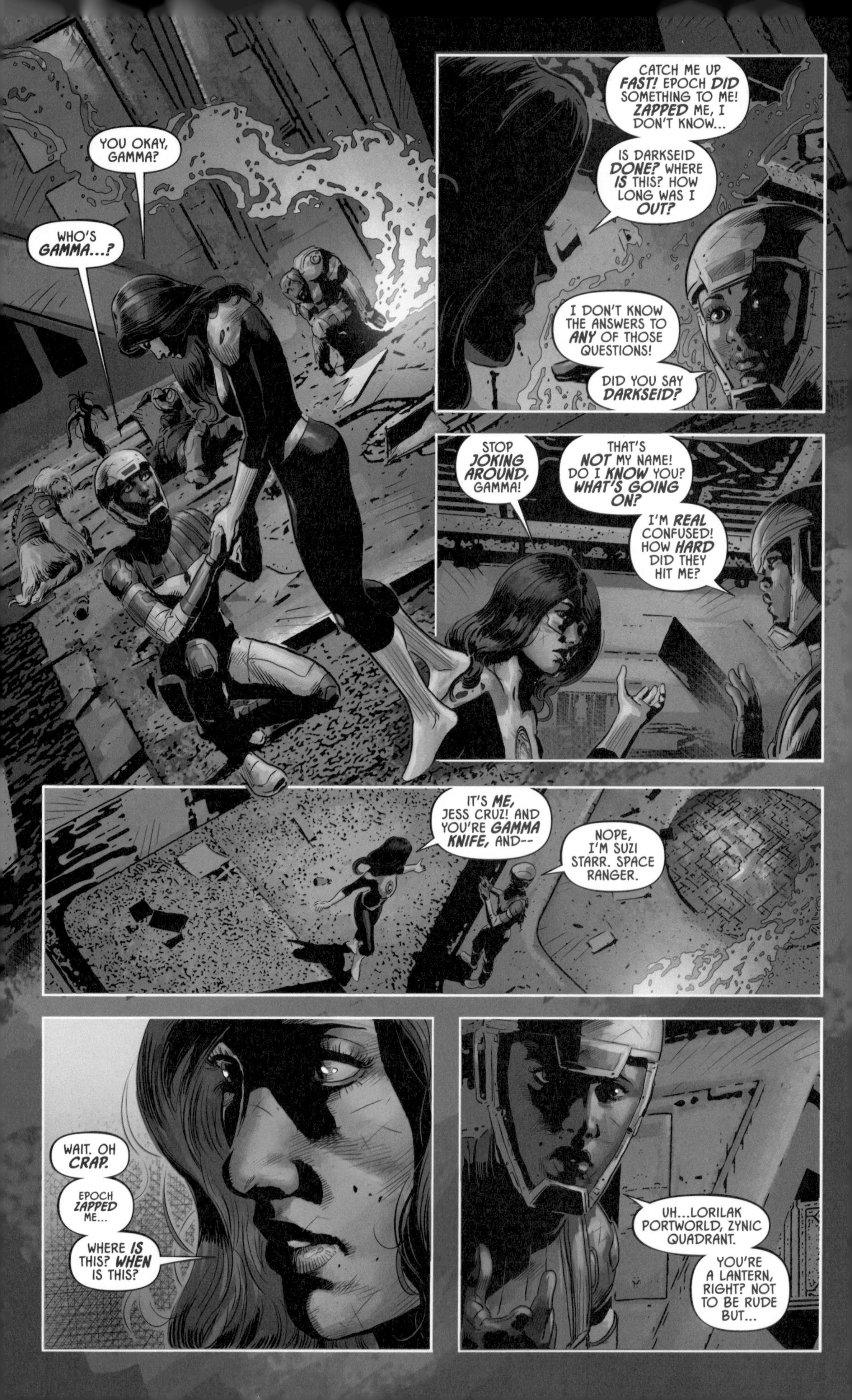
YOU OKAY, GAMMA?
WHO'S GAMMA...?
CATCH ME UP FAST! EPOCH DID SOMETHING TO ME! ZAPPED ME, I DON'T KNOW...
IS DARKSEID DONE? WHERE IS THIS? HOW LONG WAS I OUT?
I DON'T KNOW THE ANSWERS TO ANY OF THOSE QUESTIONS!
DID YOU SAY DARKSEID?
STOP JOKING AROUND, GAMMA!
THAT'S NOT MY NAME! DO I KNOW YOU? WHAT'S GOING ON?
I'M REAL CONFUSED! HOW HARD DID THEY HIT ME?
IT'S ME, JESS CRUZ! AND YOU'RE GAMMA KNIFE, AND--
NOPE, I'M SUZI STARR. SPACE RANGER.
WAIT. OH CRAP.
EPOCH ZAPPED ME...
WHERE IS THIS? WHEN IS THIS?
UH...LORILAK PORTWORLD, ZYNIC QUADRANT.
YOU'RE A LANTERN, RIGHT? NOT TO BE RUDE BUT...

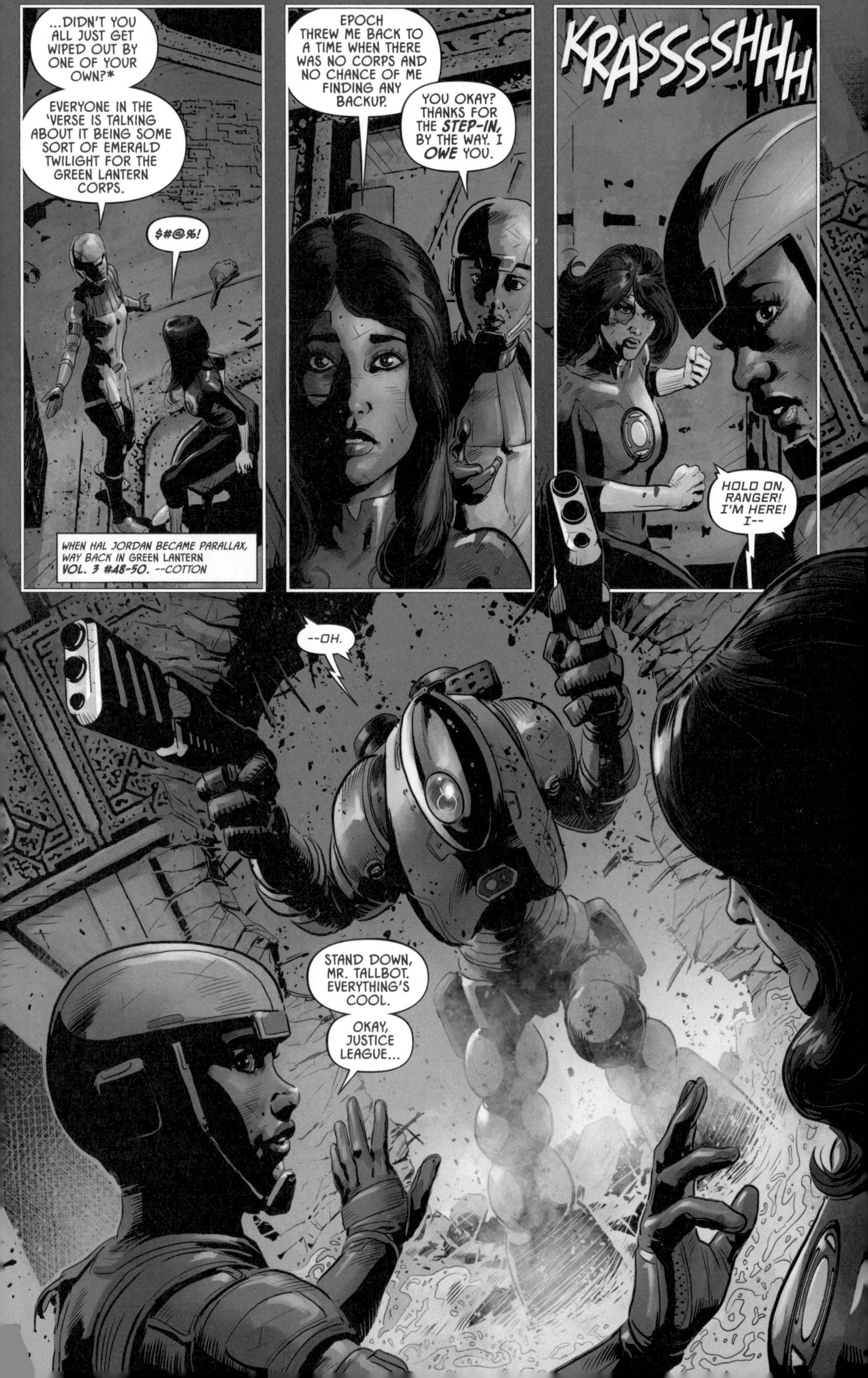
...DIDN'T YOU ALL JUST GET WIPED OUT BY ONE OF YOUR OWN?*
EVERYONE IN THE 'VERSE IS TALKING ABOUT IT BEING SOME SORT OF EMERALD TWILIGHT FOR THE GREEN LANTERN CORPS.
$#@%!
*WHEN HAL JORDAN BECAME PARALLAX, WAY BACK IN GREEN LANTERN VOL. 3 #48-50. --COTTON
EPOCH THREW ME BACK TO A TIME WHEN THERE WAS NO CORPS AND NO CHANCE OF ME FINDING ANY BACKUP.
YOU OKAY? THANKS FOR THE STEP-IN, BY THE WAY. I OWE YOU.
KRASSSSHHH
HOLD ON, RANGER! I'M HERE! I--
--OH.
STAND DOWN, MR. TALLBOT. EVERYTHING'S COOL.
OKAY, JUSTICE LEAGUE...

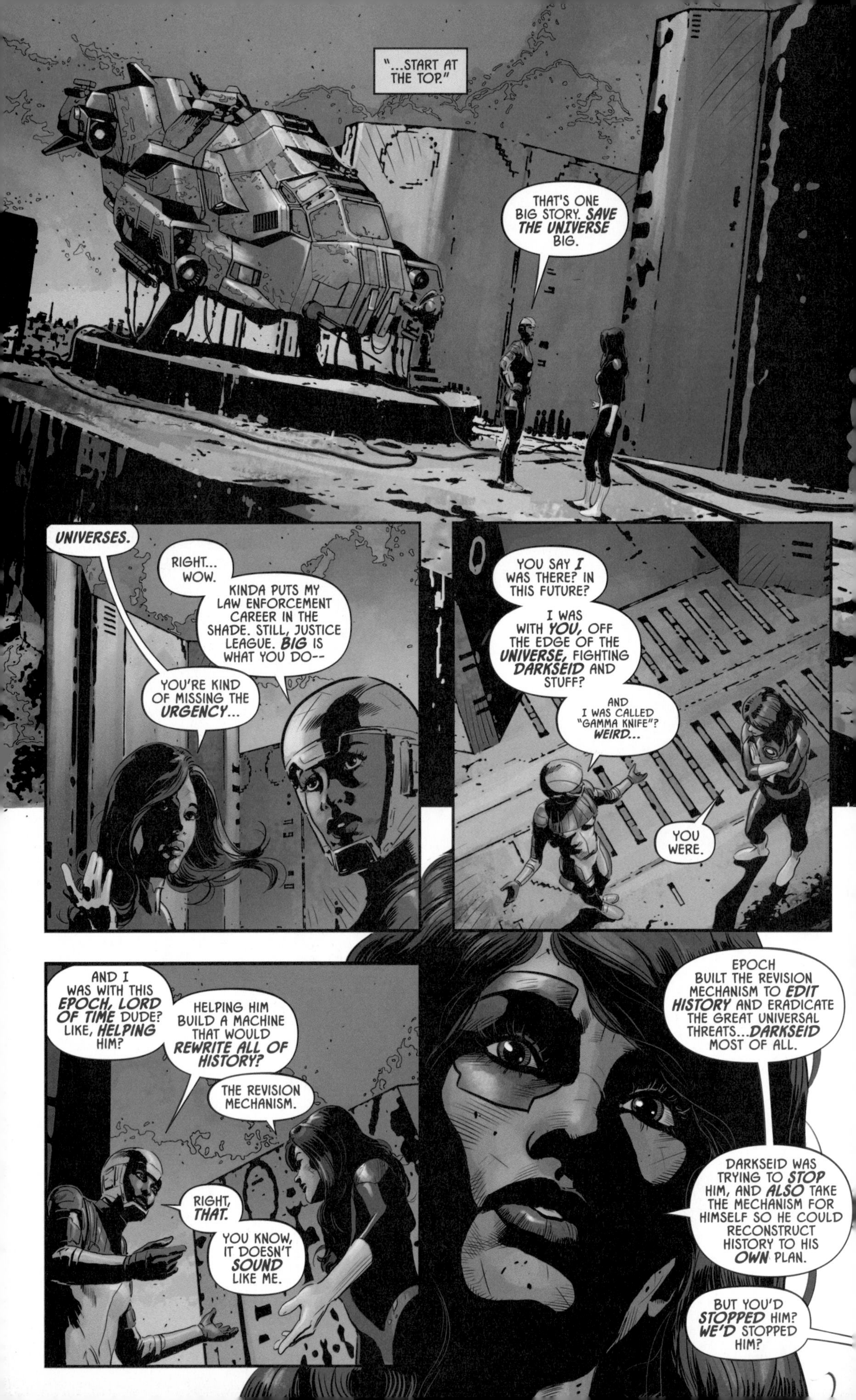
"...START AT THE TOP."
THAT'S ONE BIG STORY. SAVE THE UNIVERSE BIG.
UNIVERSES.
RIGHT... WOW.
KINDA PUTS MY LAW ENFORCEMENT CAREER IN THE SHADE. STILL, JUSTICE LEAGUE. BIG IS WHAT YOU DO--
YOU'RE KIND OF MISSING THE URGENCY...
YOU SAY I WAS THERE? IN THIS FUTURE?
I WAS WITH YOU, OFF THE EDGE OF THE UNIVERSE, FIGHTING DARKSEID AND STUFF?
AND I WAS CALLED "GAMMA KNIFE"? WEIRD...
YOU WERE.
AND I WAS WITH THIS EPOCH, LORD OF TIME DUDE? LIKE, HELPING HIM?
HELPING HIM BUILD A MACHINE THAT WOULD REWRITE ALL OF HISTORY?
THE REVISION MECHANISM.
RIGHT, THAT.
YOU KNOW, IT DOESN'T SOUND LIKE ME.
EPOCH BUILT THE REVISION MECHANISM TO EDIT HISTORY AND ERADICATE THE GREAT UNIVERSAL THREATS...DARKSEID MOST OF ALL.
DARKSEID WAS TRYING TO STOP HIM, AND ALSO TAKE THE MECHANISM FOR HIMSELF SO HE COULD RECONSTRUCT HISTORY TO HIS OWN PLAN.
BUT YOU'D STOPPED HIM? WE'D STOPPED HIM?

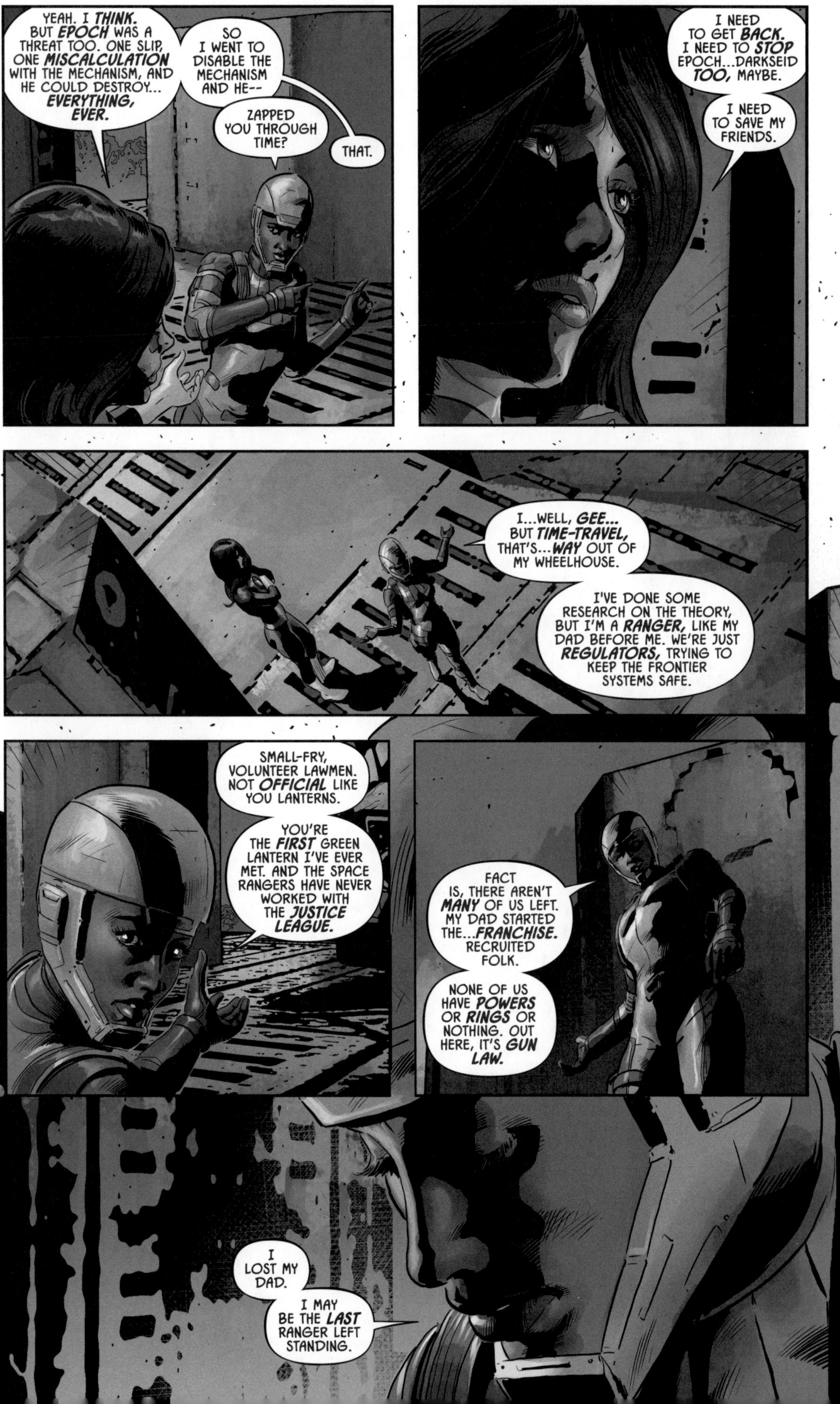
YEAH. I THINK. BUT EPOCH WAS A THREAT TOO. ONE SLIP, ONE MISCALCULATION WITH THE MECHANISM, AND HE COULD DESTROY... EVERYTHING, EVER.
SO I WENT TO DISABLE THE MECHANISM AND HE--
ZAPPED YOU THROUGH TIME?
THAT.
I NEED TO GET BACK. I NEED TO STOP EPOCH...DARKSEID TOO, MAYBE.
I NEED TO SAVE MY FRIENDS.
I...WELL, GEE... BUT TIME-TRAVEL, THAT'S...WAY OUT OF MY WHEELHOUSE.
I'VE DONE SOME RESEARCH ON THE THEORY, BUT I'M A RANGER, LIKE MY DAD BEFORE ME. WE'RE JUST REGULATORS, TRYING TO KEEP THE FRONTIER SYSTEMS SAFE.
SMALL-FRY, VOLUNTEER LAWMEN. NOT OFFICIAL LIKE YOU LANTERNS.
YOU'RE THE FIRST GREEN LANTERN I'VE EVER MET. AND THE SPACE RANGERS HAVE NEVER WORKED WITH THE JUSTICE LEAGUE.
FACT IS, THERE AREN'T MANY OF US LEFT. MY DAD STARTED THE...FRANCHISE. RECRUITED FOLK.
NONE OF US HAVE POWERS OR RINGS OR NOTHING. OUT HERE, IT'S GUN LAW.
I LOST MY DAD.
I MAY BE THE LAST RANGER LEFT STANDING.

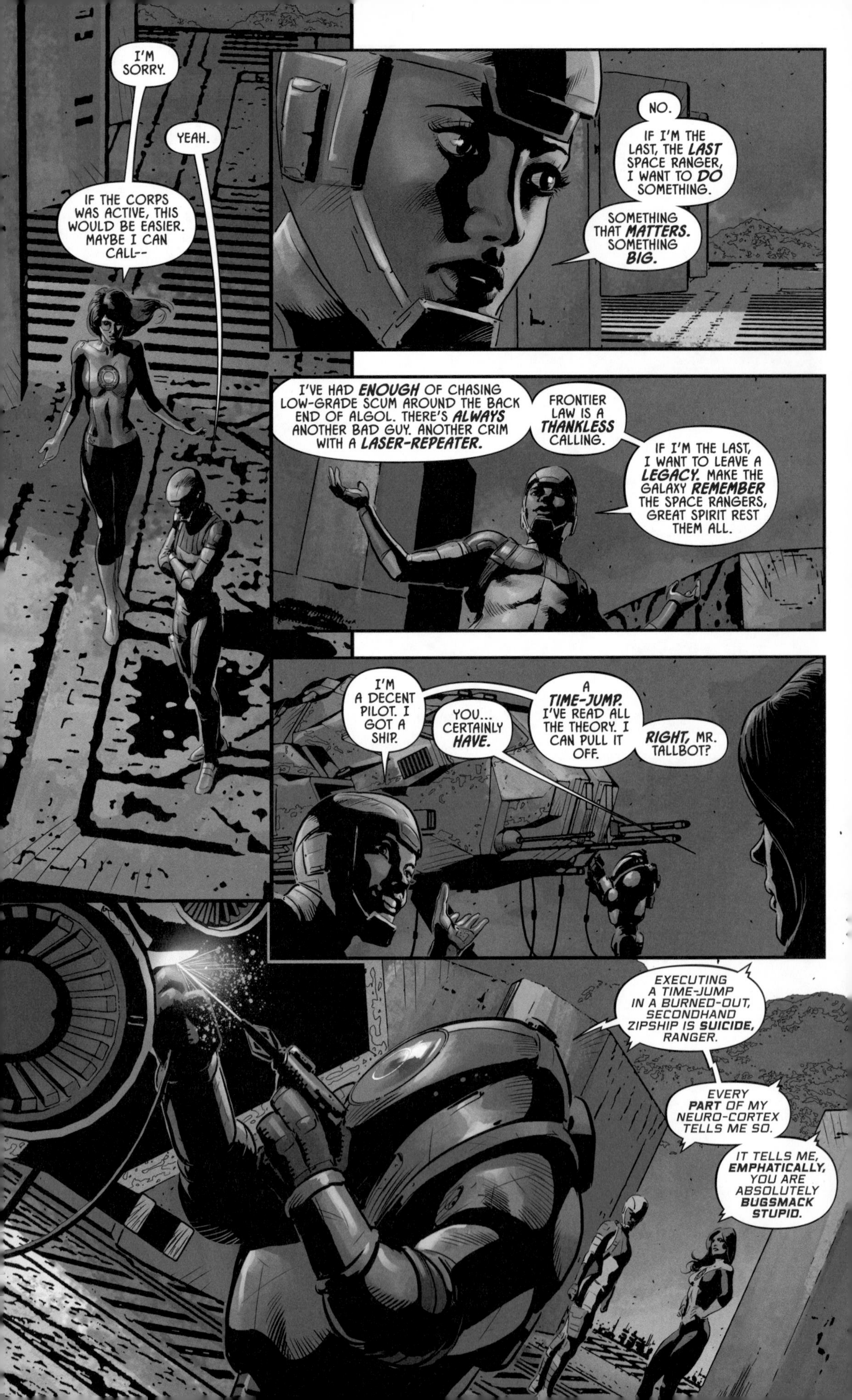
I'M SORRY.
YEAH.
IF THE CORPS WAS ACTIVE, THIS WOULD BE EASIER. MAYBE I CAN CALL--
NO.
IF I'M THE LAST, THE LAST SPACE RANGER, I WANT TO DO SOMETHING.
SOMETHING THAT MATTERS. SOMETHING BIG.
I'VE HAD ENOUGH OF CHASING LOW-GRADE SCUM AROUND THE BACK END OF ALGOL. THERE'S ALWAYS ANOTHER BAD GUY. ANOTHER CRIM WITH A LASER-REPEATER.
FRONTIER LAW IS A THANKLESS CALLING.
IF I'M THE LAST, I WANT TO LEAVE A LEGACY. MAKE THE GALAXY REMEMBER THE SPACE RANGERS, GREAT SPIRIT REST THEM ALL.
I'M A DECENT PILOT. I GOT A SHIP.
YOU... CERTAINLY HAVE.
A TIME-JUMP. I'VE READ ALL THE THEORY. I CAN PULL IT OFF.
RIGHT, MR. TALLBOT?
EXECUTING A TIME-JUMP IN A BURNED-OUT, SECONDHAND ZIPSHIP IS SUICIDE, RANGER.
EVERY PART OF MY NEURO-CORTEX TELLS ME SO.
IT TELLS ME, EMPHATICALLY, YOU ARE ABSOLUTELY BUGSMACK STUPID.

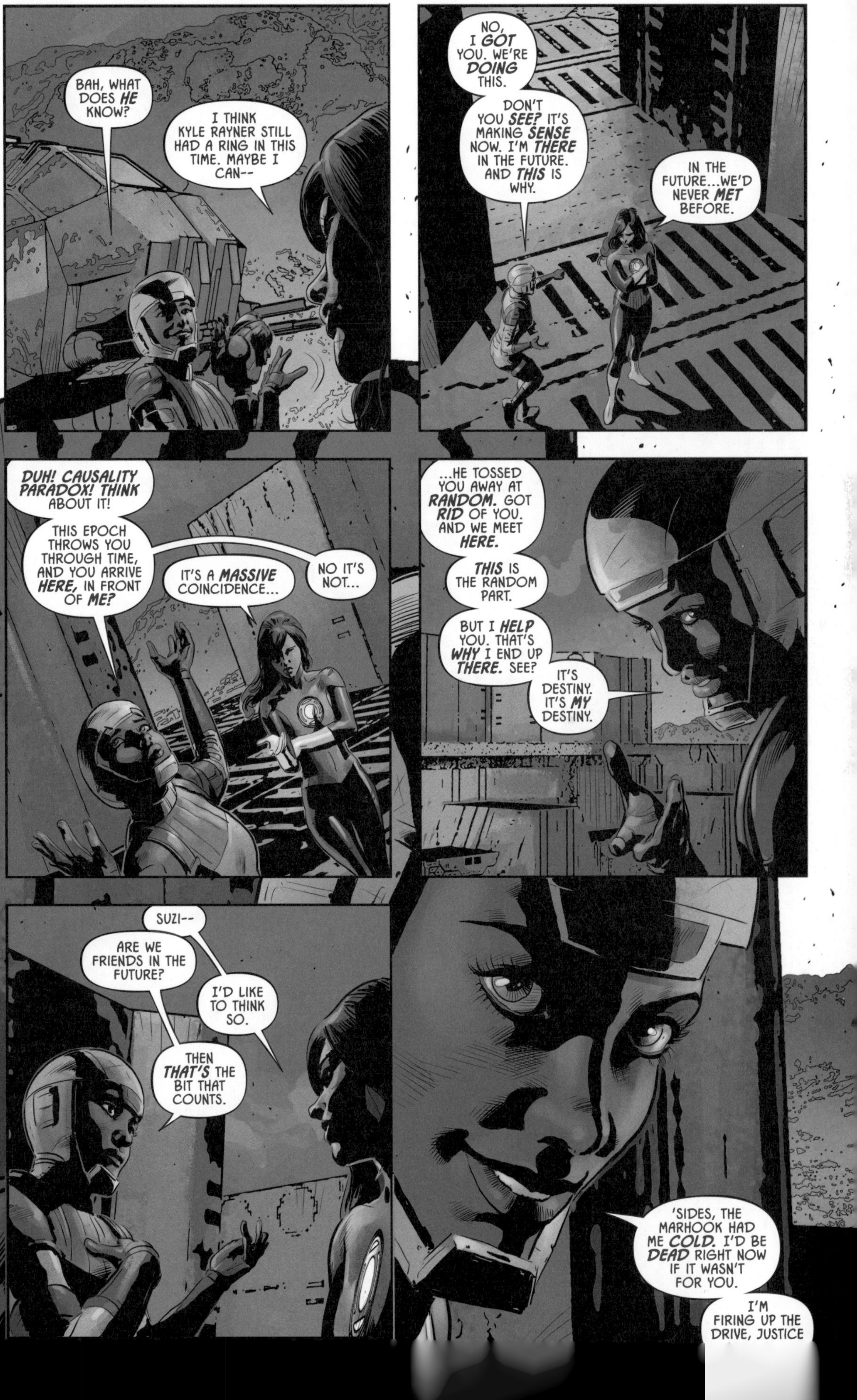
BAH, WHAT DOES HE KNOW?
I THINK KYLE RAYNER STILL HAD A RING IN THIS TIME. MAYBE I CAN--
NO, I GOT YOU. WE'RE DOING THIS.
DON'T YOU SEE? IT'S MAKING SENSE NOW. I'M THERE IN THE FUTURE. AND THIS IS WHY.
IN THE FUTURE...WE'D NEVER MET BEFORE.
DUH! CAUSALITY PARADOX! THINK ABOUT IT!
THIS EPOCH THROWS YOU THROUGH TIME, AND YOU ARRIVE HERE, IN FRONT OF ME?
IT'S A MASSIVE COINCIDENCE...
NO IT'S NOT...
...HE TOSSED YOU AWAY AT RANDOM. GOT RID OF YOU. AND WE MEET HERE.
THIS IS THE RANDOM PART.
BUT I HELP YOU. THAT'S WHY I END UP THERE. SEE?
IT'S DESTINY. IT'S MY DESTINY.
SUZI--
ARE WE FRIENDS IN THE FUTURE?
I'D LIKE TO THINK SO.
THEN THAT'S THE BIT THAT COUNTS.
'SIDES, THE MARHOOK HAD ME COLD. I'D BE DEAD RIGHT NOW IF IT WASN'T FOR YOU.
I'M FIRING UP THE DRIVE, JUSTICE

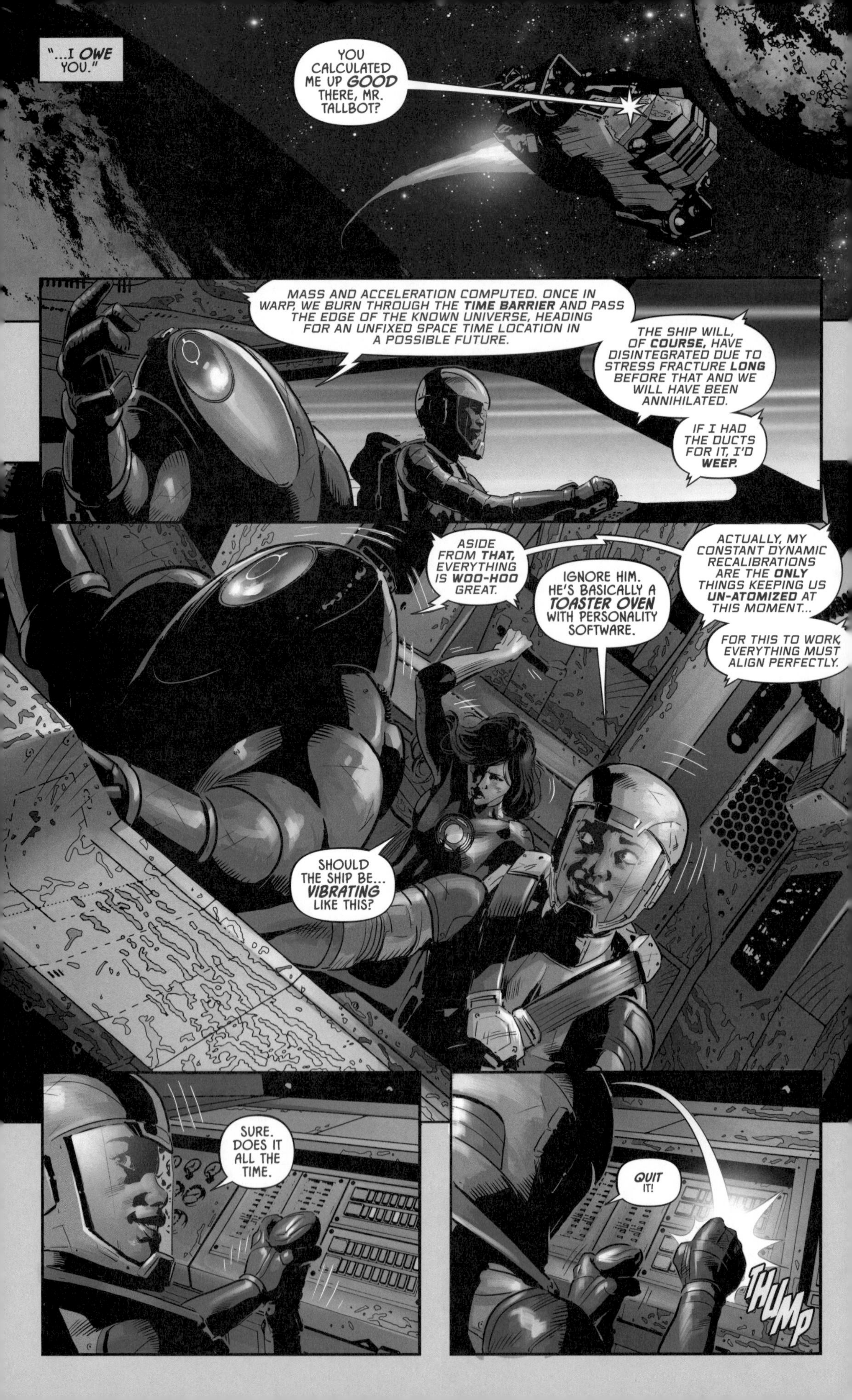
"...I OWE YOU."
YOU CALCULATED ME UP GOOD THERE, MR. TALLBOT?
MASS AND ACCELERATION COMPUTED. ONCE IN WARP, WE BURN THROUGH THE TIME BARRIER AND PASS THE EDGE OF THE KNOWN UNIVERSE, HEADING FOR AN UNFIXED SPACE TIME LOCATION IN A POSSIBLE FUTURE.
THE SHIP WILL, OF COURSE, HAVE DISINTEGRATED DUE TO STRESS FRACTURE LONG BEFORE THAT AND WE WILL HAVE BEEN ANNIHILATED.
IF I HAD THE DUCTS FOR IT, I'D WEEP.
ASIDE FROM THAT, EVERYTHING IS WOO-HOO GREAT.
IGNORE HIM. HE'S BASICALLY A TOASTER OVEN WITH PERSONALITY SOFTWARE.
ACTUALLY, MY CONSTANT DYNAMIC RECALIBRATIONS ARE THE ONLY THINGS KEEPING US UN-ATOMIZED AT THIS MOMENT...
FOR THIS TO WORK, EVERYTHING MUST ALIGN PERFECTLY.
SHOULD THE SHIP BE... VIBRATING LIKE THIS?
SURE. DOES IT ALL THE TIME.
QUIT IT!
THUMP

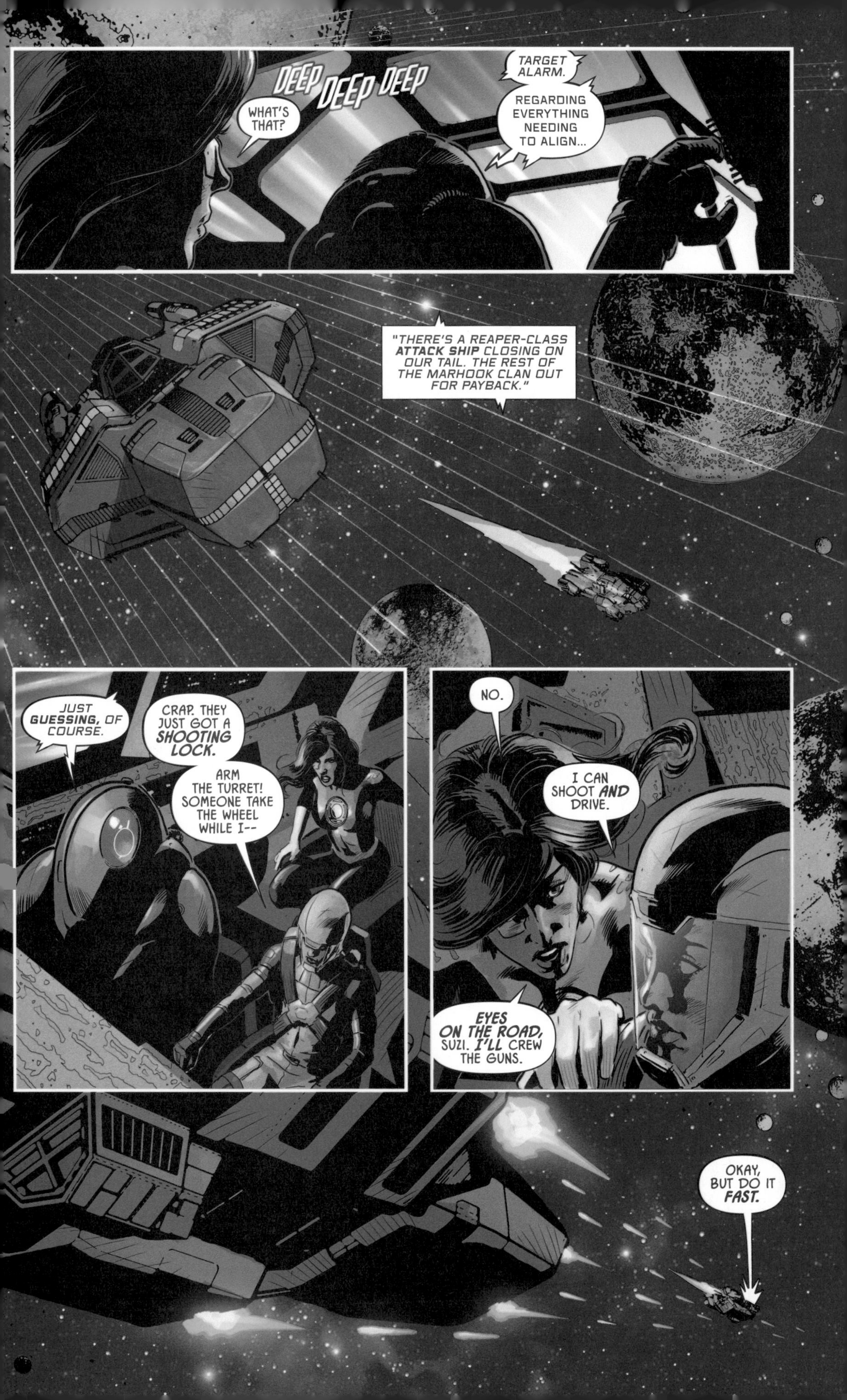
DEEP DEEP DEEP
WHAT'S THAT?
TARGET ALARM.
REGARDING EVERYTHING NEEDING TO ALIGN...
"THERE'S A REAPER-CLASS ATTACK SHIP CLOSING ON OUR TAIL. THE REST OF THE MARHOOK CLAN OUT FOR PAYBACK."
JUST GUESSING, OF COURSE.
CRAP. THEY JUST GOT A SHOOTING LOCK.
ARM THE TURRET! SOMEONE TAKE THE WHEEL WHILE I--
NO.
I CAN SHOOT AND DRIVE.
EYES ON THE ROAD, SUZI. I'LL CREW THE GUNS.
OKAY, BUT DO IT FAST.

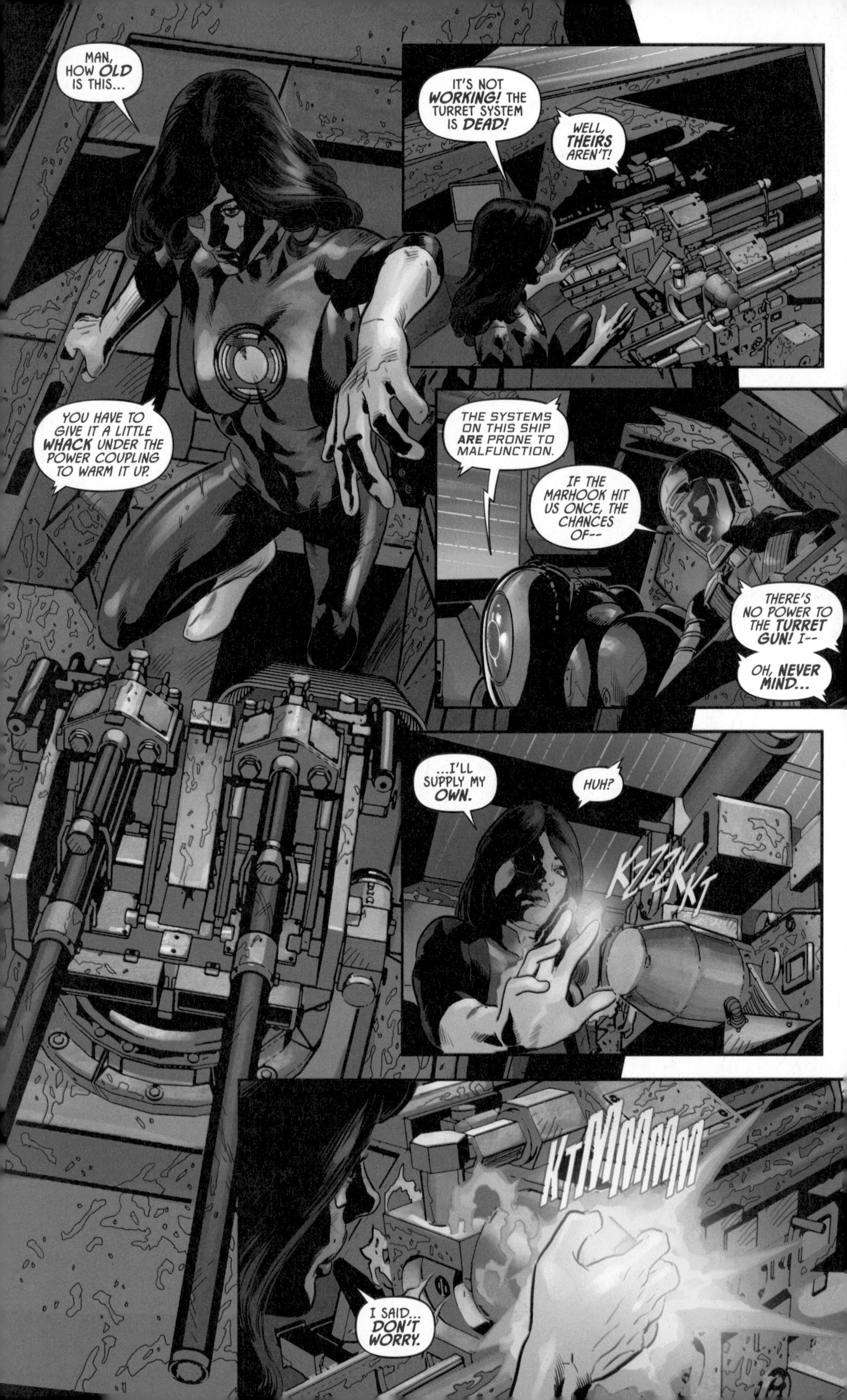
MAN, HOW **OLD** IS THIS...
YOU HAVE TO GIVE IT A LITTLE **WHACK** UNDER THE POWER COUPLING TO WARM IT UP.
IT'S NOT **WORKING!** THE TURRET SYSTEM IS **DEAD!**
WELL, **THEIRS** AREN'T!
THE SYSTEMS ON THIS SHIP **ARE** PRONE TO MALFUNCTION.
IF THE MARHOOK HIT US ONCE, THE CHANCES OF--
THERE'S NO POWER TO THE **TURRET GUN!** I--
OH, **NEVER MIND...**
...I'LL SUPPLY MY **OWN.**
HUH?
KZZZKKT
KTMMMMM
I SAID... **DON'T WORRY.**

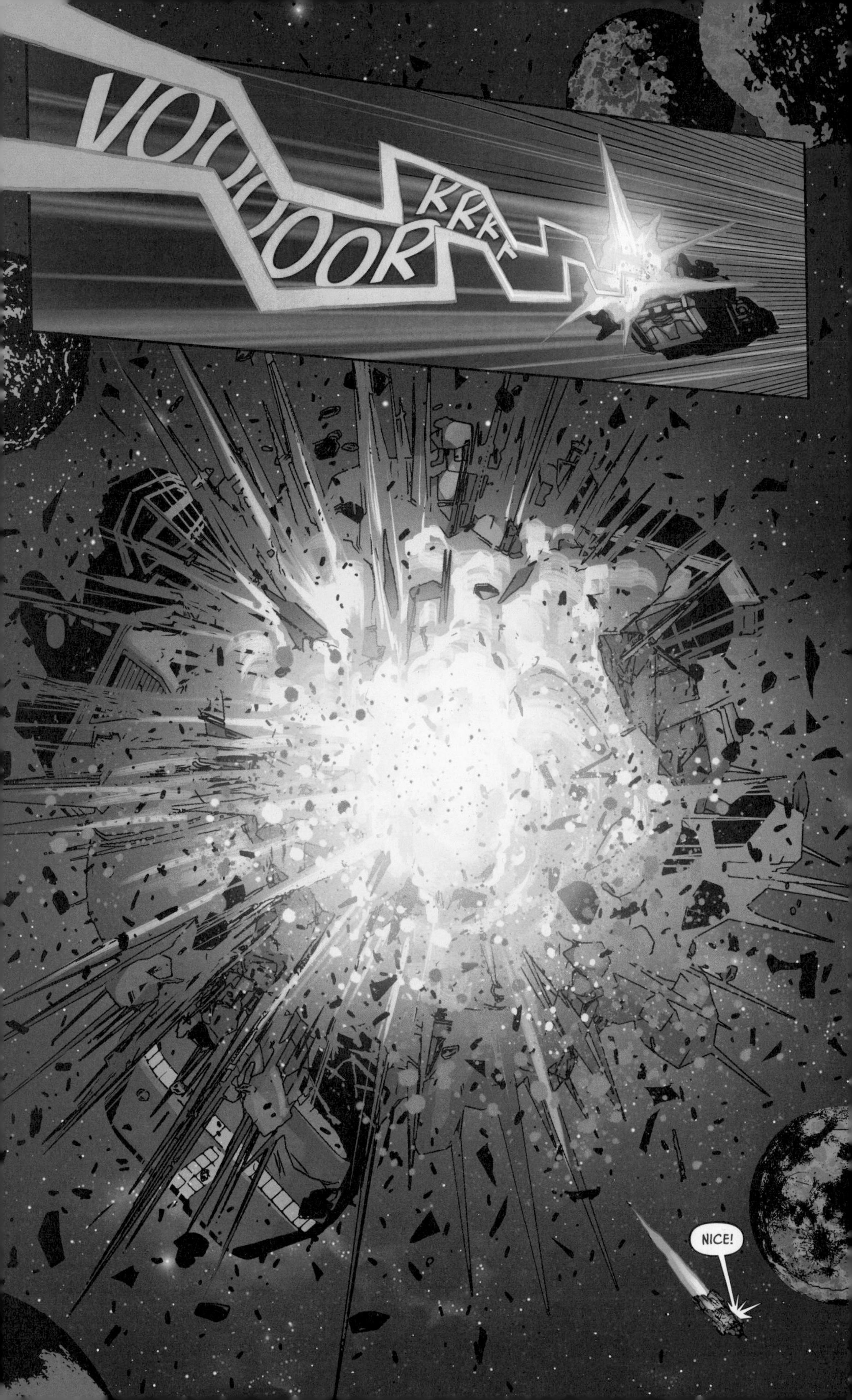
VOOOOOOR
KKKK
NICE!

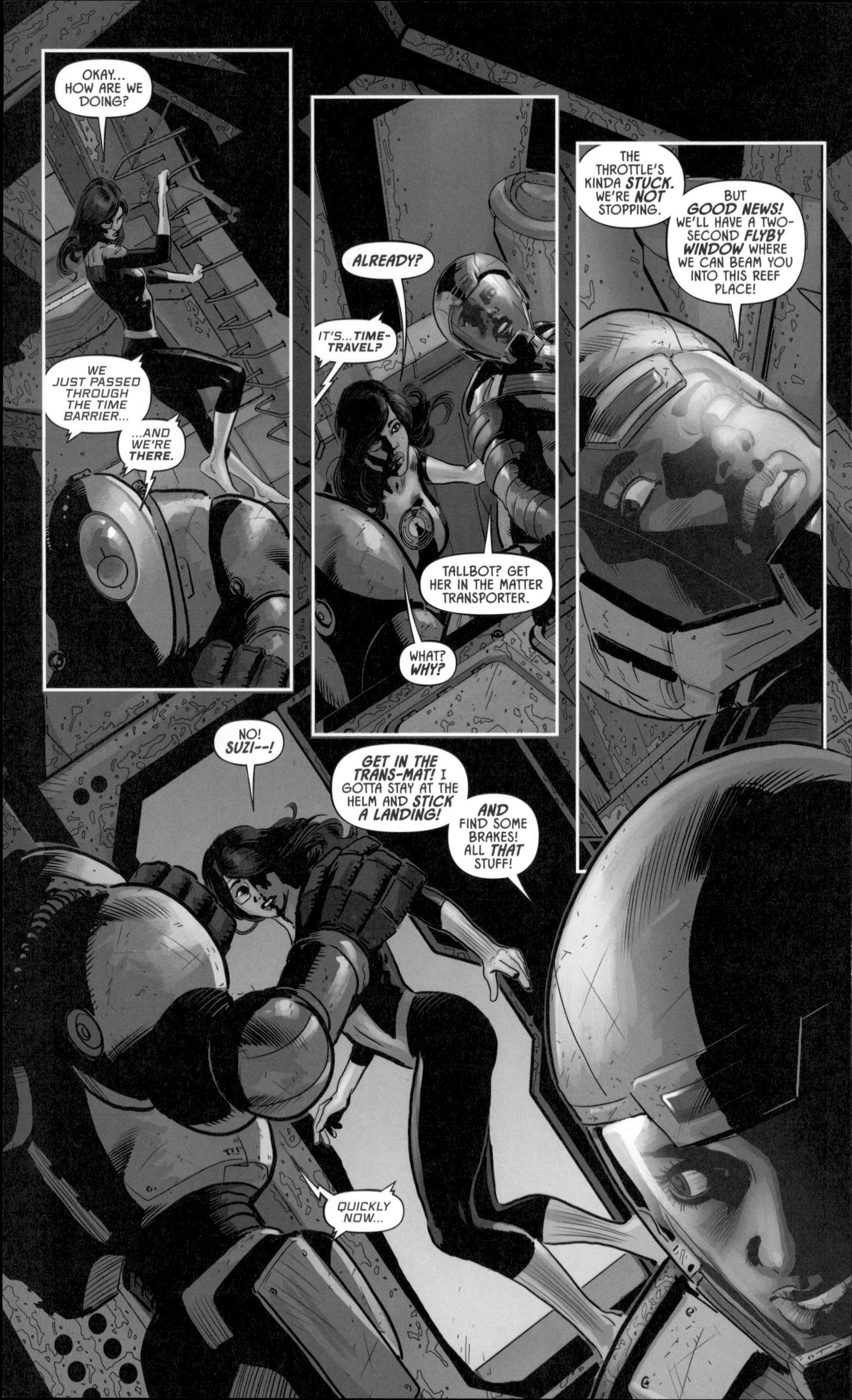
OKAY... HOW ARE WE DOING?
WE JUST PASSED THROUGH THE TIME BARRIER...
...AND WE'RE THERE.
ALREADY?
IT'S... TIME-TRAVEL?
TALLBOT? GET HER IN THE MATTER TRANSPORTER.
WHAT? WHY?
THE THROTTLE'S KINDA STUCK. WE'RE NOT STOPPING.
BUT GOOD NEWS! WE'LL HAVE A TWO-SECOND FLYBY WINDOW WHERE WE CAN BEAM YOU INTO THIS REEF PLACE!
NO! SUZI--!
GET IN THE TRANS-MAT! I GOTTA STAY AT THE HELM AND STICK A LANDING!
AND FIND SOME BRAKES! ALL THAT STUFF!
QUICKLY NOW...

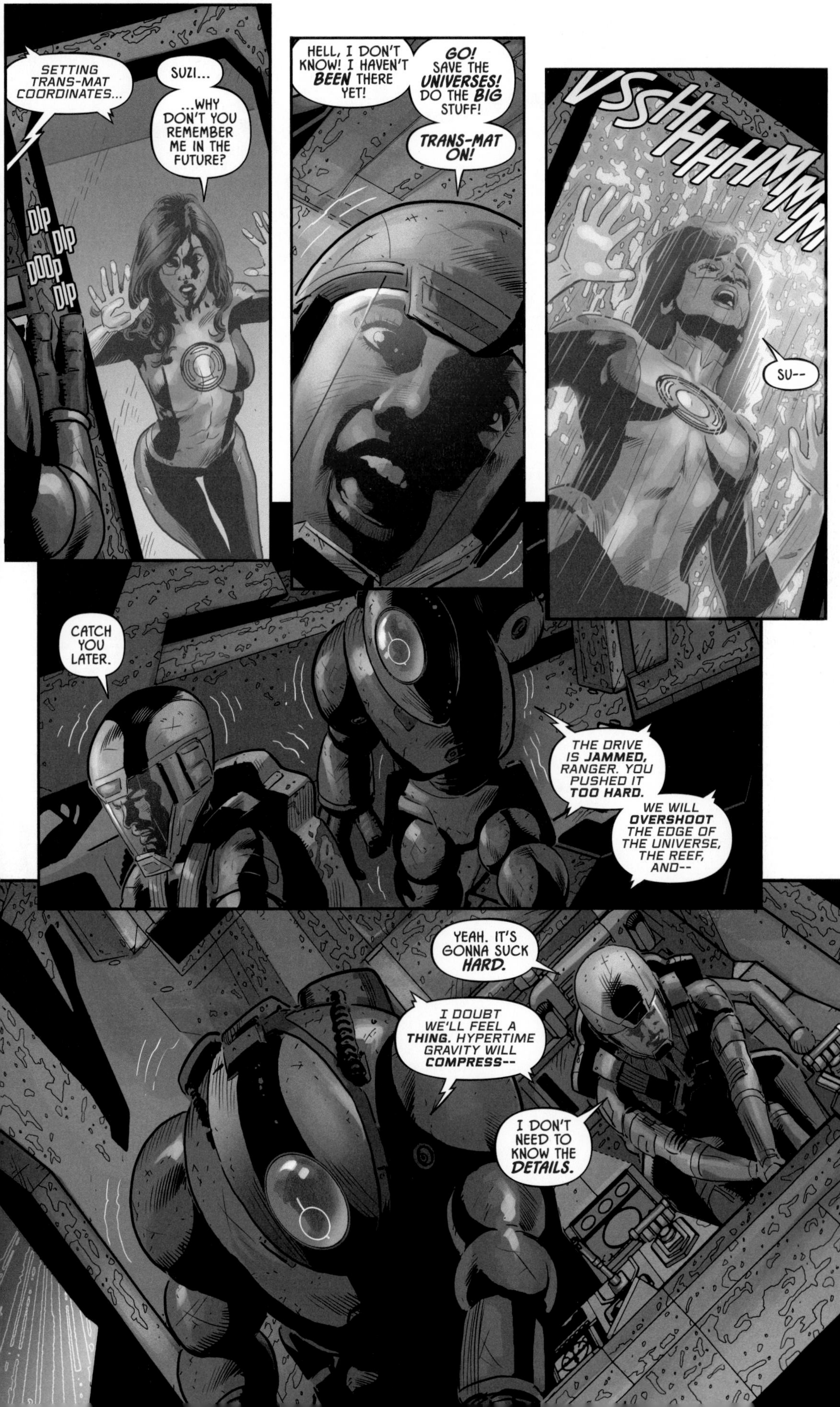

SETTING TRANS-MAT COORDINATES...
SUZI...
...WHY DON'T YOU REMEMBER ME IN THE FUTURE?
DIP DIP DOOP DIP
HELL, I DON'T KNOW! I HAVEN'T BEEN THERE YET!
GO! SAVE THE UNIVERSES! DO THE BIG STUFF!
TRANS-MAT ON!
VSSHHHHMMM
SU--
CATCH YOU LATER.
THE DRIVE IS JAMMED, RANGER. YOU PUSHED IT TOO HARD.
WE WILL OVERSHOOT THE EDGE OF THE UNIVERSE, THE REEF, AND--
YEAH. IT'S GONNA SUCK HARD.
I DOUBT WE'LL FEEL A THING. HYPERTIME GRAVITY WILL COMPRESS--
I DON'T NEED TO KNOW THE DETAILS.

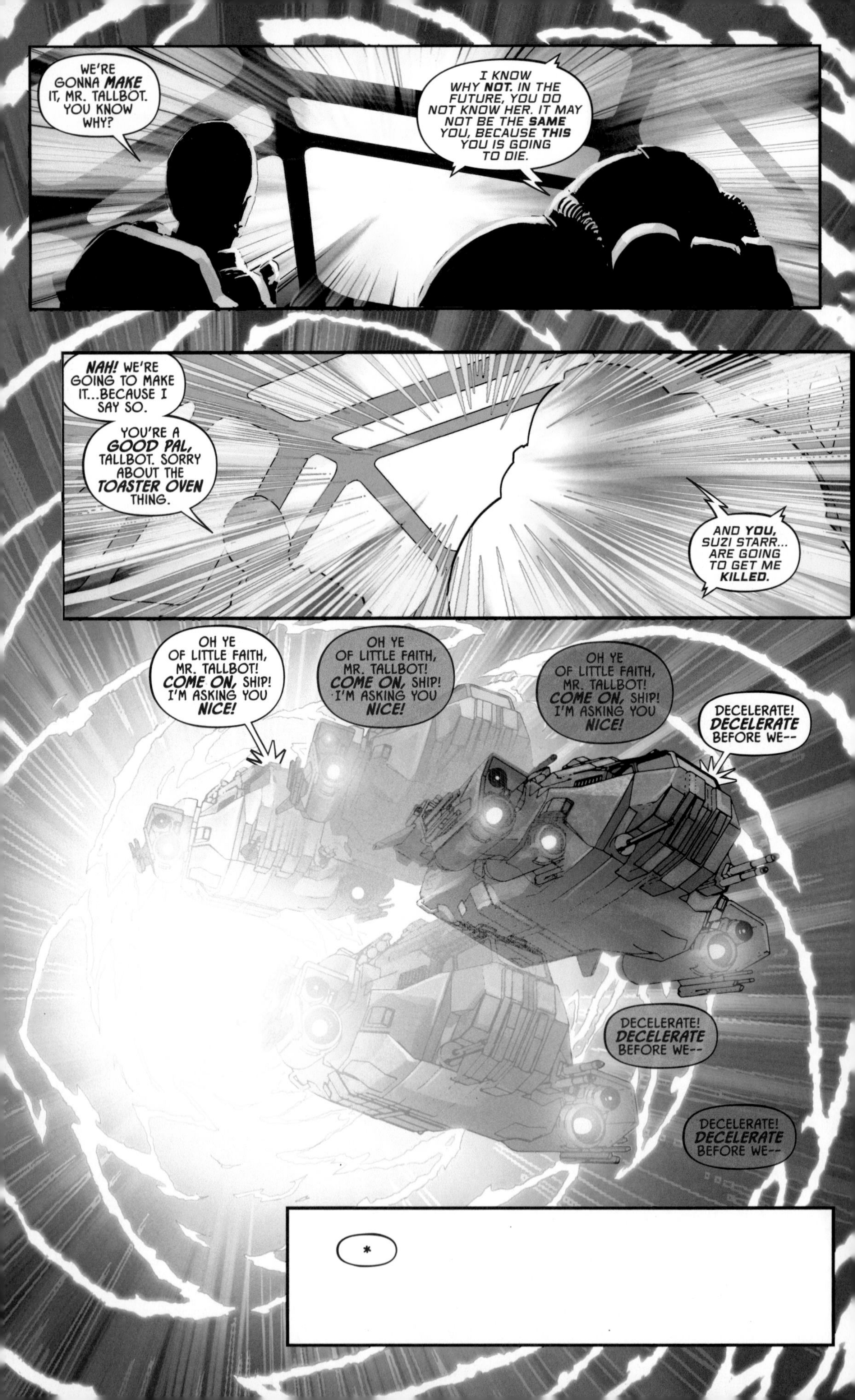
WE'RE GONNA MAKE IT, MR. TALLBOT. YOU KNOW WHY?
I KNOW WHY NOT. IN THE FUTURE, YOU DO NOT KNOW HER. IT MAY NOT BE THE SAME YOU, BECAUSE THIS YOU IS GOING TO DIE.
NAH! WE'RE GOING TO MAKE IT...BECAUSE I SAY SO.
YOU'RE A GOOD PAL, TALLBOT. SORRY ABOUT THE TOASTER OVEN THING.
AND YOU, SUZI STARR... ARE GOING TO GET ME KILLED.
OH YE OF LITTLE FAITH, MR. TALLBOT! COME ON, SHIP! I'M ASKING YOU NICE!
OH YE OF LITTLE FAITH, MR. TALLBOT! COME ON, SHIP! I'M ASKING YOU NICE!
OH YE OF LITTLE FAITH, MR. TALLBOT! COME ON, SHIP! I'M ASKING YOU NICE!
DECELERATE! DECELERATE BEFORE WE--
DECELERATE! DECELERATE BEFORE WE--
DECELERATE! DECELERATE BEFORE WE--
*

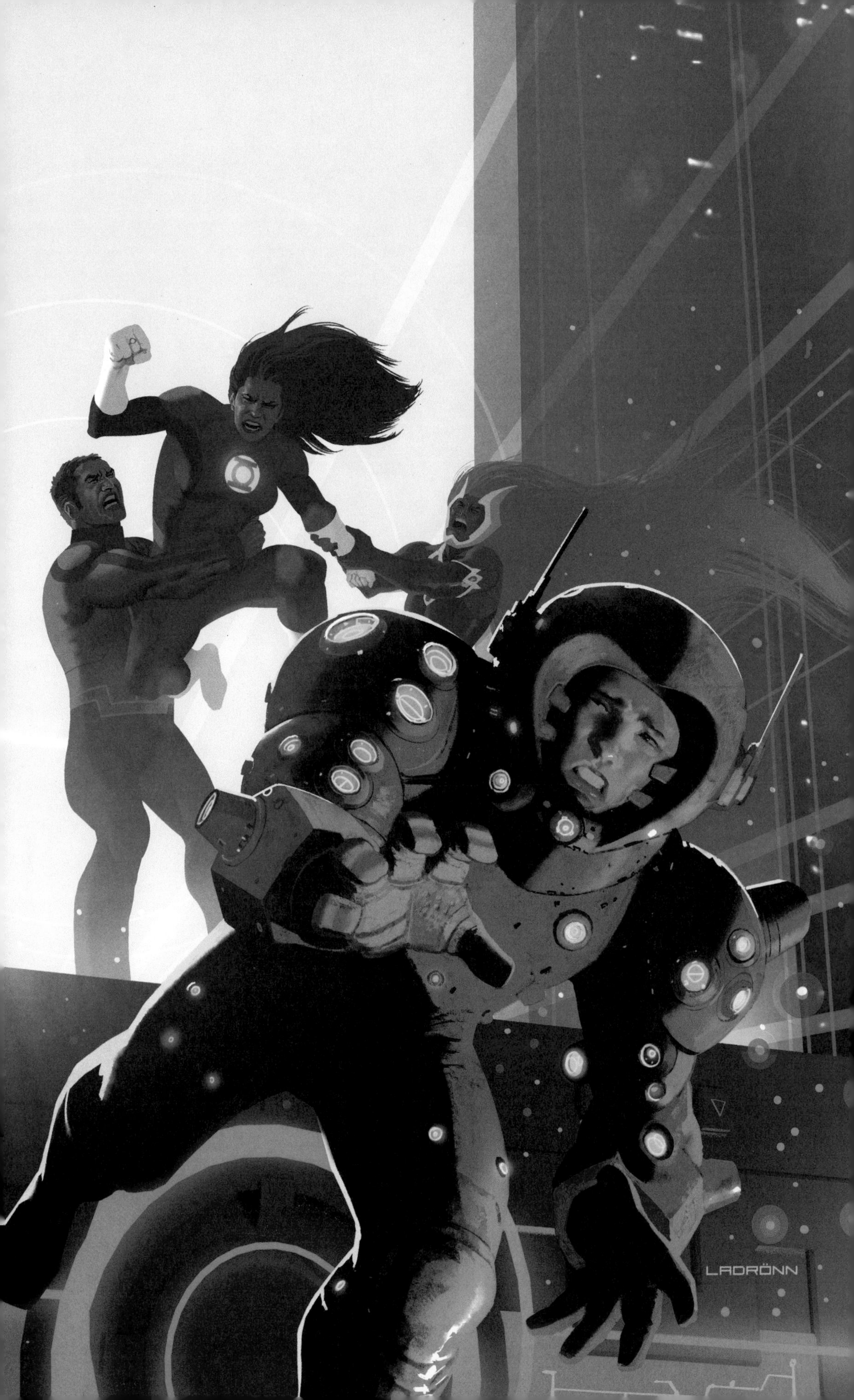
LADRÖNN

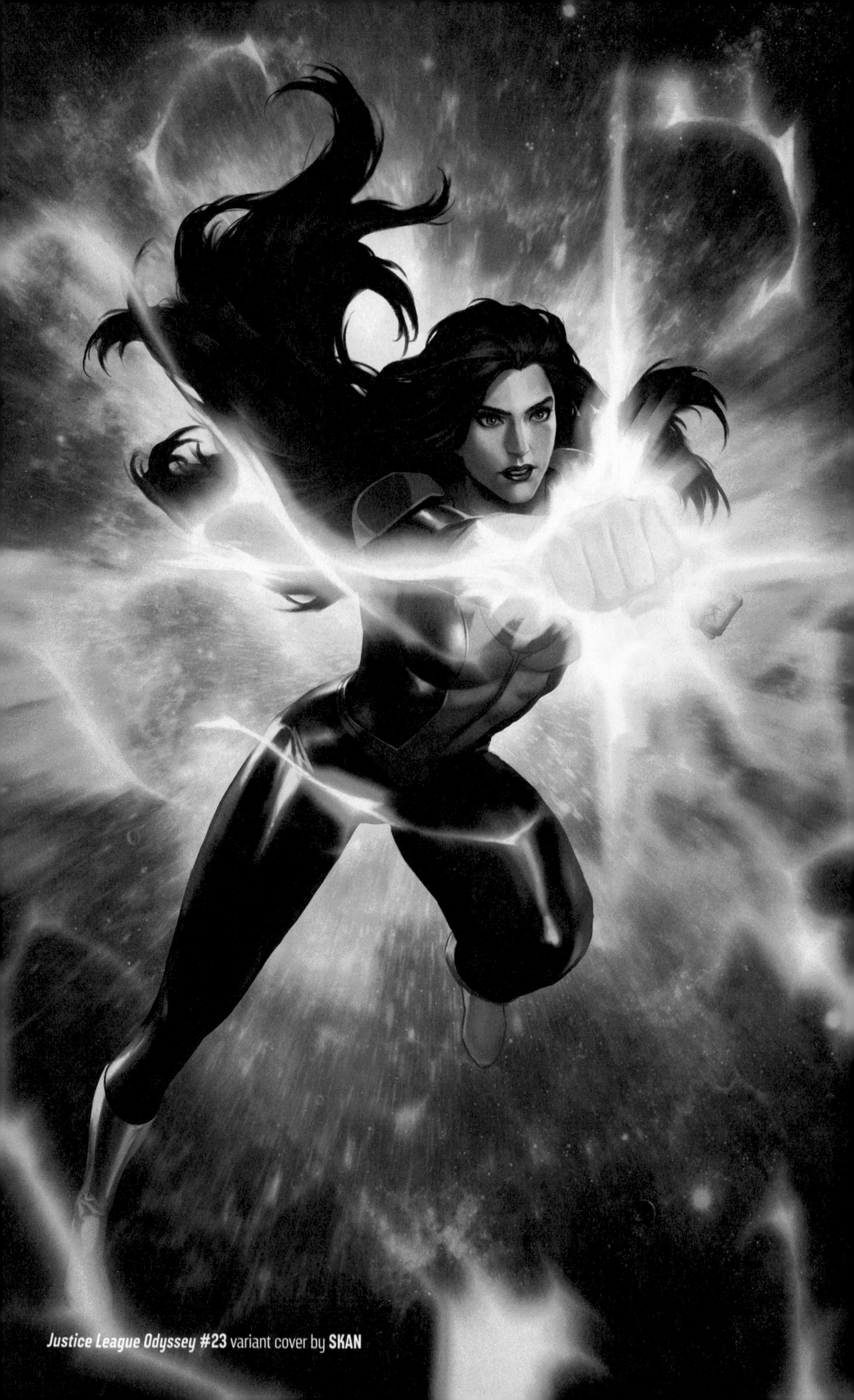

Justice League Odyssey **#23** variant cover by **SKAN**

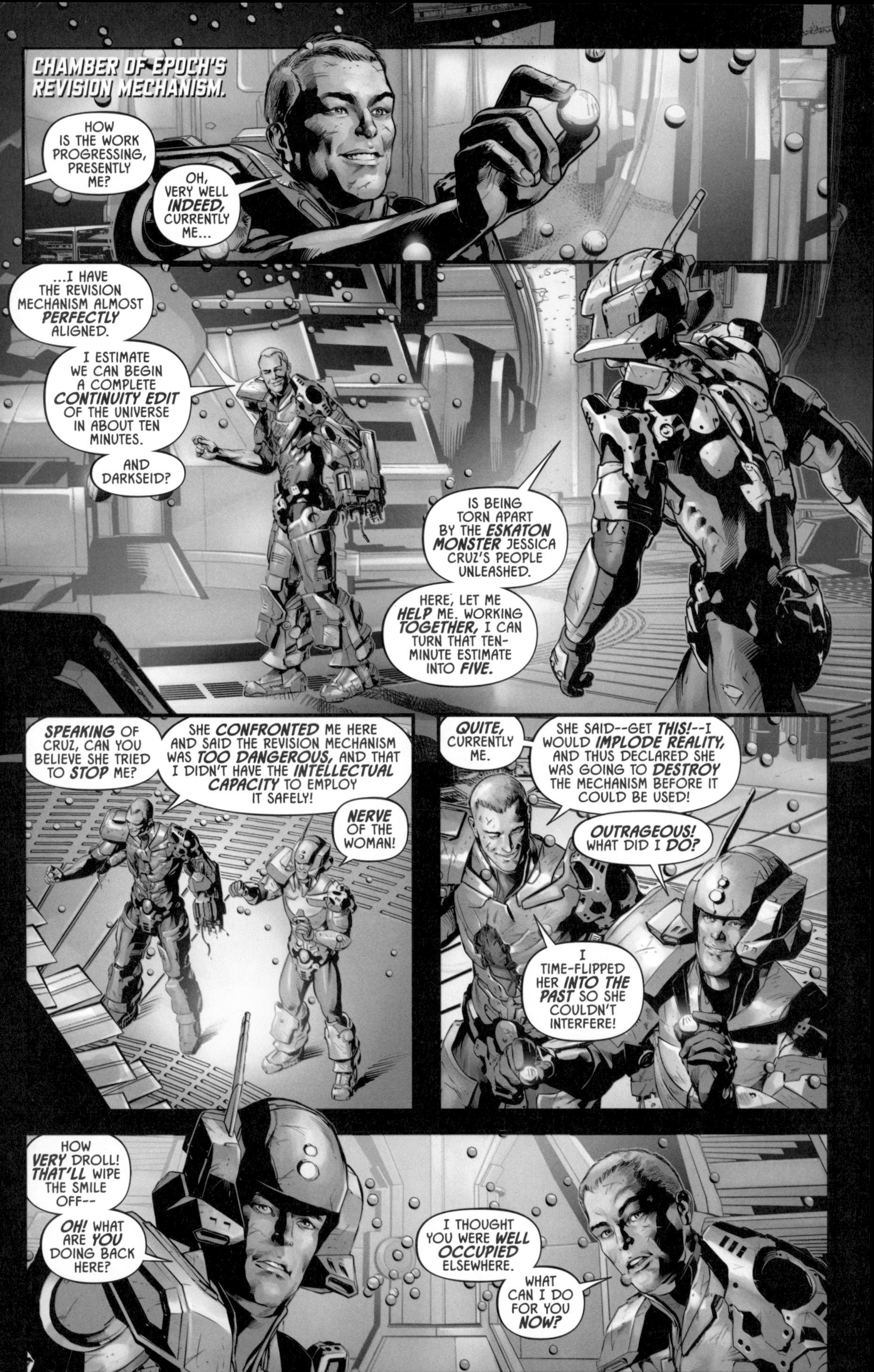
CHAMBER OF EPOCH'S REVISION MECHANISM.
HOW IS THE WORK PROGRESSING, PRESENTLY ME?
OH, VERY WELL INDEED, CURRENTLY ME...
...I HAVE THE REVISION MECHANISM ALMOST PERFECTLY ALIGNED.
I ESTIMATE WE CAN BEGIN A COMPLETE CONTINUITY EDIT OF THE UNIVERSE IN ABOUT TEN MINUTES.
AND DARKSEID?
IS BEING TORN APART BY THE ESKATON MONSTER JESSICA CRUZ'S PEOPLE UNLEASHED.
HERE, LET ME HELP ME. WORKING TOGETHER, I CAN TURN THAT TEN-MINUTE ESTIMATE INTO FIVE.
SPEAKING OF CRUZ, CAN YOU BELIEVE SHE TRIED TO STOP ME?
SHE CONFRONTED ME HERE AND SAID THE REVISION MECHANISM WAS TOO DANGEROUS, AND THAT I DIDN'T HAVE THE INTELLECTUAL CAPACITY TO EMPLOY IT SAFELY!
NERVE OF THE WOMAN!
QUITE, CURRENTLY ME.
SHE SAID--GET THIS!--I WOULD IMPLODE REALITY, AND THUS DECLARED SHE WAS GOING TO DESTROY THE MECHANISM BEFORE IT COULD BE USED!
OUTRAGEOUS! WHAT DID I DO?
I TIME-FLIPPED HER INTO THE PAST SO SHE COULDN'T INTERFERE!
HOW VERY DROLL! THAT'LL WIPE THE SMILE OFF--
OH! WHAT ARE YOU DOING BACK HERE?
I THOUGHT YOU WERE WELL OCCUPIED ELSEWHERE.
WHAT CAN I DO FOR YOU NOW?

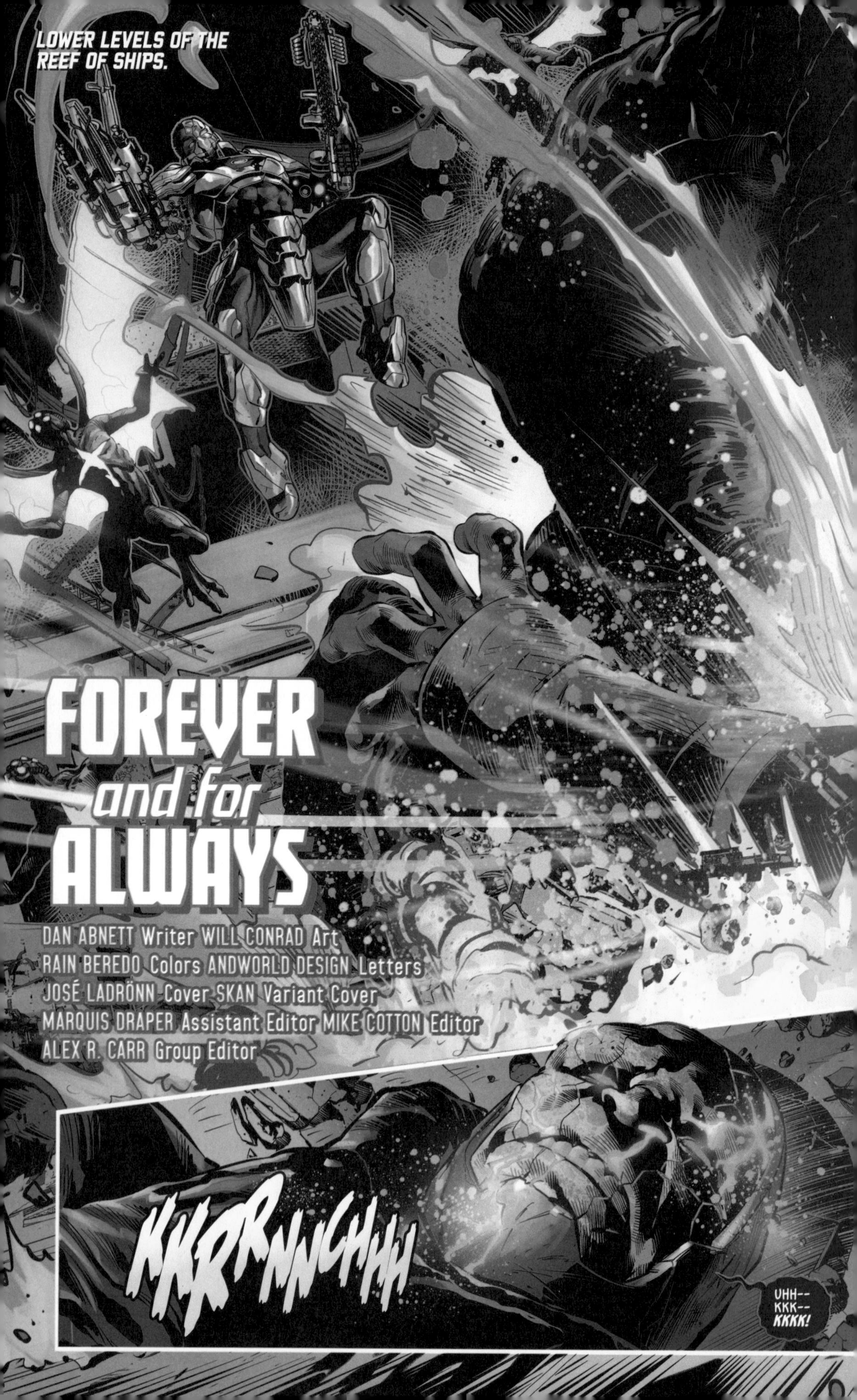
LOWER LEVELS OF THE REEF OF SHIPS.
FOREVER and for ALWAYS
DAN ABNETT Writer WILL CONRAD Art
RAIN BEREDO Colors ANDWORLD DESIGN Letters
JOSÉ LADRÖNN Cover SKAN Variant Cover
MARQUIS DRAPER Assistant Editor MIKE COTTON Editor
ALEX R. CARR Group Editor
KKRRNNCHHH
UHH-- KKK-- KKKK!

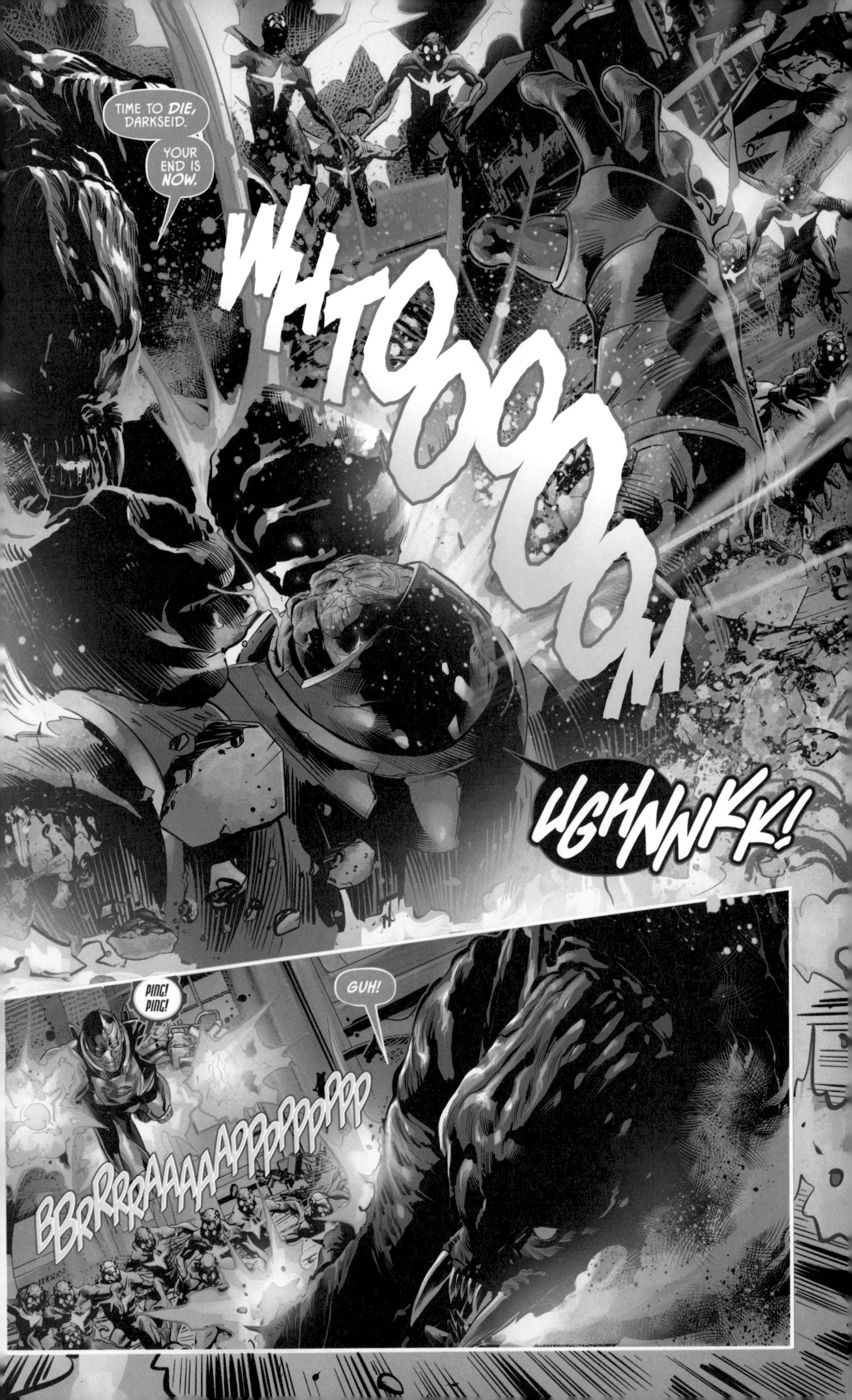
TIME TO DIE, DARKSEID.
YOUR END IS NOW.
WHTOOOOOOM
UGHNNKK!
PING! PING!
GUH!
BBRRRRAAAAAPPPPPPPP

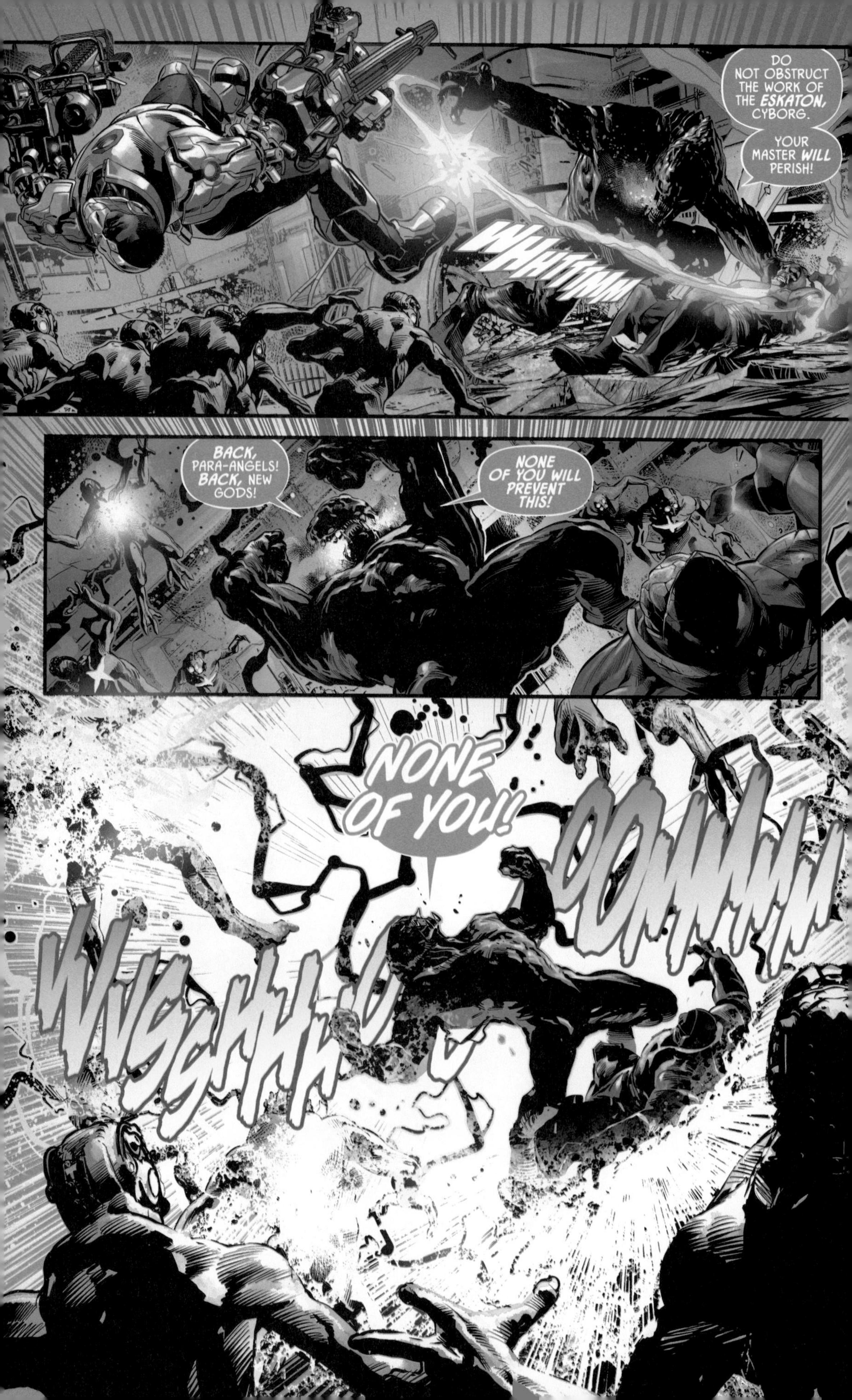
DO NOT OBSTRUCT THE WORK OF THE ESKATON, CYBORG.
YOUR MASTER WILL PERISH!
BACK, PARA-ANGELS! BACK, NEW GODS!
NONE OF YOU WILL PREVENT THIS!
NONE OF YOU!

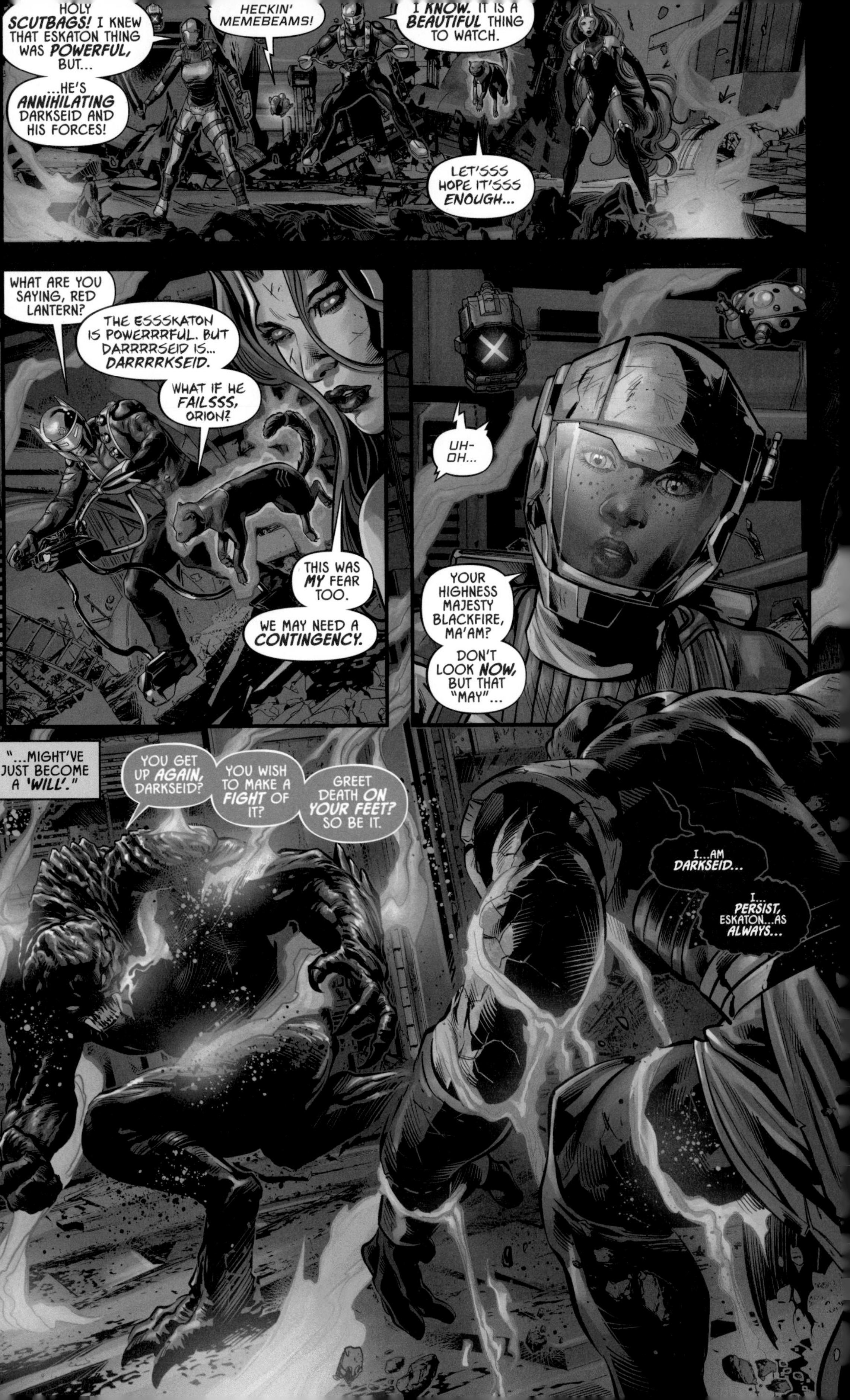
HOLY SCUTBAGS! I KNEW THAT ESKATON THING WAS POWERFUL, BUT...
...HE'S ANNIHILATING DARKSEID AND HIS FORCES!
HECKIN' MEMEBEAMS!
I KNOW. IT IS A BEAUTIFUL THING TO WATCH.
LET'SSS HOPE IT'SSS ENOUGH...
WHAT ARE YOU SAYING, RED LANTERN?
THE ESSSKATON IS POWERRRRFUL. BUT DARRRRSEID IS... DARRRRKSEID.
WHAT IF HE FAILSSS, ORION?
THIS WAS MY FEAR TOO.
WE MAY NEED A CONTINGENCY.
UH-OH...
YOUR HIGHNESS MAJESTY BLACKFIRE, MA'AM?
DON'T LOOK NOW, BUT THAT "MAY"...
"...MIGHT'VE JUST BECOME A 'WILL'."
YOU GET UP AGAIN, DARKSEID?
YOU WISH TO MAKE A FIGHT OF IT?
GREET DEATH ON YOUR FEET? SO BE IT.
I...AM DARKSEID...
I... PERSIST, ESKATON...AS ALWAYS...

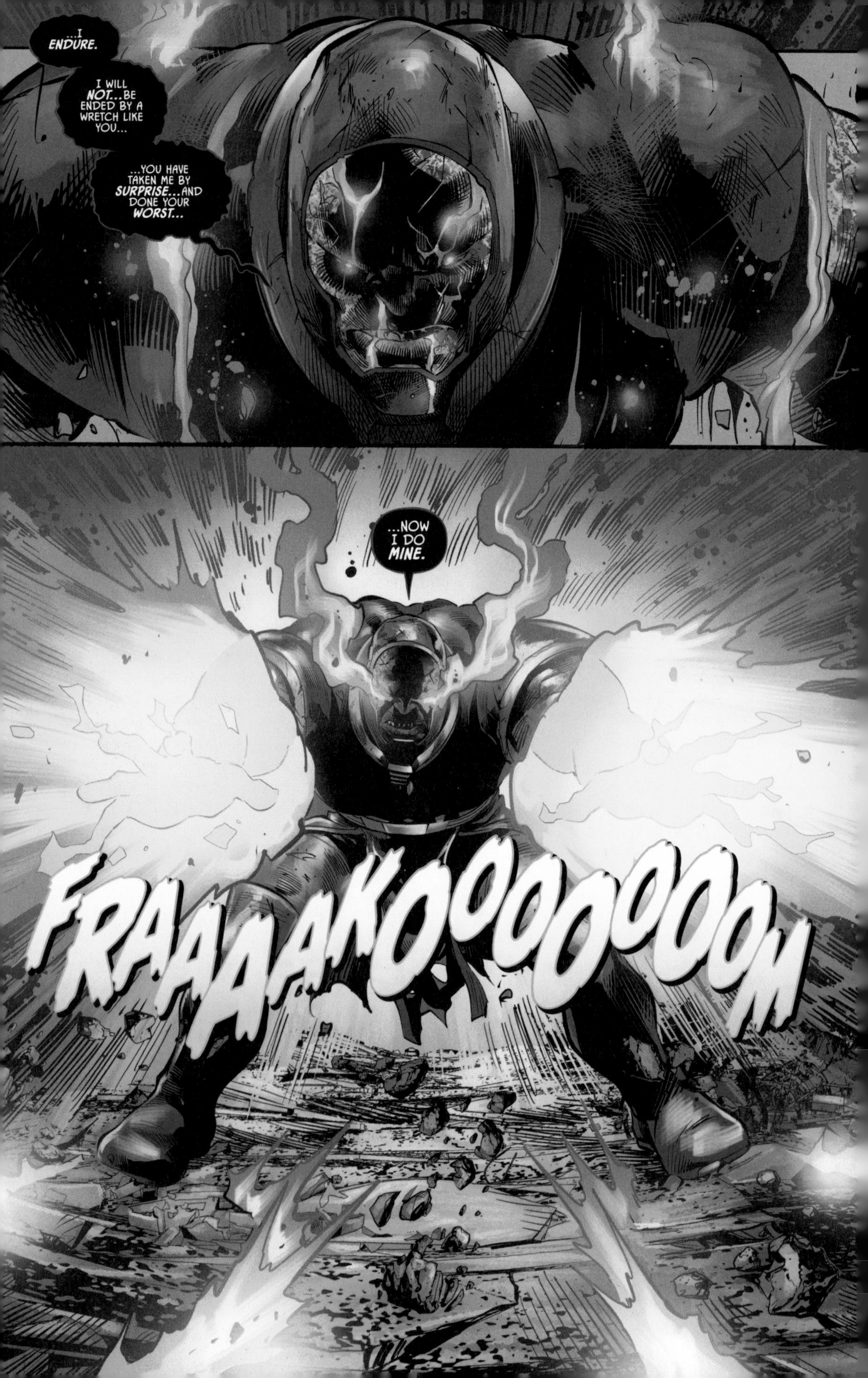
...I ENDURE.
I WILL NOT...BE ENDED BY A WRETCH LIKE YOU...
...YOU HAVE TAKEN ME BY SURPRISE...AND DONE YOUR WORST...
...NOW I DO MINE.
FRAAAAKOOOOOOOOM

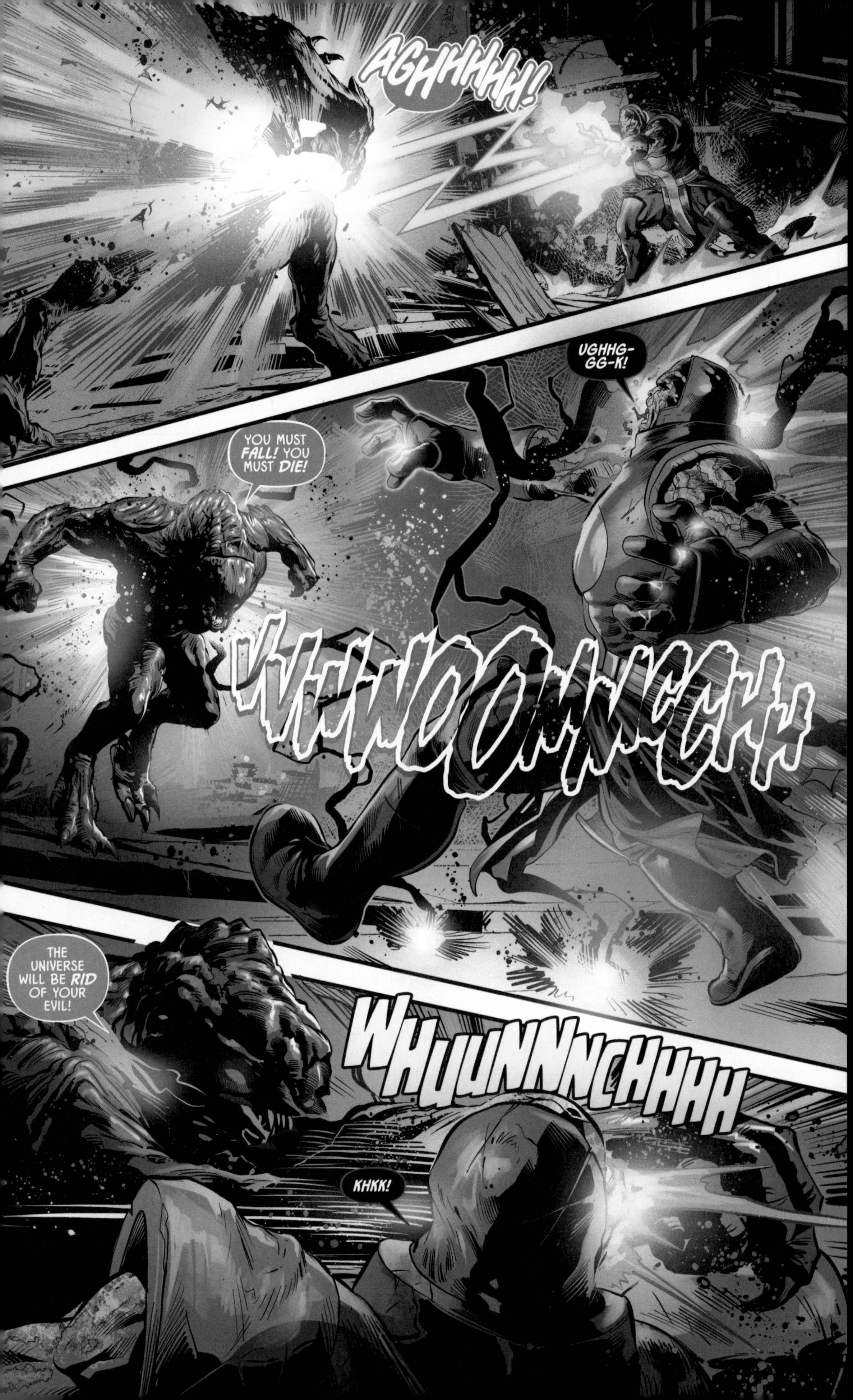
AGHHHHH!
UGHHG-GG-K!
YOU MUST FALL! YOU MUST DIE!
VVWWOOMMCHH
THE UNIVERSE WILL BE RID OF YOUR EVIL!
WHUUNNNCHHHH
KHKK!

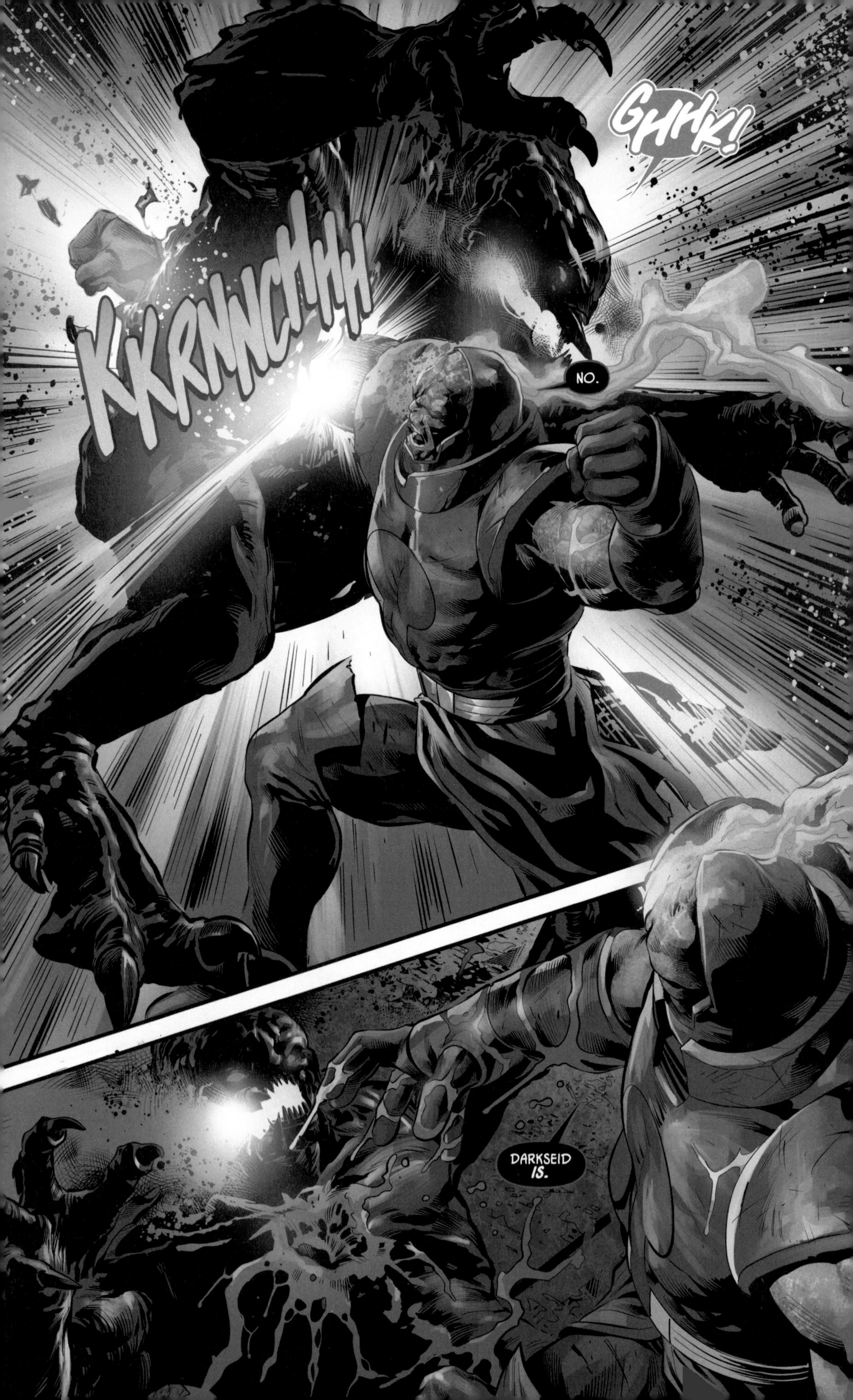
GHHK!
KKRNNCHHH
NO.
DARKSEID IS.

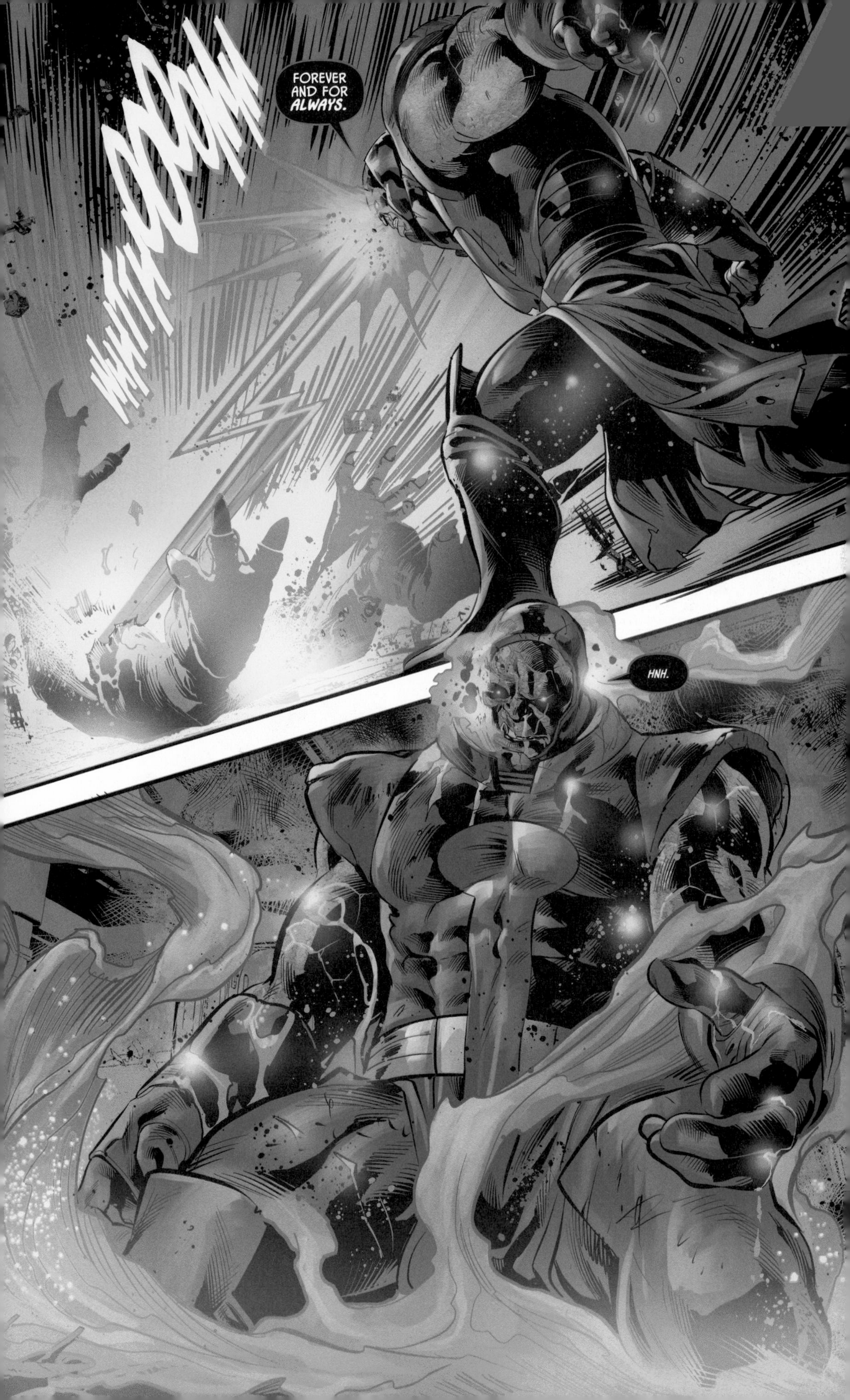
WHHHOOOM
FOREVER AND FOR ALWAYS.
HNH.

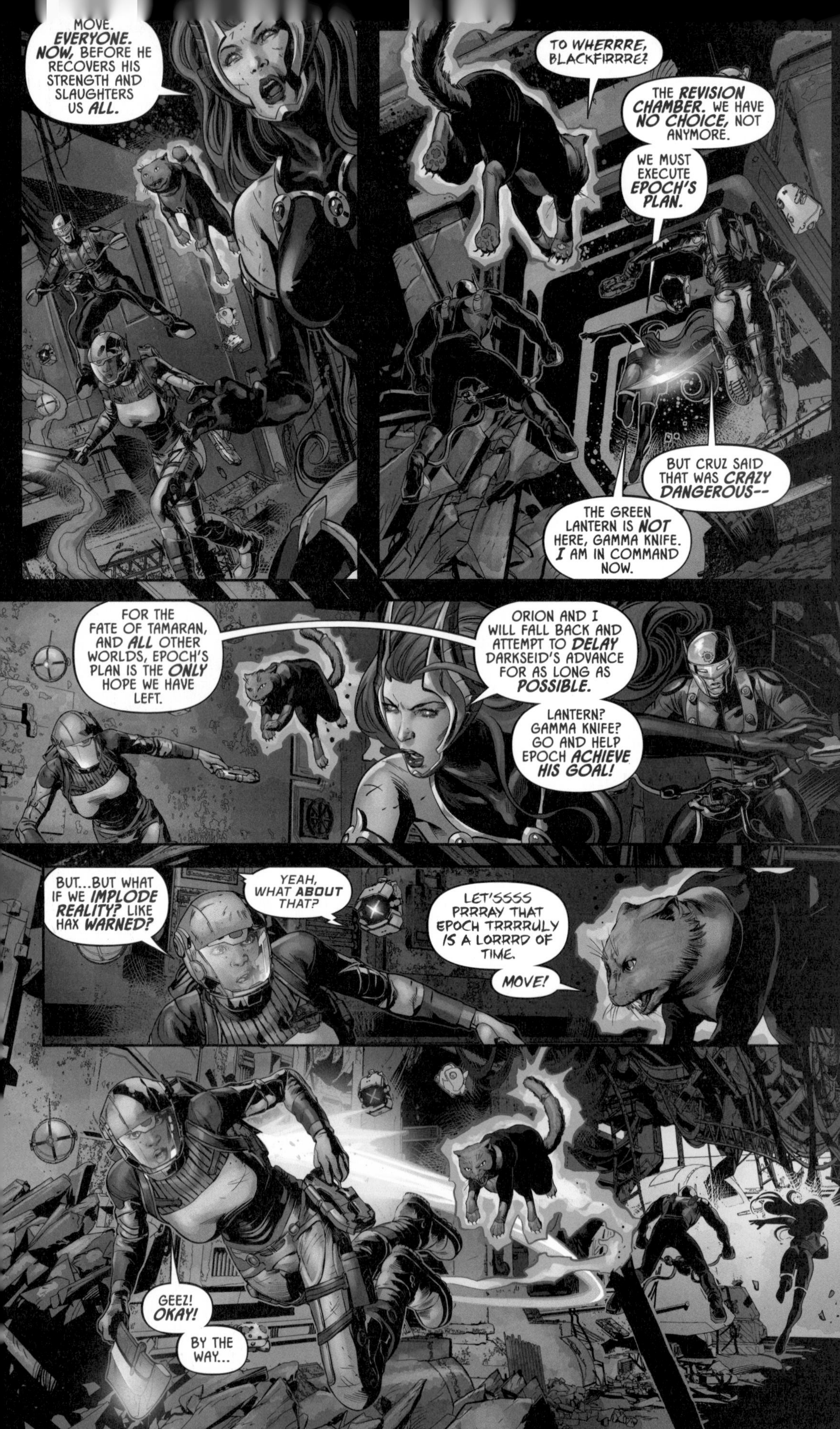

MOVE. **EVERYONE. NOW,** BEFORE HE RECOVERS HIS STRENGTH AND SLAUGHTERS US **ALL.**
TO **WHERRRE,** BLACKFIRRRE?
THE **REVISION CHAMBER.** WE HAVE **NO CHOICE,** NOT ANYMORE.
WE MUST EXECUTE **EPOCH'S PLAN.**
BUT CRUZ SAID THAT WAS **CRAZY DANGEROUS--**
THE GREEN LANTERN IS **NOT** HERE, GAMMA KNIFE. ***I*** AM IN COMMAND NOW.
FOR THE FATE OF TAMARAN, AND **ALL** OTHER WORLDS, EPOCH'S PLAN IS THE **ONLY** HOPE WE HAVE LEFT.
ORION AND I WILL FALL BACK AND ATTEMPT TO **DELAY** DARKSEID'S ADVANCE FOR AS LONG AS **POSSIBLE.**
LANTERN? GAMMA KNIFE? GO AND HELP EPOCH **ACHIEVE HIS GOAL!**
BUT...BUT WHAT IF WE **IMPLODE REALITY?** LIKE HAX **WARNED?**
YEAH, WHAT **ABOUT** THAT?
LET'SSSS PRRRAY THAT EPOCH TRRRRULY ***IS*** A LORRRD OF TIME.
MOVE!
GEEZ! **OKAY!**
BY THE WAY...

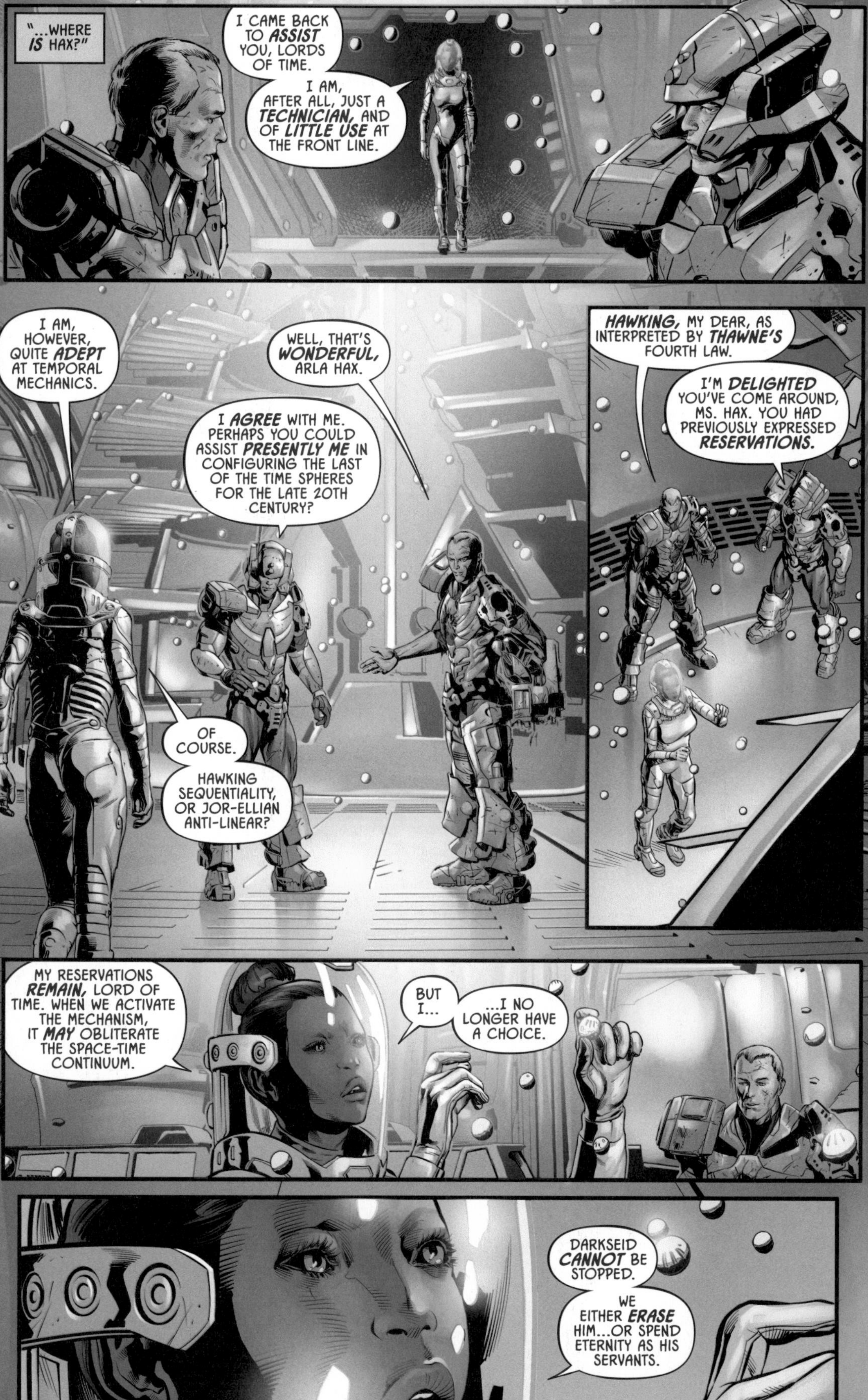
"...WHERE IS HAX?"
I CAME BACK TO ASSIST YOU, LORDS OF TIME.
I AM, AFTER ALL, JUST A TECHNICIAN, AND OF LITTLE USE AT THE FRONT LINE.
I AM, HOWEVER, QUITE ADEPT AT TEMPORAL MECHANICS.
WELL, THAT'S WONDERFUL, ARLA HAX.
I AGREE WITH ME. PERHAPS YOU COULD ASSIST PRESENTLY ME IN CONFIGURING THE LAST OF THE TIME SPHERES FOR THE LATE 20TH CENTURY?
OF COURSE.
HAWKING SEQUENTIALITY, OR JOR-ELLIAN ANTI-LINEAR?
HAWKING, MY DEAR, AS INTERPRETED BY THAWNE'S FOURTH LAW.
I'M DELIGHTED YOU'VE COME AROUND, MS. HAX. YOU HAD PREVIOUSLY EXPRESSED RESERVATIONS.
MY RESERVATIONS REMAIN, LORD OF TIME. WHEN WE ACTIVATE THE MECHANISM, IT MAY OBLITERATE THE SPACE-TIME CONTINUUM.
BUT I...
...I NO LONGER HAVE A CHOICE.
DARKSEID CANNOT BE STOPPED.
WE EITHER ERASE HIM...OR SPEND ETERNITY AS HIS SERVANTS.

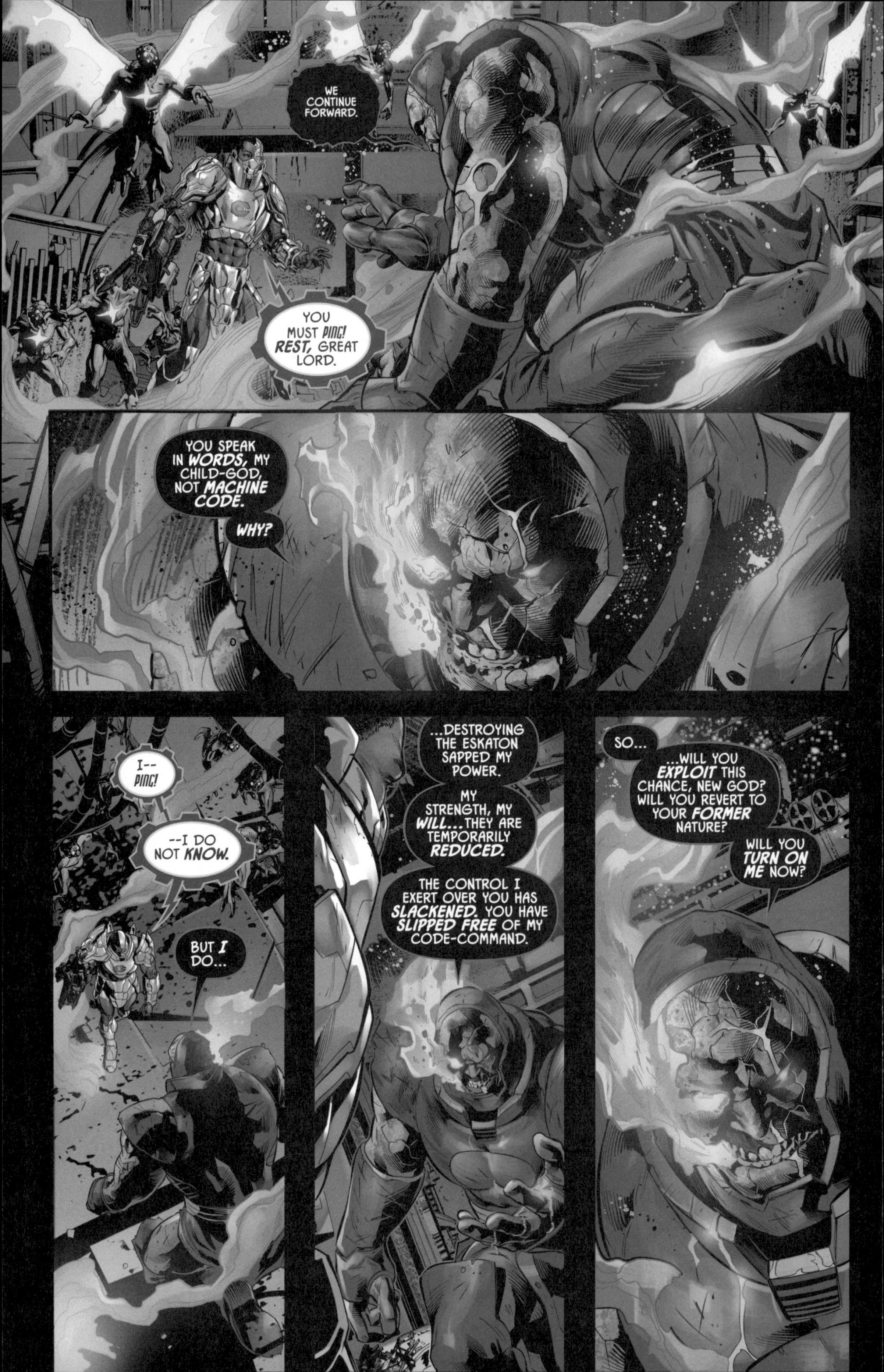
WE CONTINUE FORWARD.
YOU MUST PING! REST, GREAT LORD.
YOU SPEAK IN WORDS, MY CHILD-GOD, NOT MACHINE CODE.
WHY?
I-- PING!
--I DO NOT KNOW.
BUT I DO...
...DESTROYING THE ESKATON SAPPED MY POWER.
MY STRENGTH, MY WILL...THEY ARE TEMPORARILY REDUCED.
THE CONTROL I EXERT OVER YOU HAS SLACKENED. YOU HAVE SLIPPED FREE OF MY CODE-COMMAND.
SO...
...WILL YOU EXPLOIT THIS CHANCE, NEW GOD? WILL YOU REVERT TO YOUR FORMER NATURE?
WILL YOU TURN ON ME NOW?

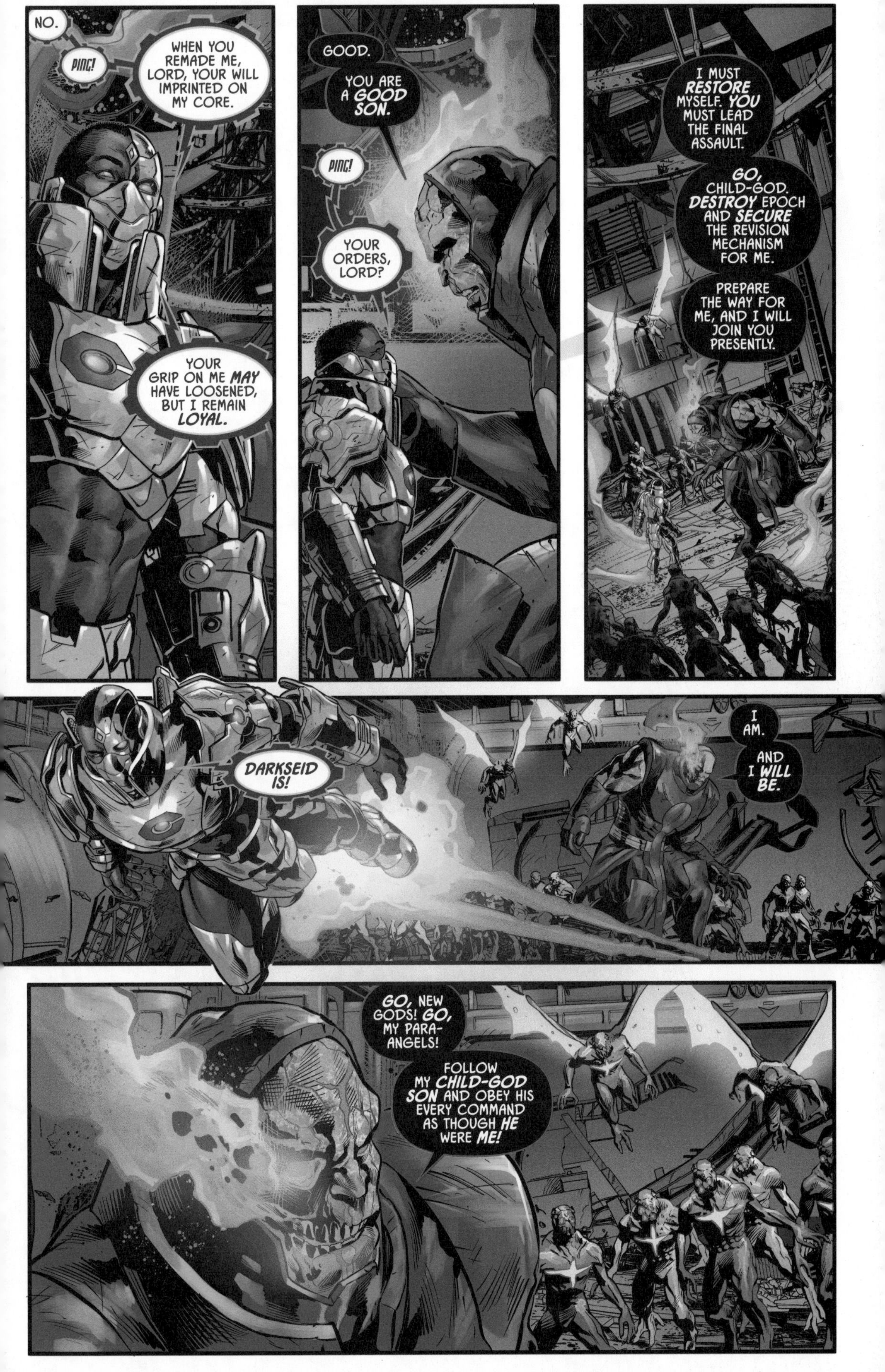
NO.
PING!
WHEN YOU REMADE ME, LORD, YOUR WILL IMPRINTED ON MY CORE.
YOUR GRIP ON ME MAY HAVE LOOSENED, BUT I REMAIN LOYAL.
GOOD.
YOU ARE A GOOD SON.
PING!
YOUR ORDERS, LORD?
I MUST RESTORE MYSELF. YOU MUST LEAD THE FINAL ASSAULT.
GO, CHILD-GOD. DESTROY EPOCH AND SECURE THE REVISION MECHANISM FOR ME.
PREPARE THE WAY FOR ME, AND I WILL JOIN YOU PRESENTLY.
DARKSEID IS!
I AM.
AND I WILL BE.
GO, NEW GODS! GO, MY PARA-ANGELS!
FOLLOW MY CHILD-GOD SON AND OBEY HIS EVERY COMMAND AS THOUGH HE WERE ME!

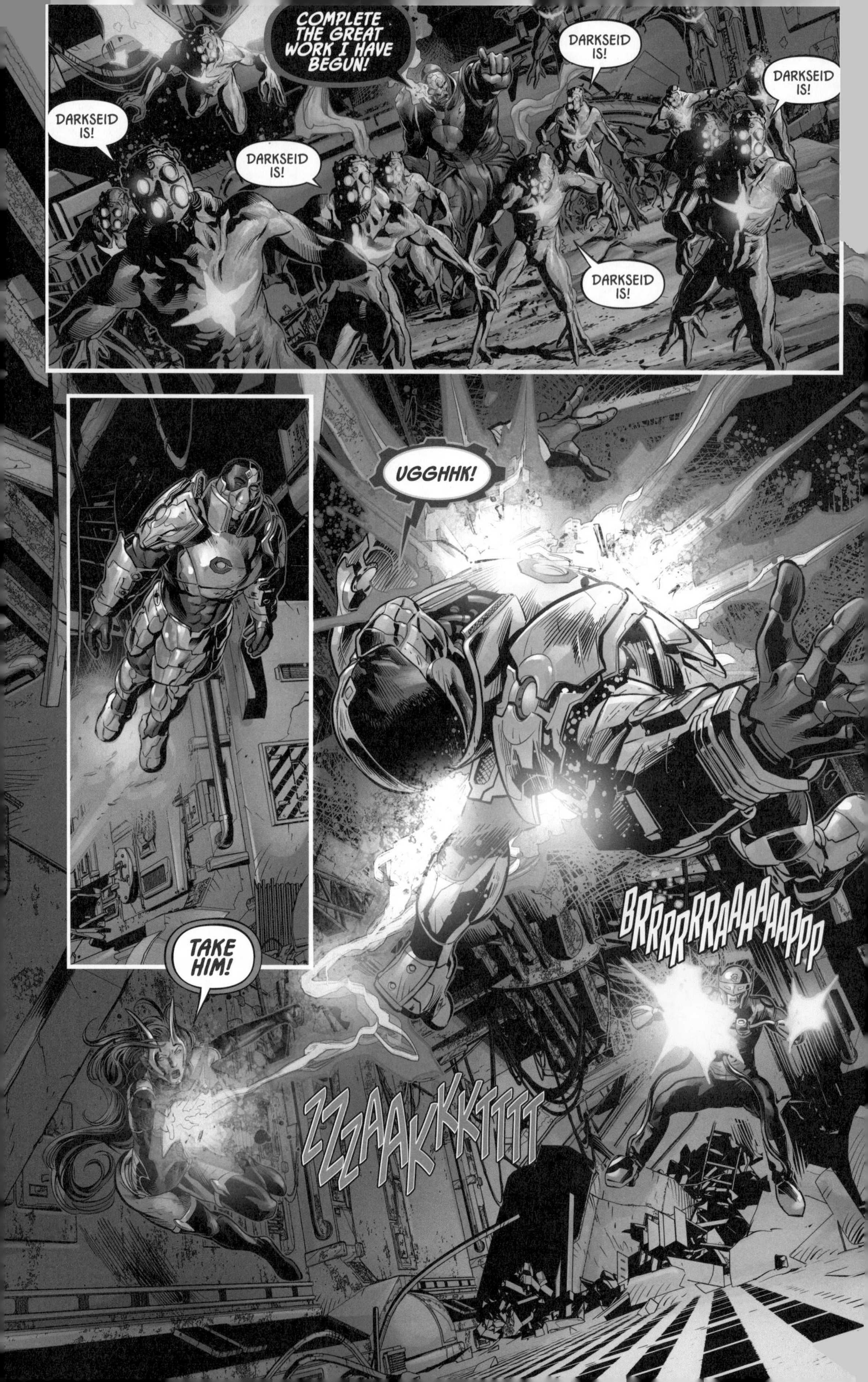
COMPLETE THE GREAT WORK I HAVE BEGUN!
DARKSEID IS!
DARKSEID IS!
DARKSEID IS!
DARKSEID IS!
DARKSEID IS!
UGGHHK!
TAKE HIM!
ZZZAAKKKTTTTT
BRRRRRAAAAAAPPP

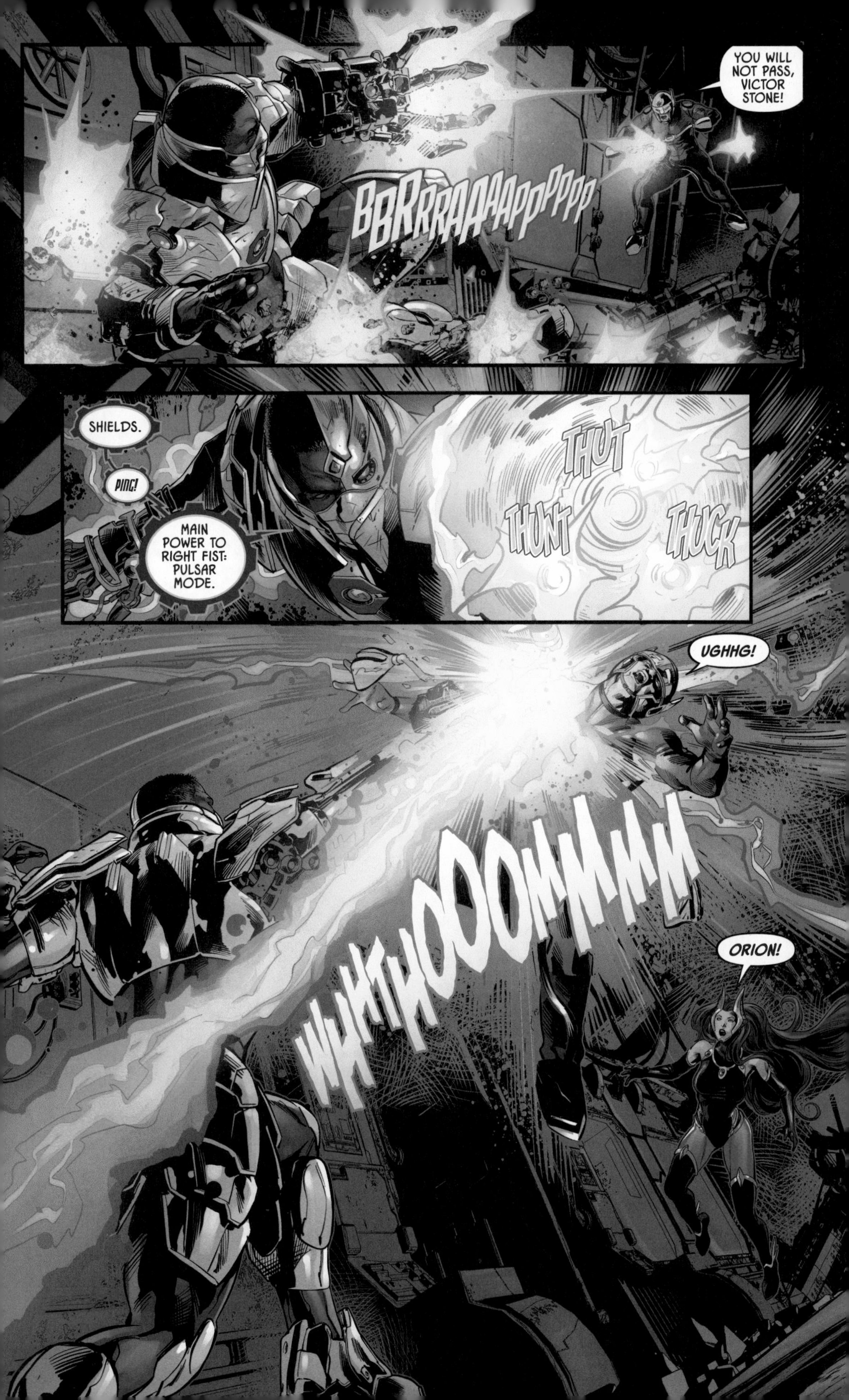
YOU WILL NOT PASS, VICTOR STONE!
BBRRRAAAAPPPPPP
SHIELDS.
PING!
MAIN POWER TO RIGHT FIST: PULSAR MODE.
THUT
THUNT
THUCK
UGHHG!
WHHTHOOOMMMM
ORION!

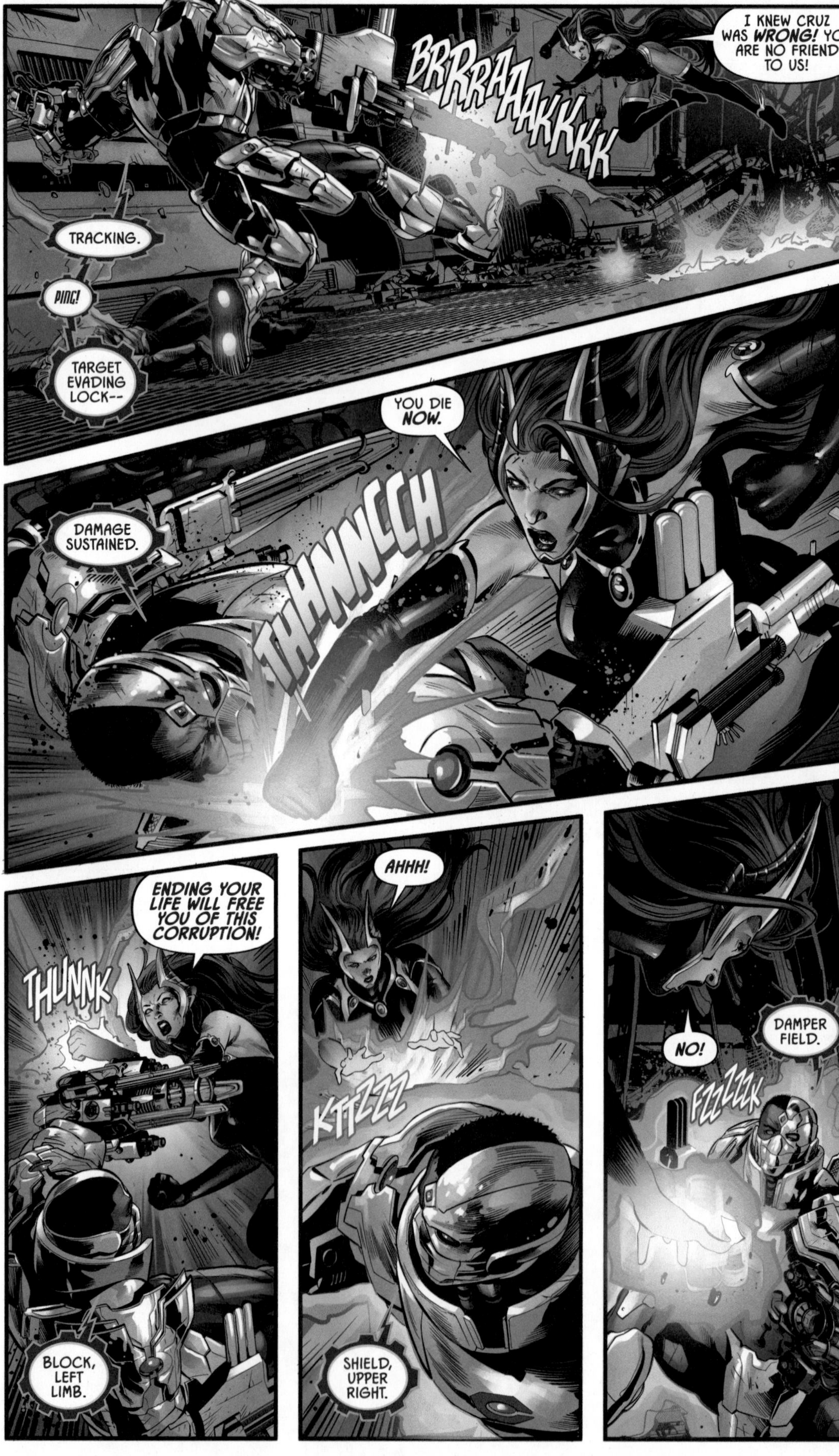

I KNEW CRUZ WAS WRONG! YOU ARE NO FRIEND TO US!
BRRRAAAKKKKK
TRACKING.
PING!
TARGET EVADING LOCK--
YOU DIE NOW.
DAMAGE SUSTAINED.
THHNNCCH
ENDING YOUR LIFE WILL FREE YOU OF THIS CORRUPTION!
THUNNK
BLOCK, LEFT LIMB.
AHHH!
KTTZZZ
SHIELD, UPPER RIGHT.
NO!
DAMPER FIELD.
FZZZZZK

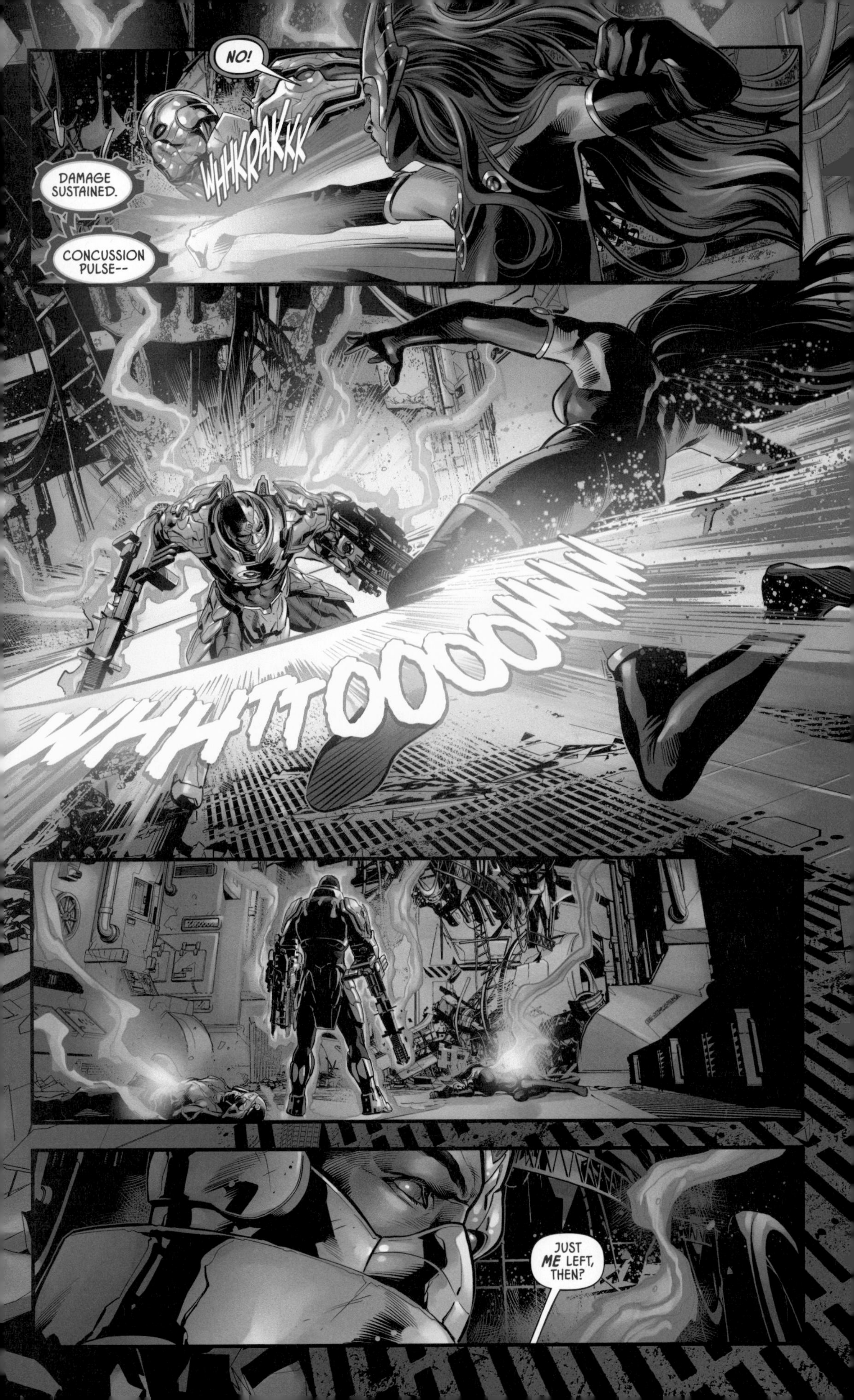
NO!
WHHKRAKKK
DAMAGE SUSTAINED.
CONCUSSION PULSE--
WHHTTOOOOMM
JUST ME LEFT, THEN?

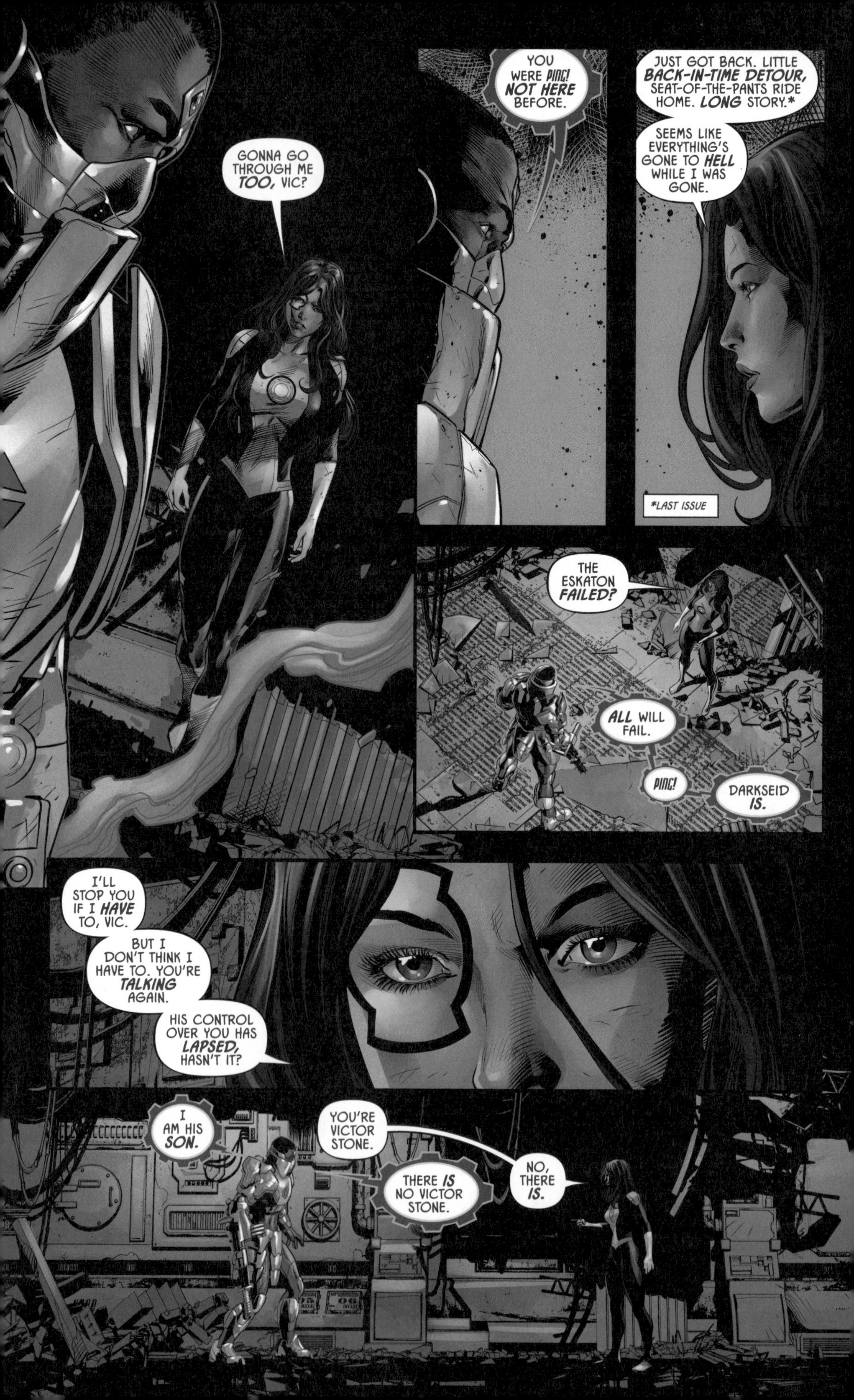
GONNA GO THROUGH ME TOO, VIC?
YOU WERE PING! NOT HERE BEFORE.
JUST GOT BACK. LITTLE BACK-IN-TIME DETOUR, SEAT-OF-THE-PANTS RIDE HOME. LONG STORY.*
SEEMS LIKE EVERYTHING'S GONE TO HELL WHILE I WAS GONE.
*LAST ISSUE
THE ESKATON FAILED?
ALL WILL FAIL.
PING!
DARKSEID IS.
I'LL STOP YOU IF I HAVE TO, VIC.
BUT I DON'T THINK I HAVE TO. YOU'RE TALKING AGAIN.
HIS CONTROL OVER YOU HAS LAPSED, HASN'T IT?
I AM HIS SON.
YOU'RE VICTOR STONE.
THERE IS NO VICTOR STONE.
NO, THERE IS.

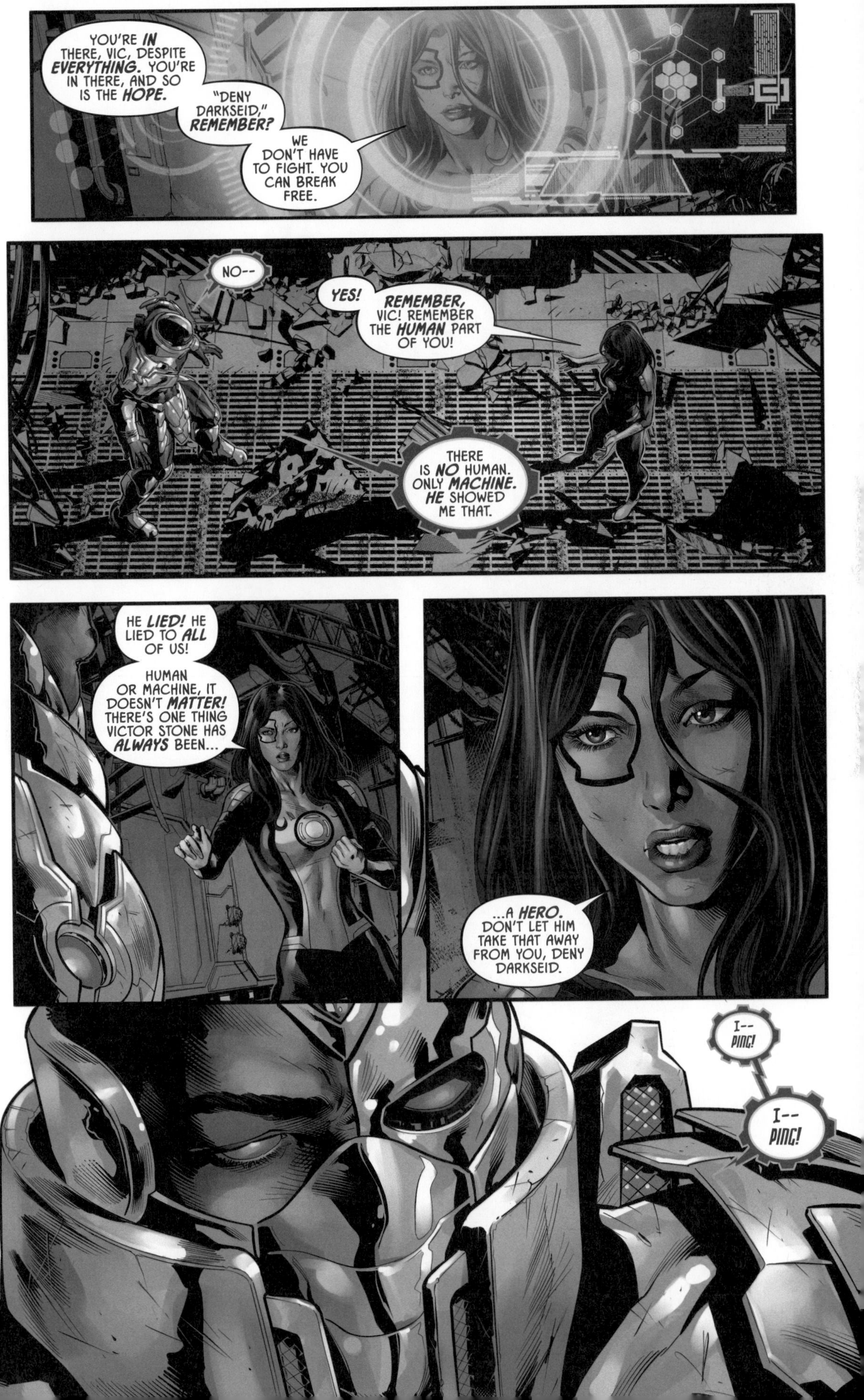
YOU'RE IN THERE, VIC, DESPITE EVERYTHING. YOU'RE IN THERE, AND SO IS THE HOPE.
"DENY DARKSEID," REMEMBER?
WE DON'T HAVE TO FIGHT. YOU CAN BREAK FREE.
NO--
YES!
REMEMBER, VIC! REMEMBER THE HUMAN PART OF YOU!
THERE IS NO HUMAN. ONLY MACHINE. HE SHOWED ME THAT.
HE LIED! HE LIED TO ALL OF US!
HUMAN OR MACHINE, IT DOESN'T MATTER! THERE'S ONE THING VICTOR STONE HAS ALWAYS BEEN...
...A HERO. DON'T LET HIM TAKE THAT AWAY FROM YOU, DENY DARKSEID.
I-- PING!
I-- PING!

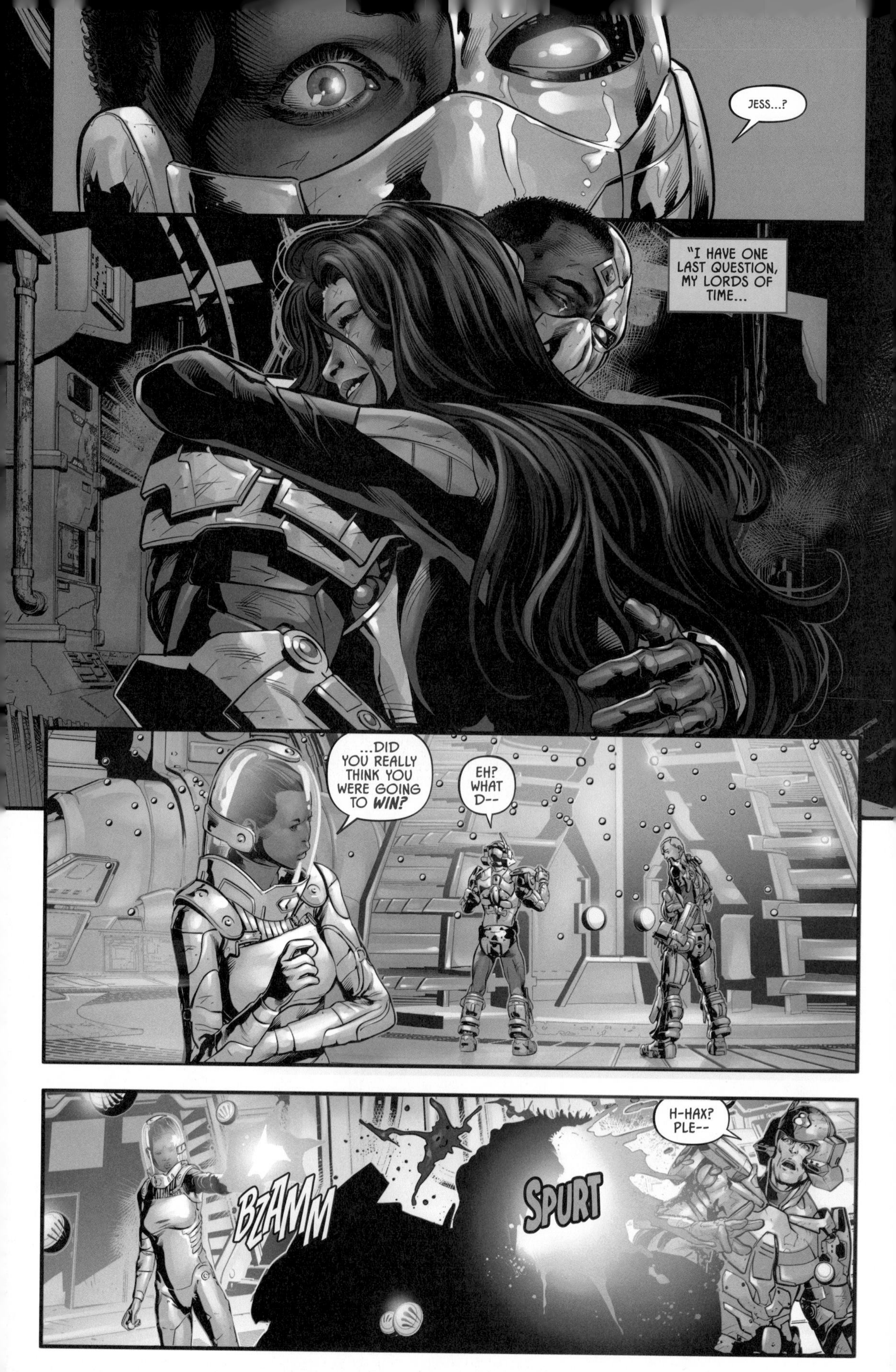
JESS...?
"I HAVE ONE LAST QUESTION, MY LORDS OF TIME...
...DID YOU REALLY THINK YOU WERE GOING TO WIN?
EH? WHAT D--
BZAMM
SPURT
H-HAX? PLE--

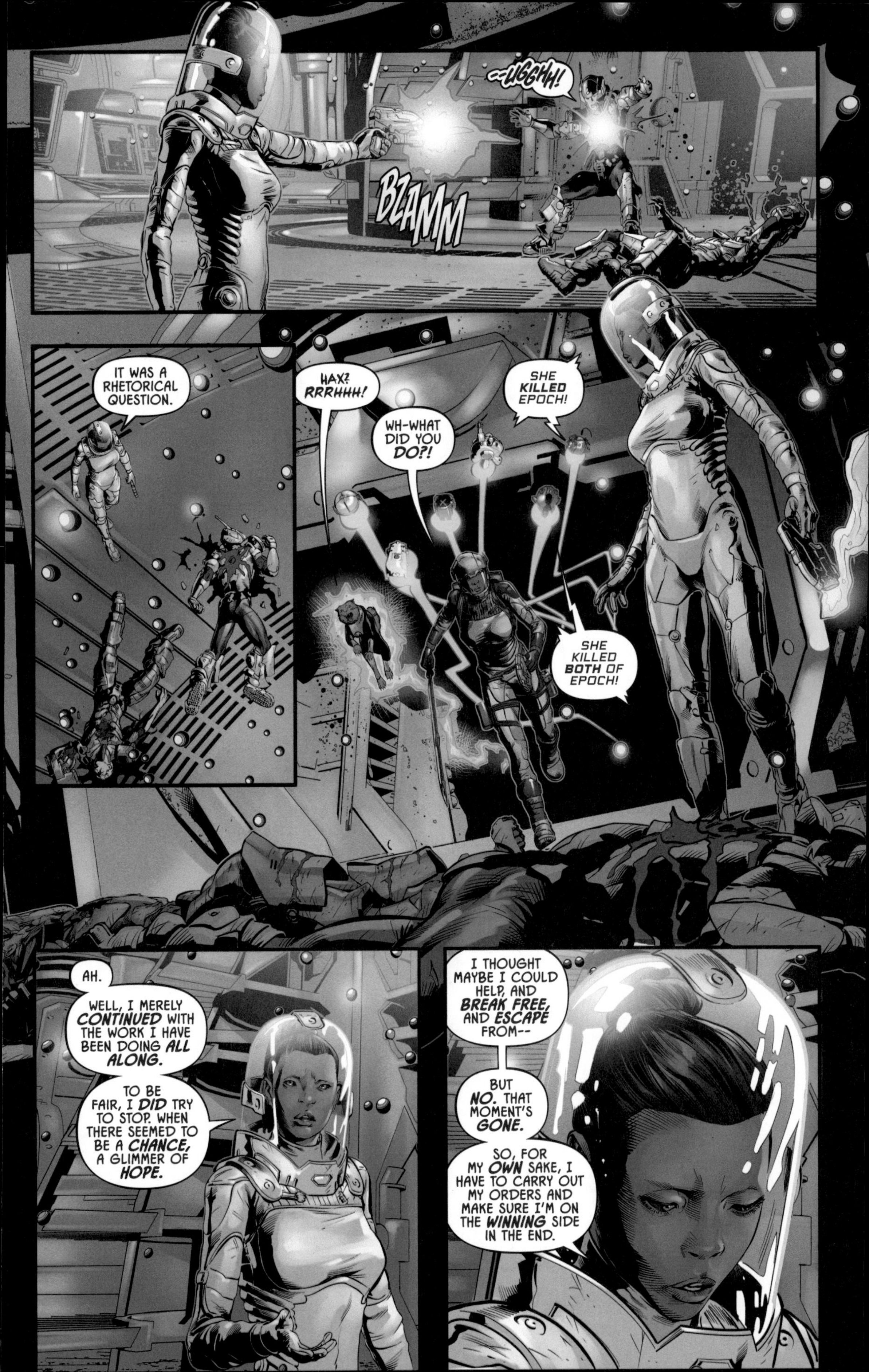
--UGGHH!
BZAMM
IT WAS A RHETORICAL QUESTION.
HAX? RRRHHH!
WH-WHAT DID YOU DO?!
SHE KILLED EPOCH!
SHE KILLED BOTH OF EPOCH!
AH.
WELL, I MERELY CONTINUED WITH THE WORK I HAVE BEEN DOING ALL ALONG.
TO BE FAIR, I DID TRY TO STOP. WHEN THERE SEEMED TO BE A CHANCE, A GLIMMER OF HOPE.
I THOUGHT MAYBE I COULD HELP, AND BREAK FREE, AND ESCAPE FROM--
BUT NO. THAT MOMENT'S GONE.
SO, FOR MY OWN SAKE, I HAVE TO CARRY OUT MY ORDERS AND MAKE SURE I'M ON THE WINNING SIDE IN THE END.

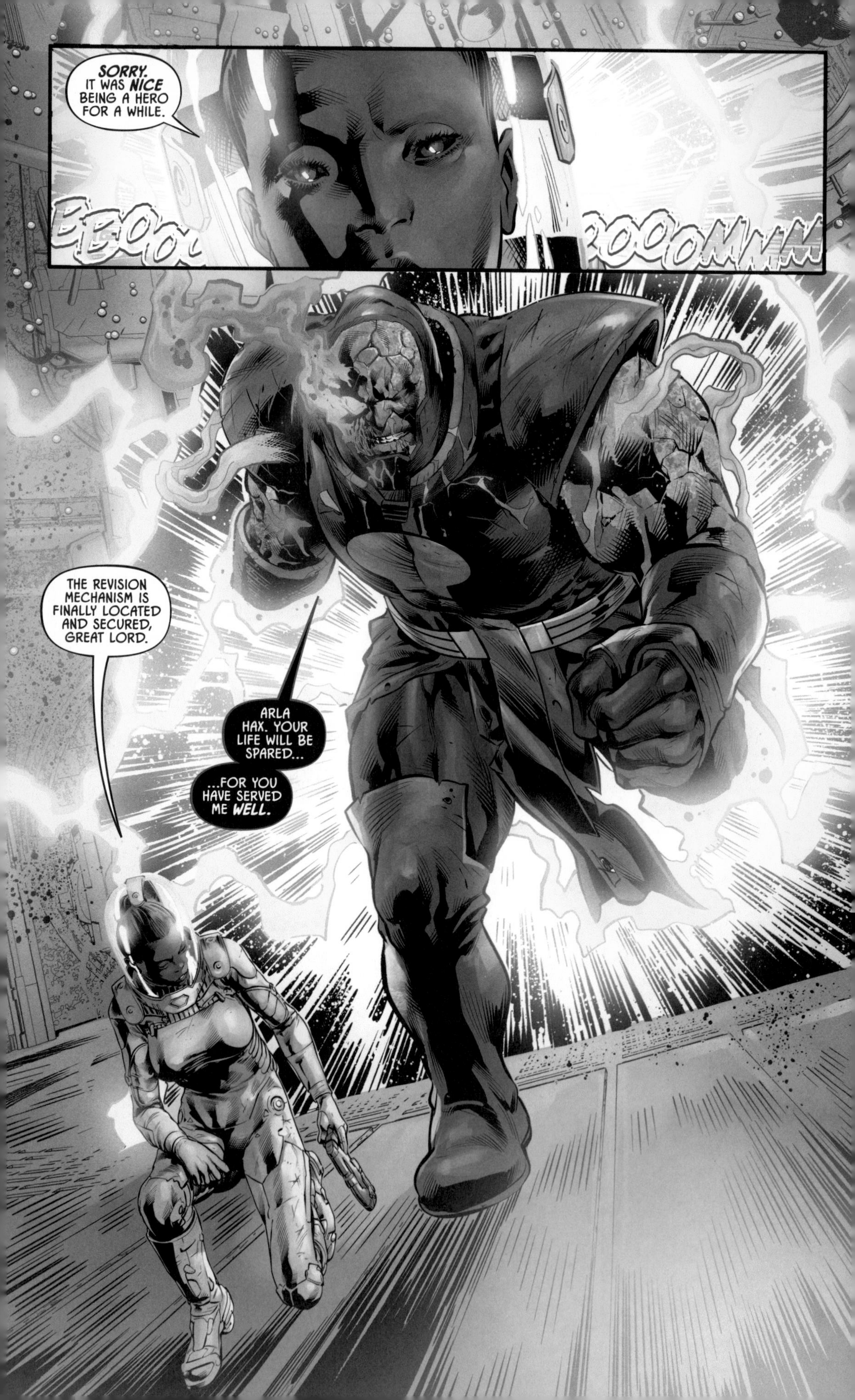
SORRY. IT WAS NICE BEING A HERO FOR A WHILE.
EEBOO
OOOOMMM
THE REVISION MECHANISM IS FINALLY LOCATED AND SECURED, GREAT LORD.
ARLA HAX. YOUR LIFE WILL BE SPARED...
...FOR YOU HAVE SERVED ME WELL.

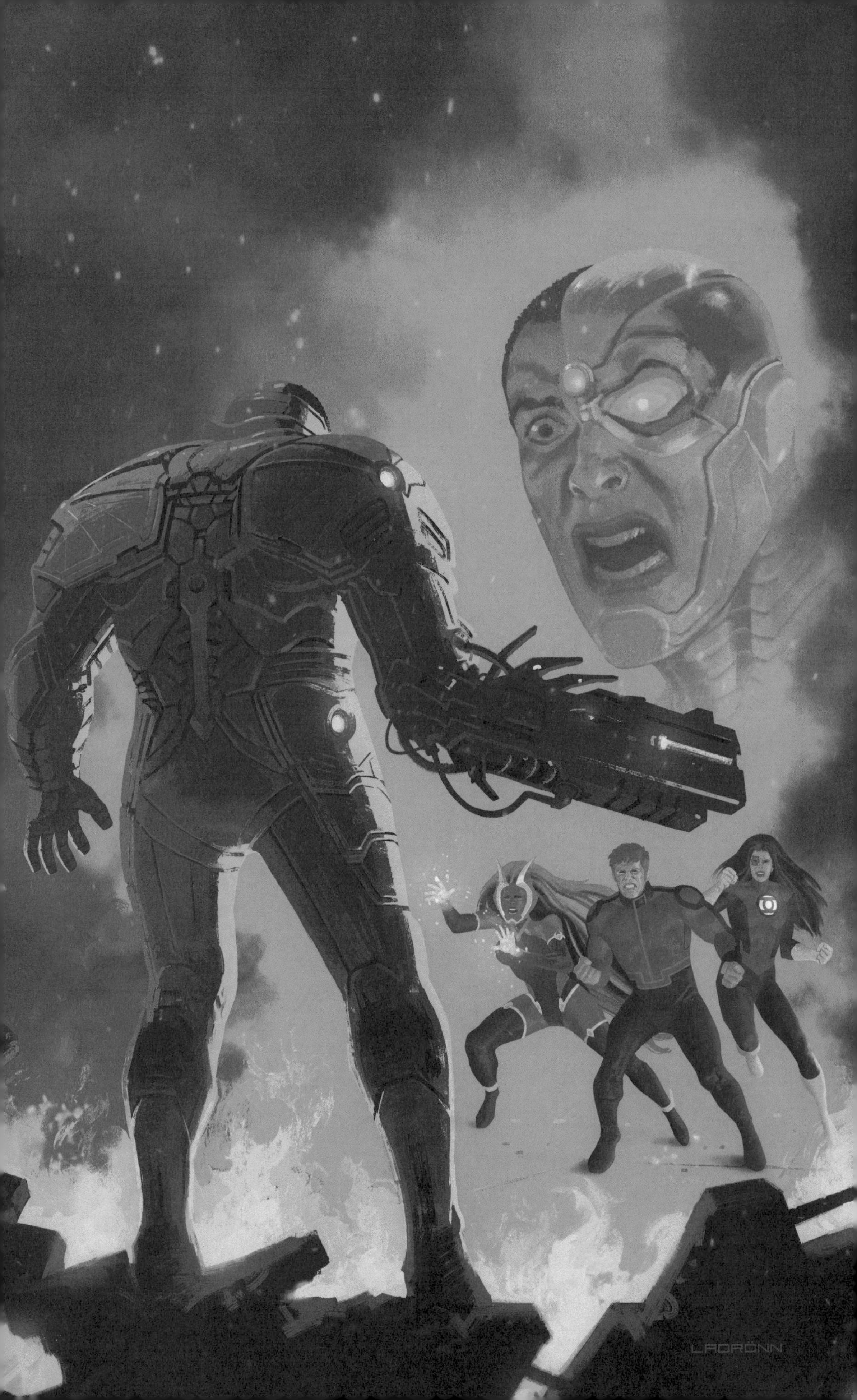
LAORÖNN

***Justice League Odyssey* #24** variant cover by **SKAN**

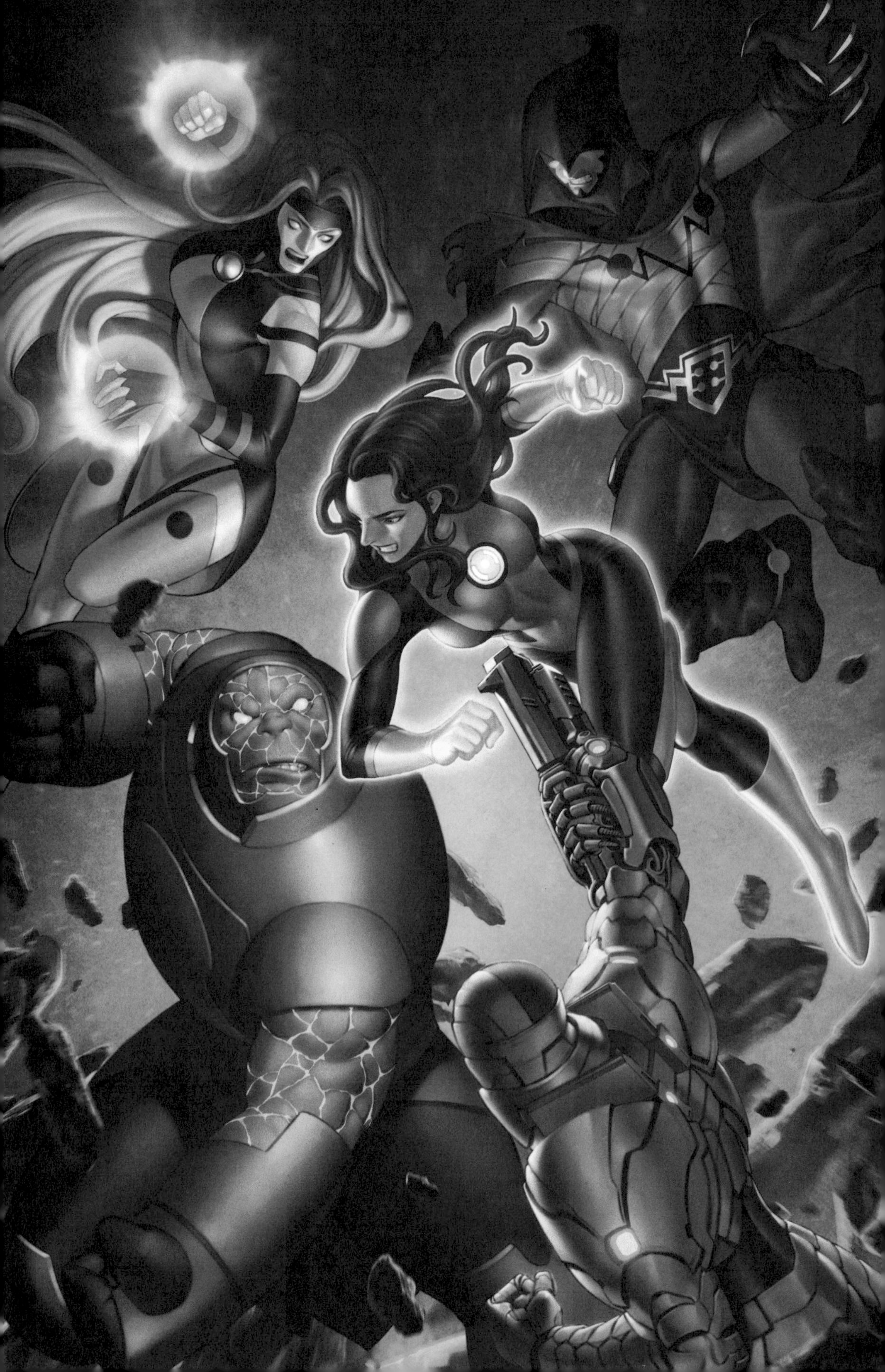

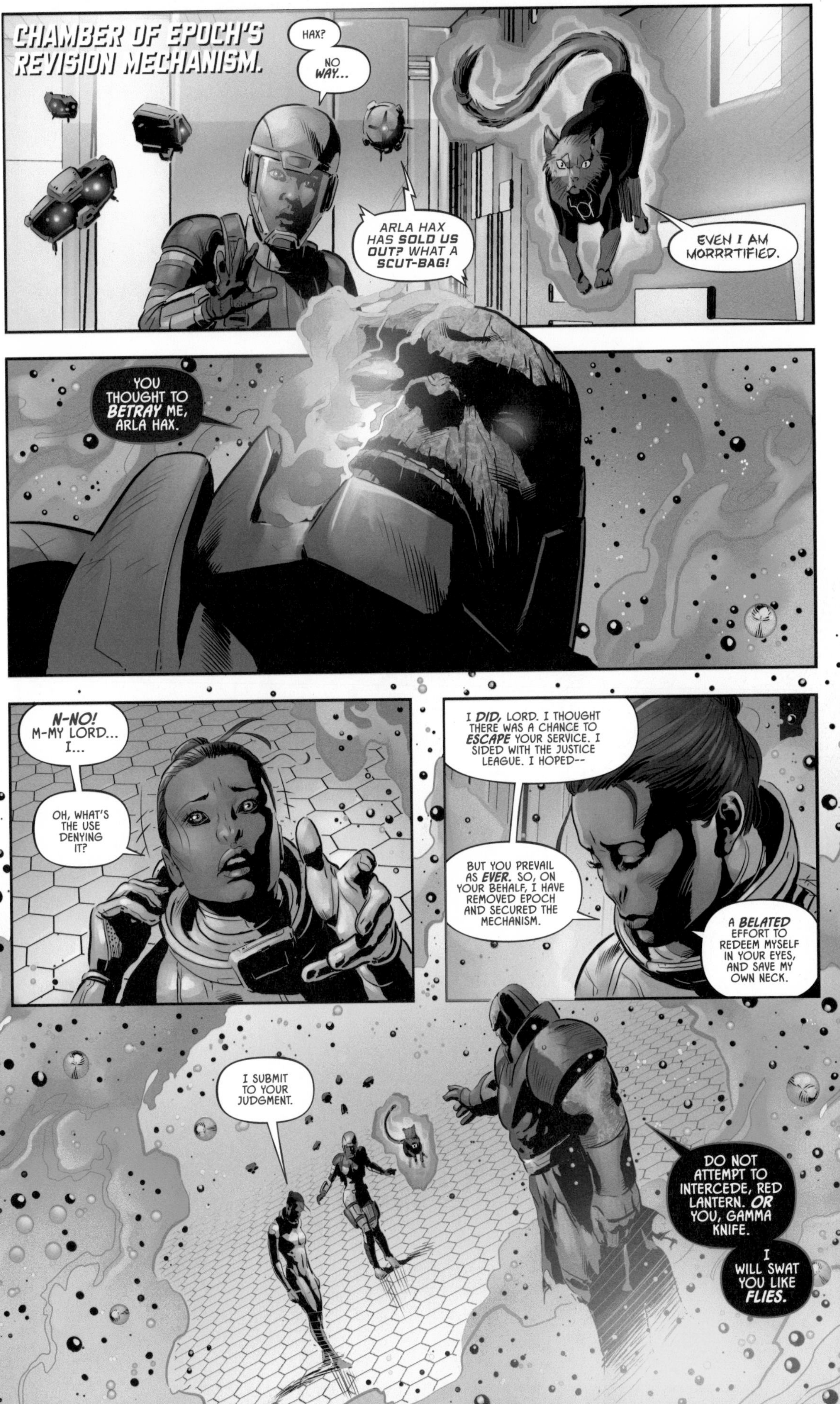
CHAMBER OF EPOCH'S REVISION MECHANISM.
HAX?
NO WAY...
ARLA HAX HAS SOLD US OUT? WHAT A SCUT-BAG!
EVEN I AM MORRRTIFIED.
YOU THOUGHT TO BETRAY ME, ARLA HAX.
N-NO! M-MY LORD... I...
OH, WHAT'S THE USE DENYING IT?
I DID, LORD. I THOUGHT THERE WAS A CHANCE TO ESCAPE YOUR SERVICE. I SIDED WITH THE JUSTICE LEAGUE. I HOPED--
BUT YOU PREVAIL AS EVER. SO, ON YOUR BEHALF, I HAVE REMOVED EPOCH AND SECURED THE MECHANISM.
A BELATED EFFORT TO REDEEM MYSELF IN YOUR EYES, AND SAVE MY OWN NECK.
I SUBMIT TO YOUR JUDGMENT.
DO NOT ATTEMPT TO INTERCEDE, RED LANTERN. OR YOU, GAMMA KNIFE.
I WILL SWAT YOU LIKE FLIES.

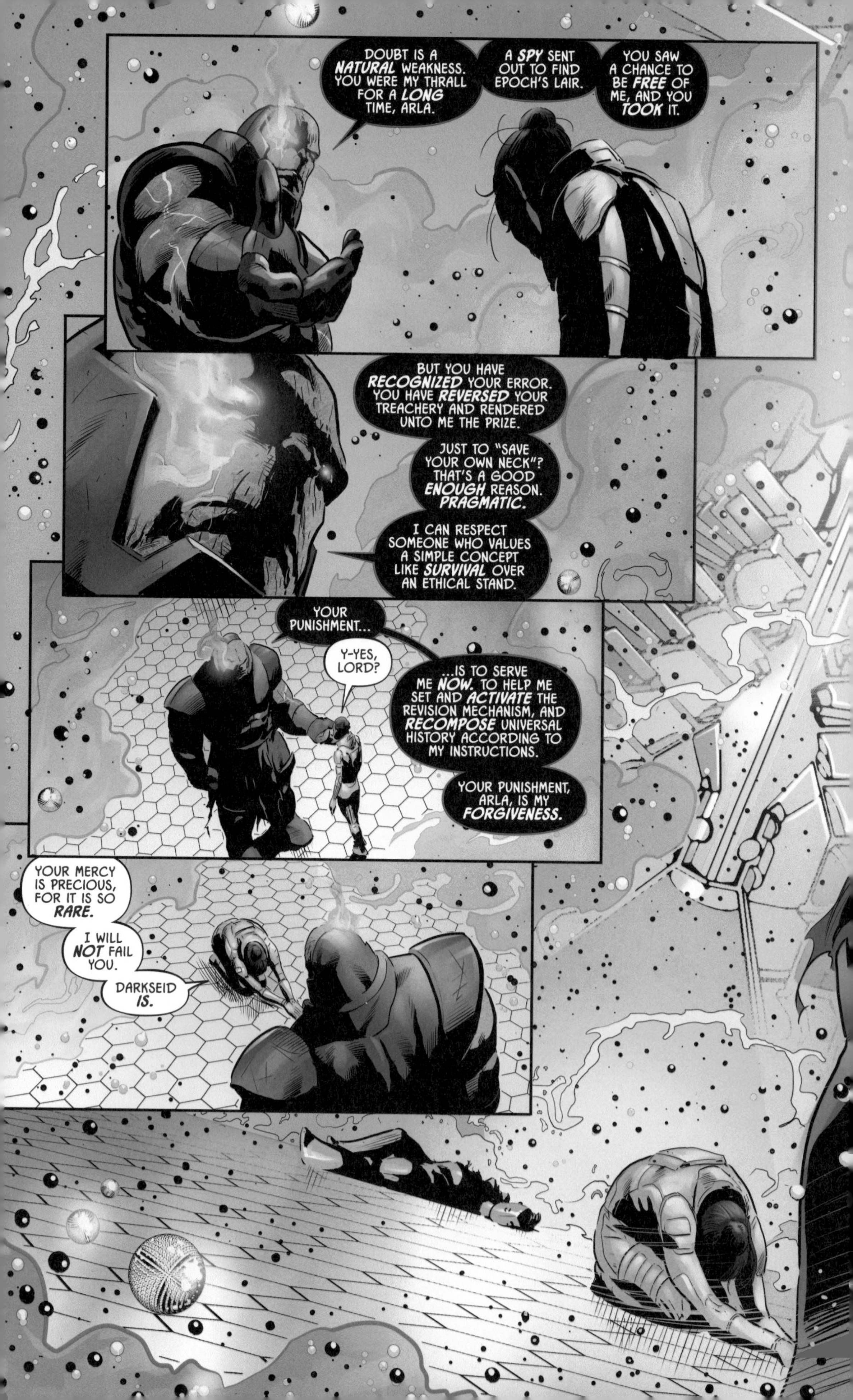
DOUBT IS A NATURAL WEAKNESS. YOU WERE MY THRALL FOR A LONG TIME, ARLA.
A SPY SENT OUT TO FIND EPOCH'S LAIR.
YOU SAW A CHANCE TO BE FREE OF ME, AND YOU TOOK IT.
BUT YOU HAVE RECOGNIZED YOUR ERROR. YOU HAVE REVERSED YOUR TREACHERY AND RENDERED UNTO ME THE PRIZE.
JUST TO "SAVE YOUR OWN NECK"? THAT'S A GOOD ENOUGH REASON. PRAGMATIC.
I CAN RESPECT SOMEONE WHO VALUES A SIMPLE CONCEPT LIKE SURVIVAL OVER AN ETHICAL STAND.
YOUR PUNISHMENT...
Y-YES, LORD?
...IS TO SERVE ME NOW. TO HELP ME SET AND ACTIVATE THE REVISION MECHANISM, AND RECOMPOSE UNIVERSAL HISTORY ACCORDING TO MY INSTRUCTIONS.
YOUR PUNISHMENT, ARLA, IS MY FORGIVENESS.
YOUR MERCY IS PRECIOUS, FOR IT IS SO RARE.
I WILL NOT FAIL YOU.
DARKSEID IS.

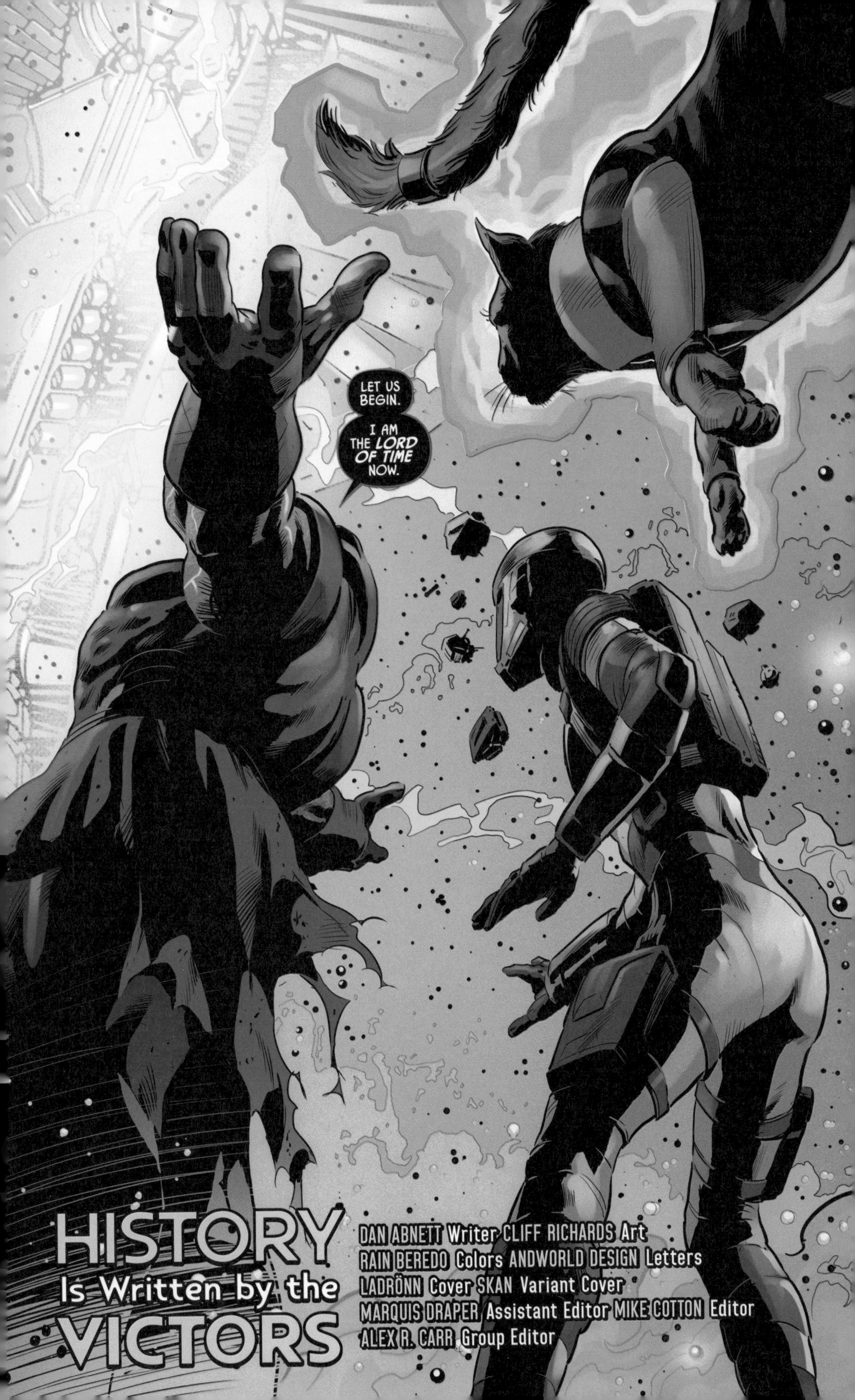
LET US BEGIN.
I AM THE *LORD OF TIME* NOW.
HISTORY Is Written by the VICTORS
DAN ABNETT Writer CLIFF RICHARDS Art
RAIN BEREDO Colors ANDWORLD DESIGN Letters
LADRÖNN Cover SKAN Variant Cover
MARQUIS DRAPER Assistant Editor MIKE COTTON Editor
ALEX R. CARR Group Editor

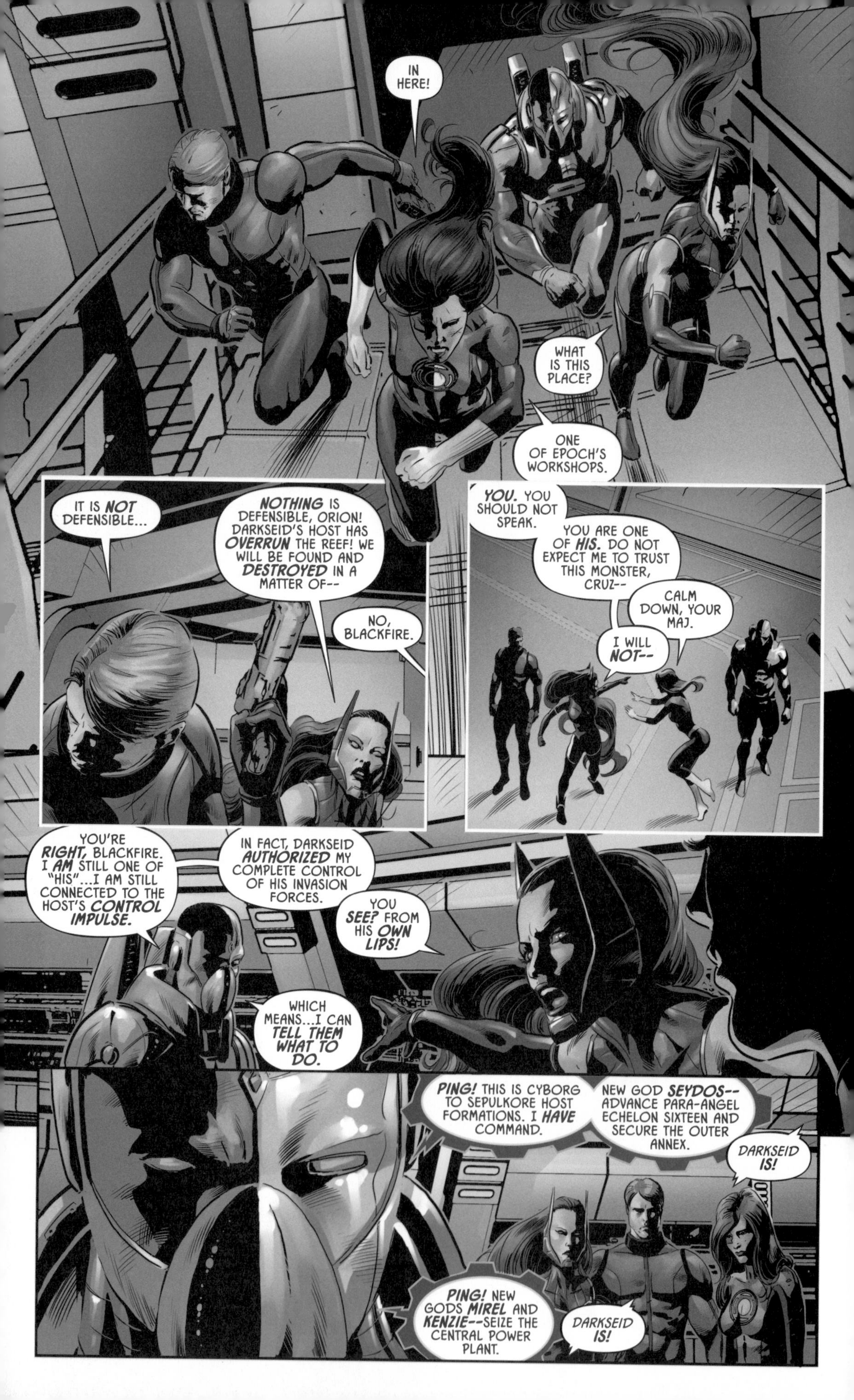

IN HERE!
WHAT IS THIS PLACE?
ONE OF EPOCH'S WORKSHOPS.
IT IS NOT DEFENSIBLE...
NOTHING IS DEFENSIBLE, ORION! DARKSEID'S HOST HAS OVERRUN THE REEF! WE WILL BE FOUND AND DESTROYED IN A MATTER OF--
NO, BLACKFIRE.
YOU. YOU SHOULD NOT SPEAK.
YOU ARE ONE OF HIS. DO NOT EXPECT ME TO TRUST THIS MONSTER, CRUZ--
CALM DOWN, YOUR MAJ.
I WILL NOT--
YOU'RE RIGHT, BLACKFIRE. I AM STILL ONE OF "HIS"...I AM STILL CONNECTED TO THE HOST'S CONTROL IMPULSE.
IN FACT, DARKSEID AUTHORIZED MY COMPLETE CONTROL OF HIS INVASION FORCES.
YOU SEE? FROM HIS OWN LIPS!
WHICH MEANS...I CAN TELL THEM WHAT TO DO.
PING! THIS IS CYBORG TO SEPULKORE HOST FORMATIONS. I HAVE COMMAND.
NEW GOD SEYDOS-- ADVANCE PARA-ANGEL ECHELON SIXTEEN AND SECURE THE OUTER ANNEX.
DARKSEID IS!
PING! NEW GODS MIREL AND KENZIE--SEIZE THE CENTRAL POWER PLANT.
DARKSEID IS!

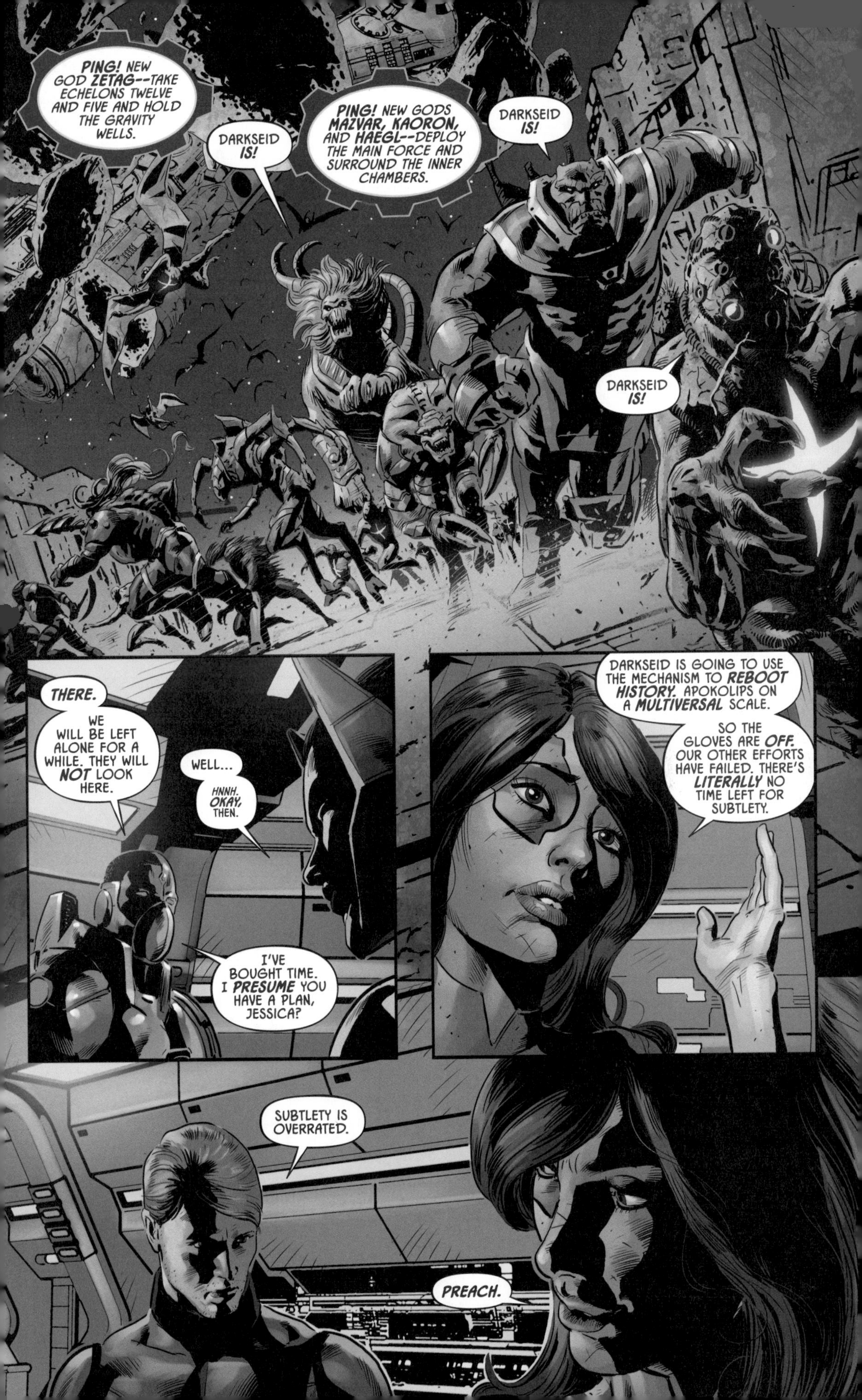
PING! NEW GOD ZETAG--TAKE ECHELONS TWELVE AND FIVE AND HOLD THE GRAVITY WELLS.
DARKSEID IS!
PING! NEW GODS MAZVAR, KAORON, AND HAEGL--DEPLOY THE MAIN FORCE AND SURROUND THE INNER CHAMBERS.
DARKSEID IS!
DARKSEID IS!
THERE.
WE WILL BE LEFT ALONE FOR A WHILE. THEY WILL NOT LOOK HERE.
WELL...
HNNH. OKAY, THEN.
I'VE BOUGHT TIME. I PRESUME YOU HAVE A PLAN, JESSICA?
DARKSEID IS GOING TO USE THE MECHANISM TO REBOOT HISTORY. APOKOLIPS ON A MULTIVERSAL SCALE.
SO THE GLOVES ARE OFF. OUR OTHER EFFORTS HAVE FAILED. THERE'S LITERALLY NO TIME LEFT FOR SUBTLETY.
SUBTLETY IS OVERRATED.
PREACH.

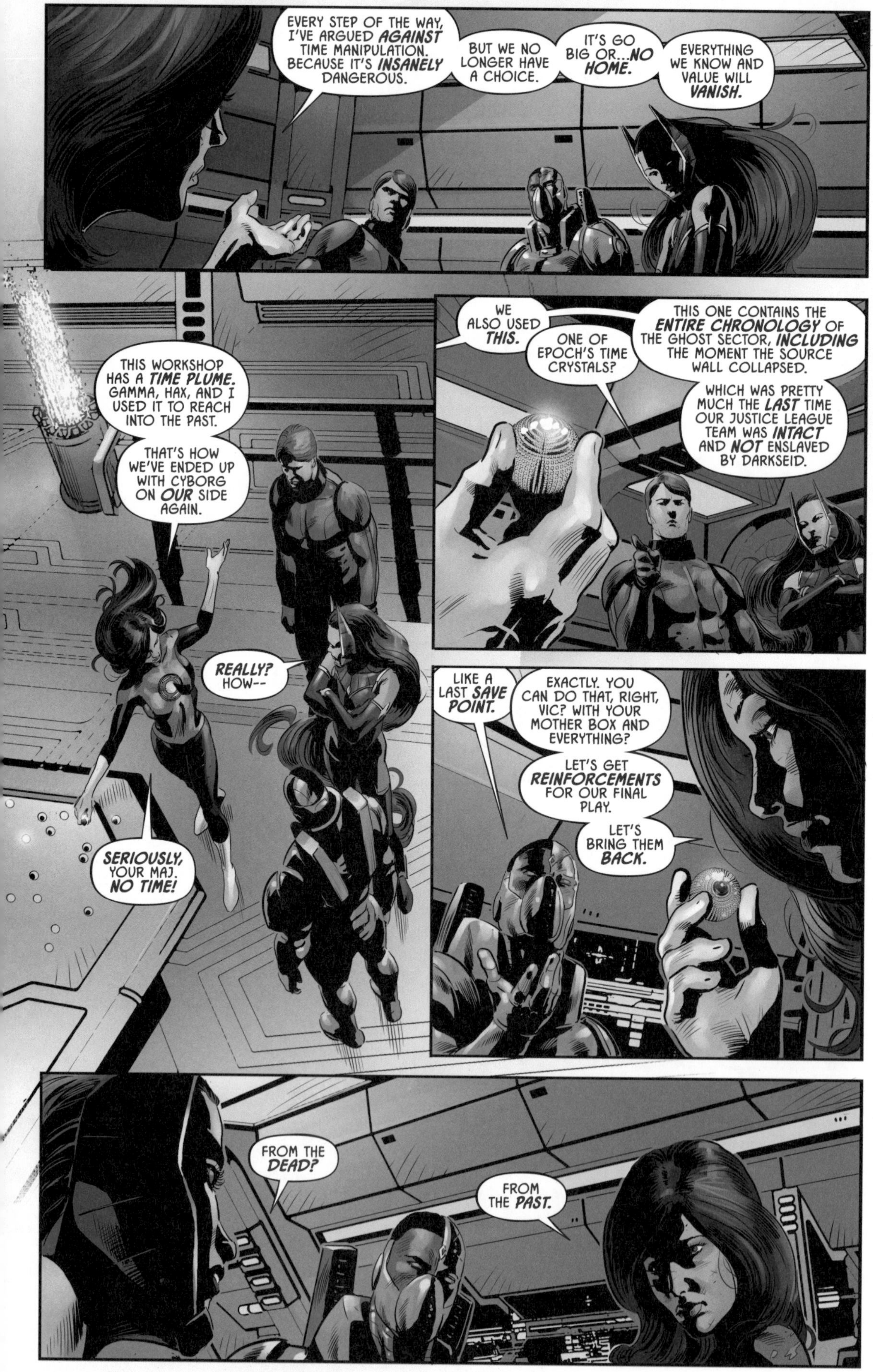

EVERY STEP OF THE WAY, I'VE ARGUED AGAINST TIME MANIPULATION. BECAUSE IT'S INSANELY DANGEROUS.
BUT WE NO LONGER HAVE A CHOICE.
IT'S GO BIG OR...NO HOME.
EVERYTHING WE KNOW AND VALUE WILL VANISH.
THIS WORKSHOP HAS A TIME PLUME. GAMMA, HAX, AND I USED IT TO REACH INTO THE PAST.
THAT'S HOW WE'VE ENDED UP WITH CYBORG ON OUR SIDE AGAIN.
REALLY? HOW--
SERIOUSLY, YOUR MAJ. NO TIME!
WE ALSO USED THIS.
ONE OF EPOCH'S TIME CRYSTALS?
THIS ONE CONTAINS THE ENTIRE CHRONOLOGY OF THE GHOST SECTOR, INCLUDING THE MOMENT THE SOURCE WALL COLLAPSED.
WHICH WAS PRETTY MUCH THE LAST TIME OUR JUSTICE LEAGUE TEAM WAS INTACT AND NOT ENSLAVED BY DARKSEID.
LIKE A LAST SAVE POINT.
EXACTLY. YOU CAN DO THAT, RIGHT, VIC? WITH YOUR MOTHER BOX AND EVERYTHING?
LET'S GET REINFORCEMENTS FOR OUR FINAL PLAY.
LET'S BRING THEM BACK.
FROM THE DEAD?
FROM THE PAST.

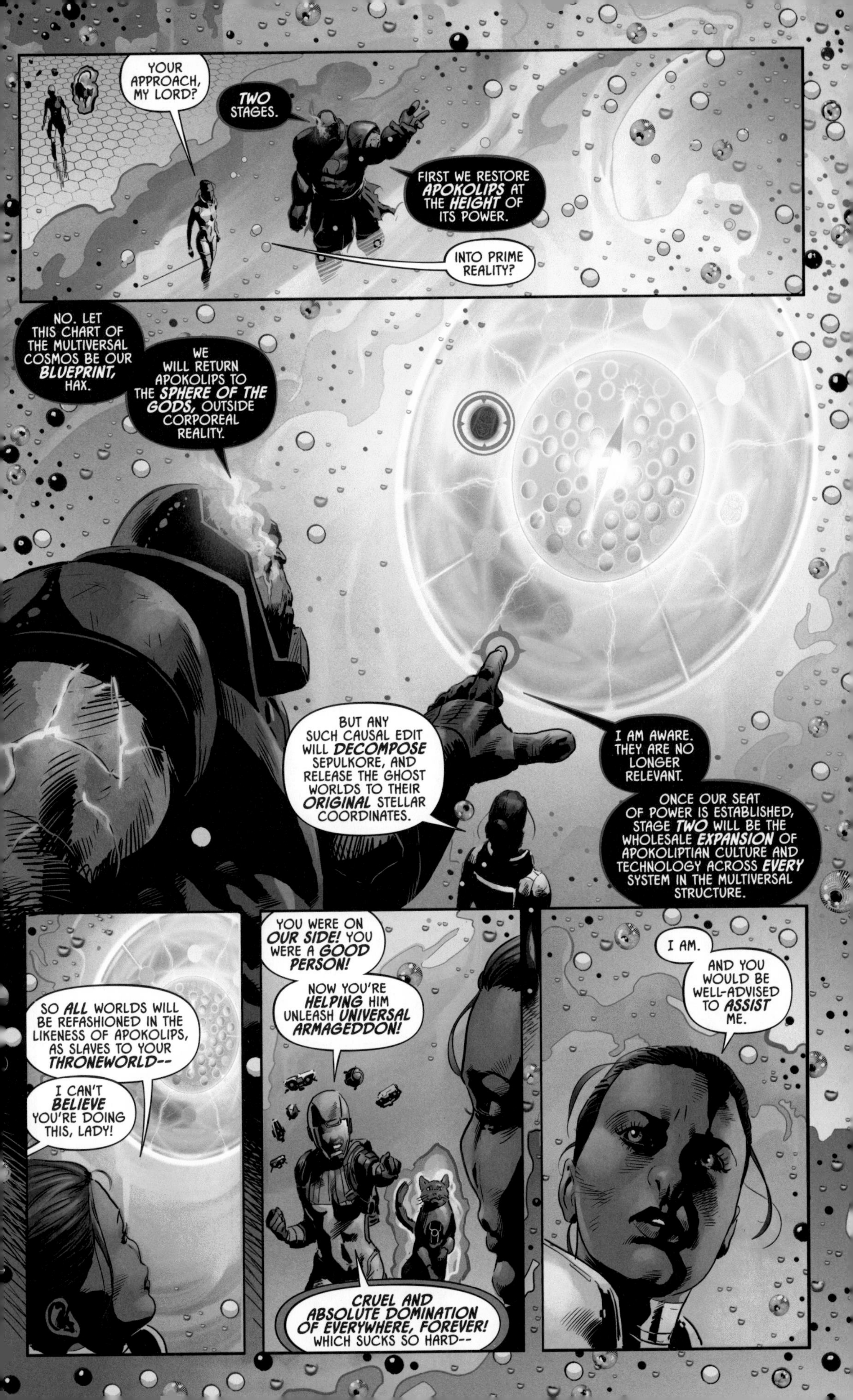
YOUR APPROACH, MY LORD?
TWO STAGES.
FIRST WE RESTORE APOKOLIPS AT THE HEIGHT OF ITS POWER.
INTO PRIME REALITY?
NO. LET THIS CHART OF THE MULTIVERSAL COSMOS BE OUR BLUEPRINT, HAX.
WE WILL RETURN APOKOLIPS TO THE SPHERE OF THE GODS, OUTSIDE CORPOREAL REALITY.
BUT ANY SUCH CAUSAL EDIT WILL DECOMPOSE SEPULKORE, AND RELEASE THE GHOST WORLDS TO THEIR ORIGINAL STELLAR COORDINATES.
I AM AWARE. THEY ARE NO LONGER RELEVANT.
ONCE OUR SEAT OF POWER IS ESTABLISHED, STAGE TWO WILL BE THE WHOLESALE EXPANSION OF APOKOLIPTIAN CULTURE AND TECHNOLOGY ACROSS EVERY SYSTEM IN THE MULTIVERSAL STRUCTURE.
SO ALL WORLDS WILL BE REFASHIONED IN THE LIKENESS OF APOKOLIPS, AS SLAVES TO YOUR THRONEWORLD--
I CAN'T BELIEVE YOU'RE DOING THIS, LADY!
YOU WERE ON OUR SIDE! YOU WERE A GOOD PERSON!
NOW YOU'RE HELPING HIM UNLEASH UNIVERSAL ARMAGEDDON!
CRUEL AND ABSOLUTE DOMINATION OF EVERYWHERE, FOREVER! WHICH SUCKS SO HARD--
I AM.
AND YOU WOULD BE WELL-ADVISED TO ASSIST ME.

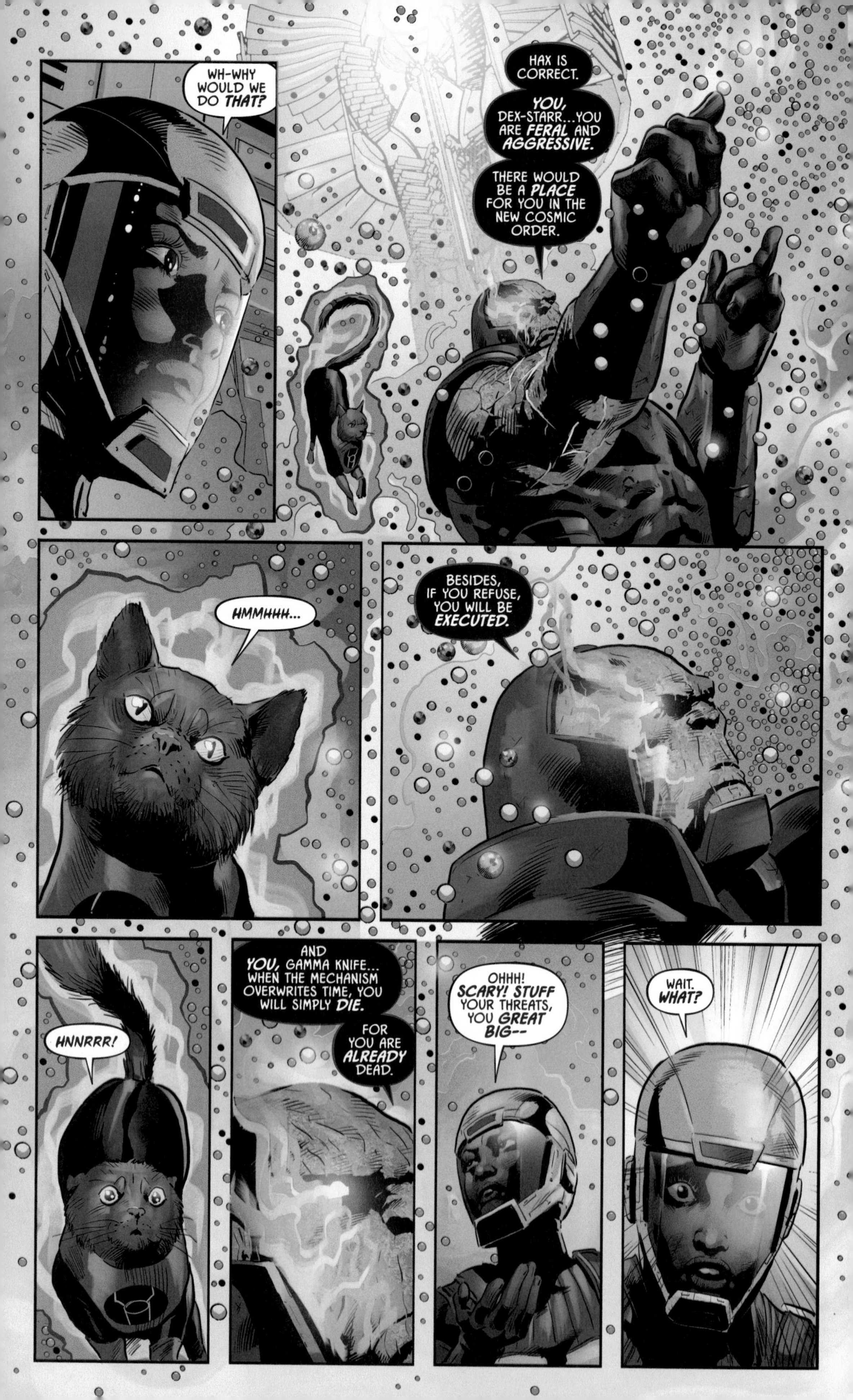
WH-WHY WOULD WE DO *THAT?*
HAX IS CORRECT.
YOU, DEX-STARR...YOU ARE *FERAL* AND *AGGRESSIVE.*
THERE WOULD BE A *PLACE* FOR YOU IN THE NEW COSMIC ORDER.
HMMHHH...
BESIDES, IF YOU REFUSE, YOU WILL BE *EXECUTED.*
HNNRRR!
AND *YOU,* GAMMA KNIFE... WHEN THE MECHANISM OVERWRITES TIME, YOU WILL SIMPLY *DIE.*
FOR YOU ARE *ALREADY* DEAD.
OHHH! *SCARY! STUFF* YOUR THREATS, YOU *GREAT BIG--*
WAIT. *WHAT?*

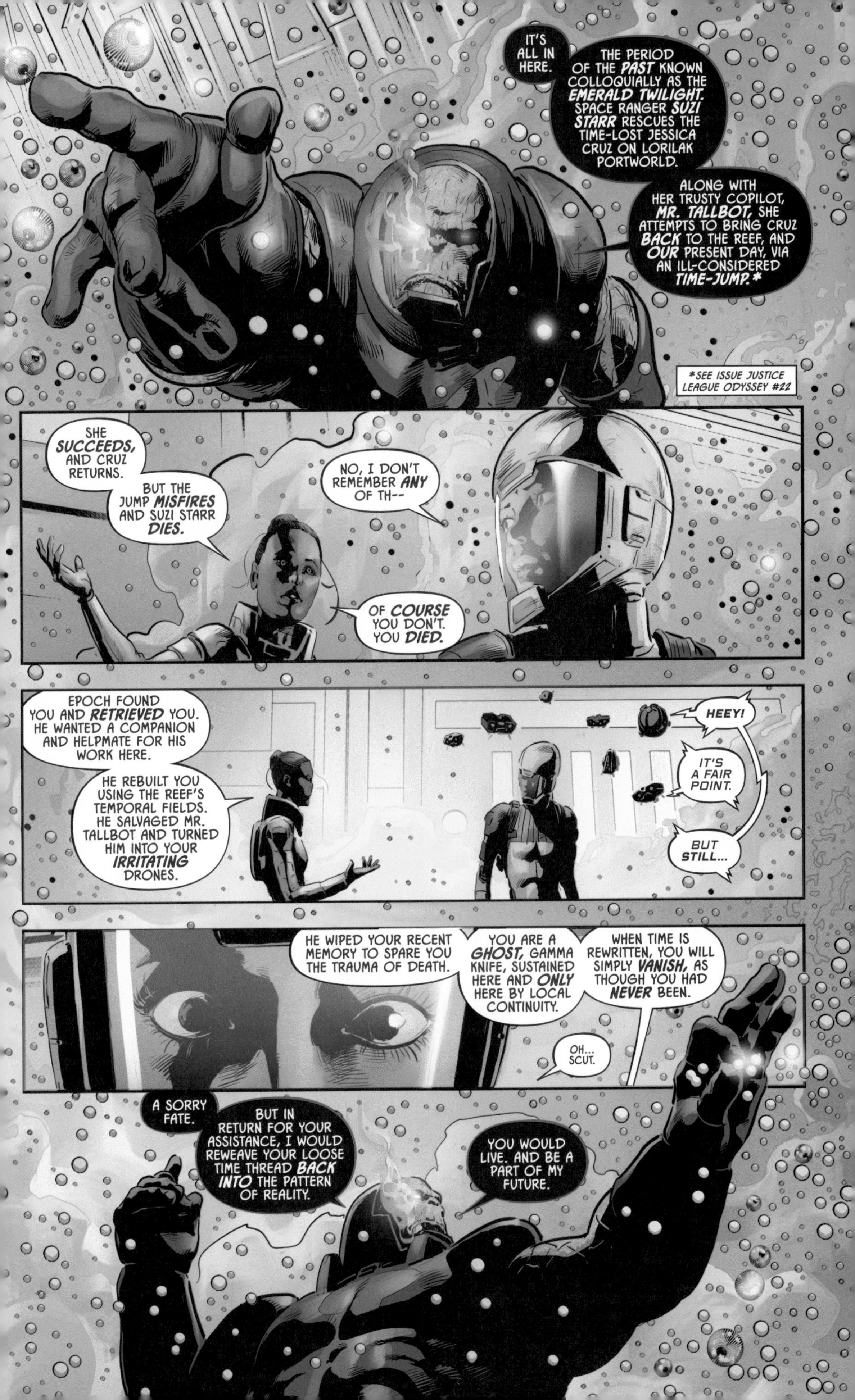
IT'S ALL IN HERE.
THE PERIOD OF THE PAST KNOWN COLLOQUIALLY AS THE EMERALD TWILIGHT. SPACE RANGER SUZI STARR RESCUES THE TIME-LOST JESSICA CRUZ ON LORILAK PORTWORLD.
ALONG WITH HER TRUSTY COPILOT, MR. TALLBOT, SHE ATTEMPTS TO BRING CRUZ BACK TO THE REEF, AND OUR PRESENT DAY, VIA AN ILL-CONSIDERED TIME-JUMP.*
*SEE ISSUE JUSTICE LEAGUE ODYSSEY #22
SHE SUCCEEDS, AND CRUZ RETURNS.
BUT THE JUMP MISFIRES AND SUZI STARR DIES.
NO, I DON'T REMEMBER ANY OF TH--
OF COURSE YOU DON'T. YOU DIED.
EPOCH FOUND YOU AND RETRIEVED YOU. HE WANTED A COMPANION AND HELPMATE FOR HIS WORK HERE.
HE REBUILT YOU USING THE REEF'S TEMPORAL FIELDS. HE SALVAGED MR. TALLBOT AND TURNED HIM INTO YOUR IRRITATING DRONES.
HEEY!
IT'S A FAIR POINT.
BUT STILL...
HE WIPED YOUR RECENT MEMORY TO SPARE YOU THE TRAUMA OF DEATH.
YOU ARE A GHOST, GAMMA KNIFE, SUSTAINED HERE AND ONLY HERE BY LOCAL CONTINUITY.
WHEN TIME IS REWRITTEN, YOU WILL SIMPLY VANISH, AS THOUGH YOU HAD NEVER BEEN.
OH... SCUT.
A SORRY FATE.
BUT IN RETURN FOR YOUR ASSISTANCE, I WOULD REWEAVE YOUR LOOSE TIME THREAD BACK INTO THE PATTERN OF REALITY.
YOU WOULD LIVE. AND BE A PART OF MY FUTURE.

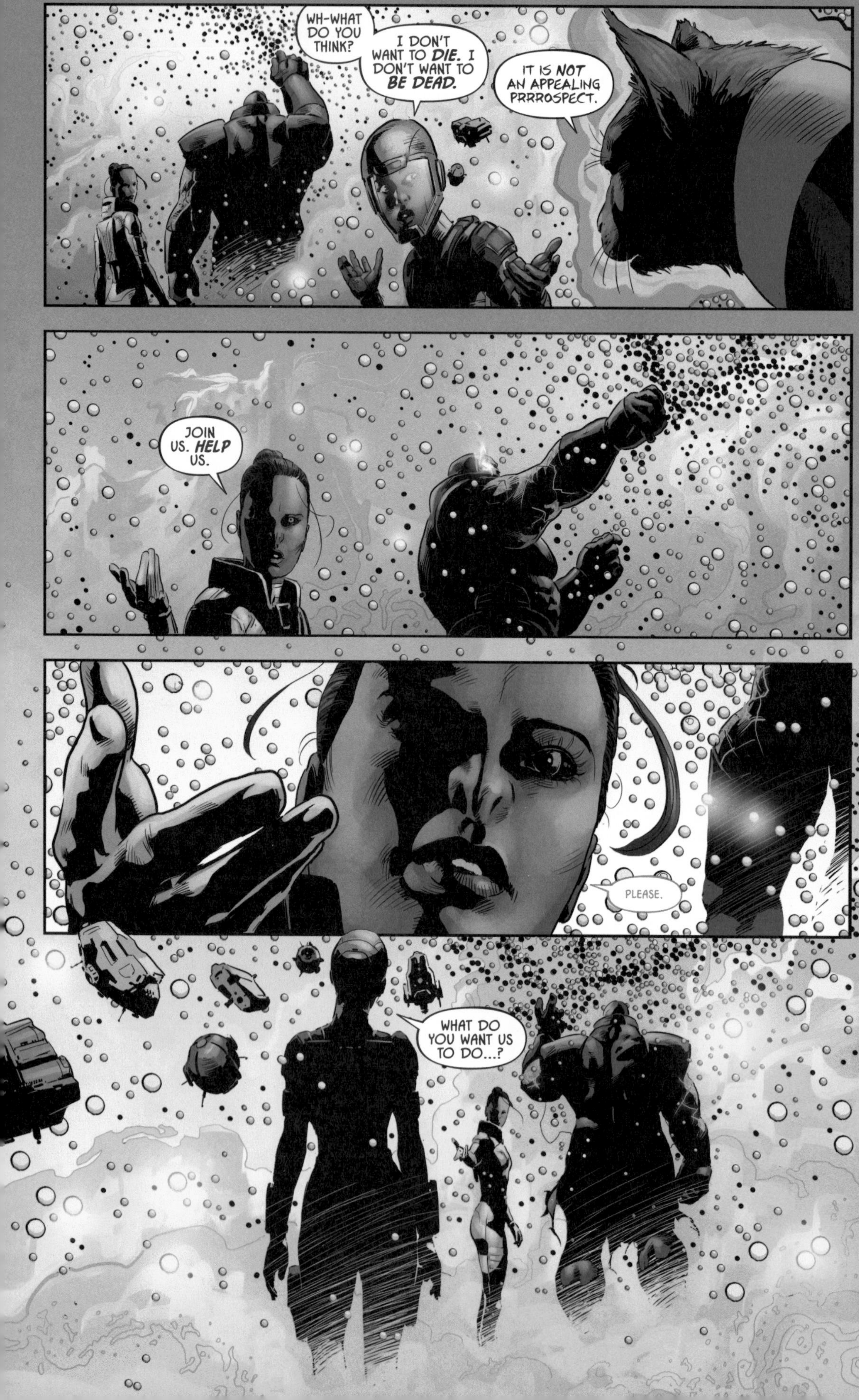
WH-WHAT DO YOU THINK?
I DON'T WANT TO DIE. I DON'T WANT TO BE DEAD.
IT IS NOT AN APPEALING PRRROSPECT.
JOIN US. HELP US.
PLEASE.
WHAT DO YOU WANT US TO DO...?

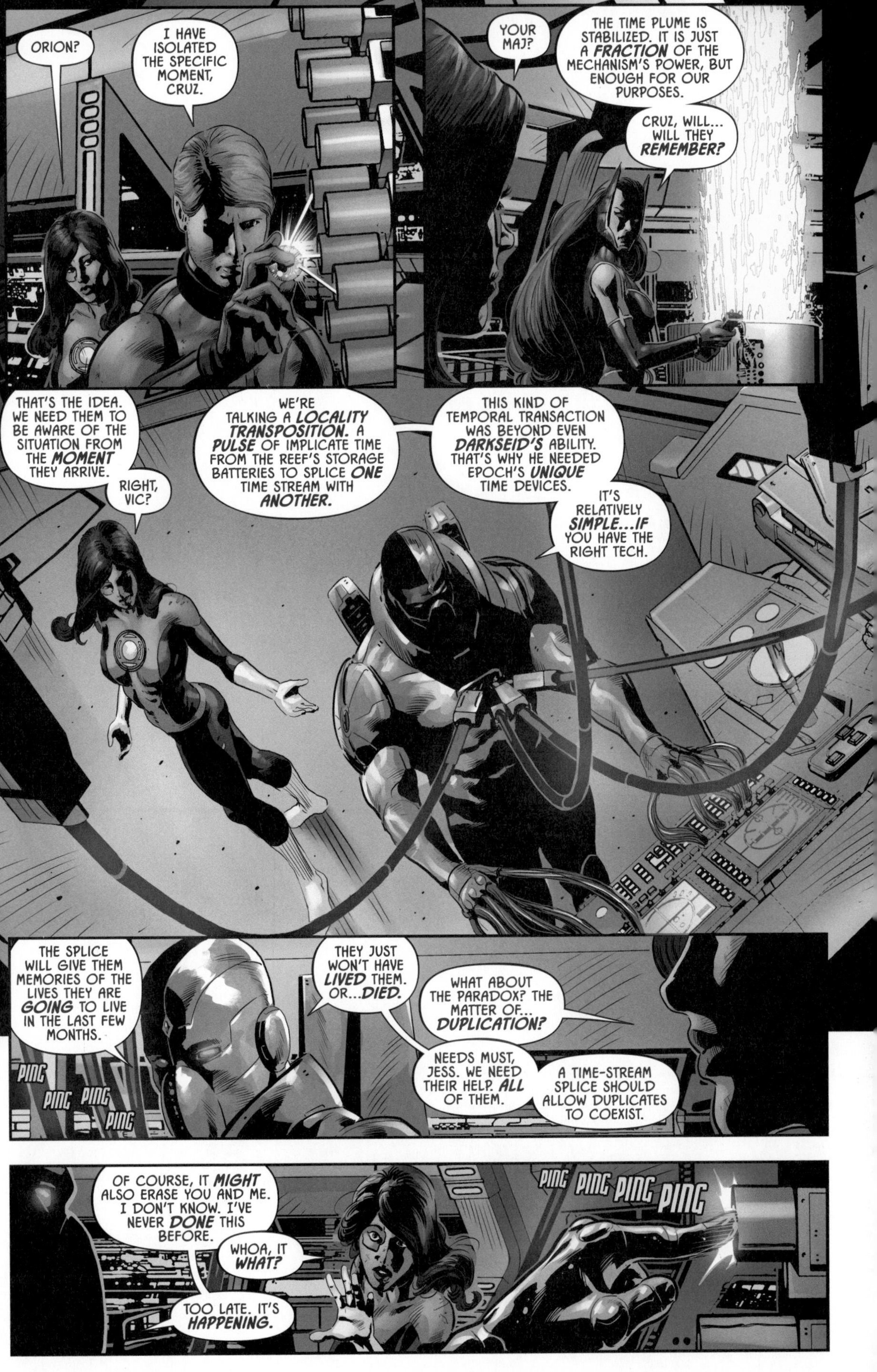
ORION?
I HAVE ISOLATED THE SPECIFIC MOMENT, CRUZ.
YOUR MAJ?
THE TIME PLUME IS STABILIZED. IT IS JUST A FRACTION OF THE MECHANISM'S POWER, BUT ENOUGH FOR OUR PURPOSES.
CRUZ, WILL... WILL THEY REMEMBER?
THAT'S THE IDEA. WE NEED THEM TO BE AWARE OF THE SITUATION FROM THE MOMENT THEY ARRIVE.
RIGHT, VIC?
WE'RE TALKING A LOCALITY TRANSPOSITION. A PULSE OF IMPLICATE TIME FROM THE REEF'S STORAGE BATTERIES TO SPLICE ONE TIME STREAM WITH ANOTHER.
THIS KIND OF TEMPORAL TRANSACTION WAS BEYOND EVEN DARKSEID'S ABILITY. THAT'S WHY HE NEEDED EPOCH'S UNIQUE TIME DEVICES.
IT'S RELATIVELY SIMPLE...IF YOU HAVE THE RIGHT TECH.
THE SPLICE WILL GIVE THEM MEMORIES OF THE LIVES THEY ARE GOING TO LIVE IN THE LAST FEW MONTHS.
THEY JUST WON'T HAVE LIVED THEM. OR...DIED.
WHAT ABOUT THE PARADOX? THE MATTER OF... DUPLICATION?
NEEDS MUST, JESS. WE NEED THEIR HELP. ALL OF THEM.
A TIME-STREAM SPLICE SHOULD ALLOW DUPLICATES TO COEXIST.
PING PING PING PING
OF COURSE, IT MIGHT ALSO ERASE YOU AND ME. I DON'T KNOW. I'VE NEVER DONE THIS BEFORE.
WHOA, IT WHAT?
TOO LATE. IT'S HAPPENING.
PING PING PING PING

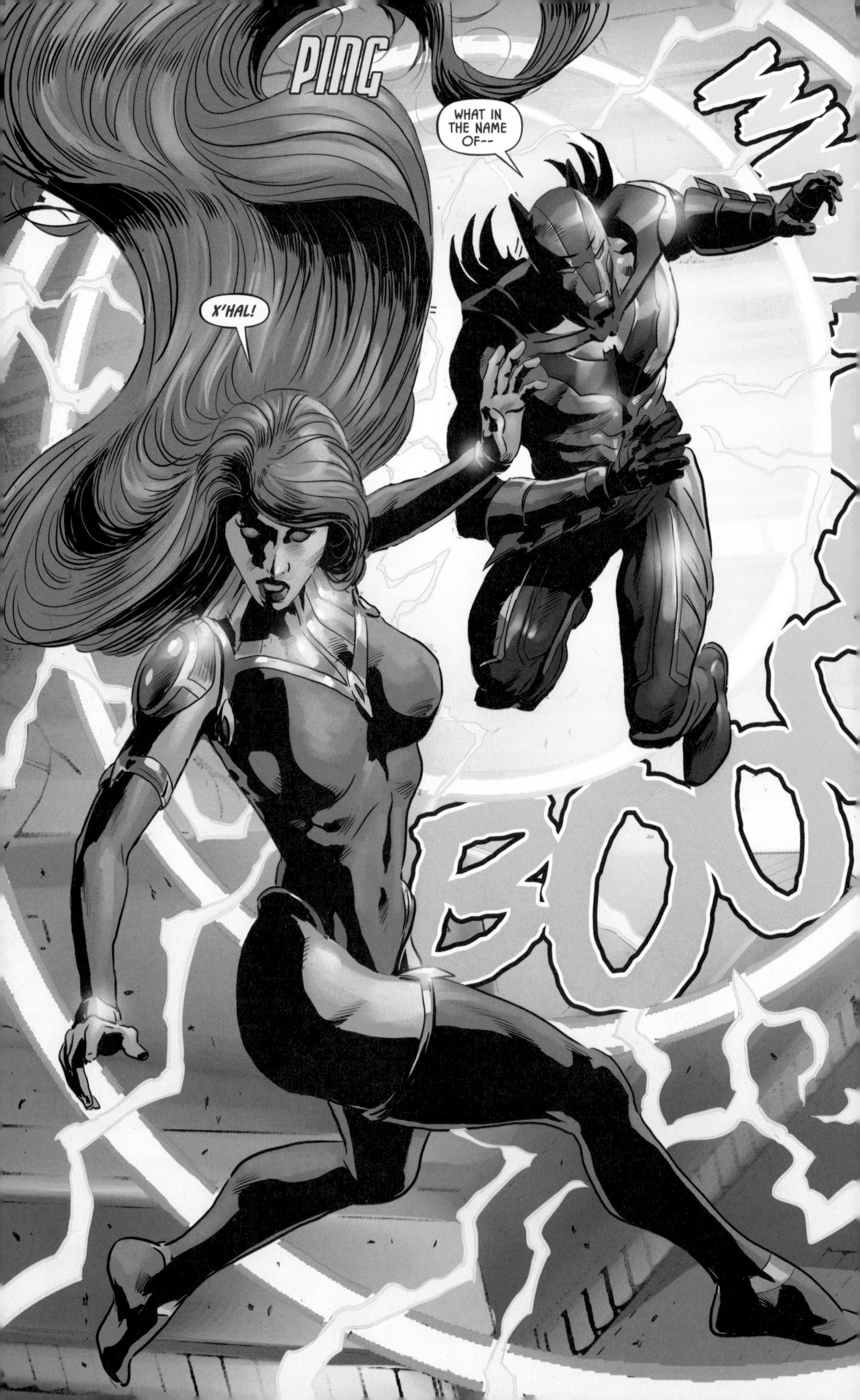
PING
WHAT IN THE NAME OF--
X'HAL!
BOO

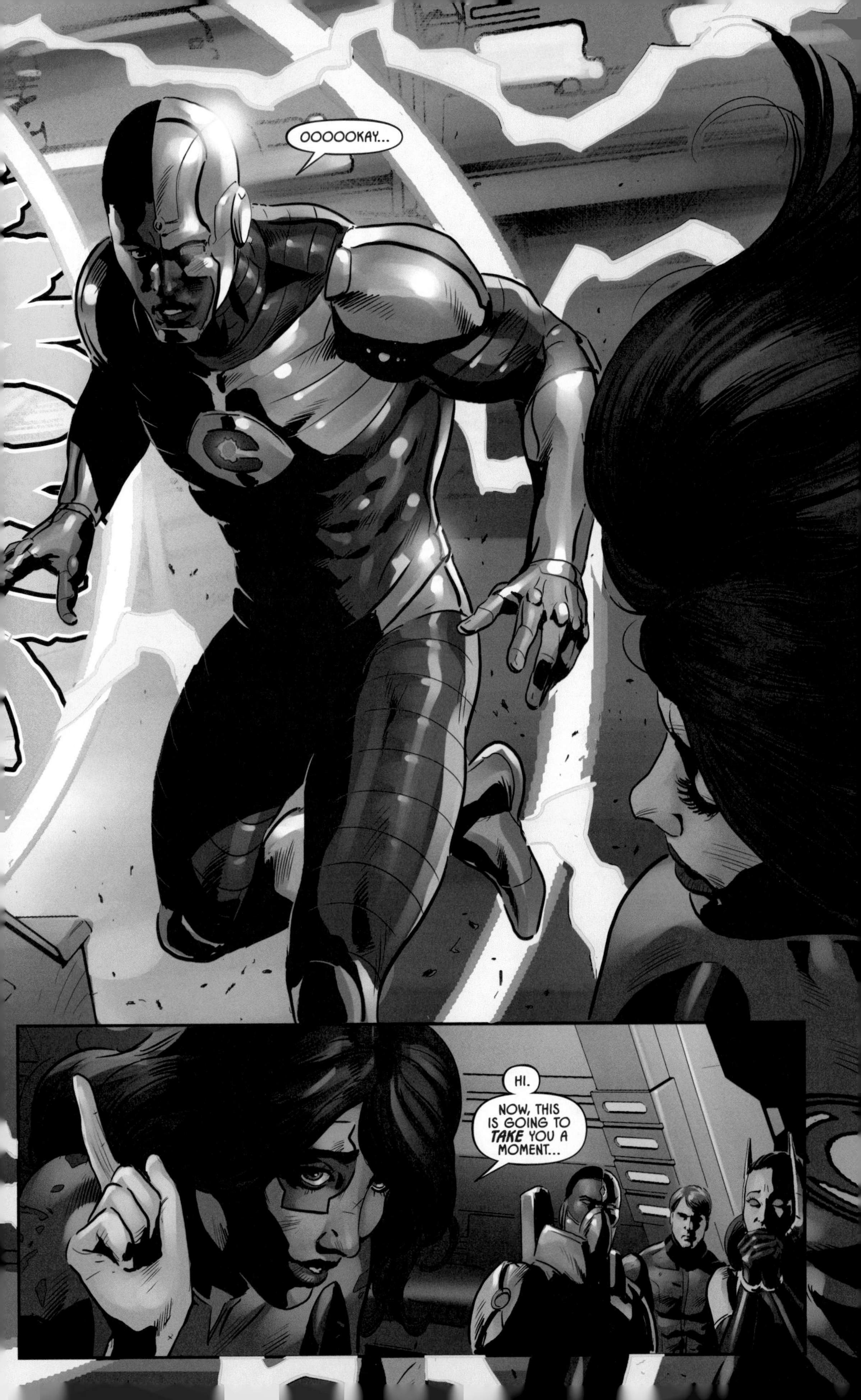
OOOOOKAY...
HI.
NOW, THIS IS GOING TO *TAKE* YOU A MOMENT...

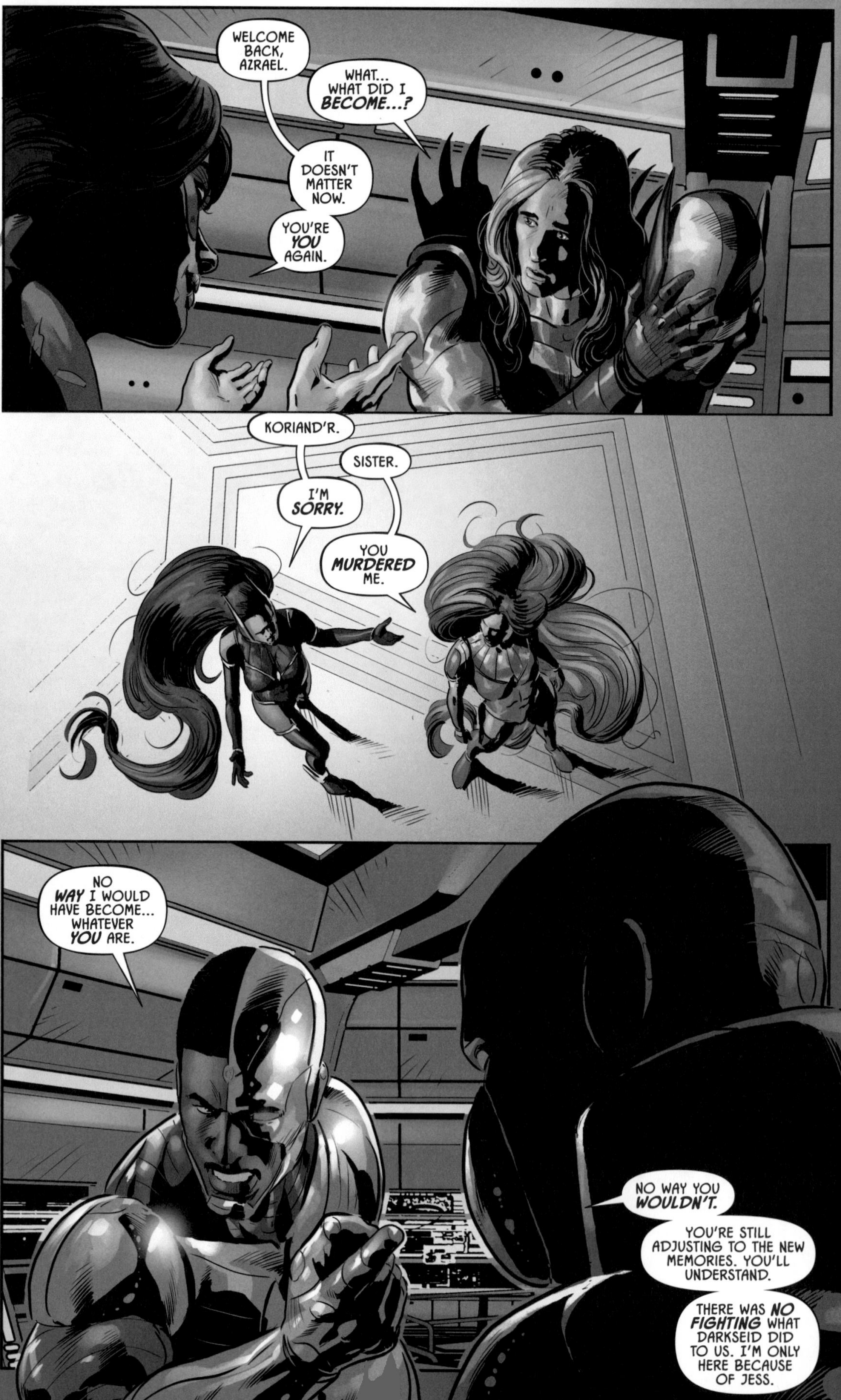
WELCOME BACK, AZRAEL.
WHAT... WHAT DID I BECOME...?
IT DOESN'T MATTER NOW.
YOU'RE YOU AGAIN.
KORIAND'R.
I'M SORRY.
SISTER.
YOU MURDERED ME.
NO WAY I WOULD HAVE BECOME... WHATEVER YOU ARE.
NO WAY YOU WOULDN'T.
YOU'RE STILL ADJUSTING TO THE NEW MEMORIES. YOU'LL UNDERSTAND.
THERE WAS NO FIGHTING WHAT DARKSEID DID TO US. I'M ONLY HERE BECAUSE OF JESS.

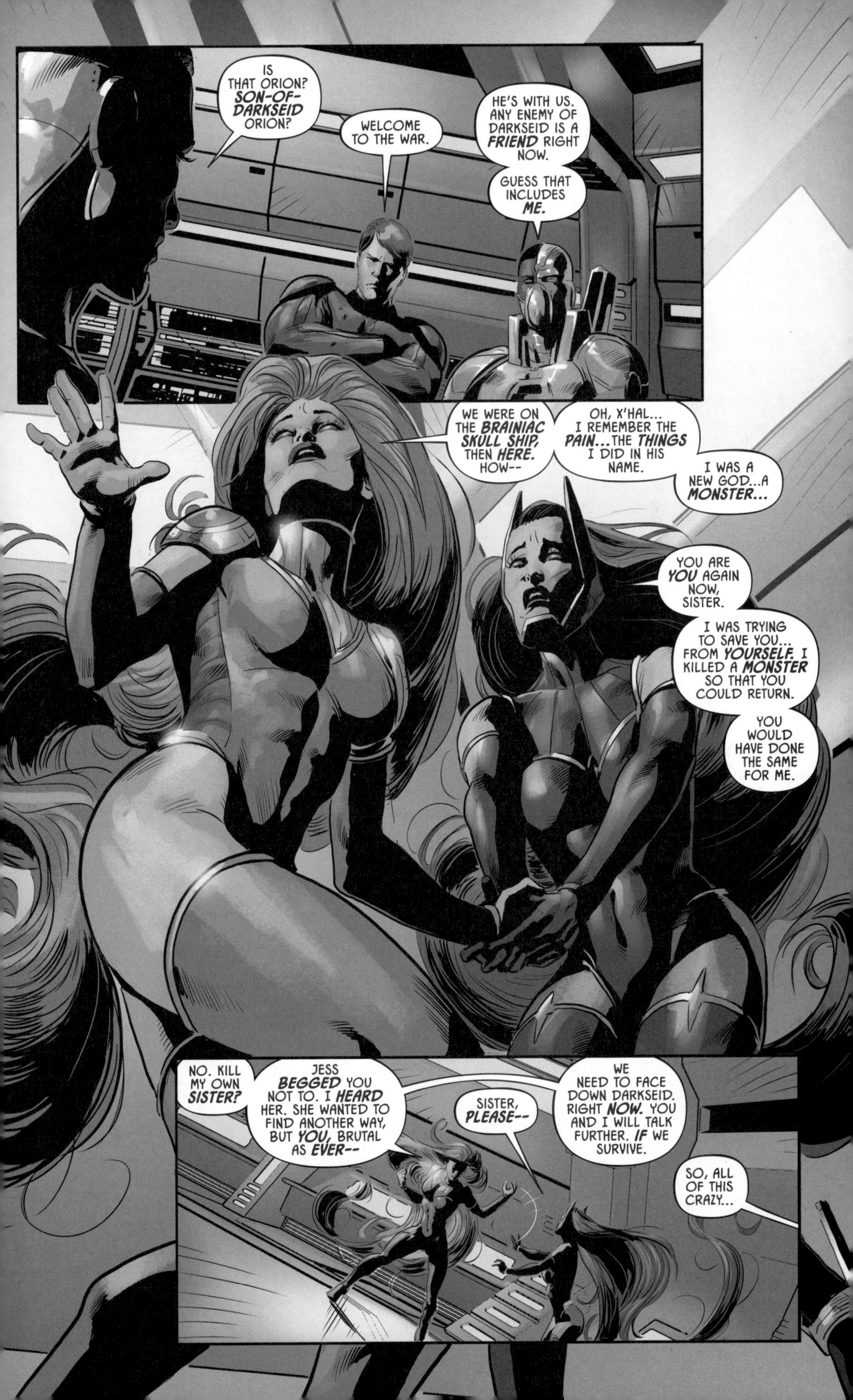
IS THAT ORION? SON-OF-DARKSEID ORION?
WELCOME TO THE WAR.
HE'S WITH US. ANY ENEMY OF DARKSEID IS A FRIEND RIGHT NOW.
GUESS THAT INCLUDES ME.
WE WERE ON THE BRAINIAC SKULL SHIP, THEN HERE. HOW--
OH, X'HAL... I REMEMBER THE PAIN...THE THINGS I DID IN HIS NAME.
I WAS A NEW GOD...A MONSTER...
YOU ARE YOU AGAIN NOW, SISTER.
I WAS TRYING TO SAVE YOU... FROM YOURSELF. I KILLED A MONSTER SO THAT YOU COULD RETURN.
YOU WOULD HAVE DONE THE SAME FOR ME.
NO. KILL MY OWN SISTER?
JESS BEGGED YOU NOT TO. I HEARD HER. SHE WANTED TO FIND ANOTHER WAY, BUT YOU, BRUTAL AS EVER--
SISTER, PLEASE--
WE NEED TO FACE DOWN DARKSEID. RIGHT NOW. YOU AND I WILL TALK FURTHER. IF WE SURVIVE.
SO, ALL OF THIS CRAZY...

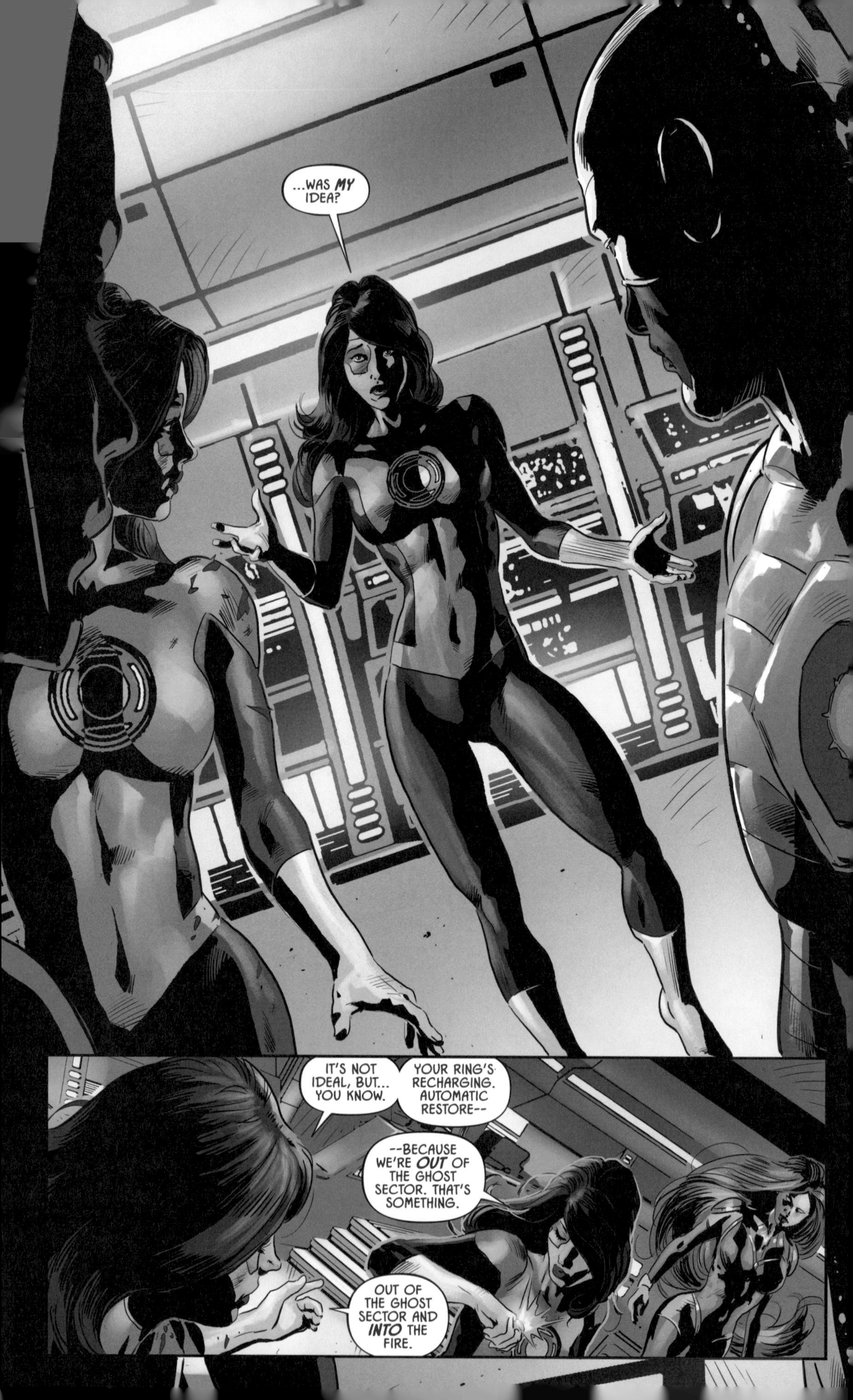
...WAS *MY* IDEA?
IT'S NOT IDEAL, BUT... YOU KNOW.
YOUR RING'S RECHARGING. AUTOMATIC RESTORE--
--BECAUSE WE'RE *OUT* OF THE GHOST SECTOR. THAT'S SOMETHING.
OUT OF THE GHOST SECTOR AND *INTO* THE FIRE.

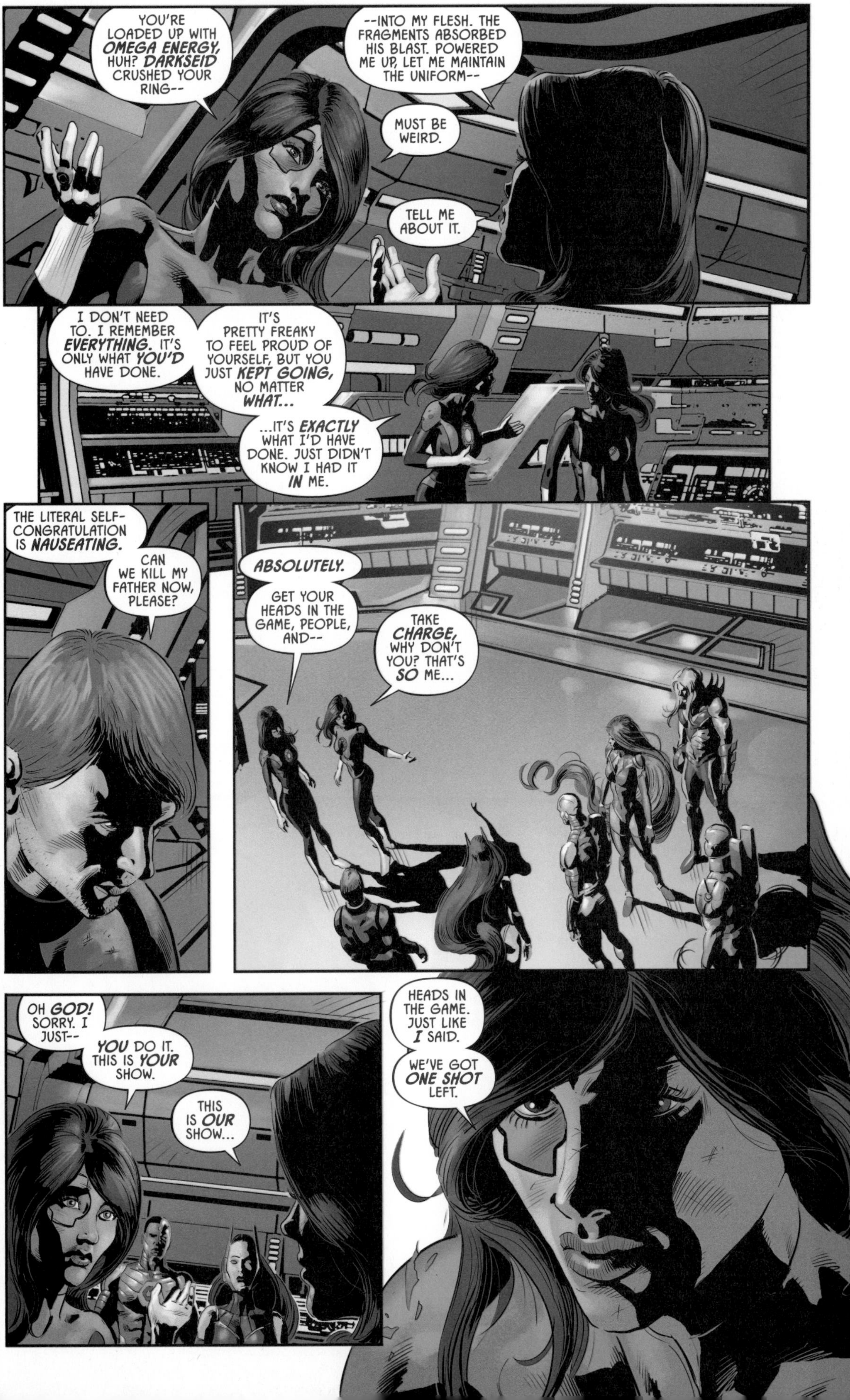
YOU'RE LOADED UP WITH OMEGA ENERGY, HUH? DARKSEID CRUSHED YOUR RING--
--INTO MY FLESH. THE FRAGMENTS ABSORBED HIS BLAST. POWERED ME UP, LET ME MAINTAIN THE UNIFORM--
MUST BE WEIRD.
TELL ME ABOUT IT.
I DON'T NEED TO. I REMEMBER EVERYTHING. IT'S ONLY WHAT YOU'D HAVE DONE.
IT'S PRETTY FREAKY TO FEEL PROUD OF YOURSELF, BUT YOU JUST KEPT GOING, NO MATTER WHAT...
...IT'S EXACTLY WHAT I'D HAVE DONE. JUST DIDN'T KNOW I HAD IT IN ME.
THE LITERAL SELF-CONGRATULATION IS NAUSEATING.
CAN WE KILL MY FATHER NOW, PLEASE?
ABSOLUTELY.
GET YOUR HEADS IN THE GAME, PEOPLE, AND--
TAKE CHARGE, WHY DON'T YOU? THAT'S SO ME...
OH GOD! SORRY. I JUST--
YOU DO IT. THIS IS YOUR SHOW.
THIS IS OUR SHOW...
HEADS IN THE GAME. JUST LIKE I SAID.
WE'VE GOT ONE SHOT LEFT.

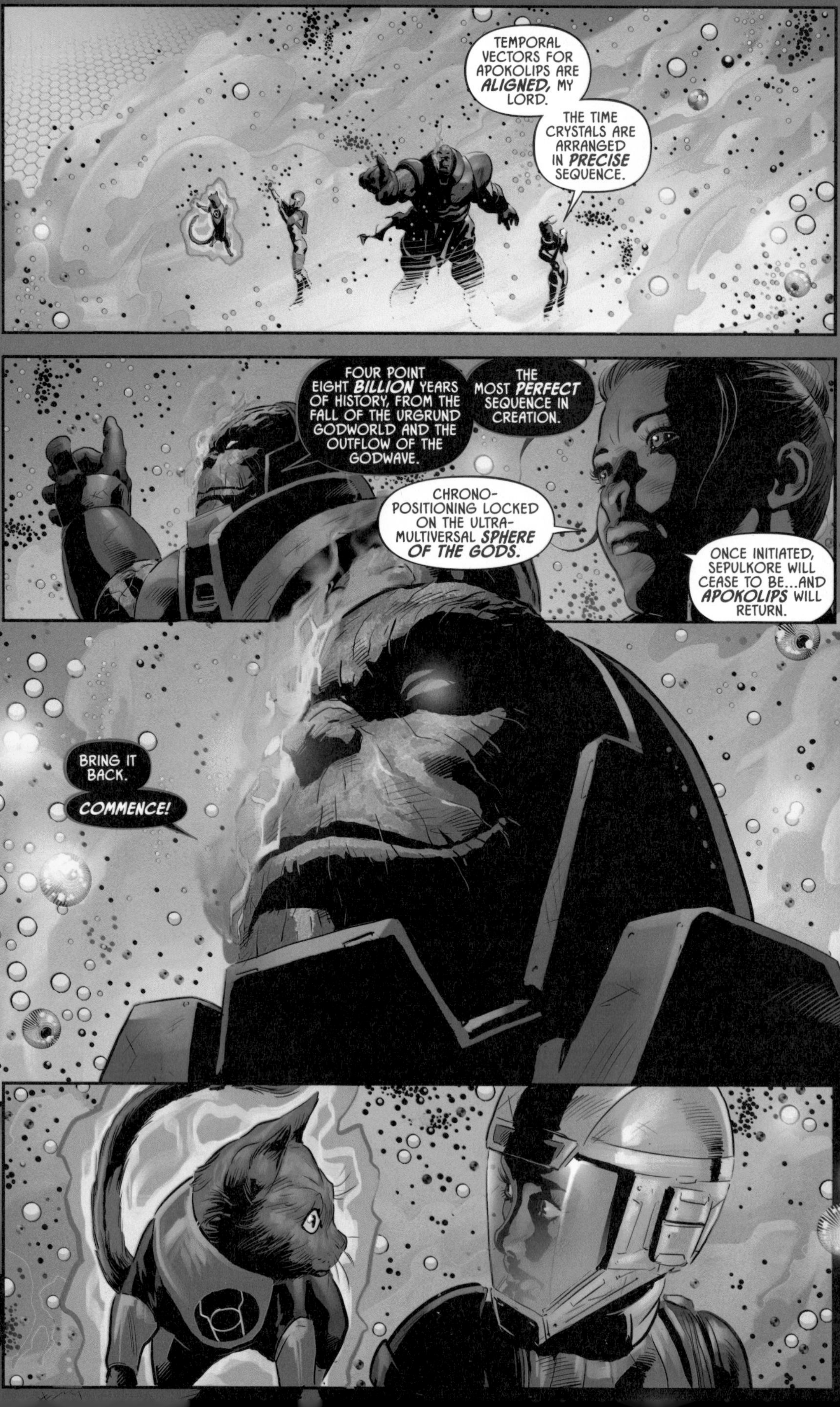
TEMPORAL VECTORS FOR APOKOLIPS ARE ALIGNED, MY LORD.
THE TIME CRYSTALS ARE ARRANGED IN PRECISE SEQUENCE.
FOUR POINT EIGHT BILLION YEARS OF HISTORY, FROM THE FALL OF THE URGRUND GODWORLD AND THE OUTFLOW OF THE GODWAVE.
THE MOST PERFECT SEQUENCE IN CREATION.
CHRONO-POSITIONING LOCKED ON THE ULTRA-MULTIVERSAL SPHERE OF THE GODS.
ONCE INITIATED, SEPULKORE WILL CEASE TO BE...AND APOKOLIPS WILL RETURN.
BRING IT BACK.
COMMENCE!

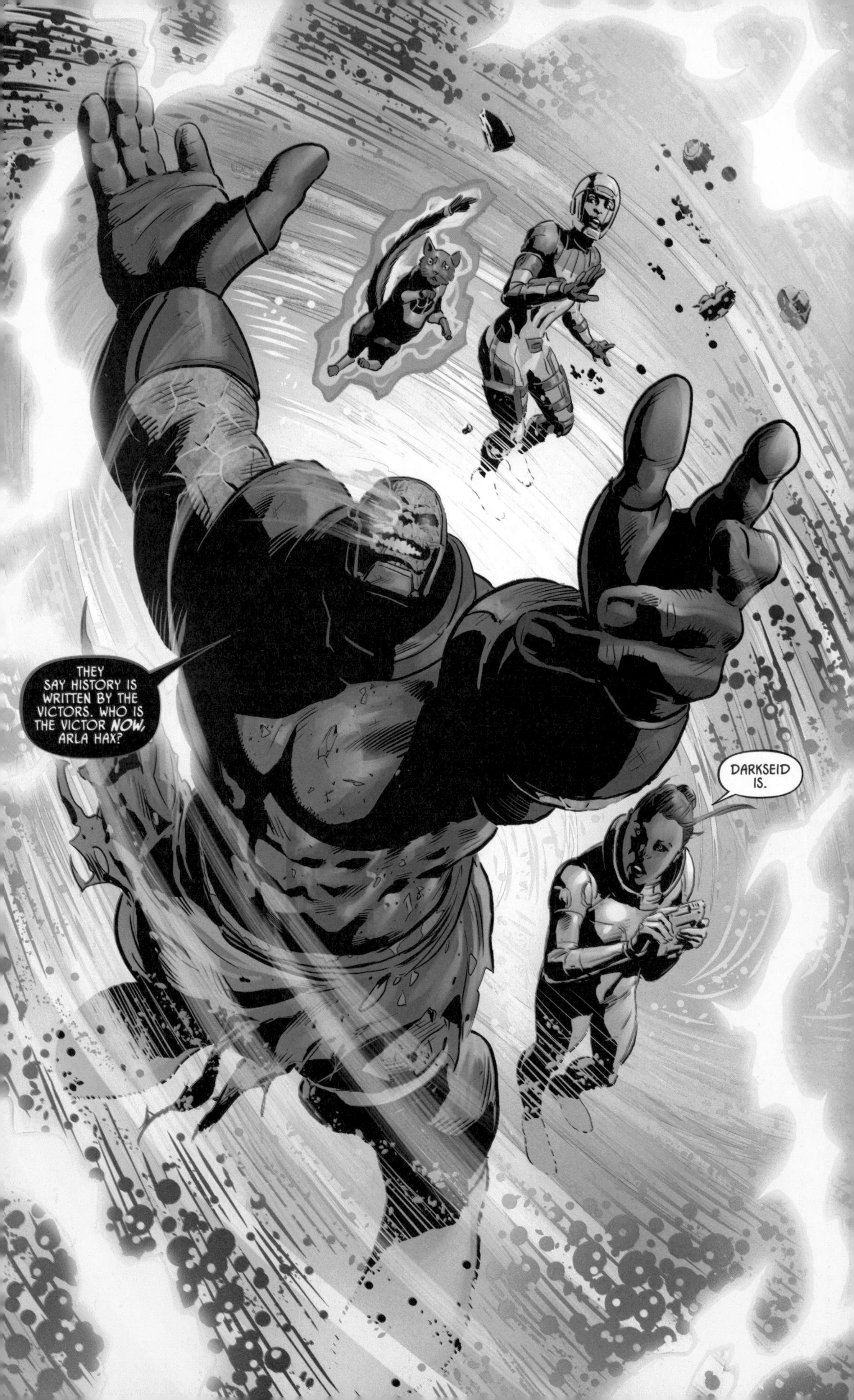
THEY SAY HISTORY IS WRITTEN BY THE VICTORS. WHO IS THE VICTOR NOW, ARLA HAX?
DARKSEID IS.

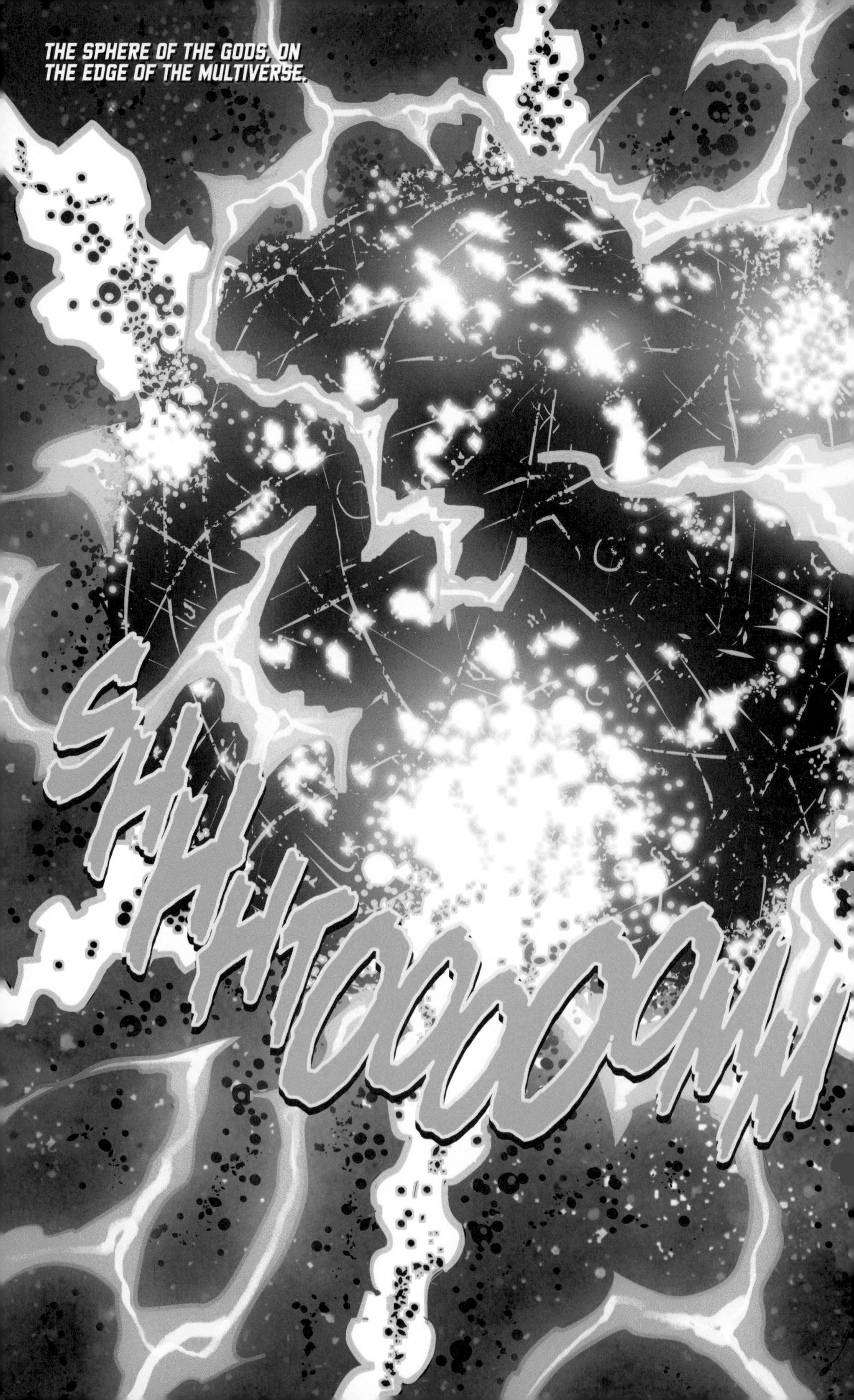
THE SPHERE OF THE GODS, ON THE EDGE OF THE MULTIVERSE.

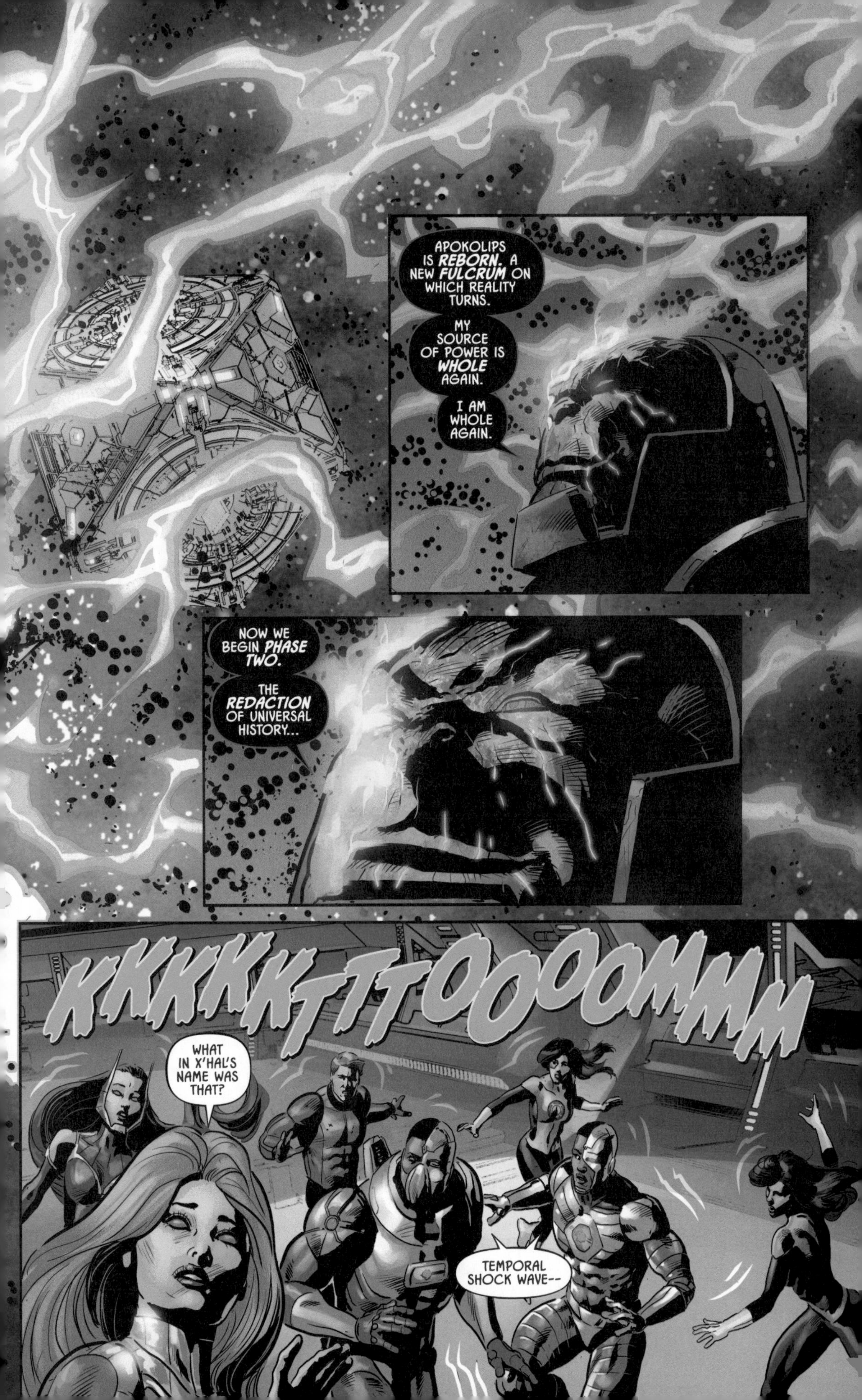
APOKOLIPS IS REBORN. A NEW FULCRUM ON WHICH REALITY TURNS.
MY SOURCE OF POWER IS WHOLE AGAIN.
I AM WHOLE AGAIN.
NOW WE BEGIN PHASE TWO.
THE REDACTION OF UNIVERSAL HISTORY...
KKKKKTTTOOOOMMM
WHAT IN X'HAL'S NAME WAS THAT?
TEMPORAL SHOCK WAVE--

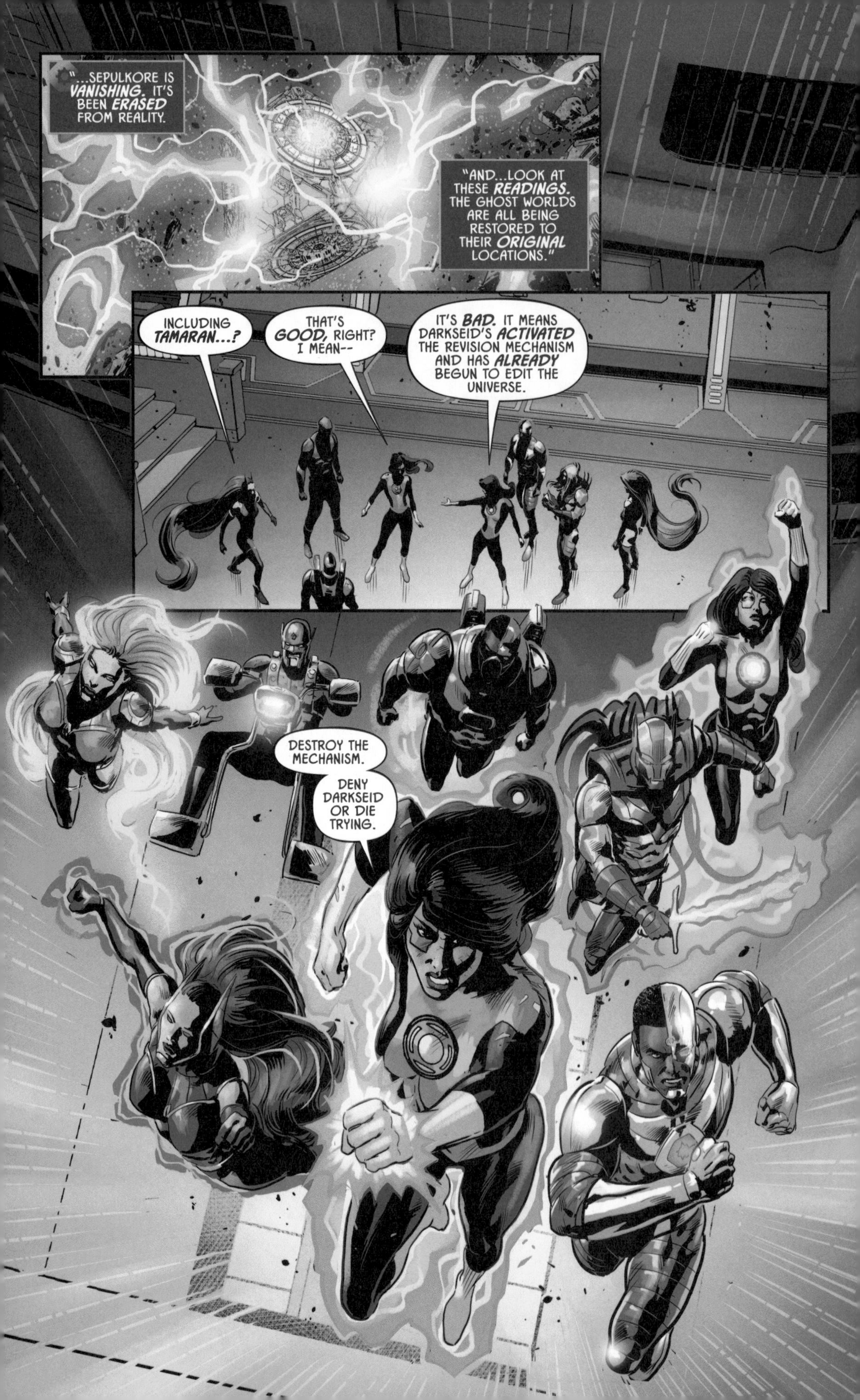
"...SEPULKORE IS VANISHING. IT'S BEEN ERASED FROM REALITY.
"AND...LOOK AT THESE READINGS. THE GHOST WORLDS ARE ALL BEING RESTORED TO THEIR ORIGINAL LOCATIONS."
INCLUDING TAMARAN...?
THAT'S GOOD, RIGHT? I MEAN--
IT'S BAD. IT MEANS DARKSEID'S ACTIVATED THE REVISION MECHANISM AND HAS ALREADY BEGUN TO EDIT THE UNIVERSE.
DESTROY THE MECHANISM.
DENY DARKSEID OR DIE TRYING.

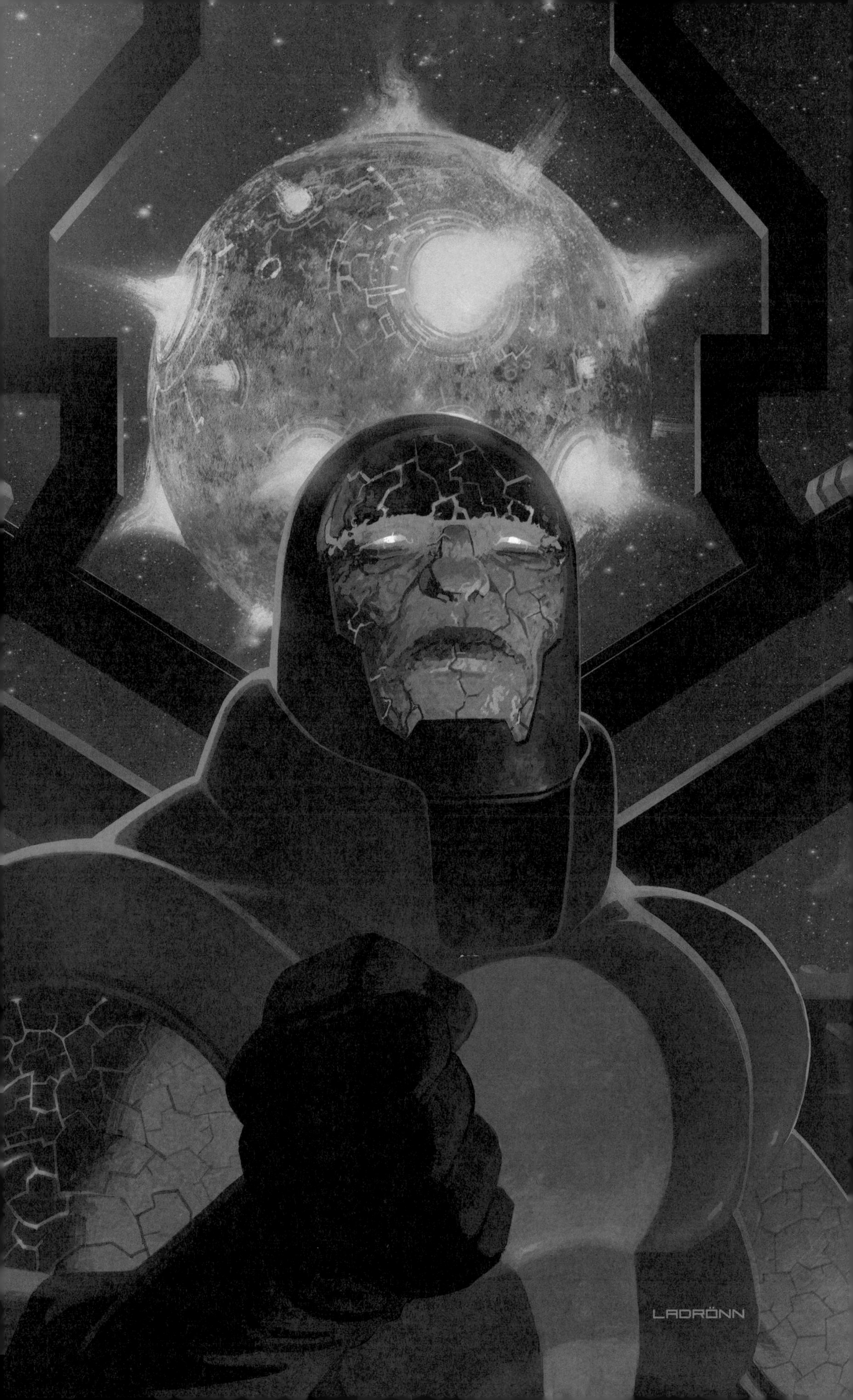
LADRÖNN

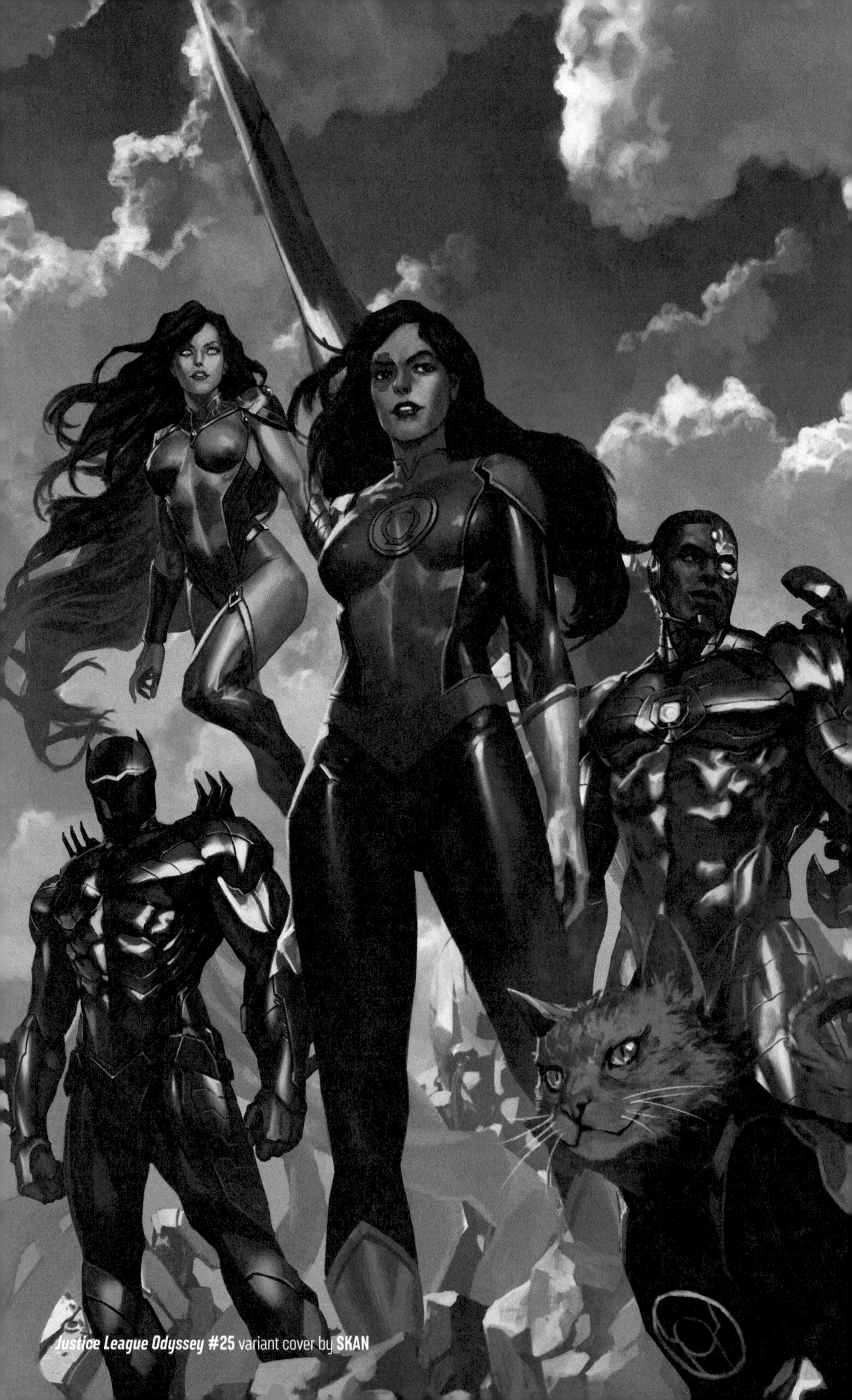

***Justice League Odyssey* #25** variant cover by **SKAN**

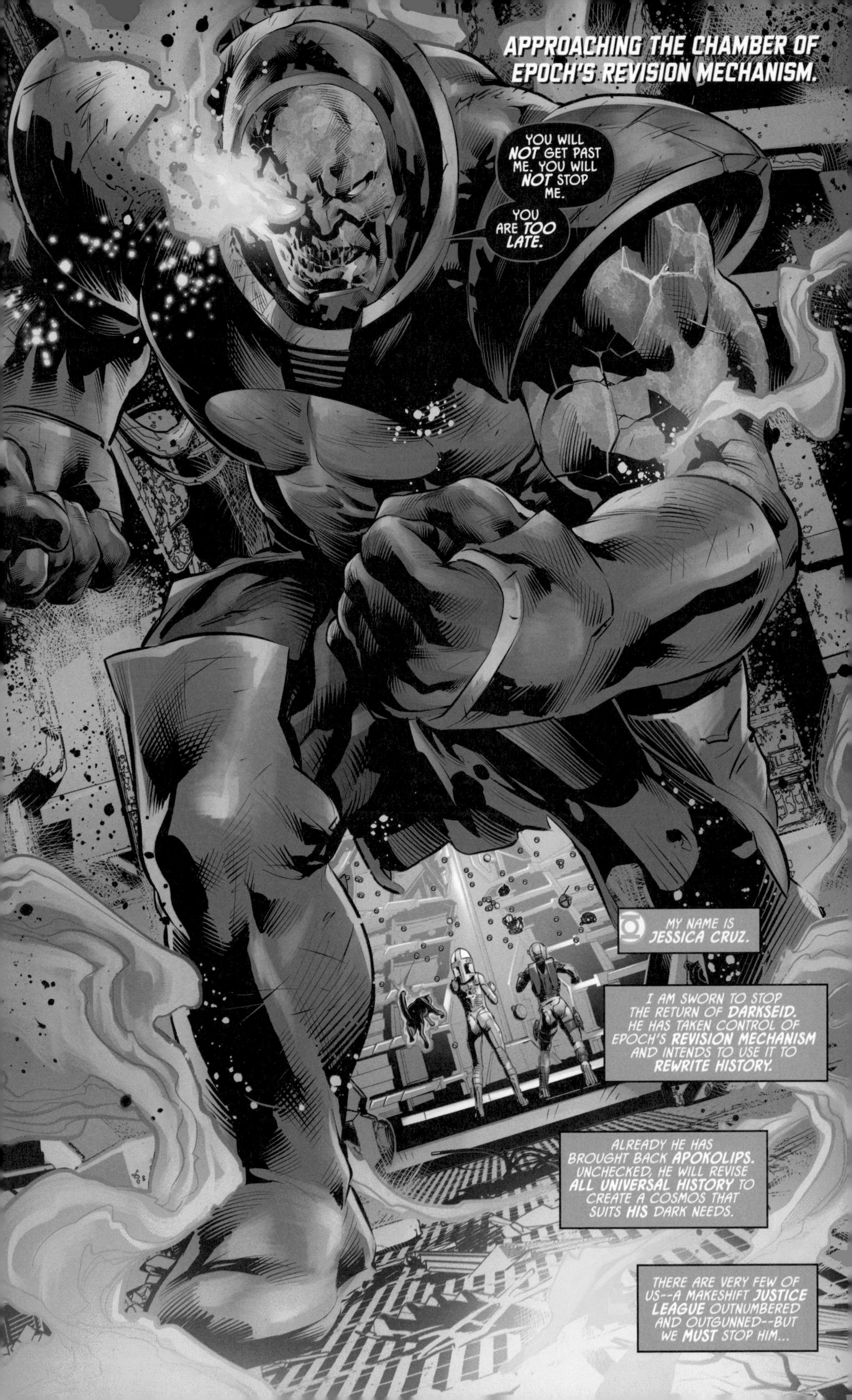
APPROACHING THE CHAMBER OF EPOCH'S REVISION MECHANISM.
YOU WILL NOT GET PAST ME. YOU WILL NOT STOP ME.
YOU ARE TOO LATE.
MY NAME IS JESSICA CRUZ.
I AM SWORN TO STOP THE RETURN OF DARKSEID. HE HAS TAKEN CONTROL OF EPOCH'S REVISION MECHANISM AND INTENDS TO USE IT TO REWRITE HISTORY.
ALREADY HE HAS BROUGHT BACK APOKOLIPS. UNCHECKED, HE WILL REVISE ALL UNIVERSAL HISTORY TO CREATE A COSMOS THAT SUITS HIS DARK NEEDS.
THERE ARE VERY FEW OF US--A MAKESHIFT JUSTICE LEAGUE OUTNUMBERED AND OUTGUNNED--BUT WE MUST STOP HIM...

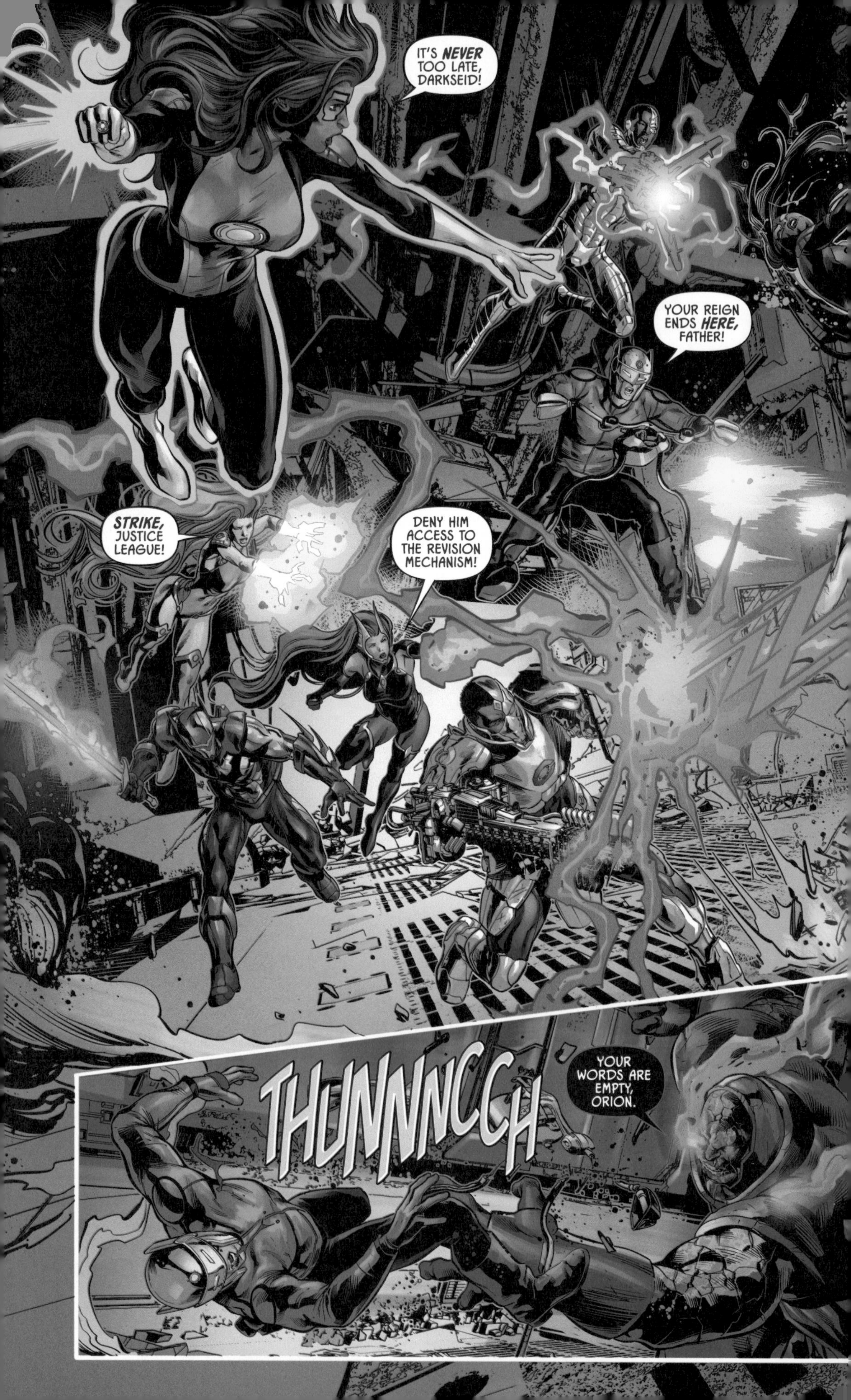
IT'S NEVER TOO LATE, DARKSEID!
YOUR REIGN ENDS HERE, FATHER!
STRIKE, JUSTICE LEAGUE!
DENY HIM ACCESS TO THE REVISION MECHANISM!
THUNNNCCH
YOUR WORDS ARE EMPTY, ORION.

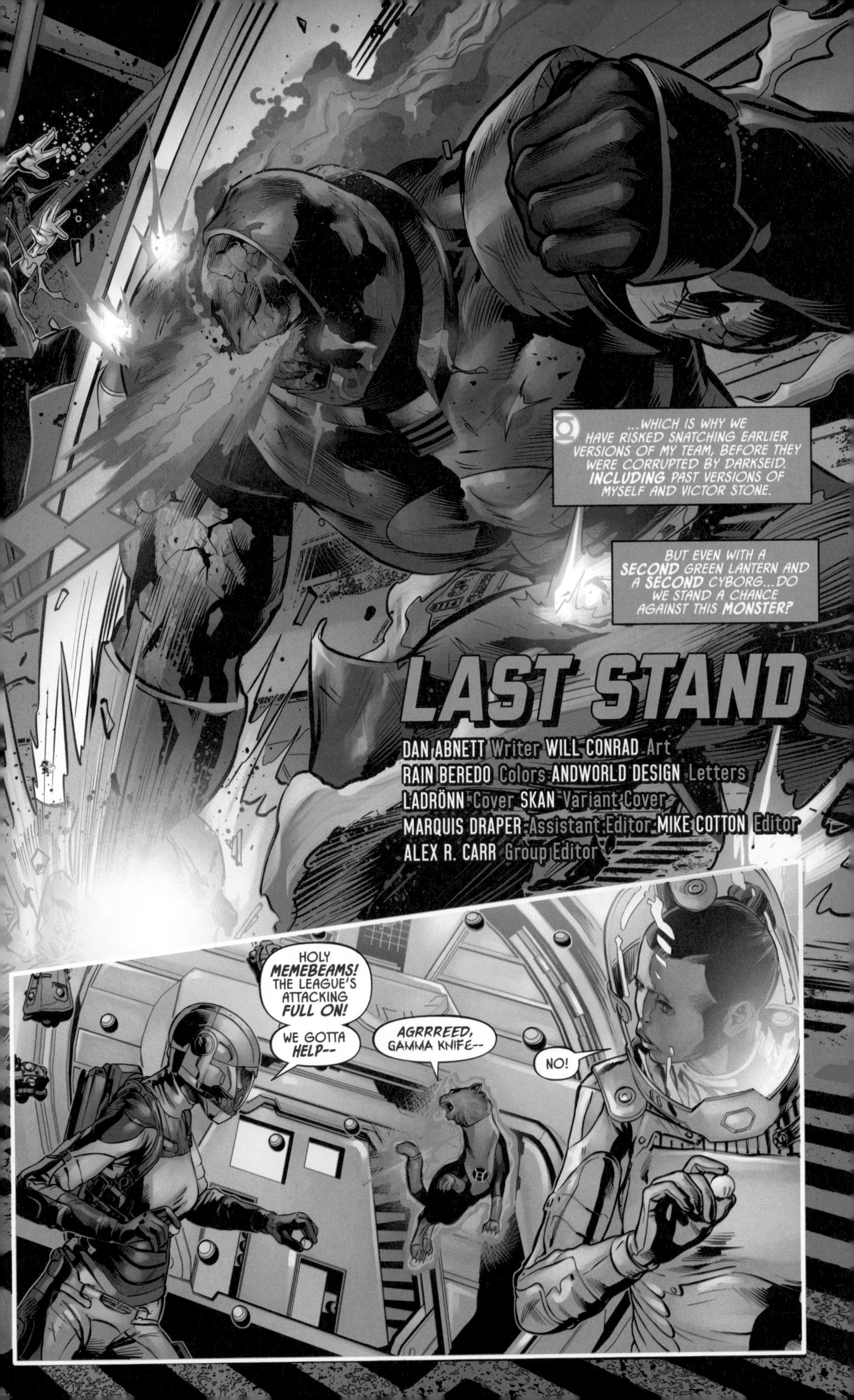
...WHICH IS WHY WE HAVE RISKED SNATCHING EARLIER VERSIONS OF MY TEAM, BEFORE THEY WERE CORRUPTED BY DARKSEID. INCLUDING PAST VERSIONS OF MYSELF AND VICTOR STONE.
BUT EVEN WITH A SECOND GREEN LANTERN AND A SECOND CYBORG...DO WE STAND A CHANCE AGAINST THIS MONSTER?
LAST STAND
DAN ABNETT Writer WILL CONRAD Art
RAIN BEREDO Colors ANDWORLD DESIGN Letters
LADRÖNN Cover SKAN Variant Cover
MARQUIS DRAPER Assistant Editor MIKE COTTON Editor
ALEX R. CARR Group Editor
HOLY MEMEBEAMS! THE LEAGUE'S ATTACKING FULL ON!
WE GOTTA HELP--
AGRRREED, GAMMA KNIFE--
NO!

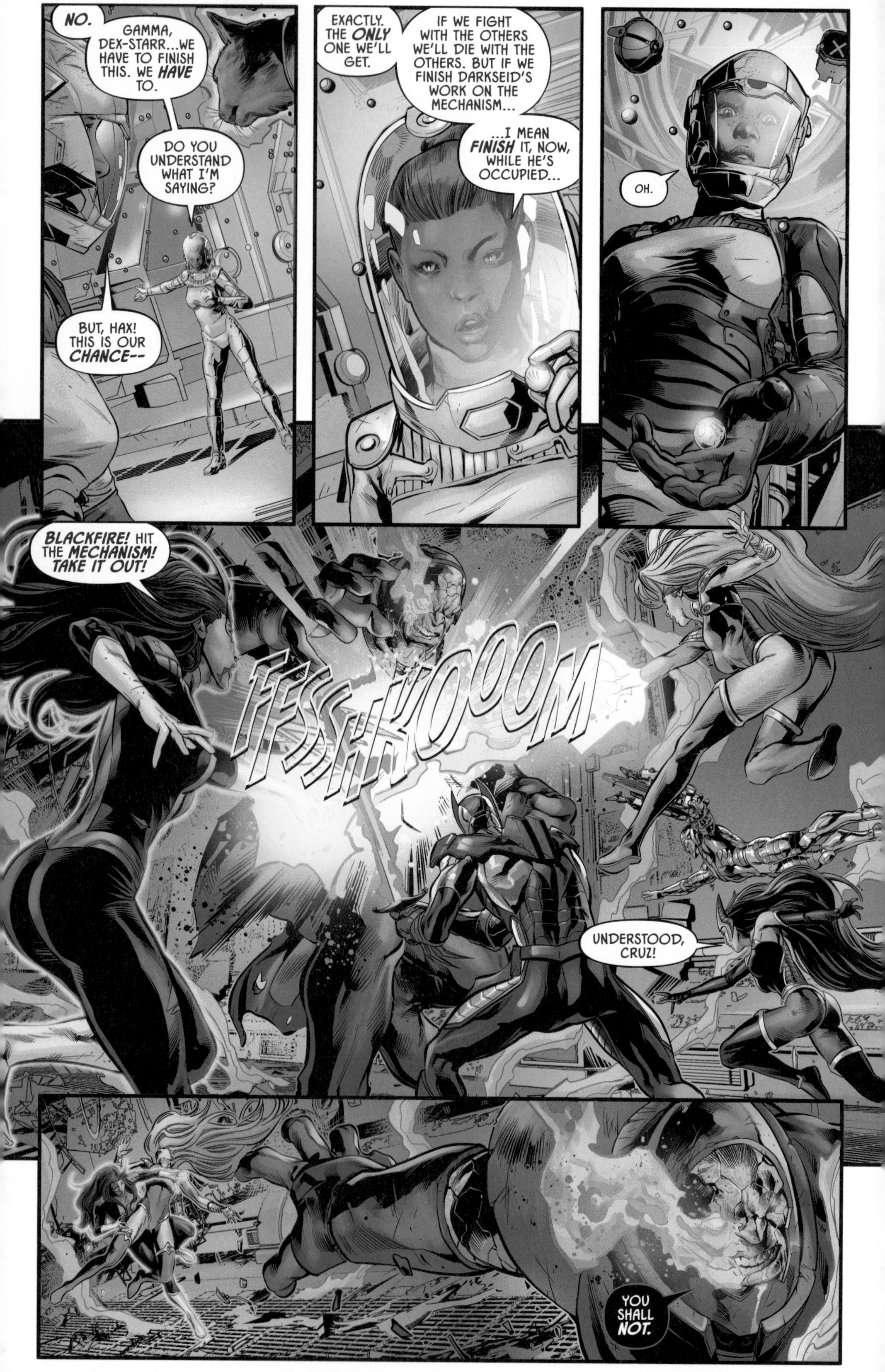
NO.
GAMMA, DEX-STARR...WE HAVE TO FINISH THIS. WE HAVE TO.
DO YOU UNDERSTAND WHAT I'M SAYING?
BUT, HAX! THIS IS OUR CHANCE--
EXACTLY. THE ONLY ONE WE'LL GET.
IF WE FIGHT WITH THE OTHERS WE'LL DIE WITH THE OTHERS. BUT IF WE FINISH DARKSEID'S WORK ON THE MECHANISM...
...I MEAN FINISH IT, NOW, WHILE HE'S OCCUPIED...
OH.
BLACKFIRE! HIT THE MECHANISM! TAKE IT OUT!
FFSHKOOOM
UNDERSTOOD, CRUZ!
YOU SHALL NOT.

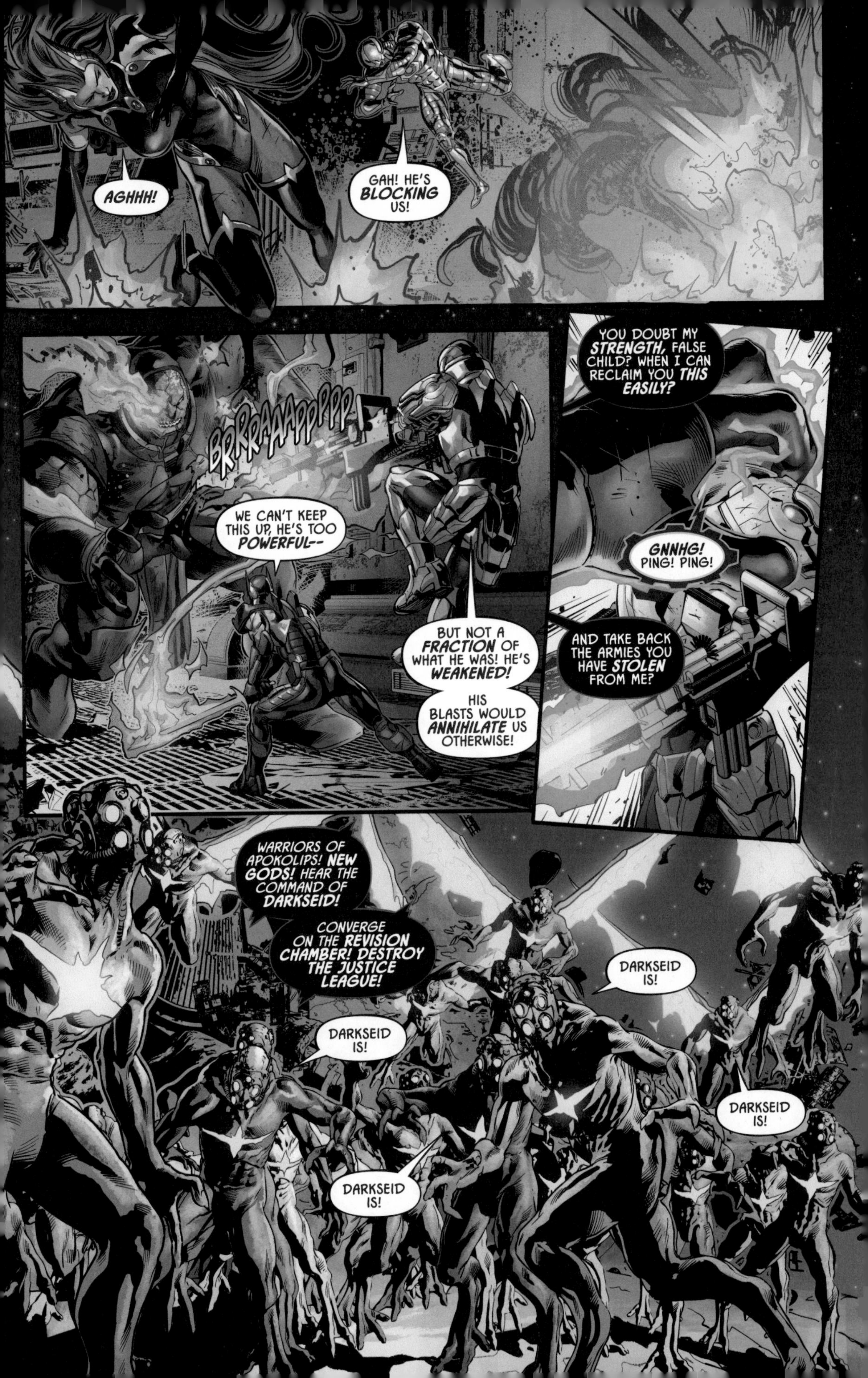
AGHHH!
GAH! HE'S BLOCKING US!
BRRRAAAPPPPP
WE CAN'T KEEP THIS UP, HE'S TOO POWERFUL--
BUT NOT A FRACTION OF WHAT HE WAS! HE'S WEAKENED!
HIS BLASTS WOULD ANNIHILATE US OTHERWISE!
YOU DOUBT MY STRENGTH, FALSE CHILD? WHEN I CAN RECLAIM YOU THIS EASILY?
GNNHG! PING! PING!
AND TAKE BACK THE ARMIES YOU HAVE STOLEN FROM ME?
WARRIORS OF APOKOLIPS! NEW GODS! HEAR THE COMMAND OF DARKSEID!
CONVERGE ON THE REVISION CHAMBER! DESTROY THE JUSTICE LEAGUE!
DARKSEID IS!
DARKSEID IS!
DARKSEID IS!
DARKSEID IS!

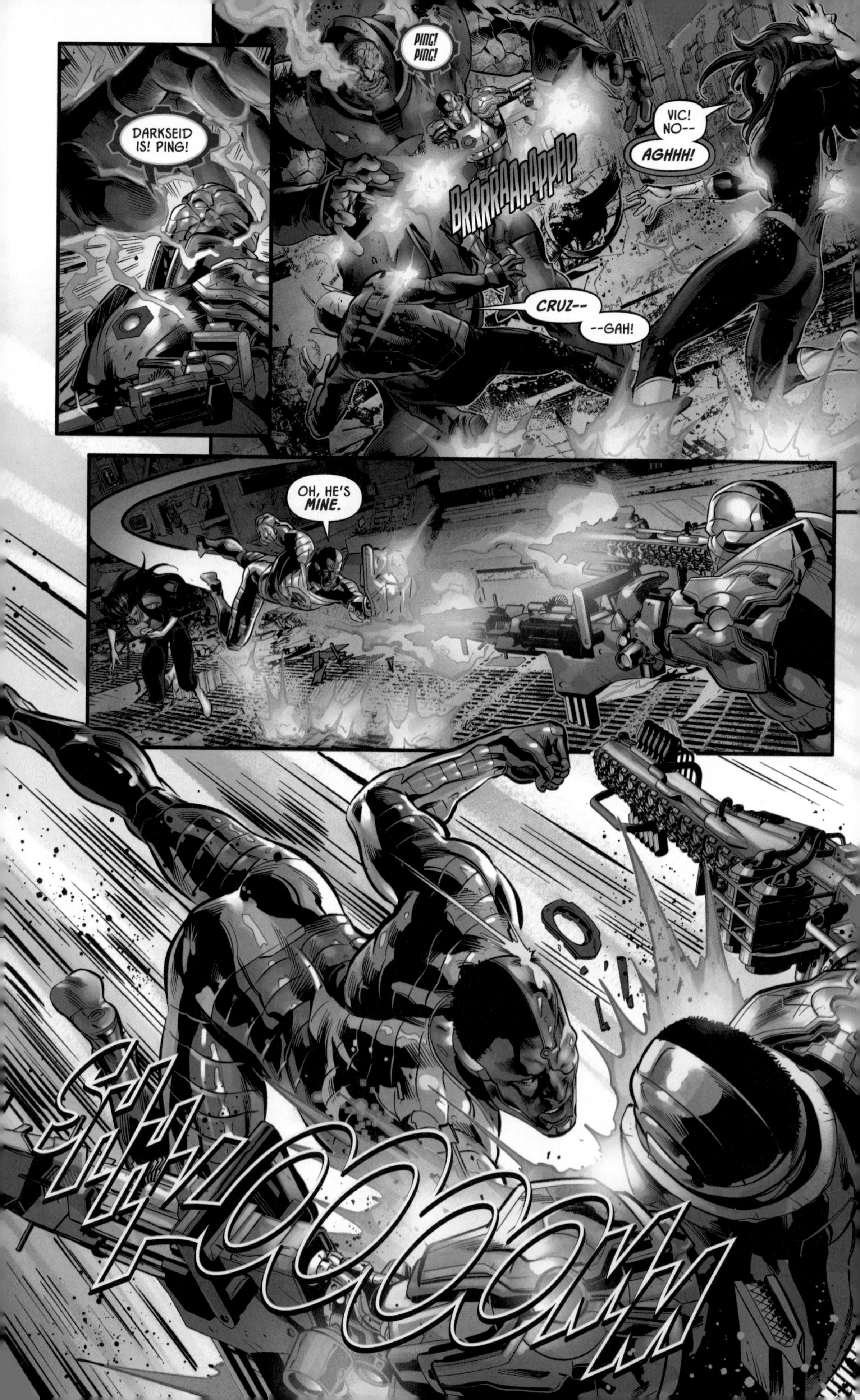
DARKSEID IS! PING!
PING! PING!
BRRRRAAAAPPPP
VIC! NO--
AGHHH!
CRUZ--
--GAH!
OH, HE'S MINE.
SHHOOOOM

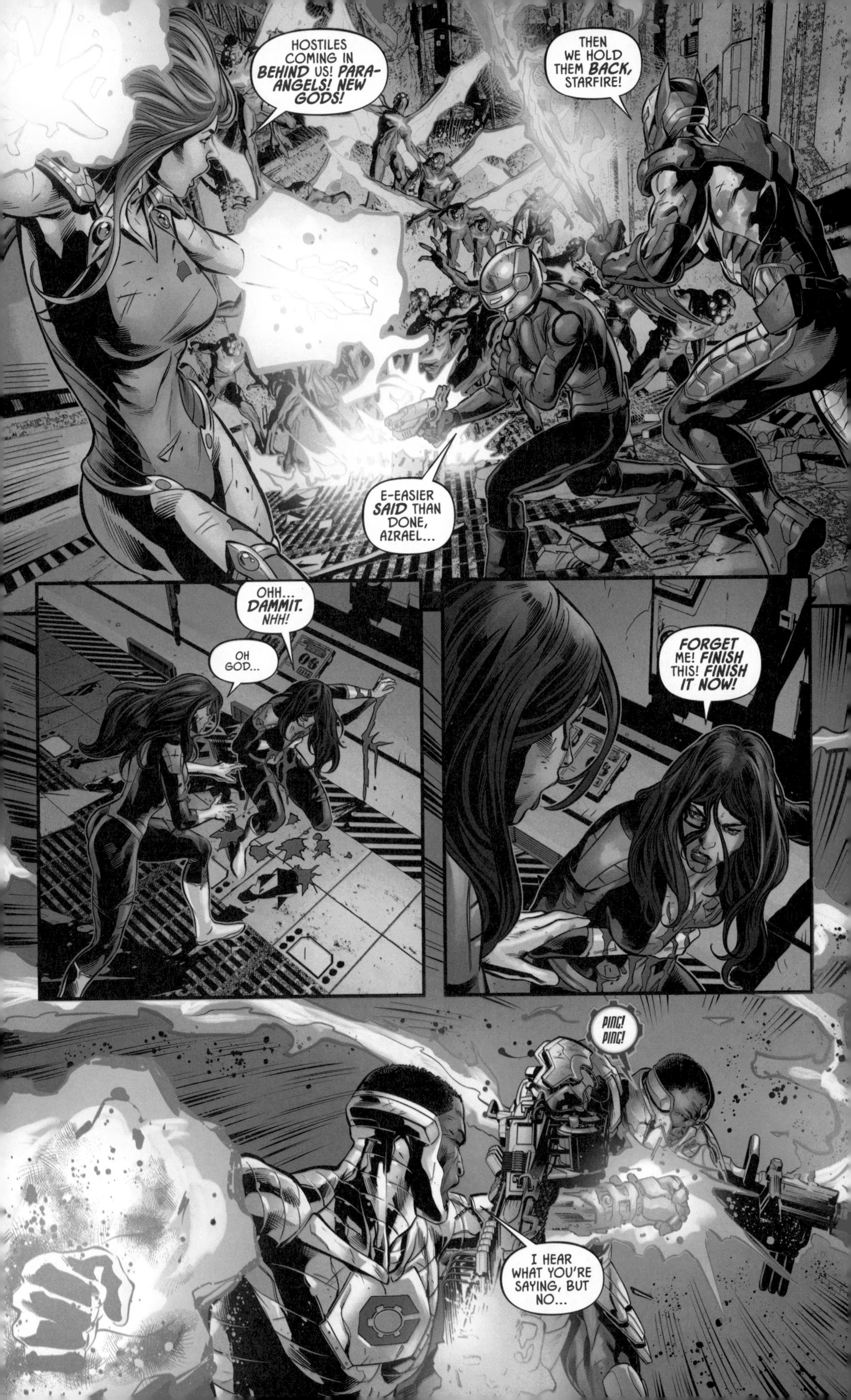
HOSTILES COMING IN BEHIND US! PARA-ANGELS! NEW GODS!
THEN WE HOLD THEM BACK, STARFIRE!
E-EASIER SAID THAN DONE, AZRAEL...
OHH... DAMMIT. NHH!
OH GOD...
FORGET ME! FINISH THIS! FINISH IT NOW!
PING! PING!
I HEAR WHAT YOU'RE SAYING, BUT NO...

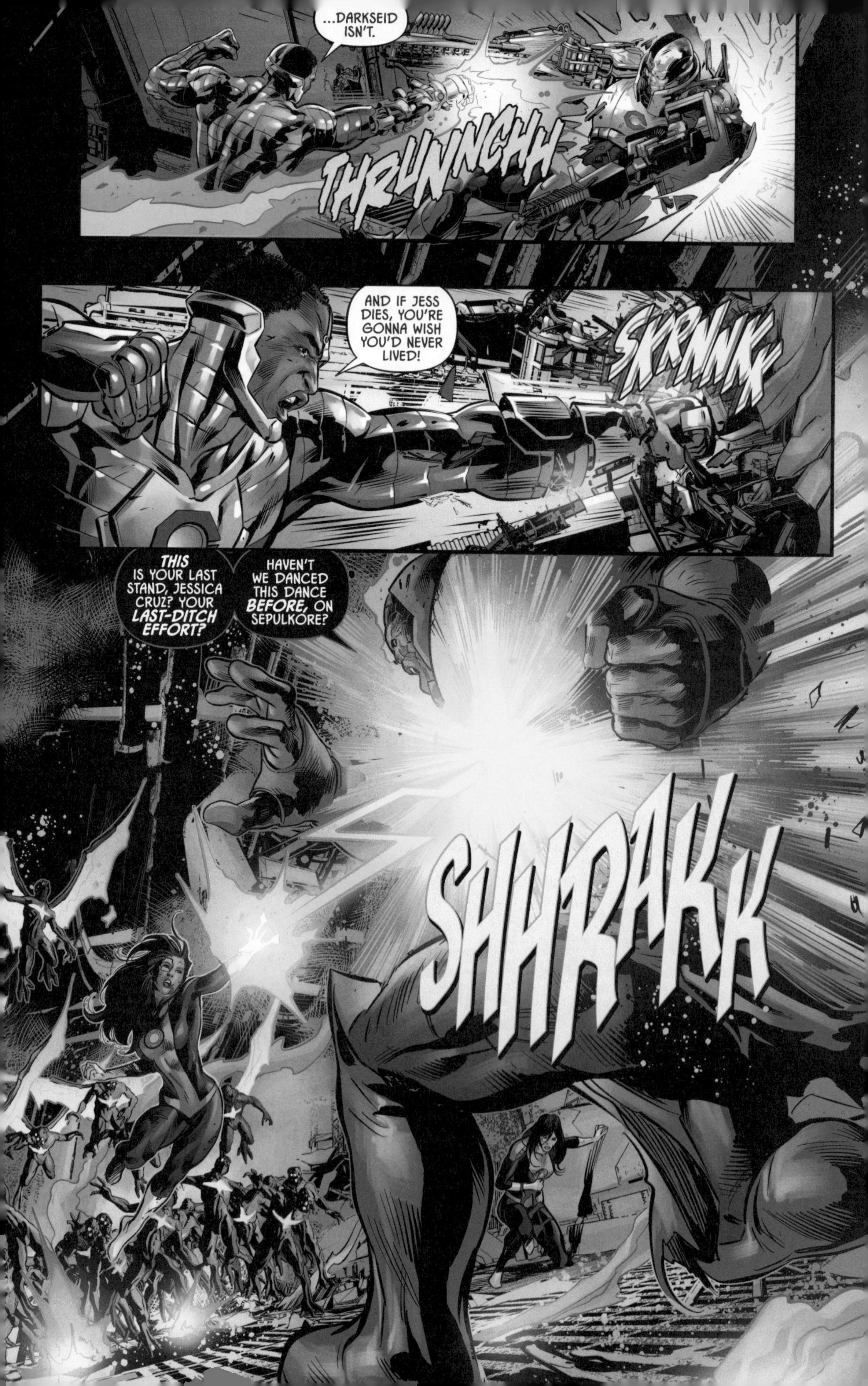
...DARKSEID ISN'T.
THRUNNCHH
AND IF JESS DIES, YOU'RE GONNA WISH YOU'D NEVER LIVED!
SKRNNK
THIS IS YOUR LAST STAND, JESSICA CRUZ? YOUR LAST-DITCH EFFORT?
HAVEN'T WE DANCED THIS DANCE BEFORE, ON SEPULKORE?
SHHRAKK

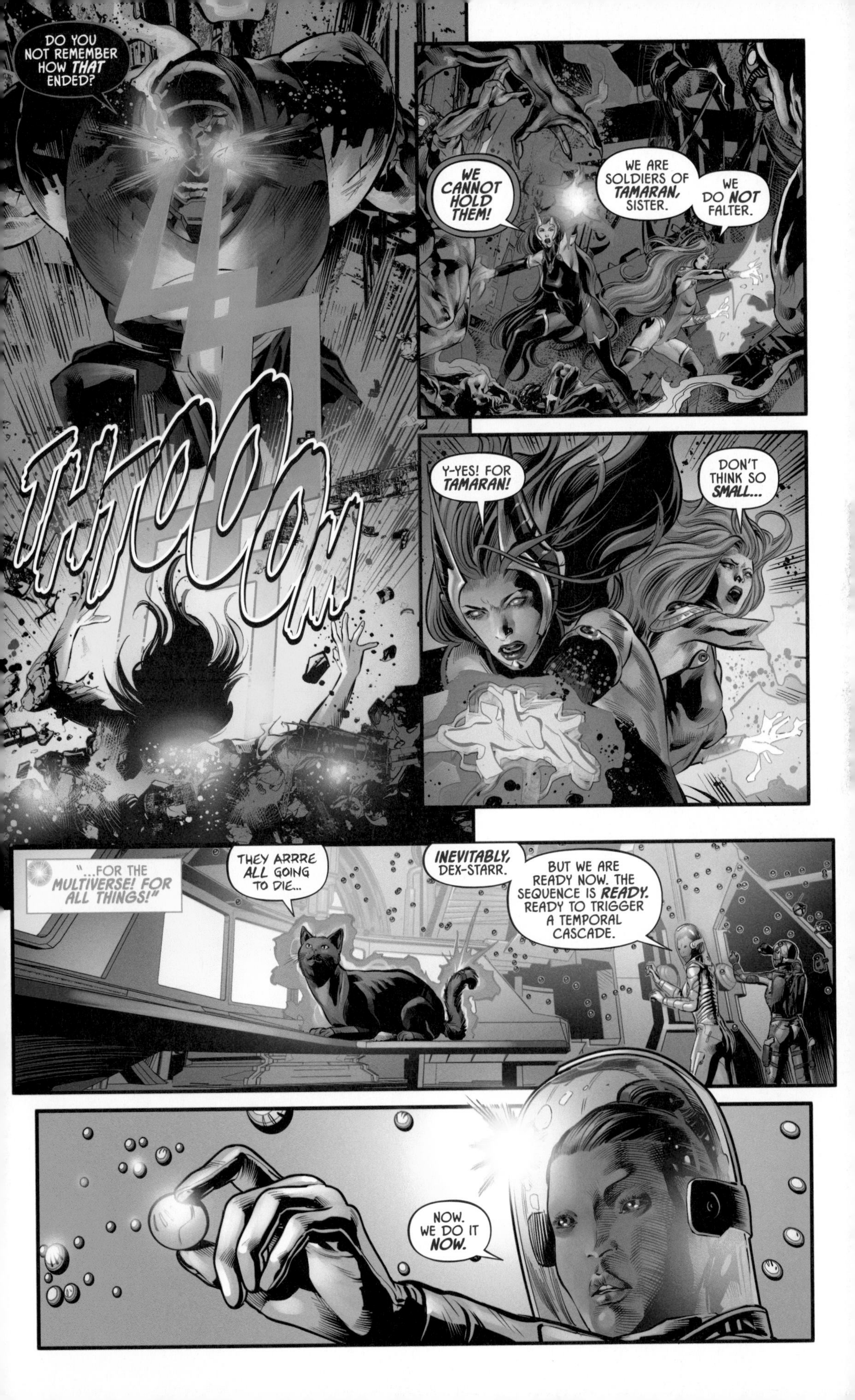
DO YOU NOT REMEMBER HOW THAT ENDED?
WE CANNOT HOLD THEM!
WE ARE SOLDIERS OF TAMARAN, SISTER.
WE DO NOT FALTER.
THOOOM
Y-YES! FOR TAMARAN!
DON'T THINK SO SMALL...
"...FOR THE MULTIVERSE! FOR ALL THINGS!"
THEY ARRRE ALL GOING TO DIE...
INEVITABLY, DEX-STARR.
BUT WE ARE READY NOW. THE SEQUENCE IS READY. READY TO TRIGGER A TEMPORAL CASCADE.
NOW. WE DO IT NOW.

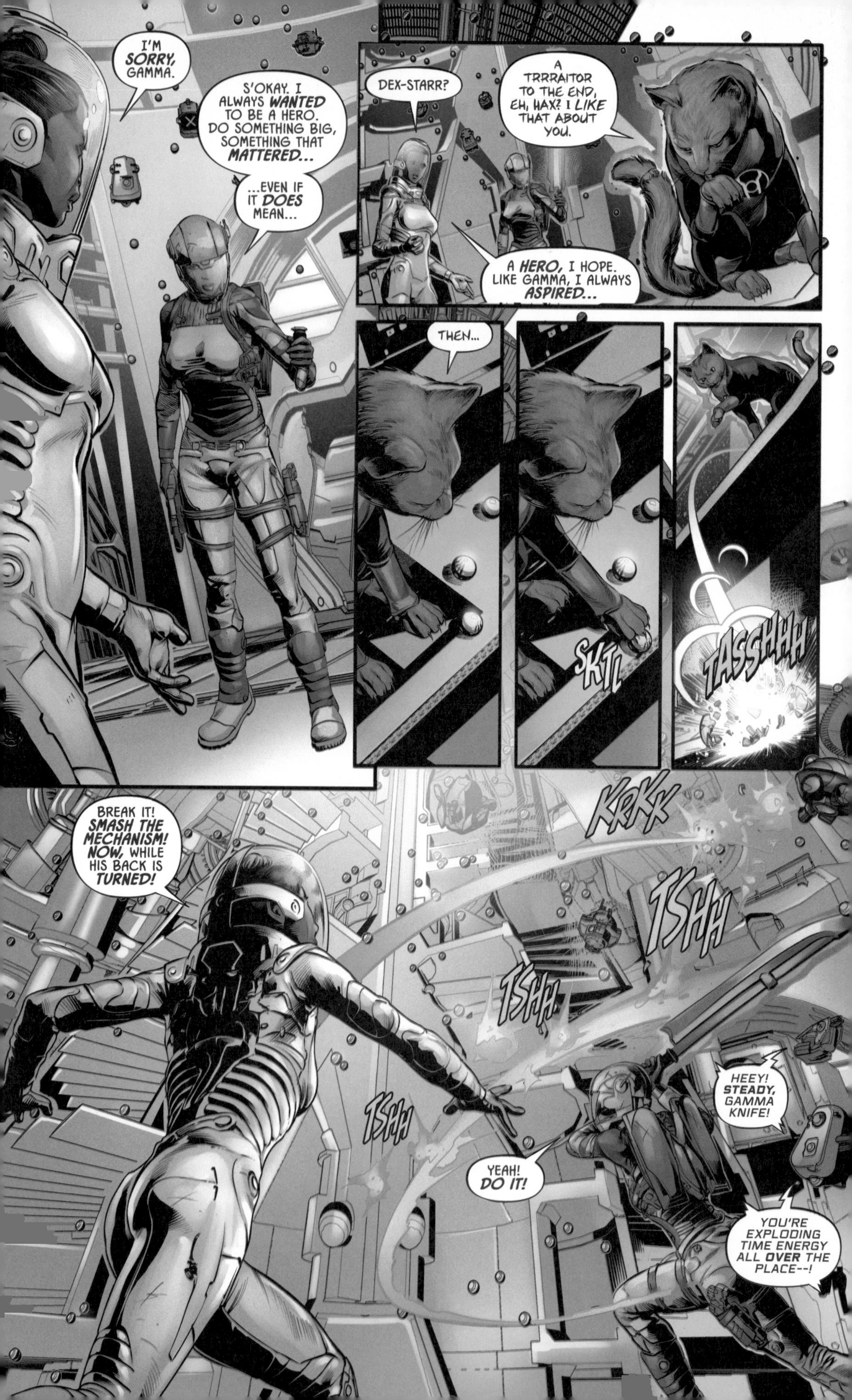

I'M SORRY, GAMMA.
S'OKAY. I ALWAYS WANTED TO BE A HERO. DO SOMETHING BIG, SOMETHING THAT MATTERED...
...EVEN IF IT DOES MEAN...
DEX-STARR?
A TRRRAITOR TO THE END, EH, HAX? I LIKE THAT ABOUT YOU.
A HERO, I HOPE. LIKE GAMMA, I ALWAYS ASPIRED...
THEN...
SKTL
TASSHHH
BREAK IT! SMASH THE MECHANISM! NOW, WHILE HIS BACK IS TURNED!
KRKK
TSHH
TSHH
TSHH
HEEY! STEADY, GAMMA KNIFE!
YEAH! DO IT!
YOU'RE EXPLODING TIME ENERGY ALL OVER THE PLACE--!

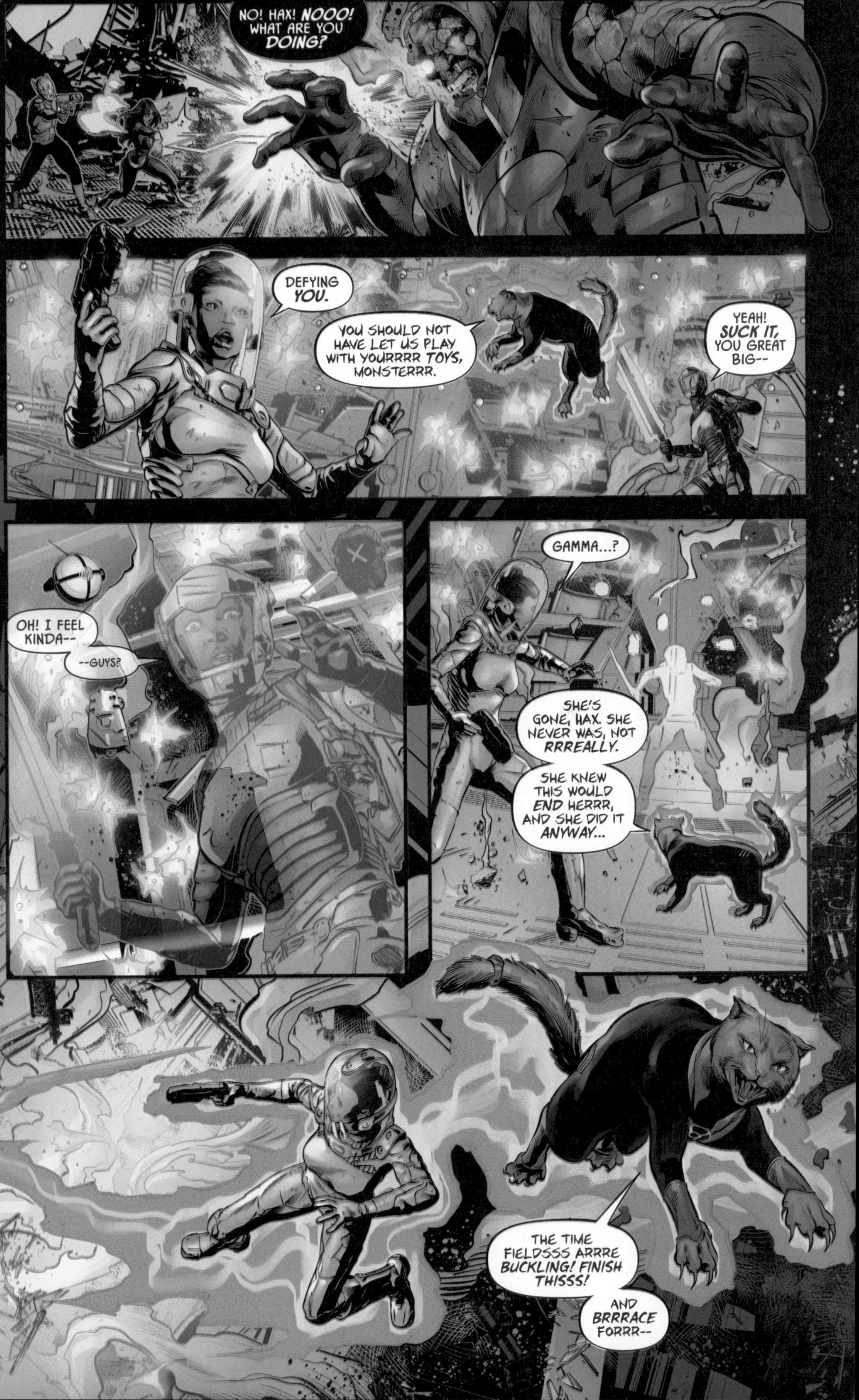
NO! HAX! NOOO! WHAT ARE YOU DOING?
DEFYING YOU.
YOU SHOULD NOT HAVE LET US PLAY WITH YOURRRR TOYS, MONSTERRR.
YEAH! SUCK IT, YOU GREAT BIG--
OH! I FEEL KINDA--
--GUYS?
GAMMA...?
SHE'S GONE, HAX. SHE NEVER WAS, NOT RRREALLY.
SHE KNEW THIS WOULD END HERRR, AND SHE DID IT ANYWAY...
THE TIME FIELDSSS ARRRE BUCKLING! FINISH THISSS!
AND BRRRACE FORRR--

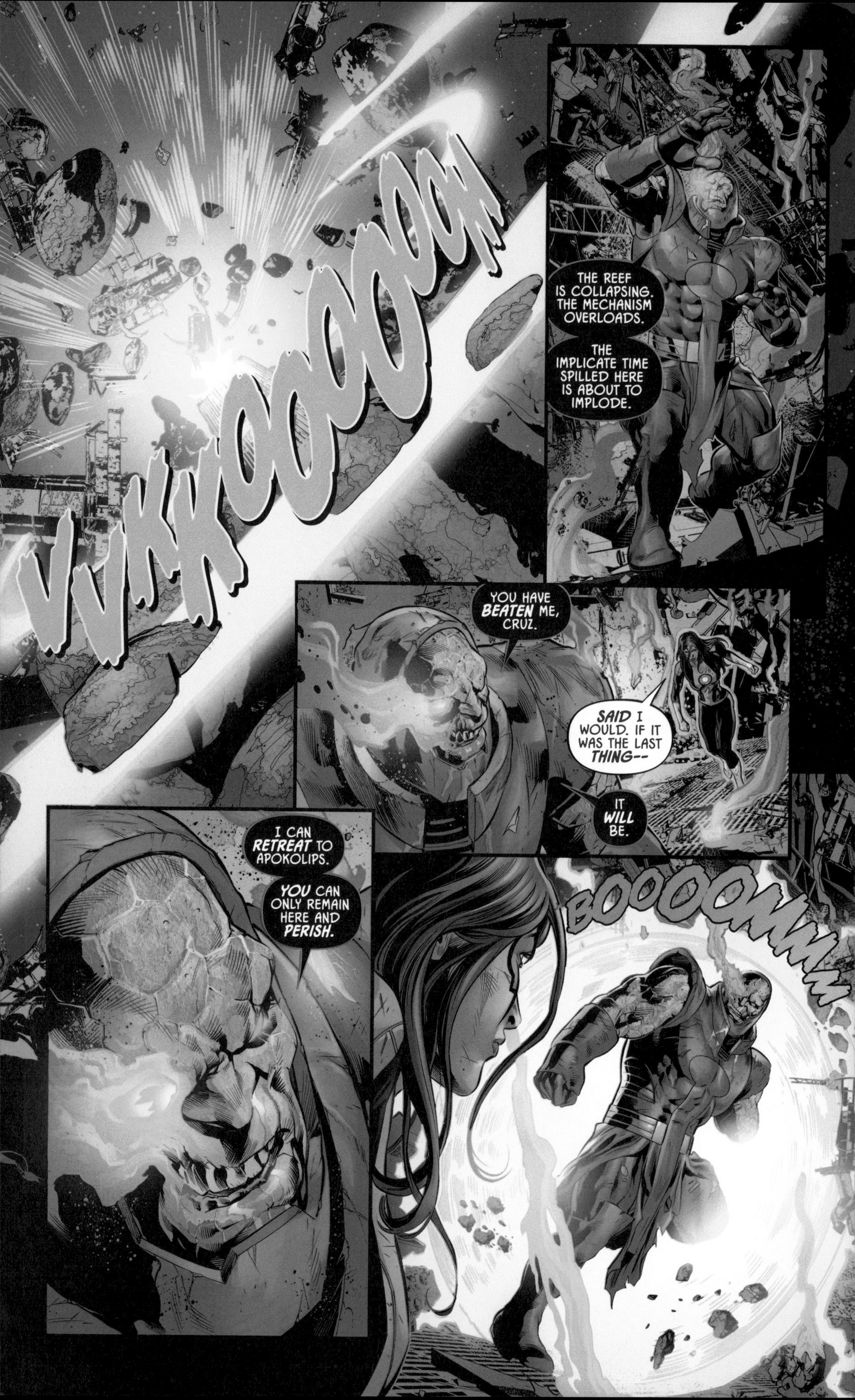
VVKKOOOOOOOOM
THE REEF IS COLLAPSING. THE MECHANISM OVERLOADS.
THE IMPLICATE TIME SPILLED HERE IS ABOUT TO IMPLODE.
YOU HAVE BEATEN ME, CRUZ.
SAID I WOULD. IF IT WAS THE LAST THING--
IT WILL BE.
I CAN RETREAT TO APOKOLIPS.
YOU CAN ONLY REMAIN HERE AND PERISH.
BOOOOMMMM

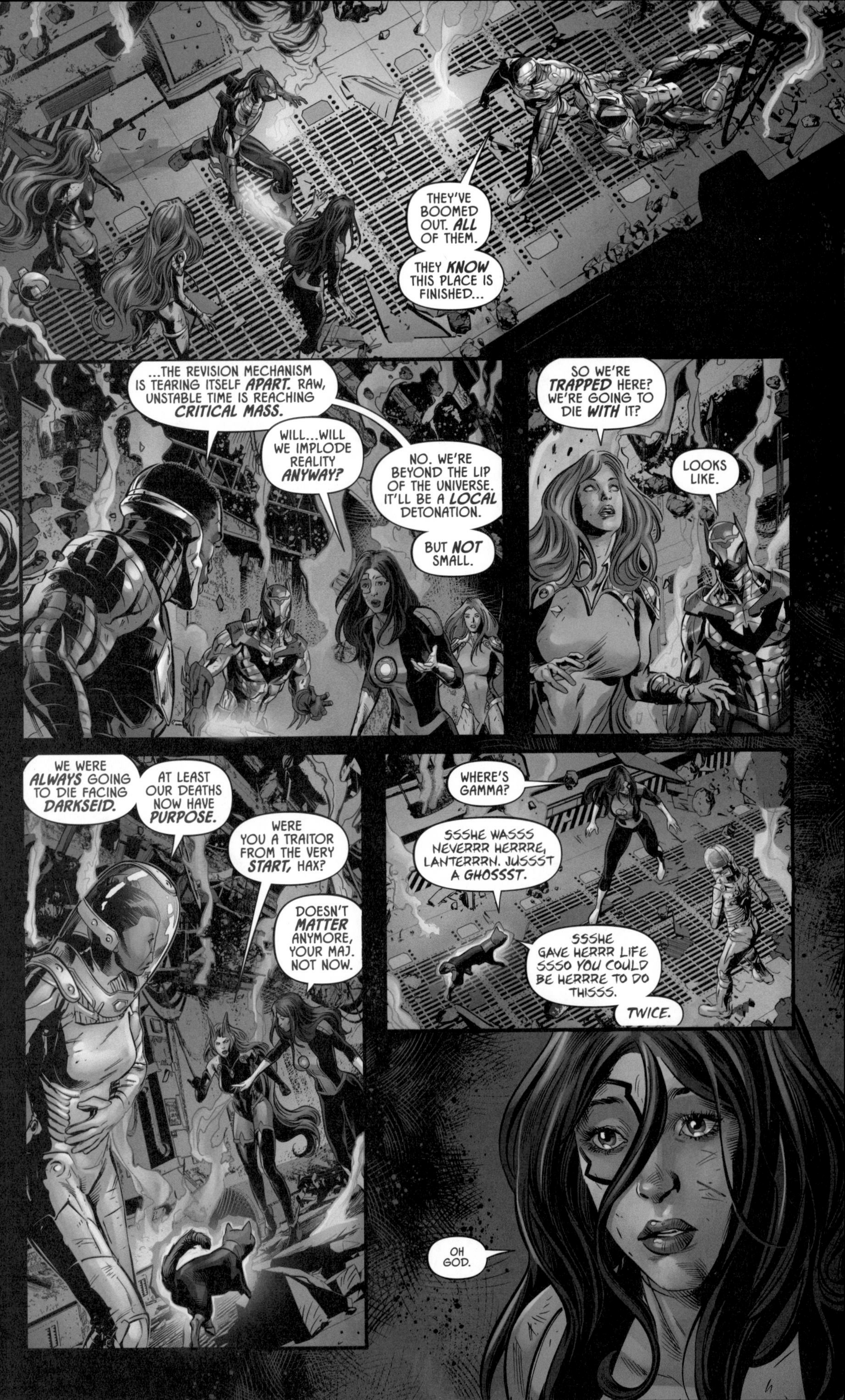
THEY'VE BOOMED OUT. ALL OF THEM.
THEY KNOW THIS PLACE IS FINISHED...
...THE REVISION MECHANISM IS TEARING ITSELF APART. RAW, UNSTABLE TIME IS REACHING CRITICAL MASS.
WILL...WILL WE IMPLODE REALITY ANYWAY?
NO. WE'RE BEYOND THE LIP OF THE UNIVERSE. IT'LL BE A LOCAL DETONATION.
BUT NOT SMALL.
SO WE'RE TRAPPED HERE? WE'RE GOING TO DIE WITH IT?
LOOKS LIKE.
WE WERE ALWAYS GOING TO DIE FACING DARKSEID.
AT LEAST OUR DEATHS NOW HAVE PURPOSE.
WERE YOU A TRAITOR FROM THE VERY START, HAX?
DOESN'T MATTER ANYMORE, YOUR MAJ. NOT NOW.
WHERE'S GAMMA?
SSSHE WASSS NEVERRR HERRRE, LANTERRRN. JUSSST A GHOSSST.
SSSHE GAVE HERRR LIFE SSSO YOU COULD BE HERRRE TO DO THISSS.
TWICE.
OH GOD.

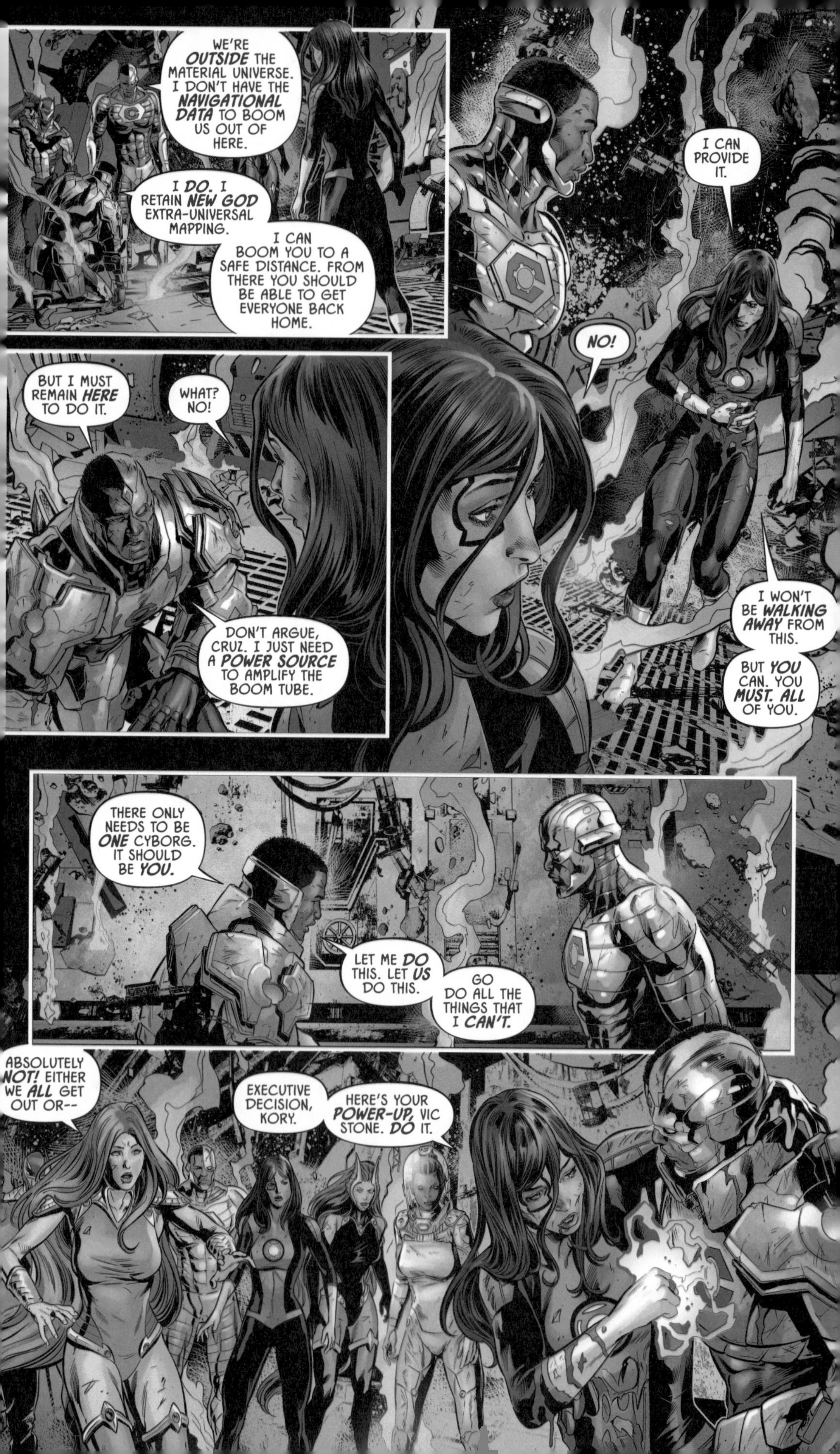
WE'RE OUTSIDE THE MATERIAL UNIVERSE. I DON'T HAVE THE NAVIGATIONAL DATA TO BOOM US OUT OF HERE.
I DO. I RETAIN NEW GOD EXTRA-UNIVERSAL MAPPING.
I CAN BOOM YOU TO A SAFE DISTANCE. FROM THERE YOU SHOULD BE ABLE TO GET EVERYONE BACK HOME.
I CAN PROVIDE IT.
NO!
BUT I MUST REMAIN HERE TO DO IT.
WHAT? NO!
DON'T ARGUE, CRUZ. I JUST NEED A POWER SOURCE TO AMPLIFY THE BOOM TUBE.
I WON'T BE WALKING AWAY FROM THIS.
BUT YOU CAN. YOU MUST. ALL OF YOU.
THERE ONLY NEEDS TO BE ONE CYBORG. IT SHOULD BE YOU.
LET ME DO THIS. LET US DO THIS.
GO DO ALL THE THINGS THAT I CAN'T.
ABSOLUTELY NOT! EITHER WE ALL GET OUT OR--
EXECUTIVE DECISION, KORY.
HERE'S YOUR POWER-UP, VIC STONE. DO IT.

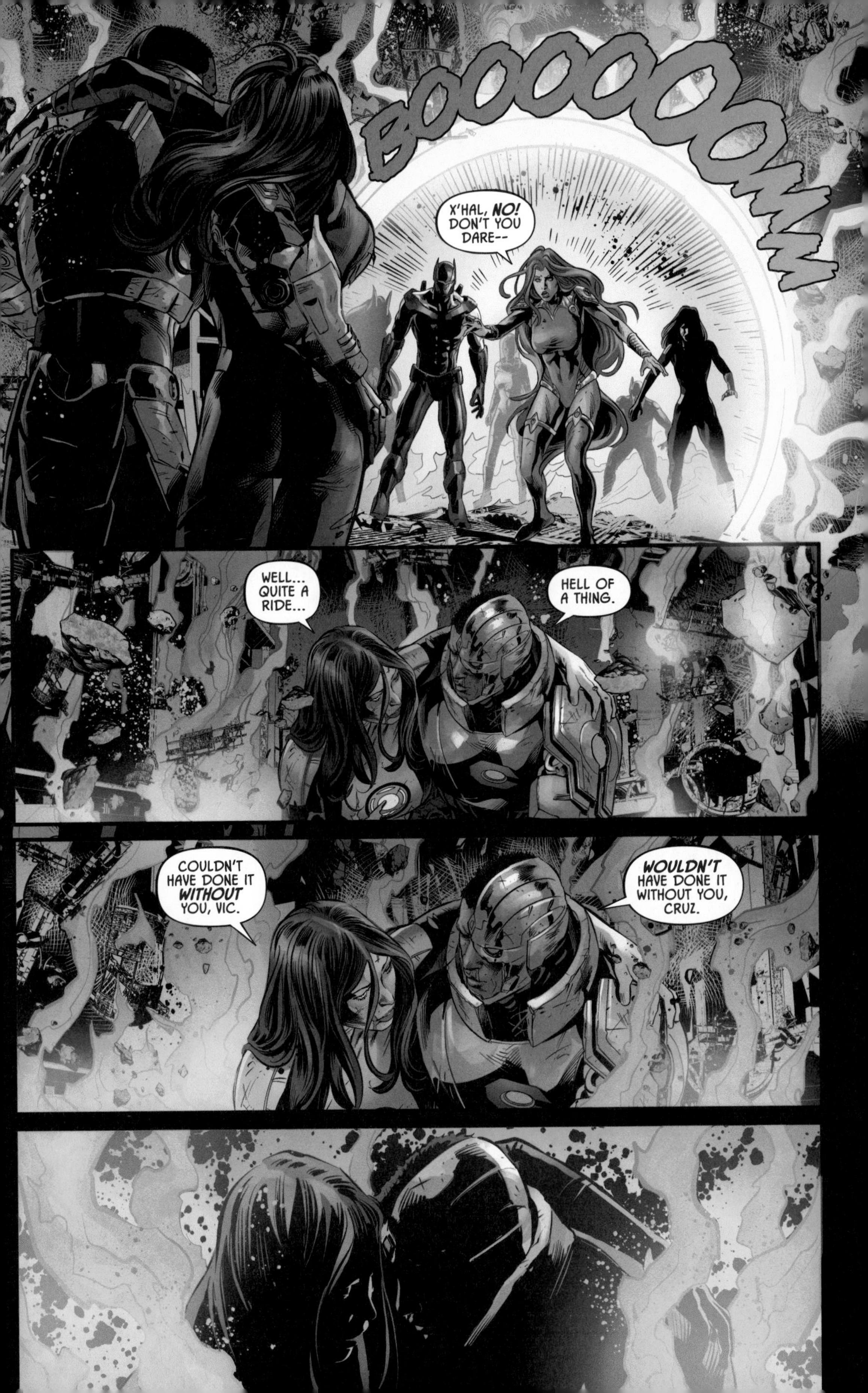
BOOOOOOMM
X'HAL, NO! DON'T YOU DARE--
WELL... QUITE A RIDE...
HELL OF A THING.
COULDN'T HAVE DONE IT WITHOUT YOU, VIC.
WOULDN'T HAVE DONE IT WITHOUT YOU, CRUZ.

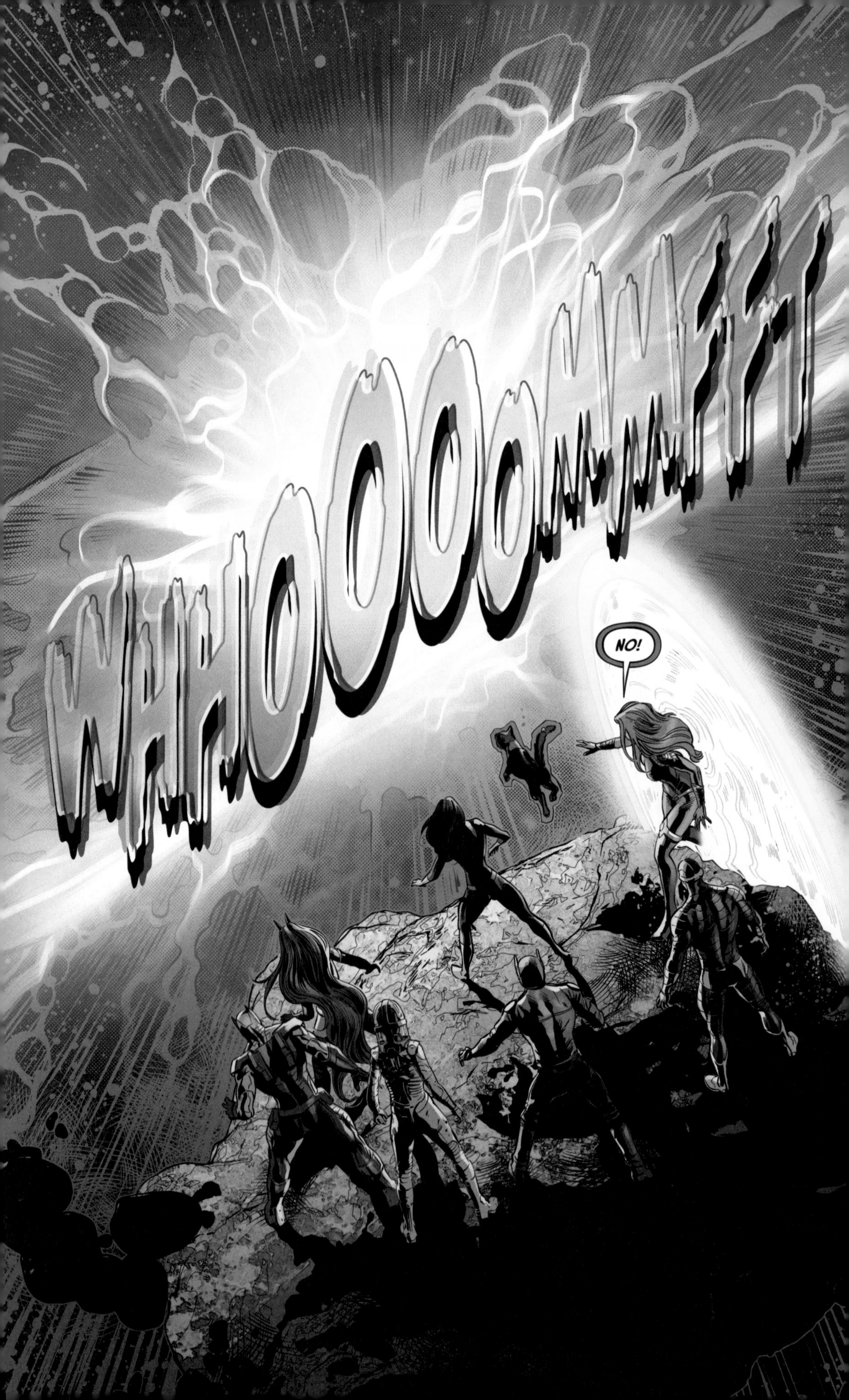
WHOOOOMMM!!
NO!

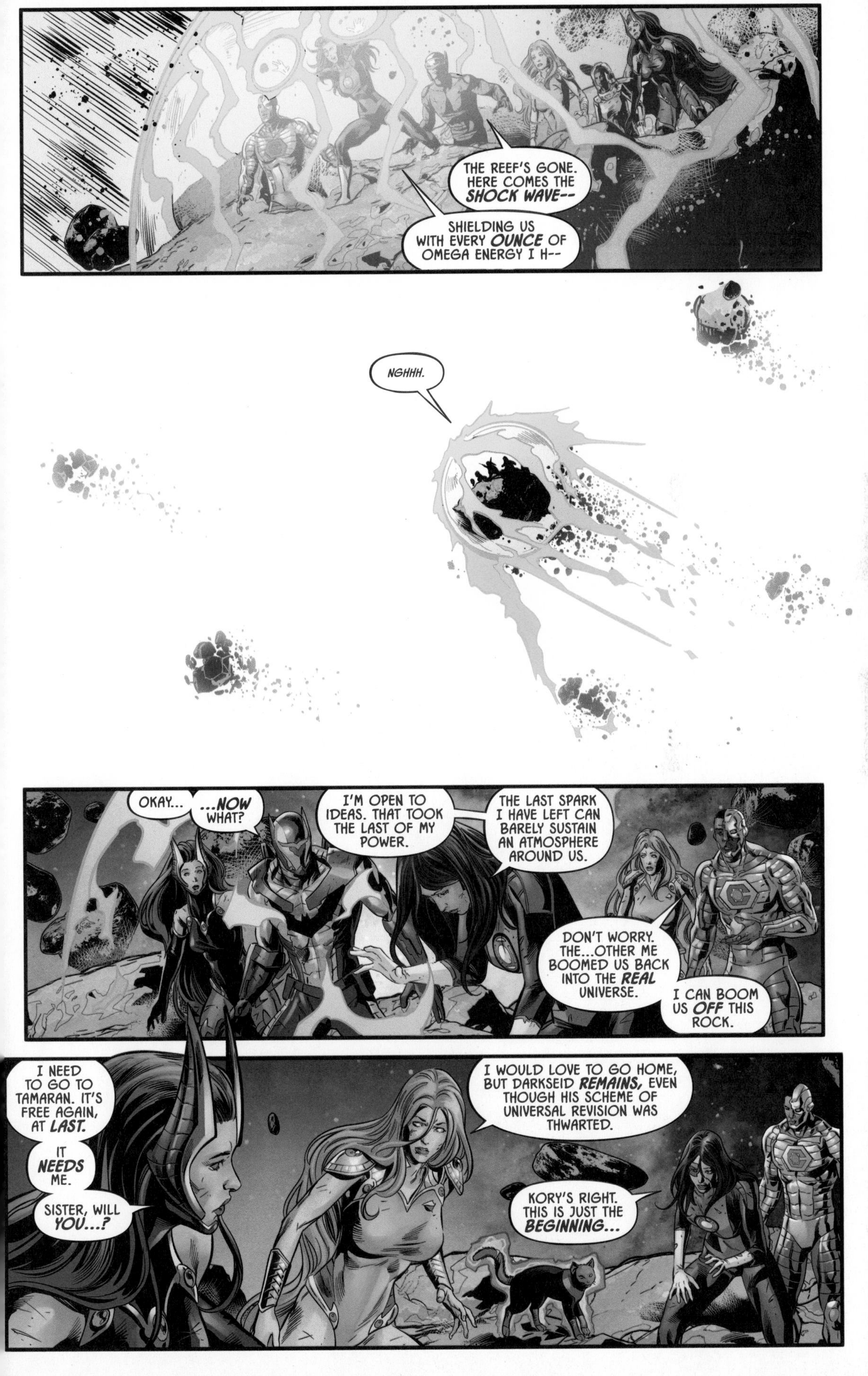
THE REEF'S GONE. HERE COMES THE SHOCK WAVE--
SHIELDING US WITH EVERY OUNCE OF OMEGA ENERGY I H--
NGHHH.
OKAY...
...NOW WHAT?
I'M OPEN TO IDEAS. THAT TOOK THE LAST OF MY POWER.
THE LAST SPARK I HAVE LEFT CAN BARELY SUSTAIN AN ATMOSPHERE AROUND US.
DON'T WORRY. THE...OTHER ME BOOMED US BACK INTO THE REAL UNIVERSE.
I CAN BOOM US OFF THIS ROCK.
I NEED TO GO TO TAMARAN. IT'S FREE AGAIN, AT LAST.
IT NEEDS ME.
SISTER, WILL YOU...?
I WOULD LOVE TO GO HOME, BUT DARKSEID REMAINS, EVEN THOUGH HIS SCHEME OF UNIVERSAL REVISION WAS THWARTED.
KORY'S RIGHT. THIS IS JUST THE BEGINNING...

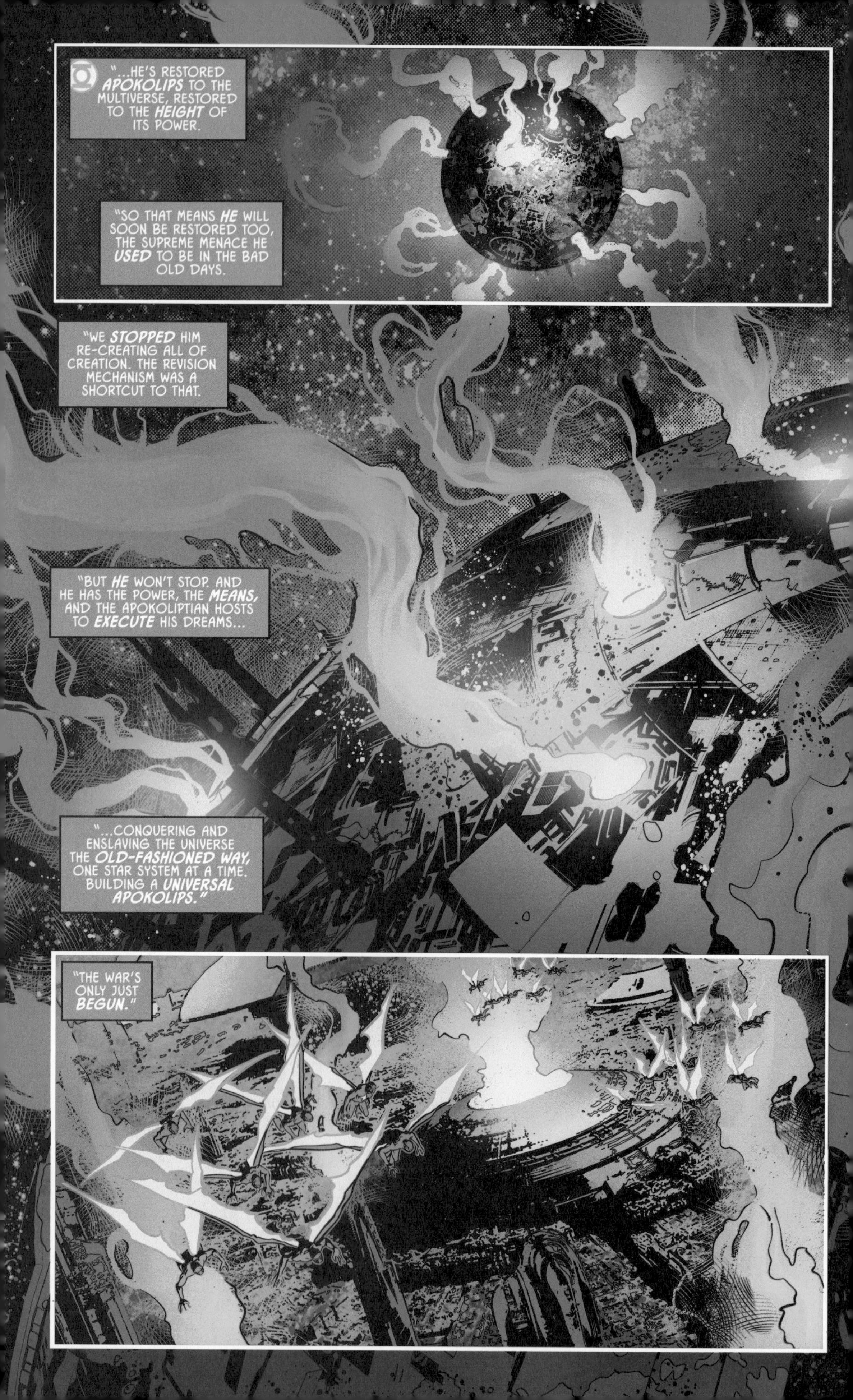
"...HE'S RESTORED APOKOLIPS TO THE MULTIVERSE, RESTORED TO THE HEIGHT OF ITS POWER.
"SO THAT MEANS HE WILL SOON BE RESTORED TOO, THE SUPREME MENACE HE USED TO BE IN THE BAD OLD DAYS.
"WE STOPPED HIM RE-CREATING ALL OF CREATION. THE REVISION MECHANISM WAS A SHORTCUT TO THAT.
"BUT HE WON'T STOP. AND HE HAS THE POWER, THE MEANS, AND THE APOKOLIPTIAN HOSTS TO EXECUTE HIS DREAMS...
"...CONQUERING AND ENSLAVING THE UNIVERSE THE OLD-FASHIONED WAY, ONE STAR SYSTEM AT A TIME. BUILDING A UNIVERSAL APOKOLIPS."
"THE WAR'S ONLY JUST BEGUN."

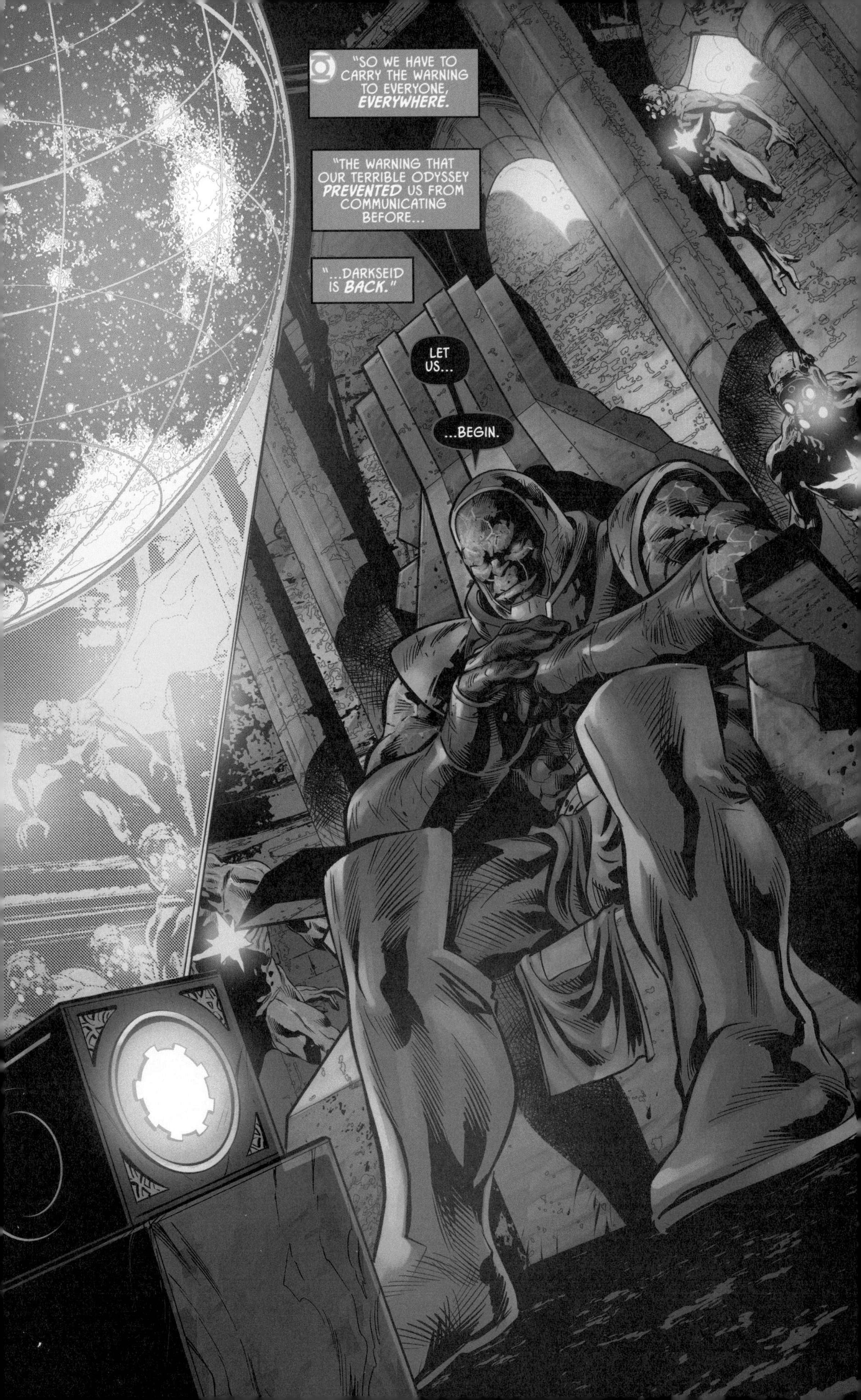
"SO WE HAVE TO CARRY THE WARNING TO EVERYONE, EVERYWHERE.
"THE WARNING THAT OUR TERRIBLE ODYSSEY PREVENTED US FROM COMMUNICATING BEFORE...
"...DARKSEID IS BACK."
LET US...
...BEGIN.

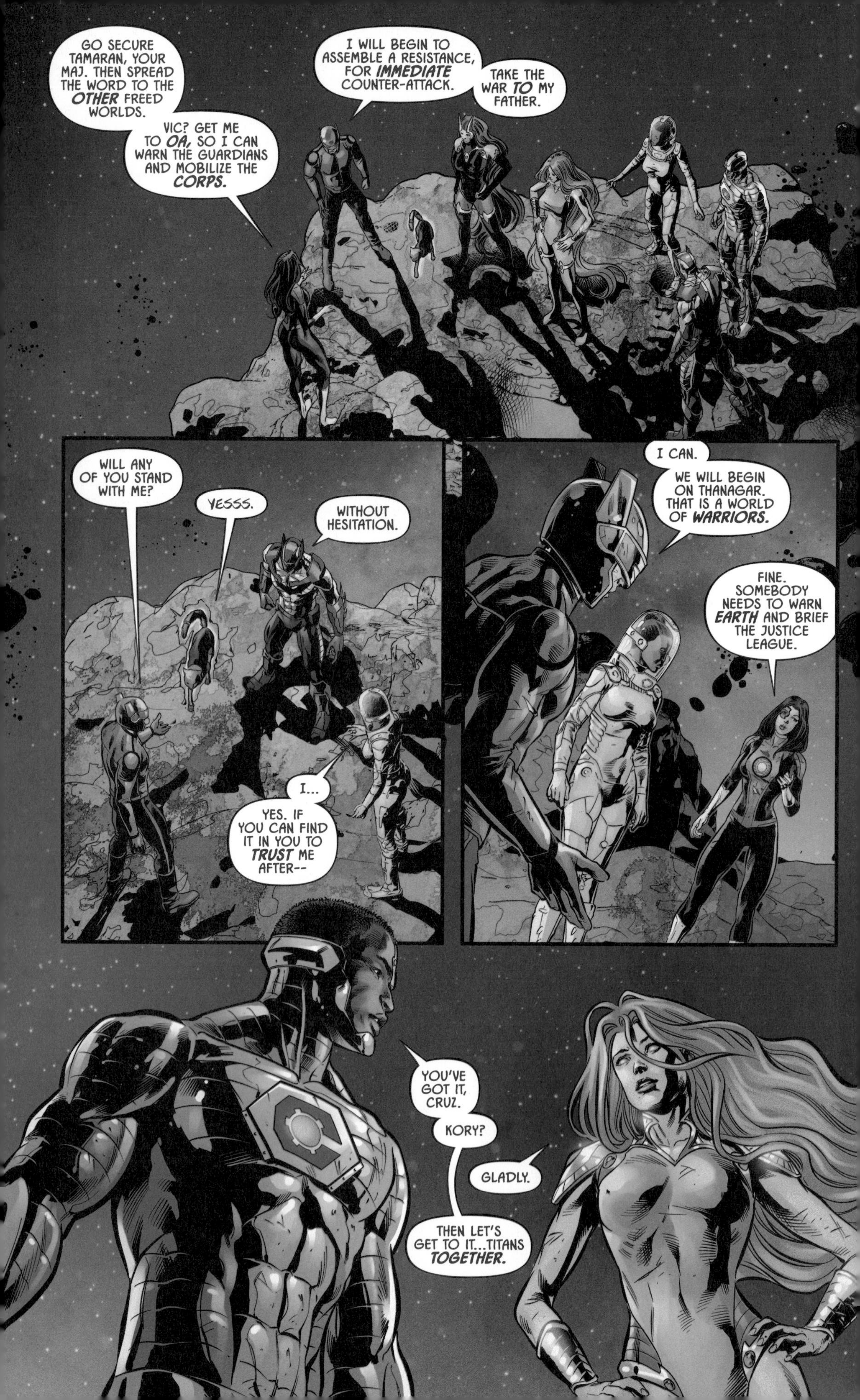
GO SECURE TAMARAN, YOUR MAJ. THEN SPREAD THE WORD TO THE OTHER FREED WORLDS.
VIC? GET ME TO OA, SO I CAN WARN THE GUARDIANS AND MOBILIZE THE CORPS.
I WILL BEGIN TO ASSEMBLE A RESISTANCE, FOR IMMEDIATE COUNTER-ATTACK.
TAKE THE WAR TO MY FATHER.
WILL ANY OF YOU STAND WITH ME?
YESSS.
WITHOUT HESITATION.
I...
YES. IF YOU CAN FIND IT IN YOU TO TRUST ME AFTER--
I CAN.
WE WILL BEGIN ON THANAGAR. THAT IS A WORLD OF WARRIORS.
FINE. SOMEBODY NEEDS TO WARN EARTH AND BRIEF THE JUSTICE LEAGUE.
YOU'VE GOT IT, CRUZ.
KORY?
GLADLY.
THEN LET'S GET TO IT...TITANS TOGETHER.

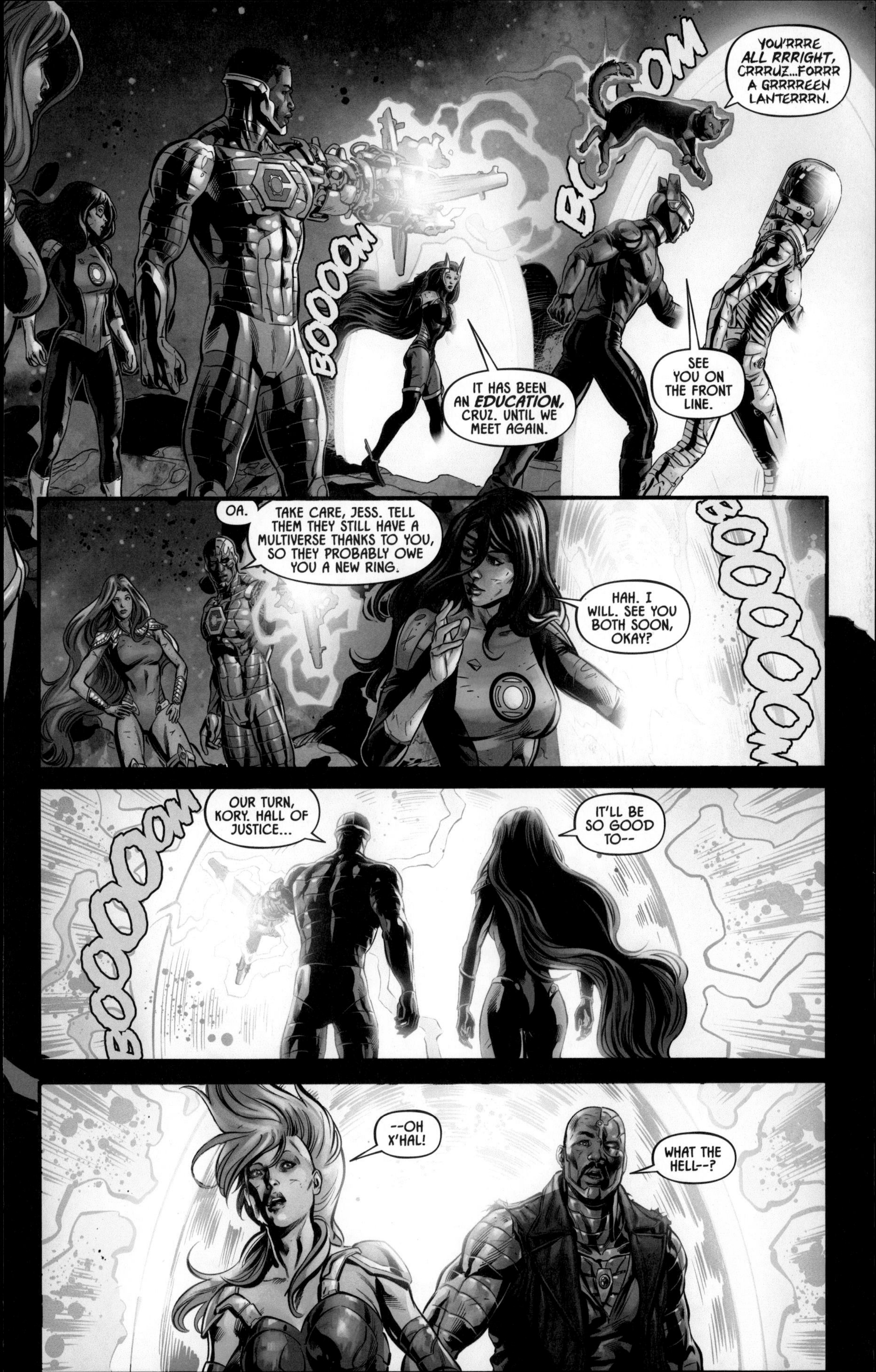
YOU'RRRE ALL RRRIGHT, CRRRUZ...FORRR A GRRRREEN LANTERRRN.
BOOOOOM
BOOOM
IT HAS BEEN AN EDUCATION, CRUZ. UNTIL WE MEET AGAIN.
SEE YOU ON THE FRONT LINE.
OA.
TAKE CARE, JESS. TELL THEM THEY STILL HAVE A MULTIVERSE THANKS TO YOU, SO THEY PROBABLY OWE YOU A NEW RING.
HAH. I WILL. SEE YOU BOTH SOON, OKAY?
BOOOOOOM
OUR TURN, KORY. HALL OF JUSTICE...
IT'LL BE SO GOOD TO--
BOOOOOOM
--OH X'HAL!
WHAT THE HELL--?

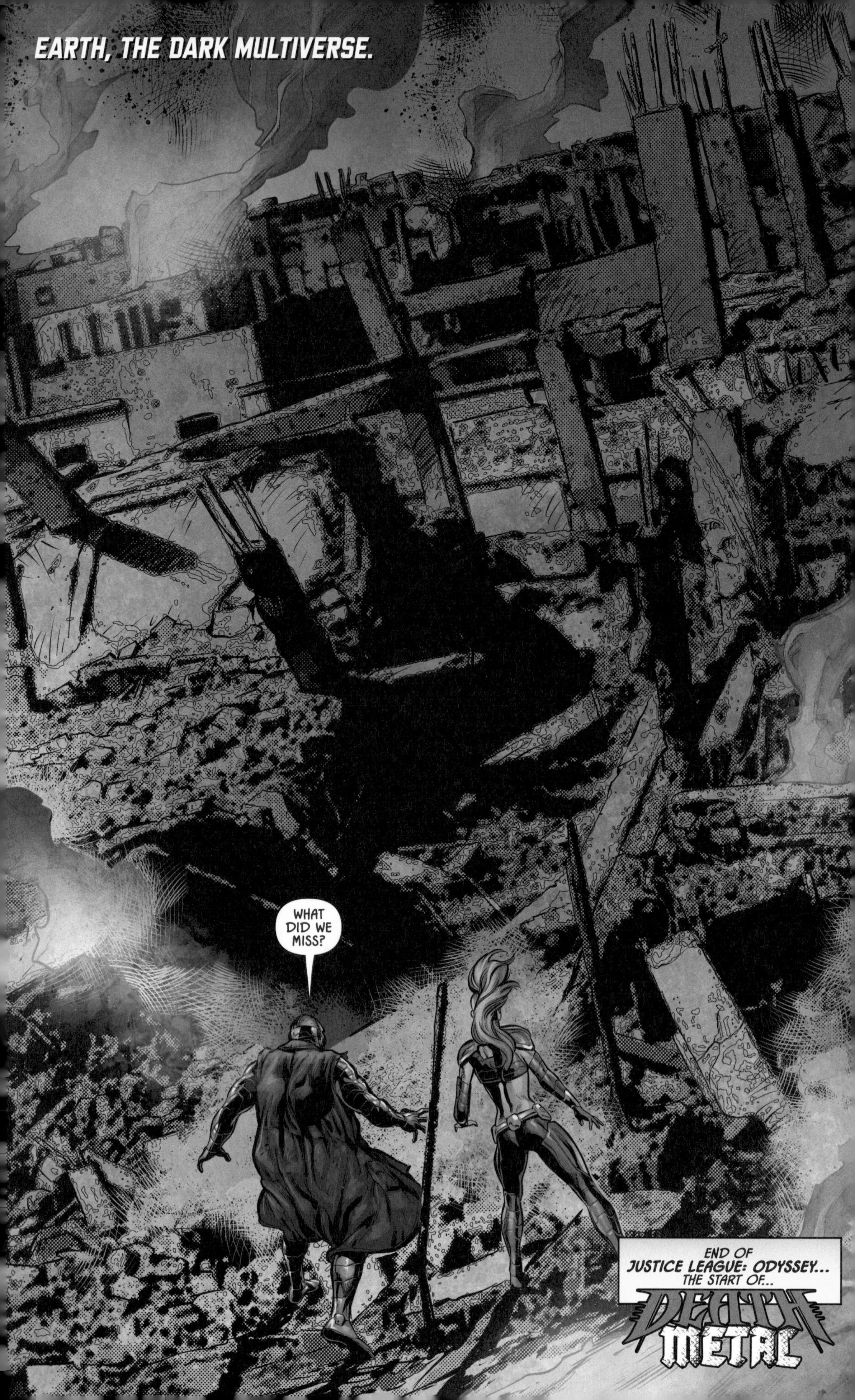
EARTH, THE DARK MULTIVERSE.
WHAT DID WE MISS?
END OF JUSTICE LEAGUE: ODYSSEY... THE START OF...
DEATH METAL

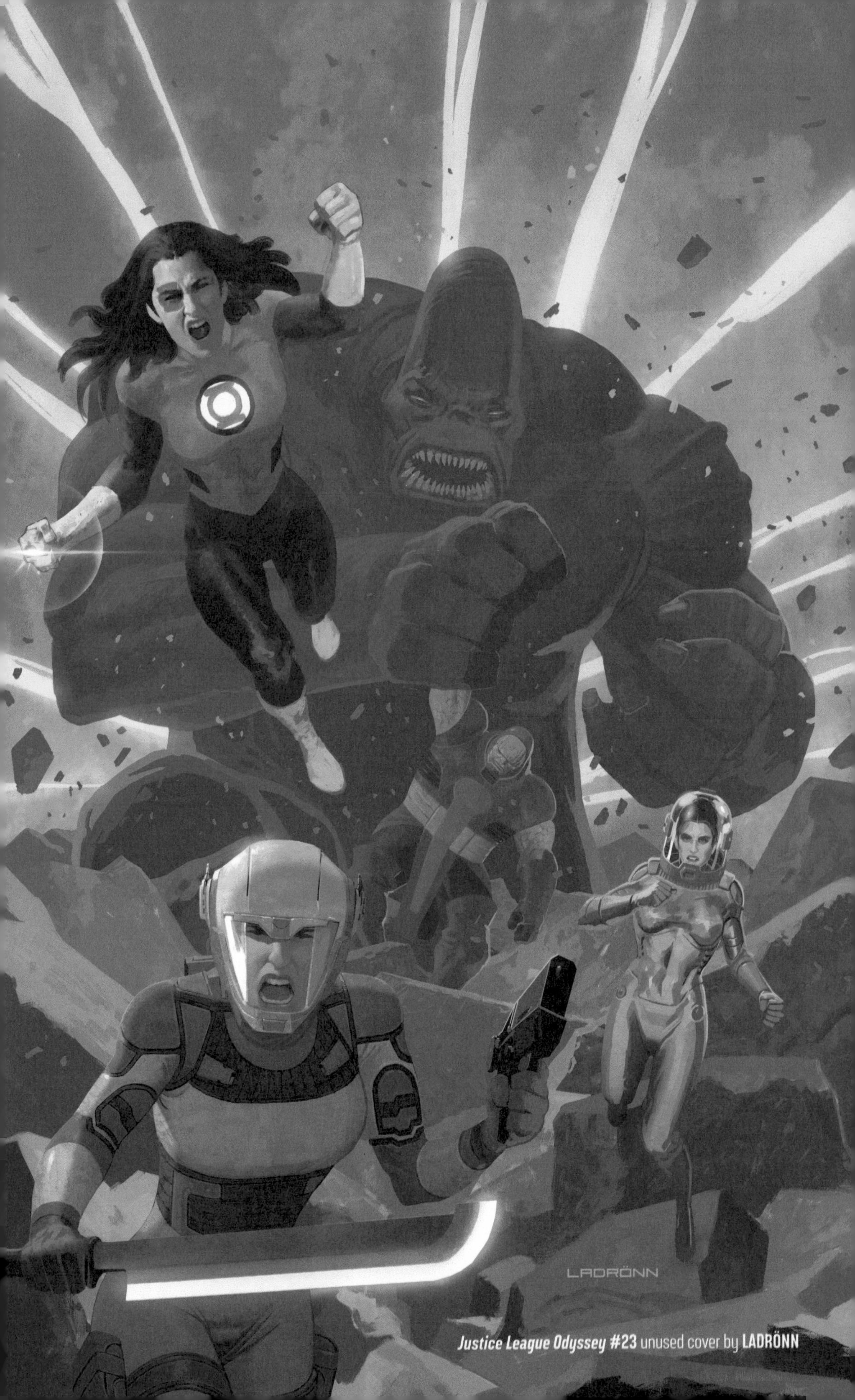
LADRÖNN

Justice League Odyssey **#23** unused cover by **LADRÖNN**

"Welcoming to new fans looking to get into superhero comics for the first time and old fans who gave up on the funny-books long ago."
– **SCRIPPS HOWARD NEWS SERVICE**

JUSTICE LEAGUE

VOL. 1: ORIGIN

GEOFF JOHNS and JIM LEE

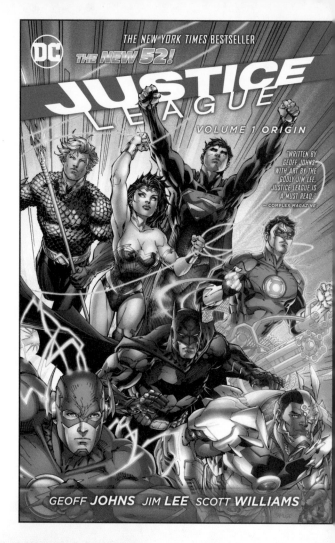

**JUSTICE LEAGUE
VOL. 2: THE VILLAIN'S JOURNEY**

**JUSTICE LEAGUE
VOL. 3: THRONE OF ATLANTIS**

READ THE ENTIRE EPIC!

JUSTICE LEAGUE VOL. 4:
THE GRID

JUSTICE LEAGUE VOL. 5:
FOREVER HEROES

JUSTICE LEAGUE VOL. 6:
INJUSTICE LEAGUE

JUSTICE LEAGUE VOL. 7:
DARKSEID WAR PART 1

JUSTICE LEAGUE VOL. 8:
DARKSEID WAR PART 2

Get more DC graphic novels wherever comics and books are sold!

Read more adventures of the World's Greatest Super Heroes in these graphic novels!

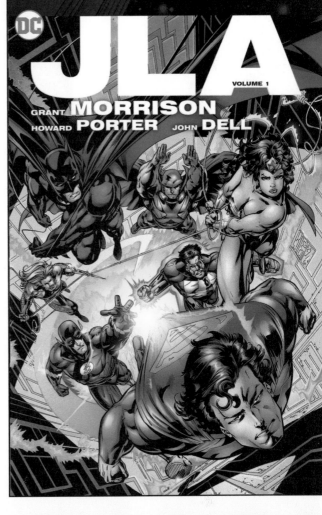

JLA VOL. 1
GRANT MORRISON and HOWARD PORTER

JLA VOL. 2

JLA VOL. 3

JLA VOL. 4

"Drips with energy."
–IGN

"Grade A."
–USA TODAY

THE NEW TEEN TITANS
MARV WOLFMAN and GEORGE PÉREZ
VOL. 1

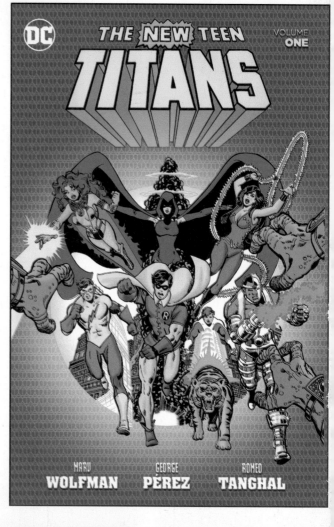

**THE NEW TEEN TITANS
VOL. 2**

**THE NEW TEEN TITANS
VOL. 3**

READ THE ENTIRE SERIES!

THE NEW TEEN TITANS VOL. 4

THE NEW TEEN TITANS VOL. 5

THE NEW TEEN TITANS VOL. 6

THE NEW TEEN TITANS VOL. 7

THE NEW TEEN TITANS VOL. 8